THE MAKING OF MODERN CORNWALL

THE MAKING OF
MODERN CORNWALL

Historical Experience and the Persistence of "Difference"

Philip Payton BSc, PhD, PhD, FRHistS

Bard "Car Dyvresow" of the Gorsedd of Cornwall
Director, Institute of Cornish Studies, University of Exeter

DYLLANSOW TRURAN

Published by Dyllansow Truran, Trewolsta, Trewirgie,
Redruth, Kernow (Cornwall)

Copyright © Dr P Payton

ISBN 1 85022 064 6

Other books published by Dyllansow Truran
The Cornish Farmer in Australia
The Cornish Miner in Australia
Cornish Carols from Australia
The Story of HMS Fisgard
Tregantle and Scraesdon: Their Forts and Railway

Typeset by Kestrel Data, Exeter
Printed and bound by Short Run Press Limited, Exeter

To the memory of
PAUL FLETCHER SMALES, MA
"Map Trevethan"
1946–1990
First amongst Cornishmen

Contents

Preface

Why is Cornwall "different"? More particularly, why has this "difference" endured, surviving centuries of rapid and often traumatic change which have served to alter radically the face of modern Cornwall? How is it that, even at the end of the twentieth-century, there remains an abiding and all-pervading sense of 'Cornishness' and separate identity?

And how does one make sense of this "Cornishness" today? At a time when support for the Rugby Union county championship was apparently declining elsewhere, why did twenty thousand and more Cornish thrice march on Twickenham, bedecked in Cornwall's black-and-gold and brandishing the black-and-white banner of St Piran? In an age when Cornwall had been considered long-since merely another administrative county, why was there not only passionate defence of the River Tamar as an historic border, but also sudden and vociferous assertion of a distinctly Cornish constitutional status? In a year when the European Elections were greeted with an embarrassing indifference in much of Britain, why did Cornwall argue so vehemently for its own seat in the Euro-Parliament?

Such questions are asked in Cornwall almost as a matter of routine, but only rarely are answers ventured; and more often than not these answers are highly subjective, slipping all too easily into personal prejudice or into the realms of the metaphysical and the romantic. Appeals to "Celtic destiny" will not do, nor even an assertion that Cornwall is ". . . still aloof and rather splendidly detached from the activity across the Tamar hailed as progress . . ." (Daphne du Maurier), nor certainly belief in ". . . the strange and compelling powers embedded in Cornwall's granite body . . . the truly mysterious and magical world of 'the timeless land' " (Denys Val Baker). Even objective histories, such as those of Halliday and Soulsby, rather dodge the issue, hoping perhaps that a sympathetic account of Cornwall's past will somehow let broader explanations of "difference" tumble out incidently, or at least leave the more sensitive reader with an intuitive grasp of the ingredients of "difference". But even these histories, with their heavy emphasis on the Medieval and the pre-modern, appeal to the image of an ancient Cornwall almost lost in the mists of time.

It seemed to me that the moment had come to confront such questions head-on, to seek to explain not only the origin of "difference" but also its persistence over time, setting such explanation against the background of other studies which had tackled similar issues elsewhere in Britain and Western Europe. The opportunity to pursue such a project in association with Polytechnic South West was seized with great enthusiasm, and this book is very much the fruit of my subsequent research. In many ways it is the fulfilment of a long-nurtured ambition, to tell the "real" story of Cornwall, and although I hope that the result is as objective as I can make it, it is a deeply personal interpretation; it is "my Cornwall".

Certainly, any lingering doubts I may have had about my approach to Cornish history were dispelled speedily by events on the international stage as my study progressed and drew to completion, not only the continuing problems of diversity in the West (especially their resurgence in the late 1980s in Scotland and Quebec) but also by the emergence of the multiplicity of "territorial", "ethnic" and "centre-periphery" issues that attended "glasnost" and "perestroika" in the East (about which I have had also the opportunity to study and write) — everything from Pan-Romanian nationalism in Moldavia and the problems of the Turkish minority in Bulgaria to the relationship between the Baltic Republics and the Soviet Union and even the constitutional demise of that polity and its replacement by the Commonwealth of Independent States, not to mention the continuing disintegration of the Yugoslavian nation-state. Troubles in the Gulf helped draw attention to Kurds, Turkmen, Baluchis, Palestinians, and other groups. At home in Britain, debate about the future shape of local government reform rekindled old aspirations and anxieties (not least in Cornwall), while the increasingly seductive notion of a "Europe of the Regions" has won much support west of the Tamar. Indeed, there is a seemingly universal consensus of Cornish opinion which insists that, whatever might happen in Britain and Europe, Cornwall should survive as a unified territorial, administrative and constitutional entity.

In writing this book I have drawn upon the professional support, advice and criticism lent by Professor David Dunkerley and Adrian Lee at Polytechnic South West and Barry Jones at University of Wales College, Cardiff. Leslie Rowse was forthcoming as always with his friendly advice, encouragement and constructive criticism. I am similarly indebted to Commander Mick Jordan for his support, and to Professor Charles Thomas and Dr Myrna Combellack Harris who afforded me invaluable assistance at the Institute of Cornish Studies. Thanks, too, should go to the ever-helpful staffs of the Polytechnic South West Library, the Royal Naval Engineering College Library, the Cornish Studies Library at Redruth, and the Royal Institution of Cornwall.

I am especially indebted to Bernard Deacon and F.L. Harris and their Murdoch House Labour History Group, to Dick and Jan Gendall and their Teere ha Tavaz Cornish studies classes, and to the participants in the Institute of Cornish Studies seminars, for opportunities to test and discuss my theories. The late Paul Smales, chairman of the Conference on Cornwall and active in so many other areas of Cornish life, was a constant source of new ideas and inspiration. Likewise, John Fleet, former Conference secretary, was eager to offer lively and stimulating discussion of contemporary Cornish affairs, as were Jim Pengelly and Peggy Morris of the Campaign For A Cornish Constituency. I am similarly indebted to those whose intellectual contributions helped provoke this book — not least Michael Hechter and Peter Berresford Ellis (both of whom I take issue with in this study!), and Derek Urwin and the late Stein Rokkan whose own work on centre-periphery relationships was to prove so important in developing my model. Additionally, authors such as A.L. Rowse, John Rowe, D.B. Barton, A.C. Todd, James Whetter,

Ronald Perry, Peter Gripaios, and Bernard Deacon have in their important contributions to Cornish Studies provided much of the secondary source material upon which I have been able and fortunate to draw. Unpublished theses, most notably those by Rosalie Eastlake, Gillian Burke, Richard Dawe, Peter Heyden, and John Rule, have also proved invaluable.

I must also thank those authors and publishers who have given permission for me to draw upon and quote from their titles; individual acknowledgements are referenced in full in the notes to each chapter and in the bibliography. Every effort has been made to discover owners of copyright, but if any omissions have occurred apologies are offered in advance and any errors in this respect will be corrected in any future editions. Also, I should thank my typist, Angela Thomas, who has had to struggle with my handwriting and who has prepared this text. As always, especial gratitude is due to Jane and Brigid and Unity for tolerating yet another project and accepting yet further demands on my time. And to Len Truran I owe a particular debt of gratitude for his continuing support and encouragement, for his co-operation and confidence in my work, and for embarking so enthusiastically upon the publication of this book.

And finally, there is a long-overdue thankyou to my parents — to my Mother for instilling in me my passion for Cornwall, and to my Father whose example and encouragement set me firmly on the road of things educational and academic.

Philip Payton,
Wheal Fortune,
Illogan,
Cornwall.

5th March 1992
St Piran's Day

xi

Introduction

A conventional wisdom emerged in the post-war era which saw the political systems of western countries in general and the United Kingdom in particular as unified, homogeneous and in several respects static, not least in terms of their territorial dimensions where a supposed overwhelming consensus of opinion in support of existing constitutional structures was assumed to guarantee the integrity of existing nation-states. However, this myth of the homogeneous state was progressively overturned by (to use Keating's phrase) " . . . the wave of 'peripheral nationalist' movements which, confounding most orthodox wisdom, swept through advanced western countries in the 1960s and 1970s . . .".[1] From Quebec to Sardinia, and from Scotland to Corsica, peripheral protest ". . . upset many of the textbook theories of politics in western nations . . .",[2] pointing not to homogeneity but to diversity, challenging rather than confirming the territorial integrity of states.

As Keating observed, this ". . . proved an uncomfortable experience for scholars and teachers . . .",[3] most especially in the United Kingdom where they were forced (as Ellis wrote) to acknowledge ". . . the inadequacy of Anglo-centric presentations of British history . . ."[4] which had often stressed unity and homogeneity in what they had assumed hitherto to be an essentially English state. Instead, British scholars were now required to develop a view of the British Isles (such as that presented by Kearney[5]) which emphasised the existence and separate experiences of four (at least) nations, establishing the importance of diversity within the territorial dimension of the state. From this emerged detailed comparative studies of the politics and history of Ireland (especially Northern Ireland), Scotland, and Wales, along with analyses attempting to elucidate and explain diversity and peripheral protest in the United Kingdom and in western countries generally.

This re-assessment helped redefine the United Kingdom as a "multi-national" state,[6] but in so doing concentrated academic attention upon the more obvious territorial issues (for example, the Northern Ireland problem, the rise of nationalism in Scotland and Wales). This had often the unfortunate (if unintended) effect of restricting the discussion of diversity to a consideration of peripheral protest alone, obscuring the fact that nationalist activity was but one symptom of a much broader pattern of diversity which warranted (but did not always receive) attention in its own right. At the same time, the preoccupation with the more obvious issues was at the expense of possibly less pressing, less easily identified, perhaps more obscure, problems. There has not, for example, been systematic or exhaustive investigation of the North of England in the territorial make-up of the United Kingdom,[7] let alone extensive discussion of the Isle of Man and Channel Islands and their relationships with the United Kingdom.

1

In particular, it is surprising that Cornwall has received only fleeting mention in otherwise detailed analyses offered by commentators such as Birch and A.D. Smith.[8] Ostensibly an integral (albeit far-flung) part of England, Cornwall has nonetheless exhibited many of the facets of diversity identified elsewhere in the United Kingdom, echoing its alleged status as part of Britain's "Celtic Fringe" and indeed inviting comparison with Scotland and Wales. This in turn invites academic inquiry of the type that has already been afforded Scotland, Wales and elsewhere. This study, then, by addressing the case of Cornwall, serves to fill a hitherto glaring gap in the elaboration of diversity within the United Kingdom. It eschews a narrow preoccupation with the surface of peripheral or nationalist protest, and takes a broader, historical perspective in its attempts to describe and explain the condition of modern Cornwall and its place in the "multi-national" state. As such, this study not only adds to the discussion of diversity within the United Kingdom, but also offers an approach which can equally be applied to other parts of the United Kingdom and indeed other regions of western Europe.

As intimated above and as discussed in greater detail later, Cornwall has attracted only limited attention from scholars anxious to investigate the new-found diversity of the United Kingdom. Notwithstanding the contributions of Lee and Rallings,[9] there has been a general if vague and rarely articulated assumption that the historical experience of Cornwall has been one of continuous erosion of ethnic identity in the face of economic exploitation and cultural imperialism, a relentless retreat from a "Celtic golden age" of economic integrity, territorial security, cultural fulfilment, and political self-determination. In other words, if Cornwall has remained at all "different" from England, then this is a "difference" that has endured *despite* Cornwall's historical experience. Eastlake, for example, has argued that:

> In each historic period, economic exploitation and cultural alienation succeeded one another, until the nineteenth century when the mining economy of Cornwall became an essential part of the English industrial system. The twentieth century offers either the prospect of total incorporation into England, or a cultural revival spearheaded by the several small, national and cultural organisations which now exist.[10]

This perspective, however, is seriously flawed — indeed it is profoundly wrong. This present study offers an alternative and fuller analysis in which it is argued that Cornwall's "difference" has endured *because of* (rather than despite) Cornwall's historical experience. Drawing upon the framework of "centre" and "periphery" developed by Rokkan and Urwin,[11] and, adapting and extending Tarrow's typology[12] of "Older" and "Second" Peripheralism (with its recognition of the central importance of industrial change in perpetuating the peripheral condition), this study contends that in each historical period the experience of Cornwall has been highly individual when compared to that of the English "centre", or indeed other areas of Britain.

In particular, this study focuses upon the period of industrialisation and de-industrialisation (Tarrow's "Second Peripheralism") and the subsequent era of post-war socio-economic movement (a "Third Peripheralism"), in the belief that the effects of industrial change were of crucial significance in determining the distinctive social, economic and political characteristics of modern Cornwall. These accounted for Cornwall's continuing "difference", and explained Cornwall's enduring (but changing) separate identity — based (as it continues to be) on a range of behaviour at variance with that of England. This study, therefore, offers an analysis which places Cornwall within the diversity of the "multi-national" state, presenting a model in which recent peripheral protest is but one index of peripheral difference, and where the historical experience of successive phases of peripherality has served to perpetuate separate identity. This is the very stuff of Cornish history; the making of modern Cornwall.

Notes and References

1. Michael Keating, *State and Regional Nationalism: Territorial Politics and the European State*, Harvester Wheatsheaf, London, 1988, p1.
2. Ibid.
3. Ibid.
4. Steven Ellis, "Not Mere English: The British Perspective 1400–1650", *History Today*, December 1988.
5. Hugh Kearney, *The British Isles: A History of Four Nations*, Cambridge University Press, Cambridge, 1989.
6. For example, see: Richard Rose, *Understanding the United Kingdom: The Territorial Dimension in Government*, Longman, London, 1982, Jaroslav Krejci and Vitezslav Velimsky, *Ethnic and Political Nations in Europe*, Croom Helm, London, 1981, pp183-192; Richard Rose, *The United Kingdom as a Multi-National State*, University of Strathclyde Survey Research Centre Occasional paper No 6, Glasgow, 1970.
7. Bulpitt notes ". . . the ever-present problem of 'the north parts' . . ." in English history; Jim Bulpitt, *Territory and Power in the United Kingdom*, Manchester University Press, Manchester, 1983, p78.
8. The Cornish make a fleeting mid-sentence appearance in A.D. Smith, *Ethnic Revival in the Modern World*, Cambridge University Press, Cambridge, 1981, p11. Birch devotes one inaccurate sentence — "Cornish nationalists in the 1980s are busily struggling to reconstruct the Cornish language, which actually became extinct in the 1930s" — in Anthony H. Birch, *Nationalism and National Integration*, Unwin Hyman, London, 1989, p70. More useful but equally brief references surface in Kearney, op. cit., especially p1 and p105.
9. For example, Colin S. Rallings and Adrian Lee, "Politics of the Periphery — The Case of Cornwall", unpublished paper presented to the conference of the PSA work group on The Politics of the United Kingdom, Aberystwyth 1977; and Adrian N. Lee, "The Persistence of Difference? Electoral Change in Cornwall", unpublished paper presented to PSA annual conference, Plymouth Polytechnic, 1988.
10. Rosalie Eastlake, "Cornwall: The Development of a Celtic Periphery", unpublished MA thesis, McGill University, 1981, abstract.

11. Stein Rokkan and Derek W. Urwin, *The Politics of Territorial Identity: Studies in European Regionalism*, Sage, London, 1982.
12. Sidney Tarrow, *Between Centre and Periphery: Grassroots Politicians in Italy and France,* Yale University Press, New Haven, 1977, p16.

Part One

The Myth Of The Homogeneous State

"The United Kingdom is a somewhat untidy state, neither federal nor completely unitary, that has no formal constitution and can only be understood in historical terms. It was created in stages, by the expansion of England . . .".

Anthony H. Birch,
Nationalism and National Integration,
Unwin Hyman, London, 1989, p77.

"History and politics, however, are rarely so tidy. It is the incongruity between culture, economics and politics which forms the essence of the centre-periphery dimension: . . . it is this incongruity which constitutes the greatest obstacle both to academic categorisation and to governmental resolution of the problems that exist".

Derek W. Urwin,
"The Price of A Kingdom: Territory, Identity and the Centre-Periphery Dimension in Western Europe", in Yves Meny and Vincent Wright,
Centre-Periphery Relations in Western Europe, George Allen and Unwin, London, 1985, p167.

". . . it is only by adopting a 'Britannic' approach that historians can make sense of the particular segment in which they may be pimarily interested, whether it be 'England', 'Ireland', 'Scotland', 'Wales', 'Cornwall' or the Isle of Man".

Hugh Kearney,
The British Isles: A History of Four Nations,
Cambridge University Press, Cambridge, 1989, p1.

CHAPTER ONE

Towards a Centre-Periphery Model

Despite the great mass of literature alluding to Cornwall's "sense of difference", "separateness" or "Celtic identity",[1] attempts by scholars to offer a serious explanation of the making of modern Cornwall have been hindered until very recently by the lack of a relevant conceptual framework within which to work. This, in turn, was the result of a conventional wisdom amongst historians and social scientists which refused to admit that "separateness" — in Cornwall, or elsewhere in the United Kingdom — was important enough to warrant extensive investigation. Indeed, the accepted view until comparatively recently was that the United Kingdom was a remarkably homogeneous state — an almost text-book example of Almond and Verba's "civic culture"[2] — such cultural or other diversity as there was being of little significance in determining the realities of social, economic or political behaviour and events. Such a view saw Cornwall as merely a part of a wider "south west", which was itself a rather amorphous region of convenience centred upon Bristol but having no particular identity or other attribute to set it apart from the rest of the country.[3] This, in turn, reflected an English tendency to treat all Britain ". . . as a mere extension of England and Englishness . . ."[4], where ". . . national identity is fluid and imprecise, floating between 'Englishness' and 'Britishness' because the centre of economic, political and ideological power in Britain is in London (and so England)."[5]

This concept of the "homogeneous state" was accepted by most historians, who frequently saw the history of the United Kingdom through English (and then essentially south-east English) eyes,[6] while social scientists were prepared to present the state as not only unitary and centralised but also centre-oriented (and therefore, in their view, homogeneous) in all its principal aspects. Blondel, for example, could claim in 1963 that "Britain is probably the most homogeneous of all industrial countries".[7] Thirty-five million people, he said, lived within the 25 most thickly populated counties of England — these represented ". . . 80 per cent of all Englishmen and two-thirds of the population of the British Isles",[8] and were of course the people who really mattered in the formation of social and political values. Blondel did admit, however, that there were geographical variations in voting behaviour — so that the south-east of England tended to be Conservative, Wales Labour and so on — but even this "geographic" factor was seen merely as one strand of a broader explanation of the influence of "tradition and environment", which was itself of less importance than considerations such as class and

7

trade union membership. As recently as 1971, Punnett could add that regional factors were less important in Britain than in the United States, Canada or Germany, although — like Blondel — he too had to admit that there were regional variations in voting behaviour. He noted, for example, that ". . . Liberal support varies quite markedly from region to region, and all six seats won by the Liberals in 1970 were in the 'Celtic Fringe' areas of north Scotland, Wales, and Cornwall".[9]

The views of Blondel, Punnett, and the many other writers who shared their conventional wisdom, were essentially Anglocentric and focussed upon the concentration of the British population in England, a concentration whose numerical dominance they translated almost without question into over-riding political importance. Liberal Members of Parliament might come overwhelmingly from the "Celtic Fringe", but what were six MPs when set in the context of a House of Commons consisting of over 600 members? Wales and Scotland might demonstrate a greater than average propensity to vote Labour, but then the combined representation of those two countries in the Commons was only a little over 100. And when Northern Ireland was considered at all in the context of "British politics" (and often it was not, despite its position as part of the United Kingdom), then it was presented as being quite outside the bounds of British political norms, a special case requiring separate treatment in isolation from what was happening elsewhere in the Union.

More recently, however, as Rokkan and Urwin have noted, ". . . the academic landscape has changed considerably . . .",[10] a change precipitated by the events of the late 1960s and 1970s when the politics of the "Celtic Fringe" were pushed more forcibly into the forefront of British politics. First of all, Northern Ireland re-emerged as a major issue after almost fifty years at the back of the British political consciousness, leading to the demise of Stormont, the imposition of "Direct Rule", the failure of "power-sharing" initiatives, and — more recently — in 1985 to an "Anglo-Irish Agreement" between London and Dublin. The same period also witnessed an upsurge in support for Plaid Cymru (the Welsh nationalists) and the Scottish National Party in their respective countries, with both parties building upon by-election successes in the mid-1960s to the point where Plaid Cymru won three Parliamentary seats in the General Election of October 1974 with the Scottish National Party winning 11 seats and gaining a startling 30.4 per cent of the Scottish vote.

In response to the growth of nationalist sentiment in Wales and Scotland, the Labour Government in 1969 appointed the Crowther (later Kilbrandon) Royal Commission on the Constitution. When the Commission reported in 1973, amongst its recommendations were devolutionary assemblies for Wales and Scotland. Spurred on by the nationalist victories of 1974 (and mindful of the need for nationalist support in the Commons), the Labour Government introduced Bills for Welsh and Scottish Devolution. But the legislation passed through Parliament with great difficulty, ending in a referendum in 1979 in which the Welsh rejected their assembly by four-to-one and the Scots failed to endorse their assembly sufficiently strongly for it to become a reality.[11] In the subsequent General Election, Plaid Cymru lost one of its seats and the Scottish National Party, in a disastrous

8

performance, saw its Parliamentary representation reduced to two. Nationalist activity continued, however, manifested not only in the behaviour of the two nationalist parties but also in the much broader attitudes and sentiments that had been moulded in Scotland and Wales.[12] By the late 1980s, in the aftermath of the nationalist by-election victory in Glasgow Govan in November 1988, the "Scottish question", was once again on the agenda of British politics.

Although it was possible for one political scientist to write in 1981 that "For the time being, devolution is a dead issue . . .",[13] the debate concerning the respective roles of central and local government continued with what Bulpitt has termed "The territorial economy of Thatcherism . . .".[14] Confrontations with Liverpool and Lothian, the abolition of the Greater London Council and Metropolitan County Councils, the controversies over the Rate Support Grant and "Rate-capping", and the introduction of the Community Charge ("Poll Tax"), all served to underline the central government's increasing problems in dealing with its local counterparts. In the same way, the Thatcher years saw an alleged economic polarisation between "North" and "South" in Britain. Statistics released in January 1987, for example, suggested that the "North" had borne the brunt of the net decline of 1.6 million jobs in the United Kingdom since 1979, the "South" (which accounted for nearly half of the population) having suffered from only six per cent of this employment decline.[15] Indeed, John Goddard concluded from these figures that ". . . regional problems strike right at the heart of the way in which Britain is governed."[16] Not only had peripheral protest emerged as a part of British political life, but also Regional Development policies — pursued consistently and often with vigour by all governments since the War — had failed in their aim of eradicating regional inequalities within the United Kingdom.

The concern for the "de-industrialisation" of the "North" had been voiced as early as 1977 (at the height of the Devolution debate) when an all-party group entitled Campaign for the North was launched. As well as drawing attention to the "North-South" economic divide, the Campaign attacked what it saw as an over-centralised United Kingdom and called for a Devolutionary Assembly for the North of England to complement those then being offered for Wales and Scotland. Significantly, the Campaign added that ". . . England is anything but homogeneous — economically, culturally or sociologically — . . ."[17] and that "Even in historical terms, England is a bit of a myth",[18] the "North" being seen as a peripheral appendage of the core or "real" England of the "South". Although in the 1970s Devolution debate many Labour MPs in the North East had opposed Scottish devolution (on the grounds that it would give Scotland an unfair advantage over equally "deprived" parts of England), by the late 1980s they had reversed their opinion, and were calling instead for assemblies for both Scotland and the North.[19]

These developments in Northern Ireland, Scotland, and Wales, along with the emerging "North-South" debate, had several important effects. First of all — and most obviously — they highlighted the shortcomings of the "homogeneous state" theory, and ushered in a new orthodoxy which stressed the diversity of the United Kingdom. Commentators became more consciously aware of the politics of the "Celtic Fringe", and of disparities and differences within England, leading Rose

9

and others to re-define the United Kingdom as a "multinational state" or "multiple complexity".[20] This was accompanied by, and indeed was a part of, a broader awareness of the significance of the "territorial dimension" of the state, a factor explored both theoretically and historically by Birch, Rose, Bulpitt, Keating and others.[21] Examination of the "territorial dimension" of the United Kingdom revealed quickly that at no time had there been a comprehensive "territorial compact" designed to define or even justify — in philosophical terms — the geographical nature and extent of the state. Instead, the "territorial dimension" had developed (and is still developing) in an essentially ad hoc manner, its lack of definition (let alone consistency) exacerbated by the non-existence of a written constitution. This development, it was argued, was connected intimately with the waxing (and waning) of the power of the state's core in southern England, and could be best understood in that light.

In expanding outwards from its southern core, the English state sought first to consolidate its control of northern England and to incorporate Cornwall (though leaving the latter with several distinguishing constitutional idiosyncrasies), moving by Tudor times to secure the northern Border against Scotland and to formalise the annexation of Wales. The Crowns of England and Scotland were joined in 1603, and in 1707 the two countries were merged by Act of Union. Although presented as the coming together of two equal partners (in marked contrast to the Anglo-Welsh Act of Union of 1536), the Union led to the demise of Scotland's Parliament and to the subordination of many of Scotland's interests to England's — despite the survival of many distinctive Scottish institutions.

The "territorial dimension" of the United Kingdom was further complicated by the relationship with Ireland, as indeed it continues to be. Ireland was brought formally into the Union in 1801 but in 1922 twenty-six counties seceded from the United Kingdom to form the sovereign and independent Irish Free State (albeit at first with Dominion status), the precursor of today's Republic. Six counties of Ulster elected to remain within the United Kingdom under a devolutionary arrangement which survived until "direct rule" was imposed in 1972. In 1985 the Anglo-Irish Agreement gave the government of the Republic a limited, consultative input into the administration of Northern Ireland, bringing the totality of the "territorial dimension" of constitutional relationships within these islands once more into the forefront of political considerations.[22] Of course, the nationalist advances in Scotland and Wales in the 1960s and 70s also brought the possibility of changes to the "territorial dimension" to the fore, and to an extent those possibilities remain alive (most especially in Scotland), whilst other factors — such as the ambiguous constitutional status of the Isle of Man and the Channel Islands, the existence of Welsh, Scottish and Northern Ireland Offices, the divergence in local government organisation between England and Scotland, and the prospect of further local government reform — point to a continuing diversity and uncertainty in the territorial relationships within the British Isles.

A second consequence of the developments of the 1960s and 70s was the increase in serious academic attention focussed upon the "Fringe" — "Celtic" and otherwise — in British politics. An extensive literature emerged to document the events in

Northern Ireland,[23] with other works seeking to chart and explain the rise of nationalism in Scotland and Wales.[24] Butt Philip found, however, that nationalism and the effects of national sentiment were not confined to any one political party in Wales,[25] a conclusion which not only emphasised the nationalist element in Welsh Liberal and Labour politics but also pointed to a distinctive Welsh political culture per se. Madgwick was able in his study of the politics of rural Wales to demonstrate the extent to which the Welsh Liberal Party was rooted deeply in Welsh culture, identifying an enduring link between Liberalism and "Welshness" which had manifested itself in (amongst other things) a consistent Liberal support for Devolution.[26] In industrial Wales the Liberal Party had been largely eclipsed by Labour. But despite Labour's centralist stance and abandonment of its early enthusiasm for "Home Rule", the party remained alive to Welsh sentiment and was often able to present itself as the protector of specifically Welsh interests and indeed as the champion of Socialist Wales against the rule of Tory England.

A distinctive political culture also became apparent in Scotland, reflected not only in the Scottish National Party but also in the activities of other groups. As in Wales, the Liberals had long been advocates of Scottish Devolution,[27] and both Miller and Berrington have noted that Scottish Conservatives (when in Opposition) have on occasions appealed successfully to Scottish national sentiment in attacking the "socialist centralisation" of Labour Government at Westminster.[28] It is Labour, however, which has increasingly adopted the role of the voice of criticism of London Government, especially after 1979 when there was a Conservative Government in power at Westminster at a time when a majority of Scottish seats were in Labour's hands. Harvie considered that Scotland had experienced ". . . political behaviour increasingly at variance with the English norm . . ."[29] and pointed to ". . . political indicators of an ever-deeper social and cultural alienation from England".[30] Labour, he said, had now been converted to the need for a Scottish assembly ". . . with which to combat de-industrialization and . . . anti-socialist centralization . . .",[31] a variant of the theme once offered by Scottish Tories! In a manner anticipated by Keating and Bleiman, the Labour Party argued that the Conservative Government ". . . lacks a Scottish mandate . . . .".[32]

Just as greater academic attention was devoted to the political cultures of Wales and Scotland, so closer examination was focussed upon the English "fringe" or "periphery".[33] Once again, distinctive features emerged from this new inquiry, highlighting a territorial distribution of class — ". . . the bosses have traditionally been identified with the centre . . .",[34] and again emphasising the role of the Liberals and subsequently of Labour as parties of the periphery. Urwin considered that "The Liberal Party may have been almost annihilated in the 1950s, but its role as defender of the 'subject-periphery' was largely taken over by Labour",[35] a view echoed by Berrington who wrote that "During the middle of the twentieth-century the periphery found political expression through the medium of the Labour Party and, to a lesser extent, through what had become a tiny Liberal Party".[36] Within the Labour Party (especially in areas such as the North East of England) this role produced inevitable tensions, given the movement's underlying centralist ideology.

With the discrediting of the "homogeneous state" paradigm, and with the new

11

concern to investigate the political cultures of both the "Celtic" and "English" peripheries, came the search for theoretical frameworks in which to explain this newly-apparent diversity. The most obviously distinctive features of peripheral politics, evident from even a cursory glance, were those provided by the various nationalist parties. An inevitable reaction, therefore, in the atmosphere of the late 60s and 70s, was to offer existing models of nationalism as interpretations of what was happening in the United Kingdom. One such model was that provided by A.D. Smith in his *Theories of Nationalism*.[37]

Building upon Kedourie's celebrated assertion that "Nationalism is a doctrine invented in Europe at the beginning of the nineteenth century",[38] and by synthesising the contributions of a remarkably diverse number of writers, Smith reviewed and analysed a series of theories to achieve his "core doctrine" of nationalism. From this "core" emerged the concept of "ethnic nationalism", a form of nationalism which Smith argued would arise (typically) in a European nation which had been incorporated into a greater nation-state or indeed divided between several states. Its aims would be to achieve self-government and to preserve its culture. In developing this view, Smith considered it important to understand the emergence of what he termed the "scientific state". This "scientific state" grew from the old "possessive state" (for example, Tudors in England or Bourbons in France) which, to serve the "political-personal ends" of its ruler, pursued policies designed to weld together and homogenise the various national groups in the state. Thus Brittany had, for the purposes of the "possessive" state, to be incorporated into France whilst England found it necessary to assimilate its "Celtic" periphery.

The "possessive" state developed gradually into the more modern "scientific state", characterised by a drive to secure administrative efficiency which necessarily made it intolerant of regional diversity. Moreover, the state was highly centralised, the culture of the metropolis or centre becoming the prototype for the whole state, and the state itself demanding a high degree of loyalty from its citizens in the implementation of its "welfare" policies. One effect of this was that the intelligentsia amongst the national minorities became "doubly socialised", on the one hand steeped in its traditional culture but on the other exposed to the new, powerful culture of the "scientific state", precipitating an acute crisis as a result of these two conflicting claims to authority and loyalty. To escape this dilemma, an individual might become a "traditionalist" — rejecting the "scientific state" and all its work — or he might become an "assimilationalist", abandoning his traditional culture in favour of the more cosmopolitan life of the centre. A third option would be to become "reformist", seeking to reform the traditional culture by reconciling it to the rationalising demands of the "scientific state". But in seeking this reconciliation, the "reformist" realises that he has in fact betrayed his traditional culture and, joining forces with the disappointed "assimilationist" whose aspirations have not been met by the "scientific state", he becomes a "revivalist" encouraging a rebirth of his native culture and ushering in a new era of scholastic interest in the language, literature and history of his national minority. This in turn leads to political demands, and thus "ethnic nationalism" is born.

There were inherent attractions in Smith's thesis for those attempting to explain

"Celtic" nationalism, not least for Celtic nationalists themselves wishing to rationalise their opposition to this newly-defined English "scientific state", and it received qualified and cautious approval from Tudur Jones in his examination of Welsh nationalism.[39] A more enthusiastic response declared that ". . . with his concept of 'ethnic' nationalism he (Smith) has captured perfectly the essence of Celtic nationalism . . .".[40] Certainly, Smith's concepts of the "possessive" and "scientific" states are of considerable importance in comprehending the conditions in which the British state acquired its "fringe" or "periphery". But in postulating the circumstances in which "ethnic nationalism" is likely to arise, he pays scant regard to the effect of economic conditions — a factor stressed by later writers on the subject.[41] Smith has retorted that ". . . they assume too close a link between nationalism and economic development . . .",[41] but in the truth the issues of industrialisation and de-industrialisation cannot be ignored. More importantly, while Smith's framework may indeed help us to understand the origins of nationalist movements, it does not address itself to the more subtle and less self-conscious behavioural "differences" observable in the social and political cultures of the "periphery". As we have seen already, in both Scotland and Wales the nationalist parties are but one part (albeit overtly and obviously) of a broader and more complex political culture exhibiting "difference" from that of England's "core". Nationalism is therefore but one index of "peripheral difference", and it is a mistake to assume otherwise.

Although still concerned to explain (amongst other things) the rise of nationalist movements in the United Kingdom in the 1960s, Hechter's study of the "Celtic Fringe" in the British state was careful to examine other manifestations of "difference" — pointing, for example, to the Nonconformist and relatively anti-Conservative nature of both Wales and Scotland.[43] Hechter's principal objective was to try to explain the persistence in Wales, Scotland and Ireland of an ethnic identity distinct from that of England in what was a modernised, highly-industrialised British state. He sought to explain the relationship between England — the "national core", as he saw it — and the "Celtic Fringe" (the "periphery") in the light of two opposing models: the "diffusion" and "internal colonial" theories. The "diffusion" theory, argued Hechter, predicted that contact between "core" and "periphery" would lead inevitably to ethnic homogenisation, the identity of the "periphery" succumbing eventually to that of the "core". By contrast, the "internal colonial" model claimed that contact could heighten ethnic differences, leading to ethnic conflict (nationalism) as groups in the "periphery" were relegated to inferior positions in what had become a cultural division of labour. Industrialisation might contribute to a decline in linguistic differences, but it certainly would not lead to cultural assimilation — nor, for that matter, to the development of regional economic equality.

Employing a blend of historical and sociological analysis, Hechter presented a wealth of empirical and statistical data to support his thesis that it was the "internal colonial" model which was appropriate to the experience of the "Celtic Fringe", concluding that the survival of ethnic distinctiveness rested upon the cultural division of labour. Again, his theoretical framework was welcomed by many observers, not least Celtic nationalists themselves, but in time serious academic objections to his work were voiced. Both Smith and Bulpitt have offered critiques, but the most sustained objection comes from Page.[44] Hechter's assumption that "diffusion" leads inevitably to homogeneity is questioned, and Page accuses Hechter of misinterpreting both Parsons and Rokkan in his attempt to suggest the link between "diffusion" and homogeneity. Far from suggesting such a connection, Rokkan had in fact emphasised the existence ". . . in the 'Celtic Fringe' of Britain . . . particularly in Wales, of opposition to the territorial, cultural and economic dominance of the English . . .".[45] Page also points to methodological problems in the "internal colonial" model and identifies significant statistical errors. He questions Hechter's ". . . assumption that there are no significant regional differences within England",[46] and concludes that Hechter has failed even to offer a satisfactory explanation for the emergence of Scottish and Welsh nationalism in the 1960s and 70s. Bulpitt has echoed Page's criticism of Hechter's ". . . free and easy attitude to the location of the Centre", but also argues that Hechter has not succeeded in his attempt to lift the "internal colonial" model from its Latin American origins and place it upon the experience of the British Isles:

> . . . his book is not really about internal colonialism at all. His real concern is to attack the diffusion theory of national development via the presentation of data which points to the persistence of peripheral sectionalism. With this general thesis (although not all the details) is it hard to disagree. But it is not an internal colonialism thesis.[47]

In other words, Hechter has merely demonstrated (albeit unsatisfactorily) the survival of diversity and regional distinctiveness within these islands — he has not provided an explanation for it.[48]

Despite these shortcomings, Hechter's analysis was useful in that it indicated the importance of regional economic inequalities — a consideration presented by Nairn in his highly polemical discussion as the "uneven diffusion" of industrial capitalism from England[49] — and talked not only of a nationalist response to English domination but also of a specific relationship between "centre" and "periphery". Although still lacking clear definitions (the "centre" was more or less synonymous with "England", and "periphery" was the "Celtic Fringe"), this suggested a framework for further contemplation. Berrington, for example, identified the south-east of England as the "centre" of the British state and reflected that,

> In the nineteenth century United Kingdom the old Celtic territories of Ireland, Scotland and Wales were obvious peripheries. South-west England is sometimes treated as a peripheral territory and the status of northern England, whose political evolution during the nineteenth century had much in common with the mainland peripheries of Celtic Britain, is uncertain.[50]

Within this paradigm of "centre-periphery" relationships, some commentators have attempted a structural analysis of the United Kingdom. Bulpitt, for example, presents an ingenious case in which he argues (in contrast to most commentators) that the creation of the United Kingdom was not "inevitable". Rather, it was the reluctant solution to problems faced by English politicians "at court" (the "centre"). Consequently, the post-Union structure of territorial government was not designed to be innovative and the "centre" relied upon a system of rather static indirect rule — through the assistance of local collaborative elites (such as the Anglo-Irish Protestants or the Scottish land-owning class) — to manage the expanded "periphery". The social and political modernisation experienced in the period 1870–1926, argues Bulpitt, had a conservative impact on territorial politics in the United Kingdom, and between 1926 and 1960 they were characterised by a "Dual Polity" in which national (or "high") and local (or "low") politics were largely divorced from one another. Contacts between "centre" and "periphery" were essentially bureaucratic and depoliticised until the 1960s when the "Dual Polity" was disturbed, first by Northern Ireland, then by the Devolution Debate, and more recently by clashes between central and local government. The erosion or the "Dual Polity" posed severe problems, for " . . . the English have never taken the Union seriously . . . exhibiting a strong distaste for positive peripheral government . . . (and) increasingly unwilling to treat territorial politics seriously".[51] As Bulpitt concludes, this is a central feature of the relationship between centre and periphery: ". . . these matters have posed an awkward dilemma for the Centre: how to run a territorial Union not taken seriously by this peculiar dominant section".[52]

Thus attitudinal and structural problems become part of the centre-periphery relationship, complementing the ethnic distinctiveness and economic inequalities stressed by Hechter or the "ethnic nationalist" response described by Smith, and suggesting the need for a framework even more wide ranging than those considered so far. For the centre-periphery relationship is all these things and more, the particular characteristics of a periphery a subtle blend of the myriad influences of its historical experience. As early as 1971 Kohr, in a volume full of rhetorical questions and picturesque analogies, had advanced his "Law of Peripheral Neglect" in explaining Welsh economic conditions, pointing to ". . . the impoverishing effect suffered by every peripheral economy serving a centre outside its natural confines . . .".[53] However, a more comprehensive analysis of the centre-periphery relationship, with an attempt at a fuller explanation and the construction of a wider framework, was only achieved with the fusion of the work undertaken by Rokkan and Urwin. Recognising the shortcomings of narrow and mono-causal explanations of peripheral protest or regional diversity, they argued for ". . . a broader approach which stresses the dichotomy between centre and periphery, seeking to place ethnic variations in a general framework of geopolitical location, economic strength and access to the loci of decision-making,"[54] with Urwin adding that:

> . . . the whole problem of territory and identity, of the centre-periphery
> dimension, goes far beyond a consideration only of ethnicity or the

sudden rise of a nationalist party . . . a more rigorous, systematic, historical and comparative perspective is necessary if we are to disentangle what is a complex mosaic.[55]

Rokkan and Urwin note that the recent developments in the periphery in the United Kingdom are mirrored in similar developments elsewhere in Western Europe, and that all Western European states are to a degree "multi-ethnic" and possess, therefore, the potential for regional or nationalist protest. They concede that an explanation for those recent developments can be sought in a model which emphasises that the continuing internationalisation of transactions and economies has led to a crisis in centre-periphery relations. The centre has found itself with decreasing resources under its exclusive control at precisely the same time that the periphery has demanded greater resources from the centre in the form of welfare, education and regional aid. The centre cannot deliver the goods, and so the periphery protests. However, Rokkan and Urwin argue that such a model sheds no light upon the origin of centre and periphery in the first place, and that it does not explain the great variation in strain between centre and periphery to be encountered in different parts of Western Europe. To begin with, ethnic tensions within states can be detected long before those "recent developments" which caught the eye of social scientists in the late 60s and 70s (indicating that a broader historical perspective is indeed required), and the degree of regional restiveness varies considerably from place to place: Scotland, Corsica and the Basque Country may have witnessed an upsurge in protest, but Sleswig, Alsace and Bavaria have become much quieter.

The key to greater understanding, insist Rokkan and Urwin, lies in the realisation that there is a symbiotic relationship between centre and periphery, that one cannot successfully analyse the one without examining the other. They begin by seeking broad definitions of centre and periphery. A "centre" is defined as a,

> . . . privileged location within a territory where key military/ administrative, economic and cultural resource-holders most frequently meet; with established arenas for deliberations, negotiations and decision-making; where people convene for ritual ceremonies of affirmation of identity; with monuments that symbolize this identity; with the largest proportion of the economically active population engaged in the processing and communication of information and instructions over long distances.[56]

In such a "centre", therefore, one would find parliaments, government ministries and military headquarters. There would be the trading head-offices of banks, corporations, insurance groups, trade unions, and stock exchanges, together with cultural centres — such as museums, theatres, universities, and archbishoprics — and the centres of communications such as rail and air, radio and television. The combined effect would be to give the centre political control, economic dominance, and the means to promote cultural standardisation, within the state.

16

By contrast,

> . . . a periphery is dependent, controlling at best only its own resources
> and more exposed to fluctuations in long-distance markets; is isolated
> from all other regions except the central one; and contributes little to
> the flow of communication within the territory, with a marginal culture
> that is fragmented and parochial . . .".[57]

Thus the periphery may be dependent on the centre, not only in economic terms,
but also for political decision-making and for cultural standardisation. It is also
different from the centre — in cultural, economic or political terms — and is
situated some distance from the centre, so that transactions are fraught with costs
and difficulties. Within the periphery, both the masses and elites experience
uncertainty, ambivalence and division. They are part of the system and yet are in
many respects marginal to it, they are aware of a separate identity but are constantly
exposed to the standardising agencies of the centre. But Rokkan and Urwin admit
that in practice the degree of dependency of periphery upon centre will vary from
one instance to another, as will the nature of that dependency (ie whether it is
primarily political, economic, or cultural).[58]

In matching these definitions of centre and periphery to the realities of state
structures, Rokkan and Urwin identify "monocephalic" and "polycephalic" states
— the former characterised by the marked dominance of one centre, the latter
exhibiting a more even and widespread diffusion of "central" features across the
territory with perhaps a chain of distinct centres with their own institutions and
elites. These two types, in turn, can be matched to the processes of state-building.
Some states have arisen out of a pursuit of "centralising strategies", where dynastic
expansion has established the territorial extent of the state — this Rokkan and
Urwin style "territorial space" which they equate with the "monocephalic" form.
Other states, however, exhibit a "federalising accommodation" and have emerged
where local groups have come together for mutual economic and political defence
but in so doing have negotiated a "covenant" to guarantee their individual rights,
interests and identities — this is styled "membership space" and equates with the
"polycephalic" form.

In practice, the states of Western Europe form many shades of "grey" between
these two extremes, reflected in state structures ranging from the unitary to the
organically federal. It is at this point in the analysis, argue Rokkan and Urwin,
that we must ". . . go back in history, to the crucial phases in centre formation
and the attempts to build territory-wide identities".[59] They achieve this by setting
a comparative overview of the territorial structures of Western Europe, examining
its centres and analysing its peripheries, in particular the latters' economic
conditions, cultural distinctiveness, political life, and propensity to mobilisation.
As well as noting that some states exhibit "territorial space" and others "membership space", with consequent variations in structure and degrees of toleration/
accommodation of peripheries (and hence varying levels of peripheral mobilisation
and protest), Rokkan and Urwin identify the creation ". . . of a number of subject

17

peripheries in the Celtic-Atlantic West . . ."[60] — the Celtic lands along with the Basque country, western Norway, the Orkneys, Shetland, Faeroes, and Iceland, the first of four sets of groupings upon an East-West gradient in Western Europe.

Their typology also deals specifically with the United Kingdom, claiming for the state a "territorial space" less extreme than that of France (or Italy) but nevertheless noting a significant degree of peripheral protest. The state is shown as having been "accommodating" to Northern Ireland, less so to Scotland and Wales, and much less so to Cornwall. Urwin stresses the significance of geography — in particular the familiar "highland"-"lowland" dichotomy — in moulding the history of the United Kingdom and ensuring that the centre would be located in London and its "lowland" hinterland, with the "highland" north and west relegated to peripheral status. In examining the development of the state, Urwin notes first the creation of the "Inner Centre" of London and the south-east. There is then an "Outer Centre", consisting of Wessex, East Anglia, and the Midlands. The periphery is similarly divided, with an "Inner Periphery" of Cornwall, Wales and northern England, and an "Outer Periphery" of Scotland and Ireland.[61]

Significantly, Urwin's discussion of centre-periphery relations in the United Kingdom notes the importance of industrialisation in perpetuating the nature of the relationship. He writes that industrialisation ". . . confirmed and redefined the United Kingdom as a strongly monocephalic state . . .",[62] with the peripheries suffering the deleterious effects of incomplete or over-specialised industrialisation: "Contemporary regional economic problems are the consequence of an economic specialization compounded after 1918 by far-reaching structural industrial change".[63] The importance of industrialisation in the centre-periphery relationship was also recognised by Tarrow.[64] He examined centre-periphery relations by analysing the contacts between local and national levels of government (in France and Italy), an essentially institutional perspective. But in offering critiques of other approaches to the problem, he attacked those "diffusionists" who did not acknowledge the essential modernity of the duality between centre and periphery in advanced societies such as those which he had examined: Tarrow insisted that in addition to the "Older Peripheralism" of territorial and cultural isolation there was, in the era of industrialisation, a "Second Peripheralism" of economic and social marginality.[65]

Although Tarrow failed to develop this analysis, his distinction between two periods of peripherality ("Older Peripheralism" and "Second Peripheralism") was profound, and worthy of closer attention. In essence, Tarrow admitted (albeit by implication) the antiquity of the peripheral condition, acknowledging the early emergence of peripheral territories as the result of the processes of state-building within the Medieval and Renaissance eras. This, the period of "Older Peripheralism", was characterised by the territorial and cultural isolation of the periphery. Geographically remote from the centre, with a degree of political or constitutional "accommodation" to reconcile itself to ultimate external control and to formalise and secure the suzerainty (or sovereignty) of the centre, a periphery was to a considerable degree territorially insulated from the centre. To this was added peripheral distinctions in language, religion, habit and perhaps socio-economic organisation, creating a cultural divide from the centre as significant as that of territory.

However, as Tarrow intimated, this territorial and cultural isolation was at length disturbed by the new forces of industrialisation within the state, with an increase in communications and economic transactions between centre and periphery, and with a new-found economic (and possibly strategic) importance of the periphery to the centre. This period Tarrow dubbed "Second Peripheralism". Its significance was that although its emergence heralded the demise of many of the attributes of "Older Peripheralism" (for example, an erosion of the mechanics of "accommodation", or a decline of the indigenous language), its new industrial order had not eradicated the condition of peripherality itself. On the contrary, argued Tarrow, the experience of industrialisation had brought in its wake economic and social marginality. Although Tarrow did not elaborate upon its characteristics, it is not difficult to develop his analysis and to argue that such marginality arose from the imperfect or over-specialised industrialisation of the periphery (a la Urwin), and was manifested in a lack of industrial diversification, early industrial collapse, and consequent de-industrialisation, emigration, and depopulation. Thus the peripheral condition was perpetuated, albeit in a strikingly different form to that which had existed hitherto.

Despite Tarrow's failure to develop his concept of "Older" and "Second Peripheralism", its value lies in its recognition that peripherality is a dynamic condition and will alter over time in response to changes in the nature of the centre-periphery relationship. That is not to say that there will not be constants of peripherality, most obviously geographical location and physical distance from the centre, or that elements of one period will not survive into and indeed influence the characteristics of the next. But it is possible to postulate a model of phases of peripherality, in which peripherality itself is constant but where its principal determining and consequent characteristics alter radically from one phase or period to the next. Such a model is inevitably multi-dimensional, with an array of cultural, social, economic, political, constitutional and other variables, and explains how it is that a peripheral territory will retain its separate (though changing) identity over time despite the often traumatic experience of movement from one phase to another. It contrasts with the uni-linear explanation offered by Hechter (where the survival of ethnic distinctiveness is the result of a "cultural division of labour"), and negates the "single variable" models advanced by observers such as Eastlake or Berresford Ellis (where cultural decline/survival is seen as the determining quality of the peripheral condition).[66]

In short, a model of phases of peripherality — involving "Older", "Second" and perhaps subsequent "Peripheralisms" — demonstrates that a peripheral territory remains distinct (in social, economic, political or other terms) from the centre *because* of rather than *despite* its historical experience. This, of course, can be tested by examining the historical experience of a particular periphery. In the context of this study, the model provides precisely the kind of framework which is required for an analysis of the making of modern Cornwall, a framework that has been lacking hitherto. Having shown that the developments of the 1960s and

70s in the United Kingdom led to the demise of the "homogeneous state" paradigm and its replacement by a new orthodoxy stressing regional diversity, and having discussed those explanations which arose to account for those developments, it is now possible to address the case of Cornwall itself. The experience of Cornwall, indeed, can only be understood against the wider background of diversity and centre-periphery relationships within the United Kingdom as a whole. That said, it offers an ideal case study in which to demonstrate the historical validity of Tarrow's "Older" and "Second Peripheralism" and the resultant model of phases of peripherality. In particular, it is possible to give detailed consideration to the movement from "Older" to "Second Peripheralism", from territorial and cultural isolation to economic and social marginalisation, and also to argue — in further refinement of Rokkan, Urwin, and Tarrow — that recent peripheral protest in Cornwall is one symptom of movement towards a further or "Third" period of "Peripheralism".

Notes and References

1. This was overwhelmingly in literary vein, for example: Daphne du Maurier, *Vanishing Cornwall: The Spirit and History of Cornwall*, Victor Gollancz, London, 1967; Denys Val Baker, *The Timeless Land: The Creative Spirit in Cornwall*, Adams and Dart, Bath, 1973; John Betjeman, *Betjeman's Cornwall*, John Murray, London, 1984; Donald R. Rawe, *A Prospect of Cornwall*, Robert Hale, London, 1986; A.L. Rowse, *The Little Land of Cornwall*, Alan Sutton, Gloucester, 1986. The theme of "difference" permeated F.E. Halliday, *A History of Cornwall*, Duckworth, London, 1959; and the "Celtic identity" approach was stated explicitly in P. Berresford Ellis, *The Cornish Language and Its Literature*, Routledge, London, 1974.
2. G. Almond and S. Verba, *The Civic Culture*, Little, Brown, Boston, 1965.
3. David St John Thomas, *A Regional history of the Railways of Great Britain — Volume 1: The West Country*, David and Charles, Newton Abbot, 5th edition, 1981, p15, noted the historical disunity of the south west: " . . . even the word region is misleading, for there was no economic, social or other unity about the West . . .".
4. Jim Bulpitt, *Territory and Power in the United Kingdom*, Manchester University Press, Manchester, 1983, p237.
5. Robert Miles, "Racism and Nationalism in Britain", in Charles Husband, *'Race' in Britain: Continuity and Change*; Hutchinson, London, 1982, p287.
6. This shortcoming was noted in Kenneth O. Morgan, *The Oxford Illustrated History of Britain*, Oxford University Press, Oxford, 1984, ppvi-viii; and Christopher Haigh, *The Cambridge Historical Encyclopaedia of Great Britain and Ireland*, Cambridge University Press, Cambridge, 1985, p7.
7. J. Blondel, *Voters, Parties, and Leaders: The Social Fabric of British Politics*, Penguin, London, 1963, 6th edition, 1974, p20.
8. Ibid, p21.
9. R.M. Punnett, *British Government and Politics*, Heinemann, London, 1968, 2nd edition, 1971, p78.
10. Stein Rokkan and Derek W. Urwin, *The Politics of Territorial Identity: Studies in European Regionalism*, Sage, London, 1982, p2.

11. John Bochel, David Denver, Allan Macartney (eds.), *The Referendum Experience: Scotland 1979*, Aberdeen University Press, Aberdeen, 1981.
12. Ibid. pp147-152; Michael Keating, *State and Regional Nationalism: Territorial Politics and the European State*, Harvester Wheatsheaf, London, 1988, pp187-192.
13. Michael Rush, *Parliamentary Government in Britain*, Pitman, London, 1981, p234.
14. Bulpitt, op. cit., p236.
15. *New Statesman*, 9 January 1987.
16. Ibid.
17. Paul Temperton (ed.), *Up North! How to Unshackle a Forgotten People*, Campaign For The North, Hebden Bridge, 1978, p19.
18. Ibid.
19. John Osmond, *The Divided Kingdom*, Constable, London, 1988, pp64-66, pp88-92.
20. Richard Rose, *The United Kingdom as a Multi-National State*, University of Strathclyde Survey Research Centre Occasional paper No 6, Glasgow, 1970; Jaroslav Krejci and Vitezslav Velimsky, *Ethnic and Political Nations in Europe*, Croom Helm, London, 1981, pp183-192.
21. Anthony H. Birch, *Political Integration and Disintegration in the British Isles*, George Allen and Unwin, London, 1977; Richard Rose, *Understanding the United Kingdom: The Territorial Dimension in Government*, Longman, London, 1982; Bulpitt, op. cit.; Keating, op. cit.
22. For example, the prospects for a developing relationship between the Republic of Ireland and the United Kingdom became a subject for speculation in studies such as: John Biggs-Davison and George Chowdharay-Best, *The Cross of Saint Patrick: The Catholic Unionist Tradition in Ireland*, Kensal, Bourne End, 1984; Kevin Boyle and Tom Hadden, *Ireland: A Positive Proposal*, Penguin, London, 1985; and Tom Wilson, *Ulster: Conflict and Consent*, Blackwell, Oxford, 1989.
23. Before 1968 there were no more than three political textbooks covering Northern Ireland — by 1984 there were over 200; see, Henry Drucker (general ed.), *Developments in British Politics*, Macmillan, London, 1984, p308.
24. A substantial Scottish literature developed, from Hanham's early study (H.J. Hanham, *Scottish Nationalism*, Faber, London, 1969) to J. Kellas, *The Scottish Political System*, Cambridge University Press, Cambridge, 3rd edition, 1986. Wales attracted similar attention, as in J. Osmond, *Creative Conflict: The Politics of Welsh Devolution*, Gomer, Llandysul, 1977; and it interesting to note that "Celtic nationalism" in Brittany also attracted some English-language attention, as in: Patricia Elton Mayo, *The Roots of Identity: Three National Movements in Contemporary Politics*, Allen Lane, London, 1974; M.J.C. O'Callaghan, *Separatism in Brittany*, Dyllansow Truran, Redruth, 1983.
25. Alan Butt Philip, *The Welsh Question: Nationalism in Welsh Politics, 1945–1975*, University of Wales Press, Cardiff, 1975.
26. P.J. Magwick, *The Politics of Rural Wales*, Hutchinson, London, 1973.
27. Hugh Berrington, "Centre-Periphery Conflict and British Politics", in Yves Meny and Vincent Wright (eds.), *Centre-Periphery Relations in Western Europe*, George Allen and Unwin, London, 1985, p183.
28. Ibid, p186; William L. Miller, *The End of British Politics? Scots and English Political Behaviour in the Seventies*, Clarendon, Oxford, 1981, pp21-26.
29. Christopher Harvie, "Scottish Politics Since 1901", in Christopher Haigh, op. cit., p304.
30. Ibid, p306.
31. Ibid.

32. Michael Keating and David Bleiman, *Labour and Scottish Nationalism*, Macmillan, London, 1979, p199.
33. The first real attempt at examining peripheral England was Geoffrey Moorhouse, *Britain in the Sixties: The Other England*, Penguin, London, 1964.
34. Derek W. Urwin, "Territorial Structures and Political Developments in the United Kingdom", in Stein Rokkan and Derek W. Urwin, op. cit., p20.
35. Derek W. Urwin, "Territorial Structure and Politics in the United Kingdom", unpublished paper presented to ECPR workshop on Politicisation of Peripheral Identities, Brussels, 1979, p35.
36. Berrington, op. cit., 186.
37. Anthony D. Smith, *Theories of Nationalism*, Duckworth, London, 1971.
38. Elie Kedourie, *Nationalism*, Hutchinson, London, 1960, p9.
39. R. Tudur Jones, *The Desire of Nations*, Christopher Davies, Llandybie, 1974, pp61-67.
40. Philip Payton, "The Ideology of Celtic Nationalism", unpublished BSc(Hons) dissertation, University of Bristol, 1975, p16.
41. For example, Tom Nairn, *The Break-Up of Britain: Crisis and Neo-Nationalism*, New Left, London, 1977.
42. Anthony D. Smith, "Nationalism, Ethnic Separatism and The Intelligentsia", in Colin H. Williams, *National Separatism*, University of Wales Press, Cardiff, 1982, p27.
43. Michael Hechter, *Internal Colonialism: The Celtic Fringe in British National Development, 1536–1966*, Routledge, London, 1975.
44. Smith, 1982, op. cit.; Bulpitt, op. cit., pp34-44; Edward Page, "Michael Hechter's 'internal colonial' model of political development in the British Isles: some theoretical and methodological problems", unpublished paper presented to PSA Conference, Aberystwyth, 1977; Edward Page, "Michael Hechter's internal colonial thesis: some theoretical and methodological problems", *European Journal of Political Research*, Vol. 6, No. 3, pp295-317.
45. Stein Rokkan, *Citizens, Elections and Parties*, Universitets for layet, Oslo, 1970, p100.
46. Page, 1977, op. cit., p14.
47. Bulpitt, op. cit., p44.
48. Hechter has himself offered substantial qualifications: Michael Hechter, "Internal Colonialism Revisited", in Edward A. Tiryakian and Ronald Rogowski, *New Nationalism and the Developed West: Towards Explanations*, George Allen and Unwin, Boston, 1985, pp18-26.
49. Nairn, op. cit.
50. Berrington, op. cit., p171.
51. Bulpitt, op. cit., p237.
52. Ibid, p238.
53. Leopold Kohr, *Is Wales Viable?* Christopher Davies, Llandybie, 1971, p2.
54. Rokkan and Urwin, op. cit., p2.
55. Derek W. Urwin, "The Price of a Kingdom: Territory, Identity and the Centre-Periphery Dimension in Western Europe", in Yves Meny and Vincent Wright, op. cit., p167.
56. Rokkan and Urwin, op. cit., p5.
57. Ibid.
58. Stein Rokkan and Derek W. Urwin, *Economy, Territory, Identity: Politics of West European Peripheries*, Sage, London, 1983.
59. Rokkan and Urwin, op. cit., p6.
60. Stein Rokkan, "Peripheries and Centres: The Territorial Structure of Western Europe", unpublished paper, 1979, p38.

61. Urwin, 1979, op. cit., p6.
62. Rokkan and Urwin, 1982, p35.
63. Ibid., p37.
64. Sidney Tarrow, *Between Centre and Periphery: Grassroots Politicians in Italy and France*, Yale University Press, New Haven, 1977.
65. Ibid., p16.
66. Rosalie Eastlake, "Cornwall: The Development of a Celtic Periphery", unpublished MA thesis, McGill University, 1981; P. Berresford Ellis, *The Celtic Revolution: A Study in Anti-Imperialism*, Y Lolfa, Talybont, 1985.

CHAPTER TWO

Towards a Cornish Explanation

The myth of the "homogeneous state" ensured that, until recently, Cornwall was rarely (if ever) afforded proper attention in her own right by historians and social scientists examining the nature of the United Kingdom. Even amongst those most likely to be predisposed towards a more sensitive appreciation of Cornwall's status and identity, there was evidence of confusion and uncertainty — perhaps even a little muddled thinking. Pelling, for example, was clear that "In Cornwall, as in Wales, a Celtic language survived until modern times",[1] and yet — almost in the same breath — he was prepared to consider Cornwall as merely a part of a wider south-west and argue that "Devon and Cornwall form a distinctive region of England".[2] He added (as if to admit his own confusion) that the south-west was a region " . . . which challenges comparison with Wales rather than with any other region of the country to which it belongs".[3] This insistence that Cornwall — although apparently "Celtic" — be considered an integral part of an English south-west led to similarly imprecise statements elsewhere, such as Waller's view that ". . . the South West has been regarded as an important part of the Liberal 'Celtic fringe' "[4] and Berrington's rather vague belief that "South West England is sometimes treated as a peripheral territory . . .".[5] Punnett, for all his adherence to the "homogeneous state", was seemingly prepared to admit that Cornwall was part of a "Celtic Fringe",[6] and Madgwick's confusion was exhibited in his persistent use of the phrase "South-West England" when it would have been more accurate to employ "Cornwall". He wrote, for example, that "The 'Celtic fringe' has long figured in accounts of politics . . . Scotland, Wales and *South-West England* are indeed peripheral in a highly-centralised, London-focussed society; and they are Celtic by historical origins".[7] Cornwall, then, was placed rather perversely in a position where the relatively few academic observers to comment on the Cornish scene were prepared to describe Cornwall as "Celtic" and yet at the same time present her as part of a wider south-west England.

However, just as events in Scotland, Wales and Northern Ireland in the 1960s and 1970s were to question the "homogeneous state" and lead to a new emphasis upon "diversity", so parallel events — albeit more modest and on a smaller scale — in Cornwall over the same decades were to draw the Cornish situation more sharply into focus. The emergence of Cornish nationalism as a cultural and political phenomenon will be discussed later, but here it is important to note that Mebyon Kernow — Cornwall's principal nationalist organisation — was founded in 1951

24

and became increasingly active during precisely the same period that Plaid Cymru and the Scottish National Party were growing in stature and support. Mebyon Kernow (Sons of Cornwall) was at first modest in its aspirations, styling itself as a pressure group (with no intention at first to contest Parliamentary seats) and arguing for a limited form of devolutionary self-government which would require only ". . . the re-organisation of the United Kingdom, not the dissolution or lessening of it".[8] The movement declared its sympathy with Cornish language and cultural groups, asserted Cornwall's identity as a Celtic nation, and won a certain credibility through its vigorous (but ultimately unsuccessful) campaign for a Cornish university. Popular support was also forthcoming as a result of Mebyon Kernow's opposition to the "Overspill" plan in the late 1960s in which Londoners were to be re-housed in Cornwall,[9] and the movement played a prominent role in Cornwall's defeat of that aspect of Local Government re-organisation which had envisaged the creation of a "Tamarside" county in which part of south-east Cornwall would have been lost to a new authority based in Plymouth.[10]

By the late 1960s, Mebyon Kernow was exhibiting an air of confidence and optimism, expressed through the pages of its journal *Cornish Nation* — "Cornwall's First Truly National Newspaper", as its banner headlines proclaimed — first published in November 1968.[11] The range of contributors to the paper revealed the degree of respect, if not support, that Mebyon Kernow had come to command in the Cornish community. Daphne du Maurier, the well-known novelist, declared herself ". . . an associate member of Mebyon Kernow . . .",[12] Dr A.L. Rowse — Cornish author and Fellow of All Souls — emphasised that "There is a wonderful opportunity for *Cornish Nation* and an important job to do",[13] and Alderman K.G. Foster, then Chairman of Cornwall County Council, assured readers that "Although I am not a member of Mebyon Kernow . . . Any effort or movement to keep our entity and maintain our viability would always have my support".[14] In a subsequent issue, Miss Du Maurier went on to express her belief that "A form of self-government for Cornwall with legislative powers . . . is . . . possible within ten years . . . a united Cornwall able to run its own affairs with minimum direction from London yet remaining part of the UK and loyal to the Crown".[15]

In pursuit of its pressure-group role, Mebyon Kernow approached local MPs. Harold Hayman, the veteran Labour MP for Falmouth-Camborne, declared his support for the movement, and two Liberal MPs — John Pardoe in North Cornwall and Peter Bessell at Bodmin — actually joined Mebyon Kernow and declared their commitment to Cornish self-government. John Nott, the Conservative Member for St Ives, later expressed his broad approval of Mebyon Kernow policies, and David Mudd — who was to become Conservative MP for Falmouth-Camborne at the 1970 General Election — joined the movement.[16] By this time, however, Mebyon Kernow was already moving towards a more party-political and overtly nationalist position, and — taking its cue from the by-election successes of Plaid Cymru and the Scottish National Party — announced during 1969 that it was to contest forthcoming Parliamentary Elections. The first target was Falmouth-Camborne, where Mebyon Kernow claimed to have more than a thousand members, but in the 1970 General Election the Mebyon Kernow candidate (Richard Jenkin) secured less than a thousand votes and the seat was won by David Mudd (albeit a member of Mebyon Kernow!).[17]

The move from pressure-group to political party led to a number of internal dissensions within Mebyon Kernow, leading first of all to a break-away but short-lived Cornish National Party and later to the similarly-named but more permanent Cornish Nationalist Party, and causing the movement to falter in the development of a Parliamentary Election strategy. In the two elections of 1974 Mebyon Kernow failed to contest Falmouth-Camborne, although a candidate — James Whetter — did contest Truro constituency on both occasion. In the first election Mebyon Kernow achieved over 800 votes, seen as comparable to the 1970 result in Falmouth-Camborne, but in the October election Dr Whetter's vote slumped to a little more than 200 as nationalist voters switched their allegiance to the successful and manifestly pro-Cornish Liberal candidate, David Penhaligon. Dr Whetter achieved a similar result in Truro when he stood as the Cornish Nationalist Party candidate in 1979, but during that year Mebyon Kernow made something of an electoral "come-back", not only winning a combined vote of over 4000 in the three seats it contested in the General Election but also achieving "10,000 Twice" — an aggregate of 10,000 votes in the Local Elections, and 10,000 votes for its candidate (Richard Jenkin) in the European Election (a result which represented an impressive 10 per cent of the Cornish component of the vote in the Cornwall and Plymouth European Parliamentary Constituency).[18]

Since 1979, nationalist party activity in Cornwall — rather like that in Wales and, until of late, Scotland — appears to have receded. But, again as in Wales and Scotland, the events of the 1960s and 70s have had an effect on Cornish life and politics, and have led observers to re-assess their interpretations of Cornish social and political culture. Compared to the re-assessment which accompanied the developments in Wales and Scotland (and Northern Ireland), the new perspectives on Cornwall are modest, muted and incomplete. Nevertheless, they exist and form the basis from which a more general explanation of the Cornish experience may be developed.

The Kilbrandon Commission on the Constitution certainly took note of Cornish events, accepting a lengthy submission from Mebyon Kernow as part of its evidence and later recommending — in the same report that advocated Devolution for Wales and Scotland — that greater use be made of the title "Duchy of Cornwall" (instead of "County") to emphasise Cornwall's distinct status and identity. Kilbrandon's recommendation also emphasised Cornwall's place in the new concern with the "territorial dimension" of the United Kingdom, reminding observers that Cornwall's territorial identity did not derive from the old Saxon heptarchy (as an ordinary English shire's might) but rather from an ancient Celtic survival which had been formalised into the "Duchy" in Medieval times when the "Principality" of Wales (with which it was linked) was also created.[19] The concern to explore and explain the constitutional significance of the Duchy status has continued apace (the Cowethas Flamank research group issued a report of the subject during 1986[20]), and equal energy has been devoted to the discussion of Stannary Law and the extent to which the degree of constitutional independence afforded to Cornwall in Medieval times by the Stannary Parliament and system still applies. This debate has attracted many popular enthusiasts,[21] but Pennington adds an academic opinion when he notes that in certain respects the Stannary Parliament ". . . had legislative powers . . . which equalled those of the national Parliament at Westminster . . ."[22] and that ". . . stannary law is still formally a part of the law of England".[23]

A further consequence of the events of the 1960s and 70s in Cornwall was the new-found appreciation of the extent to which the Liberal Party was associated with a distinctly Cornish political culture (here once again echoing the experience in Wales and Scotland). Although perpetuating the erroneous equation of "Cornwall" with "South West England", Madgwick noted that "In Scotland, Wales and *South West England*, the distinctive nature of Celtic politics has been expressed to some extent in nationalism, but most notably in support for the Liberal Party".[24] Similarly, Bogdanor noted in his study of Liberal Party politics that during the 1950s the Liberals had ". . . two areas of local strength (*Cornwall* and rural Wales) where the party contested a majority of constituencies even in 1951 and 1955",[25] leading the Liberal Party a decade later to respond to ". . . the demand for self-government . . . growing in Wales and Scotland, and to a lesser degree *in Cornwall*. The Liberal Party was sympathetic to these movements . . .".[26] Certainly, of all those Cornish MPs to join or support Mebyon Kernow, John Pardoe (especially) and Peter Bessell were those who spoke most consistently and sympathetically in favour of Mebyon Kernow policies, and Paul Tyler — briefly Liberal MP for Bodmin in 1974 — added his support for Cornish Devolution and, during the European Election campaign of 1989, for the creation of a Cornwall-only European Parliamentary Constituency. Of course, the unique relationship between the Liberal Party and Cornwall, and the importance of Cornish ethnicity in determining it, was emphasised by the emergence, popularity and enormous success of David Penhaligon in Truro constituency.

Like Pardoe and Bessell before him, Penhaligon supported Mebyon Kernow policies as a means of demonstrating his commitment to Cornish issues. But he also brought Cornish issues to the fore in the Liberal Party in Cornwall, and at times brought them to the attention of Parliament. He spoke in favour of a Cornish Assembly during the debate on Devolution, he championed the cause of the Cornish miners at the time of the tin crisis, and in the European Assembly (Constituencies) debate in December 1978 he vigorously opposed the creation of a European Parliamentary Constituency which merged Cornwall with Plymouth. He declared that Cornwall was not part of England, that Plymouth had expansionary designs upon south-east Cornwall, and that the proposed creation of a Cornwall and Plymouth constituency made

> . . . this a sad day for Cornwall. It is the first time in any election that the boundary of Cornwall, which is sacrosanct and important, has been ignored. The boundary has been denied by what many people in Cornwall see as a London-based Parliament . . . Cornwall is a Celtic

area . . . the Celts of Cornwall regard this as a sad day in their history, for it is the day when their boundary was ignored and denied.[28]

Following his tragic death in December 1986, Penhaligon was described in the *Telegraph* as ". . . a reformirg radical . . . something of a Cornish nationalist, with a healthy scepticism of London-based politicians . . .".[29] Jo Grimond considered that Penhaligon's ". . . politics were first of all Cornish . . .",[30] while David Owen thought him ". . . the personification of the Cornishman . . .".[31] The *Guardian* decided that he had been the "Voice of Cornwall".[32]

With Penhaligon setting the pace, it was difficult for other personalities and parties to demonstrate their own "Cornishness", but Penhaligon had forced his opponents to address themselves to Cornish issues. In Falmouth-Camborne, David Mudd found it necessary to "distance" himself from the Conservative Government at the height of the tin crisis, while in South-East Cornwall the local Conservative MP (Robert Hicks) adopted a more subtle and long-term process of "distancing" to demonstrate both his own "liberal" disposition within the party and his particular concern for Cornwall.[33] Even the Labour Party, which had hitherto not embraced Cornish issues to any great degree, adopted for its candidate in the Truro by-election of 1987 a Cornish-speaking Bard of the Gorsedd, one John King. In the 1987 General Election the Labour candidate for South-East Cornwall, Paul Clarke, decided to concentrate part of his local campaign upon his opposition to the processes turning Cornwall into a "Cornish Disneyland".[34] "Cornishness", then, was increasingly a quality which politicians in Cornwall had to acquire and project if they were to be judged credible by the Cornish electorate; further evidence of a distinct and active Cornish political culture.

As the events of the 1960s and 70s began to unfold, and as the attributes of Cornish political culture became more clearly observable, so certain social and political commentators became aware that Cornwall was indeed "different". As early as 1964 Moorhouse argued that Cornwall was very different to England — historically, socially, economically — and that there were real signs, not only of "difference" but also of discontent:

> For all their lobbying of MPs . . . the men of Mebyon Kernow do not appear so far to have made much impact. The English temptation is to dismiss them as a lot of cranks; and truly some of the postures they adopt invite ridicule. The cold fact is, however, that where a home-rule movement arises, at the bottom of it is generally to be found some very real grievance. Though the activities of Mebyon Kernow may be inflated out of all proportion, and though they take themselves a sight too seriously, it would be a very stupid Englishman who didn't recognise that this extravaganza expresses a fundamental resentment shared by many Cornishmen outside the movement.[35]

Thayer, in his admittedly unsatisfactory survey of the British political "fringe" in 1965, devoted half a chapter to the activities of Mebyon Kernow, describing its membership (then thought to number some 200) as ". . . well-educated and articulate . . ."[36] with ". . . the latent support of many other Cornish people . . .".[37] By 1983 Waller was able to offer a more penetrating insight into the distinctive qualities of Cornish politics, drawing attention, for example, to the importance of "personality" (as in the cases of Mudd or Penhaligon) and to the political significance of Cornwall's ". . . reputation for distrusting the English and the English parties"[38] and of the ". . . strong Nonconformist and rural radical vote, and . . . distrust of 'English' Toryism . . ."[39]. Thus, although Mebyon Kernow and its nationalist stance were the most obvious signs of "difference" in Cornish politics, it was becoming apparent that the distinctive Cornish political culture was both more broad-based and more deep-seated — involving a strongly Cornish influence in the other parties (particularly the Liberals), and exhibiting the effects of other influences such as Nonconformity and a residual rural radicalism (the latter, of course, an echo of Madgwick's assessment of rural Wales).

With this new appreciation that Cornwall was perhaps "different" in a way that Scotland and Wales were, and with observers pointing to both an embryonic nationalist movement and to a wider but very distinct Cornish political culture, came the search for theoretical frameworks in which to offer explanations of these phenomena. As noted in Chapter 1, there was already underway a parallel search for explanations of the very similar phenomena that had been observed in other nations and regions of the United Kingdom, and so it was not surprising that those seeking explanations of the Cornish experience should "borrow" models being applied at that time elsewhere. Again, given the atmosphere of the late 60s and 70s and the preoccupation with the advances of the various Celtic nationalist parties, it was not surprising that existing models of nationalism were offered as interpretations of what was happening in Cornwall as well as in other parts of the United Kingdom.

Berresford Ellis offered a straightforward nationalist interpretation. He argued that despite centuries of anglicisation, Cornwall retained a residual Celtic identity which lingered long enough to be regenerated by the "Celtic Revival" (literary and otherwise) of the late nineteenth and early twentieth centuries, leading to the rebirth of the Cornish language and — with the advent of mass politics and popular education — to the eventual emergence of political nationalism (". . . a re-awakening of Cornish nationhood").[40] He did not, however, explain what processes may have lain behind these series of events, and his apparent view of the Cornish identity revolving around the twin concerns of language and nationalist politics was so selective as to be almost unrecognisable — let alone unacceptable — to observers of the wider Cornish situation. He was content to merely express wonder at ". . . the truly astonishing rebirth of this nation"[41] and to comment that "The rise of this political national consciousness had been a remarkable achievement, after it had long been considered that Cornwall had been totally assimilated into the English ethos."[42] Surprisingly, this approach was echoed in Eastlake's discussion, which failed to note (let alone explain) the real extent of "difference" in modern Cornwall and observed rather oddly that Cornwall faces ". . . either the prospect of total incorporation into England . . ."[43], or a national revival led by Cornish cultural and political nationalists. Clearly, a more sophisticated and rigorous model was required if a satisfactory explanation was to be achieved, and one early attempt at a solution was the application of Smith's concept of "ethnic nationalism" to the Cornish case. In this, Cornwall was seen as having fallen under the centralising influences of the English "possessive" and "scientific" states:

> . . . the major Cornish cultural crisis occurred as a result of the homogenising policies of the Tudor 'possessive' State. The two Cornish rebellions of 1497 were largely a reaction to central government interference and the 'Great Prayer Book Rebellion' of 1549 was basically a protest against the introduction of the English language into Cornish services. Failure to get the Prayer Book and Bible translated into Cornish meant that the language was put into swift decline . . .[44].

This cultural crisis led, in turn, to the "double socialisation" of the intelligentsia, to the emergence of the "traditionalists", "assimilationalists", "reformists", and ultimately "revivalists", producing a Cornish "ethnic nationalism" which aimed to gain a state and preserve a culture — ". . . this is the base on which its ideology is founded".[45] As an explanation of Cornish nationalism, this had much that was attractive, but it shared the short-comings of Smith's original thesis (see Chapter 1) and presented a view of Cornish history which all but ignored the crucial phases of industrialisation and de-industrialisation, as well as failing to discuss the wider manifestations of "difference" in Cornish social and political culture.

Hechter, of course, attempted a broader examination of Celtic nationalism, but — notwithstanding the general criticisms of his model and methodology — his comments on the Cornish situation were essentially unsatisfactory. He considered that ". . . there has never been a detailed study of the anglicization of Cornwall",[46] and went on to argue that the "internal colonial" model was valid for the entire "Celtic Fringe" ". . . with the partial exception of Cornwall".[47] This qualification was due, he said, to the fact that,

> . . . the Celtic region of Cornwall became largely assimilated to English culture by the mid-seventeenth century. It was not until the seventeenth century that the English state began to seriously implement policies of cultural intolerance in the peripheral regions. Thus the relative weakness of Celtic ethnicity in nineteenth and twentieth century Cornwall is due, in part, to the fact that the integration of this region into the English economy had occurred prior to 1600.[48]

Cornwall, then, according to Hechter, was apparently straddled uncomfortably across both his "internal colonial" and "diffusion" models, a view which came in for strong criticism within Cornwall itself and which revealed Hechter's sketchy knowledge of Cornish history. Critics complained, for example, that — contrary to Hechter's belief — policies of cultural intolerance were in operation in Cornwall as early as the fifteenth and sixteenth centuries: ". . . the homogenising and centralising policies of the Tudor State were by their very nature anti-Celtic and intolerant of regional diversity. The two Cornish rebellions of 1497 and the Western Rising of 1549 can be seen as reactions to this intolerance . . .".[49] Again, contrary to Hechter's assertions , it was also argued that *after* 1600 the Cornish economy became noticeably *less* diversified and even *less* integrated with that of England, as tin (and later copper) mining became more and more important. Indeed, this lack of diversification and integration was seen as a major cause of the "Great Migration" from Cornwall in the nineteenth century.[50]

Despite Hechter's inability to address himself successfully to the case of Cornwall, his "internal colonial" model was seen by Deacon as a useful tool in seeking an explanation for the condition of modern Cornwall. Ignoring Hechter's ambivalent description of the Cornish experience, Deacon took his cue from Hechter's analysis of Wales, Scotland and Ireland, pointing to ". . . the stubborn persistence of a Cornish identity. Integrating factors have been so powerful that, by rights, a separate Cornish identity should have been obliterated long ago".[51] Like Hechter, Deacon took this to be evidence against the application of a "diffusion" model and argued instead that there was in Cornwall a ". . . pattern of resistance to assimilation . . ."[52] which could be explained within the context of the "internal colonial" model. In attempting the application of the model to Cornwall, Deacon highlighted Cornwall's "economic dualism", arguing that the Cornish economy — like other "internal colonial" or "peripheral" economies — was dependent on an external market and was based on the primary factor, principally extractive and agricultural. Sixteen per cent of Cornwall's workforce was employed in agriculture and mining in 1971, he said, compared with just over five per cent in Britain as a whole, while the fact that only 15 per cent of the Cornish workforce was engaged in manufacturing (compared with 34 per cent in Britain) ". . . illustrates the lack of secondary industry in Cornwall".[53] Mining companies treated Cornwall in a "neo-colonial" manner, the development of the Cornish transport system was directed specifically at facilitating Cornish penetration of external markets, while Cornwall had been relatively disadvantaged in mean income from as long ago as 1851. Unemployment was always consistently higher in Cornwall than the United Kingdom average.

Deacon also identified a Cornish "cultural division of labour", with Cornish people experiencing discrimination (the strength of Nonconformity reflected ". . . alienation from the culture of the core society . . .",[54] part of the "psychology of discrimination . . ."[55]) and the Cornish economy — much of it "branch factory" in nature — being controlled form outside. More importantly, there was a ". . . superimposition of cultural divisions on class division . . .",[56] with Cornish people failing to fill "top jobs" in Cornwall and being clustered generally at the lower end of the occupational/employment and housing markets. Better homes and better jobs, implied Deacon, were normally in the hands of immigrants from outside Cornwall.

Despite this seemingly enthusiastic application of the model to Cornwall, Deacon stopped short of a totally uncritical embrace of Hechter's "internal colonialism".

Hechter argued that ethnic conflict would arise from an "internal colonial" situation, but Deacon admitted that whilst there was a widespread sense of Cornish patriotism, the nationalist movement itself was quite small and had to date failed to achieve ethnic political mobilisation. In an apparent return to a "diffusionist" stance, Deacon explained that ". . . because of historical factors . . ."[57] there were few symbols of Cornish nationhood, with the Cornish people experiencing a great deal of confusion about their identity: "Many people can quite happily define themselves as both Cornish *and* English".[58] This had led (as a "diffusionist" might argue) to a ". . . weakness of Cornish ethnicity . . .".[59] Deacon also recognised that Hechter's model could not explain the recent extensive immigration into Cornwall (Hechter considered that in an ". . . impoverished and culturally alien region there is little incentive for members of the core group to migrate there in force"[60]), although he did argue that this immigration had led not to an accelerated "diffusion" but to a heightening of the "cultural division of labour" and to an " . . . informal social 'apartheid' . . .".[61] In other areas, Deacon considered that "Factual evidence can be contradictory",[62] citing the example of Cornish voting behaviour where the rise of Penhaligon in Truro (". . . based on a strongly ethnic appeal, and atypical of the English experience . . ."[63]) contrasted with the situation elsewhere in Cornwall where the traditional anti-Conservative stance had been — he contended — largely eroded by 1983, reflecting perhaps (he said) a weakening of the Cornish identity or the weight of a Tory immigrant vote.

Deacon concluded that the "internal colonial" model was ". . . a useful starting point . . ."[64] for an explanation of the relationship between the Cornish "periphery" and the English "core", especially as it highlighted the importance of economic disadvantage within that relationship. It is difficult to claim any more for Hechter, because, even leaving aside the general critiques of his model, his own doubts about the Cornish situation (albeit ill-informed, as they were) were rather reinforced by Deacon's caution and reservations. The "internal colonial" model fails to explain the many paradoxes apparent within the Cornish situation, and it is not enough to imply that Cornwall is somehow poised between the "internal colonial" and "diffusion" models: the Cornish experience deserves an explanation which is capable of application without qualification, reservation or apology.

The work of Lee and Rallings provided a refreshing corrective to the "nationalist" interpretations of the Cornish experience, taking their analysis beyond a concern for "ethnic nationalism" to try to identify a much broader manifestation of "difference" in Cornwall.[65] In marked contrast to those who saw Cornwall as part of a wider South-West England, they considered that ". . . it is Cornwall alone that is Celtic and it is Cornwall which — even on the briefest acquaintance — seems very different historically, economically, socially and politically from both Devon and the rest of the South West."[66] This "difference" had led, they argued, to ". . . the formation of an identifiable Cornish political culture . . .",[67] socio-economic differences in particular having had ". . . a residual significance in terms of contemporary Cornish politics".[68] They pointed to the social and political effects of the unusually small size of Cornish farms (the average was only 28 acres), most of which were held on tenant leases from the Duchy of Cornwall or from independent proprietors, noting that there were few landowners equivalent to the English squire in terms of status or function. They noted, too, the social and political effects of Nonconformity — which had lent Cornwall a very distinctive brand of Liberal radicalism — and considered that the "Celtic Revival" had fostered a strong Cornish sentiment which ". . . has had an important impact on the Cornish style of politics through its contribution to an apparently widespread sense of 'difference' and 'separateness' ".[69] Significantly, they considered that ". . . the historical and cultural distinctiveness of Cornwall has been eroded less by the pressures of the late twentieth century than one might expect",[70] and went on to argue that in Cornish politics there was " . . . a relatively strong sense of Cornish identity or Cornish consciousness, and a growing sense of anti-metropolitanism".[71]

This sense of identity had had an effect, argued Lee, not only on Mebyon Kernow and the other nationalists but upon the whole range of Cornish politics. The nationalists themselves had influenced the attitudes of other parties (". . . their ineffectual intervention in parliamentary elections should not be taken as an indicator of their effect on the Cornish political scene"[72]), and one measure of the distinctiveness of Cornish politics was the fact that the Liberal vote in Cornwall since the Second World War had been 15 per cent higher than the UK average, while the Labour vote was 15 per cent lower. As Lee enquired rhetorically,

> Given that the population is largely working class and economically disadvantaged — why has Labour conspicuously failed to make headway in the Cornish constituencies? Given that an increasing proportion of the electorate is either self-employed or retired 'immigrants', why have the Conservatives not benefited more in electoral terms?[73]

In answer to this and the more general questions concerning Cornwall's sense of "difference" and the distinctiveness of Cornish politics, Lee and Rallings identified two key (but interconnected) factors — the retarded "nationalisation" of Cornish politics, and the "peripheral" status of Cornwall. Using the concept first developed by Johnston to explain the reluctance and difficulty with which the constituency of Norfolk South West[74] was brought into the mainstream of English politics after 1945, Lee and Rallings claimed that in Cornwall there was also a deep-seated resistance to the "nationalisation" of local politics: anti-metropolitanism and an independent cultural background ". . . together have served to hinder the nationalisation of Cornish politics in the twentieth century".[75] This in turn was linked to the effects of Cornwall's "peripheral" status, with Lee exclaiming that,

> The history of Cornwall as one of England's peripheral areas is relatively little known, as is the fact that it is the only part of England to have given rise to and sustained a nationalist/autonomist movement that has been neither spurious nor ephemeral.[76]

Together, Lee and Rallings considered that twentieth century Cornwall was ". . . almost a classic peripheral region, given that no significant industrial development replaced the mining industry . . .",[77] a peripherality reflected in low earnings, low levels of unionisation of the workforce, high unemployment, and continuing emigration of younger age groups. Perceptively, Lee noted the importance of imperfect industrialisation and subsequent de-industrialisation in perpetuating Cornwall's peripheral status, and considered that Cornwall was ". . . Britain's first decayed industrial area".[78]

The value of Lee's and Rallings' contributions lay in their detailed observations of the Cornish political scene, which indicated that nationalist activity was but one part of a much wider Cornish political culture in which the behaviour of Cornwall was often significantly different from that elsewhere. Their awareness that the perpetuation of peripherality into the twentieth century was somehow a function of industrial change was also important, for inevitably it encouraged further analysis of the Cornish experience within a centre-periphery model which would stress the significance of industrialisation and de-industrialisation. Indeed, Lee and Rallings alluded to the concept of "Second Peripheralism" postulated by Tarrow, but failed to develop it as an explanation.[79]

Another observer of the Cornish scene to cite the validity of Tarrow's view was Wight, although his principal concern was to characterise the Cornish problem as being one of "territory versus function" in regional development. Wight identified a reigning paradigm of development "from above" in which central governments pursued regional development policies from a purely "functional" point of view, taking little account of the particular identities of the regions and using local governments merely as inferior agencies to assist in the implementation of these policies. This "functional" approach might well trigger a "territorial" response in the regions with the emergence of " . . . the opposition of various, territorially-based, interest groups to a range of official, functionally-conceived, development initiatives or strategies".[80] According to Wight this was the crux of the Cornish situation: "A Celtic nation and a county of England, Cornwall appears to be the centre of a struggle between the forces of territory and function".[81] Cornwall County Council was, he alleged, powerless to adequately represent Cornwall's particular territorial needs and demands, being an integral part of the centralist paradigm and little more than an agency for central government. Wight added that ". . . Cornish political distinctiveness has been of virtually no consequence for official regional development initiative sponsored by the central state",[82] and identified a response to this "functional" approach in the form of an alliance of interest groups — ". . . conservationists, industrialists and nationalists (who) have in common a desire to establish more effective regional control over regional development, the region in question being Cornwall".[83]

This, then, was Wight's interpretation of the events of the 1960s and 70s in Cornwall — a "territorial" response to the increasing, "functional" interference of the central government which had declared "assisted area" status for Cornwall, at the same time submerging Cornwall in a broader South West Development Area based on Plymouth. As a case-study of one particular cause of dissent within

Cornwall, Wight's analysis was clearly of value, but as a general explanation of the Cornish experience it lacked the wideranging social, economic, political and — above all — historical perspectives which Rokkan and Urwin had shown to be so necessary to the satisfactory examination of the centre-periphery relationship. Implicit in Wight's analysis, of course, was the existence of a centre-periphery relationship, and in this he shared common ground along with Lee, Rallings and Deacon. All agreed that an explanation of the Cornish situation was to be found within that relationship, although each offered a differing and specific perspective. As before (in Chapter 1), the observer is drawn to the conclusion that what is required is an all-embracing model of the centre-periphery relationship, and again one is drawn to the framework presented by Rokkan and Urwin, and to Tarrow's observations on periods or phases of peripherality.

Rokkan and Urwin, it will be remembered, offered a model which provided an overview of the territorial structures of Western Europe, describing the emergence of centres and peripheries, and identifying a number of subject peripheries in the Celtic-Atlantic West.[84] The United Kingdom was one of the territorial structures examined, being categorised as a strongly "monocephalic" state (ie with one dominant centre) exhibiting "territorial space" (having arisen out of the pursuit of centralising strategies). Geo-historical reasons had led to the centre being located in London and its "lowland" hinterland, while the "highland" zone — part of the Celtic-Atlantic West — became the state's periphery. This periphery, in turn, could be sub-divided into an "Inner Periphery" and an "Outer Periphery", the "Inner Periphery" comprising Wales, Cornwall and northern England — the first peripheral territories to have been annexed by the state's centre. Cornwall, then, emerges as an integral part of Rokkan and Urwin's grand analysis. It is part of the subject peripheries of the Celtic-Atlantic West, it exists within the monocephalic United Kingdom, and is part of the "Inner Periphery" of the "highland" zone. It has, however, been only barely "accommodated" by the centre, which has allowed few trappings or symbols of territorial identity to survive into modern times.

It follows from Rokkan and Urwin's analysis that Cornwall's peripherality is essentially a geo-political fact. Given that the United Kingdom is a highly-centralised monocephalic state with its centre located in London and environs, and given that Cornwall (from the perspective of the centre) is a remote, sea-girt peninsula at the south-western extremity of Britain, then there is a certain inevitability about Cornwall's peripheral status — unless, of course, the distribution of political power within the United Kingdom (or the European Community, perhaps) was to change dramatically, or if it were somehow possible to alter Cornwall's geographic position (a re-distribution of political power in north-western Europe might re-define Cornwall's position as "central" in the Celtic Sea).

From such an analysis, therefore, emerge certain "constants of peripherality": geographical location and geological construction, together with fundamental characteristics of the centre-periphery relationship which might endure through the ages. But of overriding importance in explaining the perpetuation of peripherality, and thus of continuing diversity and distinctiveness in the face of change, is an appreciation of the changing nature of the centre-periphery relationship itself over time. As noted in Chapter 1, Urwin stressed the effects of industrialisation and de-industrialisation in not only perpetuating but also altering the nature of the relationship, and Tarrow advanced the concept of "Older Peripheralism" (with its territorial and cultural isolation) and "Second Peripheralism" (marked by economic and social marginalisation) to demonstrate that peripherality was indeed a dynamic condition.[85] This can in turn be refined and developed to provide a model which stresses the movement of peripheral territories from one historical phase or period to the next, from "Older" to "Second" (and other "Peripheralisms" thereafter), in the manner described in Chapter 1.

In attempting here a Cornish adaptation of Tarrow's view and the adoption of such a model to explain Cornwall's historical experience, emphasis is placed upon the crucial movement to "Second Peripheralism", which occurred as a result of the rapid but incomplete and over-specialised (and ultimately fleeting) nature of industrialisation which affected Cornwall in the eighteenth and nineteenth centuries — a process that plucked Cornwall from her insular "Older Peripheralism", thrust her briefly into the world limelight of technological and economic advance, and then dropped her into the mature manifestations of "Second Peripheralism" as her mining industry collapsed and her population emigrated. Interestingly, this approach has been anticipated in part already by those who have sought descriptions and explanations of Cornwall's experience of de-industrialisation. Building upon Havinden's introductory work[86] in the field, Lewis saw that the problem of de-industrialisation was linked to the issue of peripherality, and suggested that the study of de-industrialisation in Cornwall (and the "South West") should not only elucidate the process itself but also consider ". . . how the economy and society of the region adapted to its changing economic structure."[87] This would necessitate an examination of emigration patterns, of changing employment patterns, of fluctuating wage rates, of the movement of industrial capital, and the emergence of new economic activity such as tourism. It would also, Lewis argued, mean an investigation of broader issues such as the effects on local political culture and social structure.

This study addresses itself to many of the concerns raised by Lewis, arguing that the experience of "Second Peripheralism" wrought profound changes in Cornwall, but changes nevertheless which served to perpetuate Cornwall's peripheral condition and her continuing cultural, social, economic and political "difference" from the centre. In focussing too upon the post-war experience, this study admits a further movement in peripherality, noting an emergence from the "paralysis" that had characterised the matured manifestations of "Second Periphalism", this new movement evidenced, for example, in widespread immigration into Cornwall from outside, in changing economic structures, and in the rise of peripheral protest. But this movement itself provides evidence which is at first glance conflicting, confusing, paradoxical: the face of Cornwall has altered to an extent that — as Wight observed — "Whereas the imminent 'destruction' of Cornwall is a prime issue for a concerned Cornishman, to informed outsiders the chief impression is the stubborn persistence of Cornishness in the face of anglicising influences."[88] The resolution of this paradox lies, as is argued in considerable detail in the latter chapters of this study, in the recognition that this recent movement is in fact evidence of the emergence of a "Third" phase or period of "Peripheralism". This has propelled Cornwall from its erstwhile "paralysis", but presents not "destruction" or even "anglicisation" but instead a further perpetuation of the peripheral condition, with distinctive social, economic and political features which continue to mark Cornwall off from the English centre. Cornwall, then, continues to be "different" — *because of*, rather than *despite*, her historical experience.

In conclusion, then, it can be seen that, although the myth of the "homogeneous state" had served to retard serious consideration of the Cornish situation, the events of the 1960s and 70s in Scotland, Wales and elsewhere were to an extent mirrored in Cornwall. This caused academic observers to reflect anew upon the condition of modern Cornwall, leading to a general opinion that there was an identifiably "different" social and political culture which required further examination and explanation. This led, in turn, to the application of various models (some "borrowed" from the Scottish and Welsh experience) to explain what had happened in Cornwall. Although none of the resulting explanations was comprehensive, most pointed to a relationship between an English "centre" and a Cornish "periphery", a relationship which fitted neatly into the more general centre-periphery model devised by Rokkan and Urwin. Cornwall had emerged as an integral part of the Rokkan/Urwin analysis, and this study accepts their general explanation of the processes of state-building in Western Europe and the United Kingdom. In particular, it acknowledges the key impact of industrial change in perpetuating the peripheral condition, employing the model of phases of peripherality developed from Tarrow, and explaining Cornwall's movement from "Older" to "Second" and now "Third Peripheralism". In achieving this, the intention and method has been to provide a broad historical perspective, in the manner advocated by Rokkan and Urwin.

Notes and References

1. Henry Pelling, *Social Geography of British Elections, 1885-1910*, Macmillan, London, 1962, p159.
2. Ibid., p158.
3. Ibid.
4. Robert Waller, *The Atlas of British Politics*, Croom Helm, London, 1985, p23.
5. Hugh Berrington, "Centre-Periphery Conflict and British Politics", in Yves Meny and Vincent Wright (eds.), *Centre-Periphery Relations in Western Europe*, George Allen and Unwin, London, 1985, p171.
6. R.M. Punnett, *British Government and Politics*, Heinemann, London, 1968, 2nd Edition, 1971, p78.
7. P.J. Madgwick, *The Politics of Rural Wales*, Hutchinson, London, 1973, p15. My emphasis.
8. William Greenberg, *The Flags of the Forgotten: Nationalism on the Celtic Fringe*, Clifton, Brighton, 1969, p110; P. Berresford Ellis, *The Story of The Cornish Language*, Tor Mark Press, Truro, n.d. (c.1970), p28.
9. *Cornish Nation*, November 1968; January-February 1969; November 1969.

10. *Cornish Nation*, March 1972.
11. *Cornish Nation*, November 1968.
12. Ibid.
13. Ibid.
14. Ibid.
15. *Cornish Nation*, January-February 1969.
16. Colin S. Rallings and Adrian Lee, "Politics of the Periphery — The Case of Cornwall", unpublished paper presented to the Conference of the PSA work group of The Politics of the United Kingdom, Aberystwyth, 1977, p15; Adrian Lee, "Cornwall: Aspects of Regionalism and Nationalism", unpublished paper presented to Workshop on Nationalist and Regionalist Movements in Western Europe, University of Strathclyde, 1978, p13; *Western Morning News*, 10 February 1967; 17 December 1976.
17. *Cornish Nation* January-February 1969; September 1970; December 1970.
18. *Cornish Nation* Summer 1979; D. Butler and D. Marquand, *European Elections and British Politics*, Longmans, London, 1981, p133.
19. *Royal Commission on the Constitution*, Cmnd 5460, Report Volume I, HMSO, London, 1973, paragraphs 221, 329, 1211.
20. E.J. Pengelly, *The Detectable Duchy*, Cowethas Flamank, Redruth, 1986.
21. *Cornish Stannary Gazette*, January 1975.
22. Robert R. Pennington, *Stannary Law: A History of the Mining law of Cornwall and Devon*, David and Charles, Newton Abbot, 1973, p9.
23. Ibid., p7.
24. Madgwick, op. cit., p15. My emphasis.
25. Vernon Bogdanor, *Liberal Party Politics*, Clarendon Press, Oxford, 1983, p79. My emphasis.
26. Ibid., p245. My emphasis.
27. Paul Tyler "Campaign For Cornwall '89" election leaflet, 1989; *Cornish Times* 24 March 1989.
28. *Hansard* 1161-1162, 4 December 1978.
29. *Daily Telegraph*, 23 December 1986.
30. Ibid.
31. *Independent*, 23 December 1986.
32. *Guardian*, 23 December 1986.
33. *West Briton*, 10 November 1988; *Western Morning News* 26 November 1988.
34. *Cornish Times*, 22 May 1987.
35. Geoffrey Moorhouse, *Britain in the Sixties: The Other England*, Penguin, London, 1964, pp41-42.
36. George Thayer, *The British Political Fringe: A Profile*, Anthony Blond, London, 1965, p185.
37. Ibid.
38. Robert Waller, *The Almanac of British Politics*, 2nd Edition, Croom Helm, London, 1983, p250.
39. Ibid., p265.
40. P. Berresford Ellis, *The Celtic Revolution: A Study in Anti-Imperialism*, Y Lolfa, Talybont, 1985, p141.
41. Ibid., p148.
42. Ibid., p143.
43. Rosalie Eastlake, "Cornwall: The Development of a Celtic Periphery", unpublished MA thesis, McGill University, 1981, abstract.

44. Philip Payton, "The Ideology of Celtic Nationalism", unpublished BSc(Hons) dissertation, University of Bristol, 1975, p22.
45. Ibid., p16.
46. Michael Hechter, *Internal Colonialism: The Celtic Fringe in British National Development*, Routledge, London, 1975, p65.
47. Ibid.
48. Ibid., p64.
49. Philip Payton, "The Celtic Fringe: A Review of Hechter's 'Internal Colonialism' ", *Cornish Banner*, June 1979.
50. Ibid.
51. Bernard Deacon, "Is Cornwall an Internal Colony?", in Cathal O'Luain, *For A Celtic Future*, Celtic League, Dublin, 1983, p260.
52. Ibid.
53. Ibid., p263.
54. Ibid., p264.
55. Ibid.
56. Ibid., p265
57. Ibid., p268.
58. Ibid.
59. Ibid.
60. Hechter, op. cit., p42.
61. Deacon, op. cit., p270.
62. Ibid.
63. Ibid.
64. Ibid., p271.
65. Lee, op. cit; Rallings and Lee, op. cit; Colin Rallings and Adrian Lee, "Cornwall: the 'Celtic Fringe' in English politics", ECPR Workshop, Brussels, 1979; Adrian Lee, "How Cornwall Votes", unpublished paper presented at the Institute of Cornish Studies, 1977; Adrian Lee, "The Persistence of Difference? Electoral Change in Cornwall", unpublished paper presented to PSA annual conference, Plymouth Polytechnic, 1988.
66. Rallings and Lee, op. cit., 1977, p2.
67. Ibid., pp2-3.
68. Ibid., p3.
69. Ibid., p4.
70. Ibid., p6.
71. Ibid., p8.
72. Lee, op. cit., 1977, p9.
73. Ibid., p6.
74. R.W. Johnston, "The Nationalisation of English Rural Politics: Norfolk.South West 1945-1970", *Parliamentary Affairs*, 26, 1973.
75. Rallings and Lee, op. cit., 1977, p11.
76. Lee, op. cit., 1978, p1.
77. Rallings and Lee, op. cit., 1977, p4.
78. Lee, op. cit., 1978, p6.
79. Ibid., p7.
80. Ian Wight, "Territory Versus Function in Regional Development: The Case of Cornwall", unpublished paper, University of Aberdeen, 1981, p1.
81. Ibid., p5.
82. Ibid., p13.

83. Ibid., p1.
84. Stein Rokkan and Derek W. Urwin, *The Politics of Territorial Identity: Studies in European Regionalism*, Sage, London, 1982.
85. Sidney Tarrow, *Between Centre and Periphery: Grassroots Politicians in Italy and France*, Yale University Press, New Haven, 1977, p16.
86. Michael Havinden, "The South West: A Case of De-Industrialization?", in Marilyn Palmer (ed.), *The Onset of Industrialization*, University of Nottingham, Nottingham, 1977.
87. Robert Lewis, *De-Industrialisation in the South West: Background Paper*, Department of Economic History Project on De-Industrialisation in the South West, Paper No 1, University of Exeter, Exeter, 1984, p13.
88. Wight, op. cit., p9.

Part Two

First Peripheralism — Of Territorial and Cultural Isolation

"Of all Cornwall, Duke am I,
As was also my Father.
A great lord in the country,
From the Land's End to the
Tamar"

Me yv duc in oll Kernow
Indella ytho ov thays.
Hag vhe: arluth in pov
A Tamer the pen an
vlays."

"Beunans Meriasek (The Life of St Meriasek)", 1504.
(Myrna Combellack, *The Camborne Play*, Dyllansow Truran, Redruth,
1988, p96. Original Cornish provided by Dr Combellack.)

"We are in a very wild place which no human being ever visits, in the midst
of a most barbarous race, so different in language and custom from the
Londoners and the rest of England that they are as unintelligible to these last
as to the Venetians".
The Venetian Ambassador to Castile, when in Cornwall, 1506.
(A.L. Rowse, *Tudor Cornwall*, Jonathan Cape, London, 1941, republished,
Dyllansow Truran, Redruth, 1990, p117.)

"Cornwall, as an entire state, hath at divers times enjoyed sundry titles: of a
kingdom, principality, duchy, and earldom . . .".
Richard Carew of Antony, 1602.
(F.E. Halliday [ed.], Richard Carew, *The Survey of Cornwall*, Melrose,
London, 1953, p151.)

"During the late fifteenth-century, Scotland, Ireland and Wales were left largely
to their own devices and even smaller communities such as the Isle of Man and
Cornwall, which deserve more attention than has been given to them . . .,
enjoyed a good deal of independence."
Hugh Kearney,
The British Isles: A History of Four Nations, Cambridge University Press,
Cambridge, 1989, p105.

CHAPTER THREE

The Celtic Duchy

In placing Cornwall within the diversity of the "multi-national" United Kingdom, and in assessing the experience of modern Cornwall, it is necessary — as has been argued — to examine the significance of industrial change in perpetuating the peripheral condition. But equally, it is important to explain the emergence of the peripheral condition in the first place, elucidating the circumstances in which the period of "Older Peripheralism" was established and describing the features of its "territorial and cultural isolation". As noted earlier, this "Older Peripheralism" arose form the state-building activities of the centre, resulting in the political incorporation of the periphery within the state but leaving it (the periphery) to a considerable degree insulated from the state's centre. This insulation was partly a function of geographical distance, but it was also a result of the political or constitutional "accommodation" afforded the periphery in order to reconcile its incorporation in the state and to secure within the periphery the authority of the centre. This insulation was then heightened by peripheral distinctions in language, religion, and other social or socio-economic attributes which served to emphasise the cultural dichotomy between centre and periphery.

Within what was to become the United Kingdom, the expansion and state-building activities of the English centre were lengthy and complex, observable even before the tenth century when Athelstan was hailed as "The very celebrated King who by the Grace of God ruled all England, which prior to him many Kings shared between them"[1] and "First King of the English to subdue all the nations within Britain . . ."[2]. These activities were later to involve formal annexation (as in the case of Wales), or the use of force and terror (such as the "harrying of the North" carried out by William I and again much later by Henry VIII), or a complicated blend of conquest, colonisation and treaty (as per Ireland), or even constitutional devices to lure territories otherwise too strong to succumb to incorporation (the Unions with Scotland). But in each instance incorporation was accompanied by mechanisms of "accommodation" — from the essentially symbolic Principality of Wales, through localised instruments of central influence such as the Council of the North or (much later) the Vice-Royalty of Ireland, to the very real autonomy afforded Scottish institutions.[3] Similarly, incorporation did not lead to cultural homogeneity. Not only did existing cultural distinctions endure within the peripheries, most obviously in the Celtic-speaking territories, but "accommodation" itself could on occasions heighten cultural difference (for example, in the emergence of Presbyterianism as the Church of Scotland).

To return to the focus of this study, an analysis of Cornwall's "Older Peripheralism" should, therefore, address a number of significant issues. First of all, the characteristics of this "Older Peripheralism" must be defined — how was it that Cornwall came to be a peripheral appendage to the centre of the English State, to what extent was Cornwall "accommodated" by this State (and what were the effects of such "accommodation"), and to what extent was this Cornish periphery culturally distinct from the centre (in practical terms, Celtic rather than English)? But also, having established the nature of this "Older Peripheralism", it is equally important for the purposes of this study to examine the dynamics of change which threatened Cornwall's "territorial and cultural isolation" (the impact of Tudor centralism, the increasing strategic importance of Cornwall, the emerging economic patterns) and created the conditions out of which Cornwall's "Second Peripheralism" arose. In this, the "constants of peripherality" — established in the "Older Peripheralism" and handed on to the "Second" — must also be identified.

Cornwall is a natural and self-contained geographic unit, bounded on three sides by the sea and on the fourth almost entirely cut off by the River Tamar, and this has facilitated — indeed, almost predisposed Cornwall towards — the creation within these bounds of distinct territorial and cultural units. In Roman times, for example, it seems likely that Cornwall ("Cornubia") formed an administrative sub-division ("pagus") of the south western region or canton of Dumnonia, the lands west of the Tamar occupied by a tribe known as the Cornovii.[4] Following the departure of the Legions, the precise status of Cornwall is more difficult to estimate or define. A Romano-British kingdom of Dumnonia arose from the old canton, extending roughly from Cornwall and Devon through to the western fringes of Somerset and Dorset,[5] and Cornwall emerged as its heartland as the Anglo-Saxons (the English) advanced ever-deeper into the south western peninsula. But at the same time as the English pressed ever-westwards, so Dark Age Cornwall became ever more closely drawn into the world of the Celtic Church. Again, geography played its role — ensuring that Cornwall would be touched by English influence at a much later date than the eastern districts of Dumnonia, and placing Cornwall geographically in a central position in the Celtic world with Brittany lying to the south and Wales and Ireland to the north and north-west. Communication between the Celtic lands was by sea, and Cornwall became an important landfall for seafarers, traders, and above all the "Saints" — the holy men of the Celtic Church — as they moved back and forth between Brittany and Wales or Ireland, and as the Medieval pilgrimage routes to Santiago de Compestella in Galicia (with its Celtic influence) were established.[6]

But little by little the English did come to impinge upon the life of Cornwall, and so in the period spanning from the fifth to the tenth centuries we see two significant but opposing and contradictory forces shaping the identity and destiny of Cornwall — the influence of the Celtic world (and particularly its Church) of which it was a part, and the influence of the English as they established themselves in the south west. Both influences were complex, and it is a mistake to oversimplify them and their effects upon Cornwall. It is easy, for example, to portray the "Age of Saints" as the golden age of Celtic culture, with the Celtic peoples drawn together in a common unity, sharing a common purpose and sense of identity — a model for present-day Celtic nationalists.[7] The reality was rather different.

Although the missionary zeal of the Celtic Church, diffusing outwards from its core in Ireland, did provide some sense of purpose and develop aspects of an inter-Celtic culture, it did not lead to a political sense of unity, nor did it have lasting political aspirations. Equally, the Celtic world was divided by language — the Irish, Scots and Manx speaking increasingly divergent dialects of Goidelic (Gaelic), and the Cornish, Welsh and Bretons speaking forms of Brythonic (British) from which their individual languages would eventually emerge. The precise relationship between the various Celtic lands was also complex. There is evidence of considerable Irish colonisation in Cornwall during this period, but it seems possible that the Irish came as "invaders", putting pressure upon the indigenous Cornish population, some of which may have sought refuge abroad by migrating to Brittany. Indeed, the early links between Cornwall and Brittany are especially complex, linguistic and other evidence pointing to perhaps a succession of migratory waves from south west Britain to Brittany during this period. Some of these migrants may have been from South Wales, but others were from Cornwall (reflecting even older links between Cornwall and Brittany) and from the area that is now Devon — the refugees from the latter perhaps fleeing in the face of the English advance, leaving the land relatively depopulated and accounting for the almost total lack of Celtic placenames in modern Devon.[8]

The advance of the English was equally as complex as the relationships in the Celtic world. It is tempting to portray it as a relentless westerly thrust, with Celtic Dumnonia perpetually in retreat from the time of the Battle of Durham Down (near Bristol) in 577 (which drove an English wedge between the Celts of Wales and the south west) until Athelstan established the Tamar as the boundary between Celt and West Saxon in 936. Perhaps complementing the semi-legendary exploits of the Celtic folk-hero, Arthur, the evidence suggests a tortuous and drawn-out English penetration of Dumnonia, with considerable Celtic resistance. "At the beginning of the seventh century", argues Hoskins, "the Celtic kingdom of Dumnonia was in full existence and unimpaired control of south-west Britain".[9] The English advance into Dorset had already ground to a halt and only in eastern Somerset were they making any progress. Thereafter, the English advance was two-pronged and made greater headway, the Somerset men pushing into North Devon and those in Dorset penetrating into East and South Devon, with the Exe becoming their border with the Dumnonians by 661. But large pockets of Celtic farmers remained relatively untouched in North Devon and especially in Dorset, and the English conquest of the south west must be seen as a very piecemeal process, requiring centuries of consolidation.[10]

By 682 the English had in all probability reached the River Tamar, and placename evidence suggests that they may have already crossed into that part of North Cornwall lying above the River Ottery. The Ottery, indeed, became an ethnic and linguistic border of considerable importance, with hill-forts such as Warbstow Bury (re-occupied at about this time) perhaps creating some sort of Dark Age "maginot line" along its course. An even cursory glance at an Ordnance Survey map of the district shows that to the south of the Ottery the names are overwhelmingly Celtic — Tremaine, Hendra, Trevillion, and so on — while to the north they are English (or hybrid Celtic-English) and reminiscent of those found in North Devon: Canworthy, Pattacott, Billacott. To the north west, the linguistic border twists beyond the Ottery to parallel the present-day A39 road towards Poundstock and the sea.[11]

By the end of the seventh century, then, the kingdom of Dumnonia had been pushed back into what is modern Cornwall, with English settlement already spilling over into its northern-most tip. By 710, when they fought against Geraint, the Cornish king of what was left of Dumnonia, the English felt strong enough to probe beyond the Tamar, leading to limited English settlement between the Tamar and the Lynher. But Cornwall remained independent, with its own line of chieftain-kings, and of course its Celtic Church, opposing the campaigns of the kings of Wessex until at least 815 when Egbert harried Cornwall from east to west in response to a Cornish attack across the Tamar. In 838 Egbert finally defeated the Cornish at the great battle of Hingston Down, near Callington in East Cornwall, although local native kings continued to exercise authority in western parts of Cornwall.

The eventual subjugation of Cornwall was left to Athelstan over ninety years later, a momentous event which not only fixed the Tamar as the boundary between the Cornish and the West Saxons, but also led to the eviction of the remaining Celtic population in Exeter (and perhaps the rest of Devon). It is under Athelstan, then, that we see the conscious and "official" creation of modern Cornwall, clearly delineated by its eastern border which set the limits of the "West Welsh" as clearly as did the Wye for the "North Welsh".[12] Athelstan was also noteworthy for his achievement in uniting the various kingdoms of England under one rule (his own), and for establishing his suzerainty over kings in Wales and Scotland. Athelstan's reign, then, was a significant milestone in the creation of the English State and its relations with its Celtic neighbours.

For Cornwall, the importance of Athelstan's actions cannot be stressed too greatly. Not only had Athelstan established Cornwall as a geo-political unit, but also he had set it as the territory of the "West Welsh" (the Cornish Celts) and defined its relationship with England. In short, Cornwall was firmly annexed to England and yet was not part of it, either ethnically or in terms of territorial absorption. Cornwall was not independent, and yet its existence was a political fact — albeit its status determined according to English rather than Cornish terms. Cornwall had emerged as a "satellite" of the English State, subjected but (significantly) still regarded as a security threat (as evidenced by the decision to place the Cornish shore of the Tamar estuary directly in the hands of the English king and consider it a part of Devon) and as "alien".[13] On maps, Cornwall was to appear as "West Wales" even in Tudor times,[14] while the Mappa Mundi in Hereford Cathedral depicted four constituent parts of the island of Britain: England, Scotland, Wales, and Cornwall.

Cornwall's "Older Peripheralism" grew directly from Athelstan's settlement. The raids and counter-raids across the Tamar became a thing of the past as Cornwall settled into its "territorial and cultural isolation", its territorial existence at last guaranteed and its status as a "refuge" for the "West Welsh" assured. This, of course, represented a degree of "accommodation" by the English State — a recognition that the Tamar marked the boundary between two peoples, and should remain so — and this was accepted at the Norman Conquest, the Domesday Book (for example) noting the Tamar border without question.[15] Athelstan's attempts at "accommodation" were also reflected in his creation of a Cornish See, centred on St Germans, with Conan the Cornishman as its first Bishop, although Cornwall was to lose its independent diocesan status as early as 1050.[16]

Other forms of "accommodation" had greater longevity, however, and came into their own in the Medieval period as government administration became more complex and sophisticated. Specifically, this "accommodation" centred upon the twin institutions of the Duchy and the Stannaries, which together gave Cornwall a unique relationship with the Crown and afforded a special constitutional identity. The Duchy grew out of the earlier Earldom of Cornwall, which was in itself a singular institution and was probably created as an "accommodating" successor of the earlier line of Cornish kings.[17] Certainly, at the time of the Norman Conquest in 1066 the Earldom was held by one Cadoc (or Condor), a native Cornishman, and it was to him that the Cornish owed their first loyalty — the King of England holding no land directly in Cornwall, in marked contrast to the situation in English counties where it was usual for the King to hold territorial possessions. The imposition of Norman feudalism, of course, changed the nature of land holding, and the victorious William of Normandy lost little time in replacing Cadoc with Robert, Count of Mortain, as Earl of Cornwall. Thereafter, Cornwall was granted to a succession of Earls who were, in practice, the King's "favourites"; in the absence of an Earl, Cornwall was held by the King as a distinct entity. The Earldom (and subsequent Duchy) was associated from earliest times with Tintagel, the site chosen for the construction of a castle and linked (by Geoffrey of Monmouth[18]) with the Arthurian tradition, reflecting perhaps an earlier significance of Tintagel as a seat of power — at once a means of "accommodation" and a method of confirming the "legitimacy" of English and Norman rule in Cornwall.[19]

The Duchy of Cornwall was created out of the Earldom in March 1337 by Edward III for the maintenance of his seven year-old son. Edward III was conscious that he was building the Duchy upon an ancient tradition, announcing that he was advancing ". . . our most dear first begotten Edward . . . to be Duke of Cornwall, over which awhile ago Dukes for a long time successively presided as chief rulers".[20] A succession of Charters during 1337 and 1338 defined the constitutional status of the Duchy and set the power and privileges of the Duke. Today, when it is possible to point to the distinct and quite separate activities of the County of Cornwall (which administers local government) and the Duchy of Cornwall (an essentially commercial organisation which manages the Duke's land holdings in Cornwall and elsewhere), it is customary to emphasise the difference between the County and the Duchy.[21] In the fourteenth century there was no such distinction, the Duchy itself — as late as 1855 — describing the status conferred by the Medieval Charters:

> . . . the three Duchy Charters are sufficient in themselves to vest in the Dukes of Cornwall, not only the government of Cornwall, but the entire territorial dominion in and over the county which had previously been invested in the Crown . . . not only all the territorial possessions of the Crown in Cornwall, but every prerogative right and source of revenue . . . ."[22]

Henry V's Parliament in 1422 affirmed that ". . . the County of Cornwall should always remain as a Duchy to the eldest sons of the Kings of England . . . ,[23] and — in assessing the extent of the Duchy's rule in Cornwall — Pearse has argued that,

> Under the ancient earldom Cornwall had been to a considerable extent independent, enjoying privileges in the shape of a measure of autonomy and freedom from direct interference by the central government in many of its affairs. This sense of autonomy and separateness was now strengthened. From 1337, when Prince Edward was seven years old, until he died in 1376 the only forms of government known to Cornwall were, at first, that of his household and, later, of his council.[24]

Julian Cornwall agrees that,

> A Celtic survival not yet assimilated into the English nation, Cornwall also possessed a unique institution which again helped to foster the illusion of autonomy, namely the Duchy, the birthright of the King's eldest son. The administrative structure of the Duchy constituted in effect a miniature government complete with a hierarchy of officials . . .[25]

This remained true throughout the Medieval period, and Mary Coate has noted that even in seventeenth century Cornwall, on the eve of the Civil War, the Duke's ". . . prerogative was hardly distinguishable from that of the Crown".[26] As the Duchy itself explained, ". . . from earliest times Cornwall was distinct from the Kingdom of England, and under separate government . . ."[27] so that ". . . the Duke was quasi-sovereign within his Duchy".[28]

As a vehicle of "accommodation" the Duchy was highly successful. Although, as A.L. Rowse has noted, "Something of the status of conquest remained",[29] the Duchy created an aura of semi-independence and was regarded as having antecedents which stretched back into the mists of time. In this, as in so many other respects, the Duchy mirrored the Principality of Wales, which had been created in 1307 and was an attempt by the English Crown at an "accommodation" of the Welsh. It was no co-incidence that the Prince of Wales was also the Duke

48

of Cornwall (and that this personage was no less than the heir to the Throne) and a constitutional link was thus created between Cornwall and Wales, so "That Cornwall, like Wales, was at the time of the Conquest, and was subsequently treated in many respects, as distinct from England".[30]

Quite apart from enhancing Cornwall's sense of constitutional separateness, the Duchy exercised a strong influence over Cornish society and economy, often with results that served to mark even further the differences between the Cornish experience and that which obtained east of the Tamar. As Hatcher wrote of the Duchy of Cornwall in the Middle Ages, "Much of what is significant . . . provides a contrast with the general experience of English medieval history".[31] And it would be an error to underestimate the all-pervading influence of the Duchy — in addition to the 17 Duchy manors (mostly in East Cornwall) owned directly by the Duchy, the castles of Launceston, Trematon, Tintagel, and Restormal, along with the boroughs of Launceston, Lostwithiel, Tintagel, Helston, Camelford, Grampound, Liskeard and Saltash, were under the control of the Duke, as were the shrievalty and havenership of Cornwall, the county and hundred courts, feodary, and the entire Stannary organisation. In addition, the Cornish were obliged to fulfil ". . . the host of duties stemming from the Duke's position as a great feudal lord".[32] All of this was administered with considerable efficiency from the Duchy capital of Lostwithiel.

The 17 Duchy manors (later increased to several dozen) were managed in a manner that ". . . differed so markedly from the structure of manors in other parts . . .",[33] that they had little in common with the classic English manor. Indeed, Hatcher has gone so far as to suggest that this peculiarly Cornish system ought not really to be called "manorial" at all.[34] There was, for example, no exploitation of demesnes, the absence of demesne farming meaning that lands were entirely in the hands of Duchy tenants. Equally significantly, there was no trace of the open-field, strip-system of agriculture (so typical of English manors) on any of the Duchy properties — a reflection of the Cornish form of land settlement that the Duchy had inherited, as was the fact that population settlement tended to be scattered in small hamlets rather than grouped in "nucleated" villages as was often the case east of the Tamar.

Most importantly, the Duchy operated a system of tenancy quite different from the normal English pattern. Instead of the familiar categories of "free, villein, or cottar", the Duchy operated tenancies that were "free, conventionary, or villein". Most of the Duchy land, in fact, was held in conventionary tenure. This was not the classic hereditary (and bonded) security of tenure with attendant rents and obligations, but instead a seven year lease at a free market rent with only negligible services but no renewal as a right. Those tenants who were "free" had very few obligations, and only a minority of tenants were villeins bound to their land. Moreover, the number of villeins declined (although, ironically, villeinships survived in Cornwall longer than most other parts!) for the Duchy pursued a policy of not renewing them when for various reasons they had lapsed. The result of all this was that, in Medieval Cornwall, a class of independent and potentially mobile peasants was created, a precursor of the independently-minded small tenant farmer which came to characterise Cornwall in later centuries, and indeed which is still much in evidence today.[35] And, just as the Duchy created the independent small farmer, so it served to inhibit the emergence of a strong and influential (and potentially rival) local gentry (ie a local elite) — a major factor in shaping the economic, social and political future of Cornwall, a fact noted by observers as diverse as Henderson and Rowse, Pelling and Cornwall.[36]

Although the ultimate economic effect of the Duchy may have been to drain off much of the surplus wealth of a land already short of resources, the initial impetus provided by the Duchy was for the diversification of economic activity in Cornwall. By the fifteenth century it featured shipping (a fair proportion of Cornish exports were carried by Cornishmen in Cornish ships), fishing, shipbuilding, quarrying, and textile manufacture, all of which stimulated agriculture by providing a market for it. But even at that date tin mining was emerging as a central feature of the Cornish economy, the relative mobility of the Cornish population facilitating its development, a hint of the overwhelmingly important role that mining would come to acquire in future centuries.[37]

The importance of mining was also reflected in the power of the Stannaries, which — like the Duchy (under whose jurisdiction they fell) — emerged in the Medieval period as a device by which the Crown was able to "accommodate" Cornwall. It appears that the Stannaries grew out of a body of ancient customary rights and privileges enjoyed by the tinners of Cornwall and Devon, similar to the "free mining" status enjoyed by miners in areas as diverse as the Mendip Hills, the Forest of Dean, Derbyshire, Alston Moor, France, the Low Countries, and Germany. Pennington considers that Stannary Law evolved from three sources — Cornish, Anglo-Saxon, and Norman — with "Cornish customary law . . . being kept alive from generation to generation . . .".[38] But the Stannary system, as it developed in the Middle Ages, went much further than mere "free mining" to provide Cornwall with what Rowe has said " . . . might almost be termed territorial semi-independence . . .",[39] the Stannary Parliament operating in a manner that (as Lewis wrote) ". . . scarcely differed from that at the House of Commons . . ."[40] at Westminster.

The Crown's direct interest in the Stannaries was as a result of "tin coinage", the tax payable to the King on smelted tin, which was probably first imposed as early as the late eleventh century. Consequently, when the Duchy of Cornwall was created in 1337, it was only natural that the Stannaries should become part of its structure. The first attempt at describing the status and administration of the Stannaries came in 1198, and this was followed in 1201 by the first Charter of the Stannaries which arose from the ". . . desire of the Cornish tinners to be separated from those of Devon . . ."[41] (there was already a traditional distinction, and perhaps hostility, between the two) and the economic desire to see the scope of the Stannaries extended. The Charter also established the four districts — or "Stannaries" — in which Stannary Law might operate: Foweymore (modern Bodmin Moor), Blackmore (the Hensbarrow Downs about St Austell), Tywarnhaile (the area around Truro and St Agnes), and Penwith-and-Kerrier in the far west. There was, however, no attempt at defining where the boundaries of these

Stannaries might be, and — as was sometimes argued — almost the whole of Cornwall was metaliferous and likely to be subject to the attention of miners, and so the jurisdiction of the Stannaries could if needs be be extended to encompass all Cornwall.[42]

In 1305 Edward I, in two separate Charters (one for Cornwall, and one for Devon), defined the privileges enjoyed by the tinners. Most important of these was that tinners were not to be hailed before the ordinary courts (except for the most serious charges) but were to be tried in Stannary Courts (irrespective of whether the suit was to do with mining) before a jury consisting of tinners (for a mining suit) or half tinners and half "foreigners" (non-miners) for a non-mining suit. The Charters also offered a liberal interpretation of the right of "bounding", under which a tinner might establish a tin "bound" on certain types of land, and gave the tinner exemptions from local taxation and imposts.

Like the Duchy tenancies, one effect of the Stannary Charters was to create a class of independent workers, living and working according to their own rules, answerable only to their own kind, and jealous of their rights and privileges. It was not surprising, then, when the Cornish tinners took exception to the attempts by Prince Arthur (the Duke of Cornwall) in 1496 — the year before Cornwall rose in full and open rebellion — to enforce stricter rules governing the recording of tin bounds and blowing (smelting) houses and the marking of tin ingots. As Pennington noted, ". . . such rules appealed little to the conservative and independent Cornish spirit",[43] and they were largely ignored, being no doubt a source of further outrage in the deteriorating climate which led to the Cornish Rebellion of 1497. In a move which perhaps further provoked the Cornish, Henry punished the tinners for disregarding Prince Arthur's rules by suspending the Stannaries.

Henry VII's lenient treatment of the Cornish rebels in 1497 has often given rise to comment, and in the light of this leniency it is interesting to consider his Charter of Pardon of 1508. This Charter restored the Cornish Stannaries (on the payment of a fine of £1,100!), but also created new, widespread powers affecting both the privileges of the tinners and the legislative capacity of the Stannary Convocation or Parliament.[44] These seem curiously at odds with the general Tudor concern to centralise government and dilute local usages and, coming so soon after the crisis of 1497, can be seen as renewed attempts to seek the "accommodation" of Cornwall, hinting at a resentful and potentially still-rebellious Cornwall in urgent need of pacification.

In restoring and enhancing the rights of the Cornish tinners, the Charter of Pardon of 1508 extended the definition of "tinner" (and hence the jurisdiction of the Stannaries and Stannary Law) to include almost anyone connected in some way or another with the tin trade — not only those involved with the extractive process itself, but also the owners of blowing-houses, the purchasers of black or white tin, gentlemen tin bounders, and so on. The Stannary Parliament of 1588 was to extend the definition still further, to include groups such as carpenters, smiths, colliers and other artisans with tin-trading connections, a definition upheld consistently by later Parliaments.[45]

The restoration and enhancement of the tinners' rights was accompanied by an extension of the Stannary Parliament's legislative powers, lending the Cornish Convocation much greater authority than that enjoyed by its Devon equivalent.[46] The Charter of 1508 made provision for the nomination of 24 "Stannators" (who would comprise the body of the Parliament or Convocation), the Mayors and Councils of Lostwithiel, Truro, Launceston, and Helston nominating six Stannators each. The Parliament thus constituted was given, amongst other things, the right to allow or disallow ". . . any statute, act, ordinance, provision, restraint, or proclamation . . . made by the King, his heirs, successors, or the Prince of Wales, Duke of Cornwall, or their Council . . . to the prejudice of any tinner, or other person having to do with black or white tin".[47] It was this right of veto which gave the Parliament its ultimate power, and provided that aura of semi- independence noted by Rowe and other observers.

The "accommodation" afforded Medieval Cornwall by the Duchy and the Stannaries was reflected, as Jenner noted, in the use of the phrase "Anglia et Cornubia" (much like the modern "England and Wales") in Government documents — a recognition of Cornwall's distinct status.[48] But "accommodation" went further than mere recognition, for it also led to the perpetuation — indeed, enhancement — of those attributes which continued to set Cornwall apart. In the absence of any native Cornish peerage, the Duchy assumed a distinct and important political role, leading (for example) to the extraordinary situation whereby Ducal influence had helped to provide Cornwall with no fewer than 44 Members of Parliament by the end of the reign of Elizabeth I.[49] More importantly, as we have seen, there were significant effects at the societal level, leading to the creation of the classes of independent tenant farmers and tinners which were to have such an important influence upon the developing character of Cornwall. The independence of the Cornish tinner, for example, led directly to the emergence of the "tribute" and "tutwork" forms of employment in which part of the entrepreneurial function was performed by the miner himself — the miner bidding for the area or "pitch" he was to work, providing his own equipment and materials, and being paid according to the value of the ore won ("tribute") or the amount of ground mined ("tutwork"). And as mining grew in importance in the Cornish economy, so its status as "lead industry" lent its practices and attitudes an authority which commanded respect and often imitation throughout Cornwall, an influence of considerable importance in shaping the socio-economic characteristics of modern Cornwall.[50]

"Accommodation" helped reconcile Cornwall to her relationship with the English State, in a manner typical of emerging centre-periphery relationships, but of equal importance to Cornwall, her identity, and her peripheral status was the degree to which she remained "Celtic" (and thus "un-English") in culture and outlook. The Athelstan settlement, with the fixing of the Tamar border and the creation of a Cornish See, had meant that Cornwall would not be subjected to the same processes of colonisation and assimilation that had led to the anglicisation of the rest of South West Britain. Instead her population was left relatively untouched, able to pursue its existing life-style relatively unhampered. One consequence of this was that the pattern of settlement remained remarkably unchanged, the Cornish living in scattered hamlets (in contrast to the English nucleated village) and their cultivated land remaining enclosed from early times (unlike the English strip system), a pattern that is still observable today. As Balchin has written,

> This is the Celtic under-writing. Small settlements of only two or three farmhouses and labourers' cottages, carrying Celtic names, are common at cross-roads. In some will be found the parish church, but often this stands alone, with only the rectory or vicarage nearby. Between the hamlets stretches open farmland of mixed pasture and arable, in which the fields are characteristically small irregular-shaped enclosures bounded by massive granite or slate-walled hedges. Set down in this chequerboard pattern of fields, at remarkably regular intervals, are isolated farmsteads, joined to each other by narrow and often tunnel-like lanes where trees and bushes grow on the top of monumental hedgebanks.[51]

This pattern of scattered settlement and early enclosure can be seen in each of the Celtic lands. As Muir has noted, there were clear economic reasons for this which, over time, led to a deep Celtic distrust of close settlement:

> In the Celtic lands . . . the population, like the resources, was more thinly spread . . . Substantial villages were rarely found. They did not grow naturally from the thin leached soils and various attempts to seed the countryside with feudal villages scorned the traditions of settlement that were deeply rooted in Celtic societies and were doomed to failure.[52]

In Cornwall, the "attempts" to create nucleated villages were largely confined to the small area of English settlement north of the Ottery (where the linguistically-hybrid Kilkhampton is a good example of a nucleated village created around the core of an earlier Celtic hamlet) and the strategically-placed centres of English influence elsewhere in Cornwall where the suffix "-ton" is found added to existing Celtic placenames (eg Helston, Callington), and where the atypical existence of open-field, strip agriculture may also evidence English settlement. For the rest, the Cornish eschewed close settlement. Even in the Middle Ages, when there were strong economic motives for the establishment of speculative market towns, "The Cornish never took kindly to town-life".[53] Those towns that did exist in Medieval Cornwall were, as Henderson showed, highly artificial creations which the Cornish did not trust — in the tax assessments of 1327, for example, half the burgesses of Penryn were "foreign" (ie non-Cornish), while more than half at Tregony and Grampound were "foreigners".[54] As noted earlier, the Duchy estates — with their scattered hamlets and complete absence of open fields — epitomised the Cornish settlement pattern; and, of course, the relative isolation in which Cornish families lived served to heighten their profound sense of independence. Even in north-eastern Cornwall, with its Anglo-Saxon placenames, "foreigners" in the towns were often — as in in the rest of Cornwall — given surnames such as "Anglicus" or "Le Engleys", ie "English".[55]

Medieval Cornwall was also "Celtic" in that the Cornish language continued to be spoken throughout much of the land, the language of the common people but also — before the Reformation — the language of ecclesiastical scholarship and the vehicle through which the broader aspects of Celtic culture (for example, folk tales and the Lives of the Saints) were perpetuated. For, despite the loss of the Cornish See and the supremacy of Rome, the Church in Cornwall retained much of its Celtic ambience. Celtic crosses, reminiscent of the Irish "High Crosses" with their wheel-heads and intricate tracery and "knot" work, were erected at holy places across the land, holy wells were venerated and tended, and the cults and relics of the Celtic Saints assumed central roles in the religious life of the Cornish. St Piran, as patron of Cornish tinners, was revered across Cornwall, Nicholas Roscarrock (the seventeenth century Cornish Catholic) noting that on St Piran's Day the Saint's relics would be carried up and down the land, with pilgrims from all over Cornwall making their way to his shrine in Perranzabuloe.[56] St Petroc was likewise revered, and across Cornwall the Lives were remembered and Feasts celebrated of local Saints such as Meriasek, Winwaloe, Uny, Paul Aurelian — most of whom were real historical figures of usually Breton or Welsh, and sometimes Irish, origin.[57] The Cornish enthusiasm for their Saints and churches reached its high-point in the fifteenth century, when many churches were rebuilt with the characteristic three-stage Cornish towers and acquired their ". . . instantly recognisable Cornish identity".[58]

Glasney College — a collegiate church, near Penryn — emerged as the centre of religious scholarship in the Cornish language, where, it seems, the "Cornish Ordinalia" (a long mystery cycle of three separate plays) was written circa 1400.[59] Written in Cornish, the "Ordinalia" took three days to perform, the normal venue being an open-air "plen an gwarry" or playing place. The passion poem "Pascon Agan Arluth" (Passion of Our Lord) dates from about the same time, and other "miracle plays" designed for out-door performance include "Gwreans an Bys" (the Creation of the World) written circa 1530–40 and "Beunans Meriasek" (the Life of Meriasek) of about 1500.[60]

The sympathetic attitude of the pre-Reformation Church in Cornwall towards the Cornish language has assisted modern scholars in assessing the extent to which the language was spoken in Medieval Cornwall.[61] When Bishop John de Grandisson preached in the far-western parish of St Buryan in 1328 or 29, his sermon had to be translated by an interpreter for the benefit of the monoglot Cornish. And, although it is reasonable to assume that English was by that time already making significant inroads in East and North Cornwall, it is interesting to note that in 1339 a certain J. Polmarke was appointed to preach in the Cornish language at St Merryn, near Padstow. In 1354–55 Grandisson appointed two penitentiaries for Cornwall — one in Truro for those who spoke only Cornish, and one at Bodmin in East Cornwall for those who spoke English and Cornish.[62] As late as

1538 the Bishop of Exeter decreed that the Epistle or Gospel of the day should be read in Cornish in those parishes where English was not understood,[63] and even in 1560 it was directed by the Bishop that those who had no English might be taught the Catechism in Cornish.[62] Indeed, at Gorran Haven in mid-Cornwall in 1587 an interpreter had to be employed in a court case because certain local fishermen could not speak English,[65] and a few years later in 1595 inhabitants of the neighbouring parish of St Ewe were said to be bi-lingual.[66] In 1542 Andrew Borde described the state of the language thus: "In Cornwall is two speches; the one is naughty Englyshe, and the other Cornyshe speche. And there be many men and women the which cannot speake one word of Englyshe, but all Cornyshe".[67]

The Celtic identity was also perpetuated through Cornwall's continuing links with Brittany, which endured as strong as ever until as late as the sixteenth century. Of all the Celtic tongues, Cornish and Breton are the closest cousins, in that period mutually intelligible and giving the monoglot Cornishman a much closer feeling of affinity with his Breton counterpart than with an English-speaker of neighbouring Devon.[68] Like Cornwall, Brittany had survived the encroachments of the Norman, French and English states, retaining her status as an independent Duchy until the Treaty of Union with France in 1532 established her as a semi-independent component of the French kingdom. A great many of Cornwall's Saints and Feasts were Breton in origin, and St Michael's Mount had an almost exact counterpart and mirror-image in Mont St Michel (on the marches of Brittany and Normandy), the relative geographic positions of Cornwall and Brittany allowing considerable two-way movement between the two Duchies for the purposes of religious pilgrimage or of trade. Bretons came to Cornwall as sailors and fishermen, but many actually settled in Cornwall, creating an even greater sense of partnership and alliance. Many of these Breton settlers were to be found in the western districts where the Cornish language was strongest — St Ives, Towednack, Zennor, Lelant, and Constantine (in which parish as late as 1558 there were still nine Breton families resident) — but they were also numerous in the east of Cornwall: at Fowey, Polruan and East Looe; in the Hundreds of Trigg and West Wivel some 79 Bretons were registered in 1552–24.[69] The extent to which these settlers were ingrained in Cornish society is reflected even today, in Cornish surnames of Breton origin such as Tangye, Harvey, and Britton.[70]

The links between Cornwall and Brittany were also reflected in their common claims to the Arthurian cycle, and to the associated legends such as those of Mark and Trystan and Isold, with Medieval Celtic belief insisting that King Arthur was not dead but would come again. A fascinating insight into the strength of this conviction is provided in the story of a visit of the canons of Laon to Cornwall in 1113. Not only were they shown the supposed sites of Arthurian association, but were also involved in a fracas at Bodmin Priory when it was suggested — much to the annoyance of the Cornish — that Arthur might not be alive.[71] That the ire of the Cornish should be so quick to rise, and that they might turn so quickly to violent ways, is perhaps surprising — even given the general barbarity of the era, heightened during periods of upheaval such as the civil war between Stephen and Matilda or the later Wars of the Roses. But there does seem to have been, as

Rowse has said, a mood of "feudal anarchy" in Medieval Cornwall (reflected in the records of the Court of Star Chamber where the Cornish occupy a surprisingly disproportionate place) especially during the Wars of the Roses when — as Kearney has commented — the divisions in the English "centre" allowed the "periphery" greater freedom of action.[72]

In curious contrast to the order and efficiency of the Duchy administration, but mirroring the strong sense of independence felt by Cornish folk, there does seem so often to have been a general disregard for the law, with the Cornish in a sense "beyond the pale" like the feuding society of Gaelic Ireland or the turbulent Highlands and Borders of Scotland. The often impecunious lesser-gentry (there was no peerage) acted in their own interests often without restraint, the career of the notorious (but no doubt typical) Sir Henry Bodrugan at the end of the fifteenth century providing an insight into the feuding and lawlessness of the time, and the Killigrews of Arwenack (at Falmouth) turning quite openly to piracy, as did the "Gallants of Fowey" and other Cornish sea-faring folk — under Elizabeth, this excessive behaviour was formalised into privateering and into adventuring abroad.[73] Mary Coate sums all this up rather picturesquely, describing ". . . a definite Cornish personality, conservative, with the antagonism to change bred by racial difference and geographical isolation, but quickened with a restless and active spirit which drove the Cornishman to adventure abroad and to litigation and lawlessness at home".[74] But the turbulence of Cornwall (or Ireland or Scotland) was not so much a Celtic trait, as a reaction to peripheral status — to being not quite within the law's writ — and, in Cornwall's case, a further manifestation of that independent spirit which in later centuries still would show itself in "wrecking" and in smuggling.

However, that there was an element of "antagonism" in Cornish behaviour is likely, and we have occasional glimpses of the Cornish attitude to outsiders. Writing in the reign of Elizabeth, Norden noted that the Cornish seemed ". . . to retain a kind of concealed envy against the English, whom they yet affect with a kind of desire for revenge for their fathers' sakes, by whom their fathers received the repulse".[75] Similarly, Carew — a native Cornishman — wrote in 1602 that the Cornish were still ". . . fostering a fresh memory of their expulsion long ago by the English",[76] with Mary Coate noting that in the Civil War Cornish ". . . racial prejudice would be directed against the Parliamentarian invaders . . . (a) primitive instinct to defend their homes from the 'foreigner' ".[77] As Carew commented, the inquisitive visitor from across the Tamar would often be rebuffed with the phrase "Meea navidna Cowza sawsnek"[78] — I will not speak English!

For their part, the English were equally aware that Cornwall was a land apart. Hatcher has written that "Cornwall was a remote and somewhat forbidding county to most Englishmen in the middle ages",[79] pointing to the exclamation by Bishop John de Grandisson in 1327 that Cornwall was ". . . not only the ends of the earth, but the very ends of the ends thereof"![80] Not many years later, in 1342, the Archdeacon of Cornwall resigned, confessing himself unable to communicate with the Cornish — this was not only a question of language, for ". . . the folk of these parts are quite extraordinary, being of a rebellious temper, and obdurate in the face of attempts to teach and correct."[81] Polydore Vergil, writing for Henry VIII in 1543, considered that "Britain is divided into four parts — whereof the one is inhabited by Englishmen, the other of Scots, the third of Welshmen, and the fourth of Cornish people,"[82] with Hopton adding in 1616 that "England is divided into three great Provinces, or Countries, and every of them speaking a severall and different Language, as English, Welsh, and Cornish . . .".[83] Sometimes these English perceptions were themselves antagonistic, as in 1644 when the besieged Parliamentarian garrison in Plymouth declared that it was " . . . eager to be avenged on the cursed Cornish who are as very heathen as the ignorant Welsh that know no religion nor God, but the King is more than God in that country and Wales"![84]

Cornwall, then, was considered a distinct entity by both Cornish and English, and this was a rational reflection of what they saw around them — a peripheral society appended to the English State. This was Cornwall in its "Older Peripheralism" of "territorial and cultural isolation", which had arisen out of the Athelstan settlement that had fixed the Tamar as the Cornish border and set in motion a process of "accommodation" that had led to the creation of the Duchy and the Stannary. This "accommodation" afforded a certain aura (and indeed reality) of territorial semi-independence, and enhanced the Cornishman's sense of individual independence by preserving the ancient pattern of scattered settlement and establishing classes of independent tenant farmers and tinners. The isolation of this "Older Peripheralism" was heightened by linguistic and cultural difference, in which the Cornish continued to look often towards Brittany rather than England, and by the Cornish assumption that they were often "beyond the law". A.L. Rowse has summed up the characteristics of this condition with an elegance and accuracy that cannot be bettered. Cornwall was, he says,

> . . . a homogeneous society of its own, defined by language and having a common heritage underneath, like Brittany or Wales of Ireland, reaching back beyond Normans and Saxons, beyond even Romans in these islands, to an antiquity of which its people were still dimly conscious. Some memory of all this they carried in the legends of their race that haunted them. They remembered that they were a conquered people.[85]

However, peripherality is a dynamic condition, based upon a symbiotic relationship between centre and periphery, and as the English centre developed apace in the Tudor era with what Rokkan and Urwin have termed the emergence of the "territorial space" of its "centralising strategies", so the "Older Peripheralism" of Cornwall came under threat. Again, Rowse has captured and elucidated the essence of the experience:

> From being a far-away, insignificant corner of the land, sunk in its dream of the Celtic past, with its own inner life of legends and superstitions and fears, its memories of Arthur and Mark and Tristan,

lapped in religion and the cult of the saints, it was forced in the course of the Elizabethan age into the front-line of the great sea-struggle with Spain. Inevitably the small backward-looking society struggled against the process: the Rebellions of 1497 and 1549 were to Cornwall what the '15 and '45 were to the Highlands.[86]

Rowse has described Tudor England as then ". . . the most taut and vigorous national society in Europe",[87] a society characterised by the twin imperatives of centralism and expansionism. In a manner identified by both Smith and Rokkan and Urwin, the Tudors moved swiftly to strengthen their personal power and their instruments of government. This necessitated a much greater degree of control over their subject peripheries — Cornwall, Wales, Ireland, and the North and the Borders — a process which involved military action and political treaties, but which was also manifested in more systematic taxation and the enforcement and administration of the Reformation. Hand-in-hand with centralism went English expansionism, which took Tudor England first to its Celtic peripheries and then beyond the seas to North America and elsewhere. Rowse has identified the Tudor attempts at the assimilation of the Celtic fringe as an integral part of the expansionist process, pointing to:

> . . . the expansion of that society, both by the state and by individual enterprise, first into the margin of backward societies at home — Cornwall, Wales, the Borders, with the sweep of a sickle on the map; into Ireland, where the process involved conquest and colonization; then across the oceans, to our first contacts with Russia, the Canadian North . . . (and) the colonization of North America.[88]

In practice, however, the attempts at unification, uniformity and pacification within these isles were only partially successful, and England's foreign policy led her to vulnerable isolation. Inevitably, Tudor England came into conflict with other European powers, most notably Spain, and here was further reason for attempting control in the Celtic peripheries, which were geographically and strategically vulnerable, where lingering Catholicism and anti-English sentiment might play into an enemy's hands. And geography also dictated that the Celtic West (and most especially Cornwall) would have a central role to play in the conflicts with Spain and other powers: as points of first defence against potential invaders and as points of first departure for the projection overseas of English power. In the colonisation of North America, too, the West would be best-placed to assist in the practical process of settling the new lands.

For Cornwall, the effects of this centralism and expansion were traumatic, at first disturbing and at length destroying that "Older Peripheralism" of "territorial and cultural isolation", and laying the foundations from which a new form of peripherality would emerge. Cornish reaction against increasing intervention in Cornwall's affairs was evident as early as 1496, when the tinners refused to accept new regulations imposed by Prince Arthur — a state of affairs serious enough to warrant Henry VII's suspension of the Stannaries, which was in itself further provocation of the Cornish.[89] In 1497 came still greater provocation, the demand from Henry for taxes to finance his war against Scotland. In contrast to the normal practices of the fifteenth century, tax rebates were not to be allowed for the poorer districts (of which Cornwall was one), a move which would create hardship and resentment in Cornwall. But more significant was the fact that Cornwall considered itself to be a special case, the Cornish arguing that a Scottish war was not their concern and that the defence of the Border was properly the responsibility of the people who lived there, as indeed it had been since time immemorial. Such arguments, however, cut little ice with King Henry, with his desire to dilute local usages and privileges.

So intense was the Cornish sense of outrage, that the people rose in rebellion against the taxation, the Lizard Peninsula in the west finding a strong, popular leader in the form of Michael Joseph "An Gof" ("The Smith") of St Keverne, and the folk at Bodmin in the east flocking around Thomas Flamank, a clever and persuasive lawyer.[90] Many of the indigenous lesser gentry joined the ranks of this impromptu army of tinners and agriculturalists, as it moved across the Tamar intent upon demonstrating to Henry that this taxation of Cornwall was not only unjust, but illegal. This first Cornish Rebellion of 1497 proved to be one of the greatest crises of Henry VII's reign, the rebel army marching as far as Blackheath — on the outskirts of London, threatening the English military and political establishment at its heart in Greenwich Palace — before its defeat at the hands of the King's forces on June 27th of that year. An Gof, Flamank and the other leaders were executed, but Henry dealt leniently with the rest of the Cornish insurgents, allowing them to return home to Cornwall. The Cornish, however, were not yet beaten — the pretender, Perkin Warbeck, having heard of the rebellion, made his way to Cornwall where he was proclaimed Richard IV at Bodmin. In the wake of Blackheath, Cornishmen flocked to his standard, eager for the chance of revenge, and once more a Cornish rebel army crossed the Tamar. This time, however, it reached no further than Somerset, where Warbeck lost his nerve, deserting his army and leaving it to melt back across the border. Again, Henry's treatment of the rebels was remarkably light, the King preferring retribution in the form of fines (which Cornwall could ill-afford) rather than blood.

It is difficult to gauge the mood of the Cornish in the aftermath of 1497. They may, to some extent, have sunk back into their introspective isolation. But Henry VII's Charter of Pardon of 1508 hints at a Cornwall still restless and in need of appeasement, and — having drawn attention to themselves as conservative opponents of Tudor centralism — the staunchly Catholic Cornish were identified by the government as a potential source of opposition to the Reformation: in 1539 the (admittedly short-lived) Council of the West was established to enforce the Reformation and to tighten the government's control of the region.[91] Although Cornwall had not joined that essentially North Country revolt, the "Pilgrimage of Grace", there were Cornishmen who were sympathetic to its cause — notably one Carpyssack of St Keverne who was arrested and probably hanged for expressing his beliefs in 1537 — while Exeter was perpetually afraid of a Cornish insurrection.[92] In 1548 there was a near-rebellion in Helston, led by St Keverne and Constantine men, when the officious and unpopular Protestant commissioner, William Body, was murdered by an angry mob as he endeavoured to remove "Popish" images from the parish church.[93]

Cornish opposition to the process of Reformation came to a head in 1549, when the Act of Uniformity of that year determined that the new English-language Service should replace the old Latin Service in churches. There were disturbances at Penryn and Marazion in West Cornwall, and at Bodmin the Cornish Catholics found a leader in the form of Humphrey Arundell of Helland. Discontent turned to open rebellion, as the Cornish drew up a petition to the King, declaring that the new Service was like "a Christmas game"[94] and that ". . . we will have our old service of Mattins, Mass, Evensong and Procession in Latin as it was before. And so we the Cornish men (whereof certain of us understand no English) utterly refuse this new English".[95] Cranmer retorted that there were more people in Cornwall who spoke English than Latin, but he was missing the point, for Latin was familiar (although not understood) all across Cornwall, whereas English was not. In addition, as Carew noted in 1602, the Creed, the Ten Commandments, and other elements had been said in Cornish since time immemorial, something that they feared would be lost with the introduction of the English Prayer Book.

The Cornish rebels crossed into Devon, joining forces with those Devonshire men who had also risen against the Prayer Book, and laid siege to Exeter. But within a month the siege had been partially lifted, and the rebels suffered a stinging defeat at Fenny Bridges when confronted by Edward VI's vastly superior army. The Cornish fought several rearguard actions as they retreated into Cornwall, but the great "Prayer Book Rebellion" was already over. This time, in contrast to 1497, a terrible revenge was meted out. Arundell and the other leaders were of course executed, but there were also hangings up and down Cornwall as retribution was sought. Priests implicated in the rebellion were singled out for particular attention. The vicars of Poundstock, Pillaton, Uny Lelant, and Gulval were certainly executed, and amongst those attainted were the vicars of St Cleer, St Keverne, St Neot, and St Veep: we notice here the considerable geographic spread, the involvement of the clergy by no means confined to the monoglot Cornish-speaking west of Cornwall.

The "Prayer Book Rebellion" of 1549 was a symptom of the Cornish reaction to Tudor centralism, but it was also a catalyst in the process of the erosion of Cornwall's "Older Peripheralism". The English Service was indeed introduced, and although some Cornish usages were allowed to continue, the Prayer Book and Bible were never translated into Cornish and the language was put into swift decline. Likewise, although some Catholic usages lingered on in the remotest parts, the Cornish Catholics soon became a small and persecuted minority. A rift appeared between Protestant Cornwall and Catholic Brittany, made all the more apparent now that the English and French States were religiously and politically antagonistic towards one another. Bretons no longer came to Cornwall to settle, and the age-old links between the two areas began to disintegrate. The Reformation, too, had led to the dissolution of the monasteries, and amongst those institutions suppressed was Glasney College, depriving Cornwall of an important source of literature and learning in the Cornish language. Henry VIII had promised to make amends by creating a new Cornish See at Bodmin or St Germans, but that never came to pass, Henry instead spending his money in the war against France.[96]

By the seventeenth century the language was retreating into the far west, already becoming a curiosity for travellers and scholars.[97] A visitor to St Just-in-Penwith in 1667 claimed that he could find only one man who could actually *write* Cornish, although in 1680 William Scawen reported that the principal language of the Penwith and Lizard peninsulas was still Cornish. Scawen was the first of a group of Cornish scholars concerned for the future of the language, and in the late seventeenth and early eighteenth centuries there emerged in the Penzance area a group of enthusiasts — Keigwin, Gwavas, Tonkin, Pender, the Bosons — working in Cornish. But their efforts did little to stem the decline, John Boson writing in 1700 that Cornish was ". . . only spoken from Land's End to the Mount and towards St Ives, and Redruth and again from Lizard towards Helston and Falmouth."[98] The lesser-gentry had already abandoned the language, and as political and economic contact with England increased, so it would fall into further disuse.

As the language declined, so Cornwall became more involved in the confrontation with Spain. Henry VIII had built the impressive castles of Pendennis (at Falmouth) and St Mawes as a defence against marauding Spaniards and Frenchmen, and under Elizabeth the Cornish "sea-dogs" were in the forefront of the Spanish fight and found favour at court[99] — Edmund Tremayne as Clerk of the Privy Council, William Killigrew as groom of the Queen's chamber, Henry Killigrew as a senior diplomatic envoy. The almost legendary Sir Richard Grenville of the "Revenge" was a Cornishman, and many Cornish seamen were amongst the lieutenants of Hawkins and Drake, most notably Pascoe Giddy of Saltash and Peter Carder of Veryan. In 1583 Cornwall played its part in the Armada saga: "In the war with Spain Cornwall was in the front line", argues Rowse, ". . . and in the 1590s the conflict was on her doorstep . . .".[100] In July 1595 a force of Spaniards landed at Mousehole, sacking Penzance and the surrounding settlements. At the same time, the Cornish were involved in the expansion outwards to the Americas: John Rashleigh of Fowey accompanied Sir Richard Grenville to Virginia in 1585 (and later fought against the Armada), Humphrey Gilbert sailed from Cawsand to Newfoundland in 1583, and Anthony Rouse of Halton in East Cornwall was amongst the first to settle in America.[101] At another level, Cornish fishermen played a central role in the opening-up and exploitation of the Newfoundland fisheries.

But despite all the turbulence and change, elements of this "Older Peripheralism" lived on into the seventeenth century — finding a final expression in the attitudes and events of the Civil War in Cornwall. As modern research has shown, the Civil War was often fought over local grievances rather than the "constitutional crisis",[102] and this was especially so for Cornwall and the South West — geographically separated as they were from the rest of the action. As Halliday has said, at times the Civil War in the West looked like a private quarrel between Cornwall and Devon, and always — as Coate has shown — the local patriotism and conservative but independent spirit of the Cornish were vital to the conduct of the war in Cornwall.[103] This was apparent at several levels — in the contrast between Royalist Cornwall on the one hand and fiercely Puritan Devon and Somerset on the other, in the devoted attachment of the Cornish to their local leaders, in the behaviour of the Cornish Army, and in the great hostility shown by the Cornish people to the "foreign" Parliamentarian Army when it ventured into Cornwall.

Seventeenth century Puritans were quick to point to "Popish" tendencies in Cornwall, but it is a mistake to paint too simplistic a picture of Cornish religion in that era. Whilst the Anglican Church in Cornwall may have become deeply conservative (Mass was still being celebrated at St Columb Major as late as 1590), Catholicism had declined for want of leadership and in the face of persecution, and there was in fact a growing band of Puritan Cornishmen — centred mainly around Lord Robartes in South East Cornwall. Politically, the Cornish (with their influential 44 MPs at Westminster) were for the most part moderate "constitutionalists", but with the outbreak of war Cornwall declared for King Charles, the minority of Parliamentarian sympathisers taking refuge in Puritan Plymouth. By way of contrast, Devon and Somerset — where Puritanism was much more deeply embedded — declared for Parliament.

Recruiting for a new, Royalist Cornish Army began in earnest in October 1642, and from the beginning it was distinguished by the close links, indeed affection, between men and leaders, and by the sense of common cause that had emerged. Mary Coate wrote of ". . . the passionate attachment of the Cornish to their own county and their own race . . ."[104] and explained that ". . . again and again this local patriotism, born of racial difference and geographical isolation, knit together in a common unity men of differing political and religious opinions".[105] Sir Bevill Grenville, of Stowe in North Cornwall, emerged as a focal point for these sentiments.[106] A moderate "constitutionalist" himself, he brought together the various factions, set himself up as a champion of Cornwall, and led the Cornish to victory at the battles of Braddock Down and Stamford Hill in Cornwall, and out across the Tamar towards Bristol. The "Cornish Foot" had already made a name for itself at Stamford Hill, and at the Battle of Lansdowne — near Bristol — it again carried the day, but at the terrible price of the loss of Sir Bevill Grenville in the fight. As Coate remarked, ". . . the Cornish were stunned by the loss of Sir Bevill Grenville",[107] and, although the "Cornish Foot" distinguished itself again at Roundway Down and at Bristol, things were never the same again. Two more of the Cornish leaders, Slanning and Trevanion, were killed at Bristol, and with the capture of the city ". . . ends the history of the Cornish army as a fighting force".[108]

Thereafter, the Cornish were disinclined to cross the Tamar out of Cornwall (even in the heady days of 1643 some had to be bribed to cross the river), particularly while Plymouth remained a threat. In 1644 Sir Richard Grenville attempted to raise new Cornish levies to prevent the advance of Essex through Devon, but they refused to march out of Cornwall — even when the King called upon them to attack Plymouth.[109] Essex, meanwhile, had decided to invade Cornwall (the export of tin was paying for the King's munitions, and had to be stopped) but he had underestimated the determination of the Cornish to defend their homes. His forces were defeated at Lostwithiel and Fowey, Essex himself noting the hatred of the Cornish for the Roundheads: ". . . the country people being violent against us, if any of our scouts or soldiers fall into their hands they are more bloody than the enemy".[110]

In 1645 the King sent his eldest son, Prince Charles, to take charge of the deteriorating situation in the West, but Fairfax's army was already marching westwards. Fairfax was at Bodmin by March 1646 (with the Prince forced to flee overseas) where he noted the strength of Cornish sentiment, writing that "Prince Charles is called the Duke of Cornwall altogether by the Cornish".[111] He was confident of victory, however, for Grenville's energies had been ". . . directed more to the saving of Cornwall than to the preservation of the Royalist cause".[112] In fact, the Royalist forces surrendered at Tresillian Bridge on 12th March, with Sir John Arundell holding out in Pendennis Castle until the August. The Civil War was over in Cornwall, with the brief exception of a Cornish rising in May 1648 (which was put down in the so-called "Gear Route" near Helston), the intrigues of Royalist sympathisers such as the Trelawny family, and the pro-Royalist mutiny of the Isles of Scilly garrison from September 1648 to May 1651.

In the events and attitudes of the Civil War in Cornwall, there were many echoes of the passions and motives of 1497 and 1549, not least the hostility to interference from outside agencies. But, as in 1549, the effect of the Cornish actions was to redouble the efforts of the central government (now firmly in the hands of the Parliamentarians) in dealing with Cornwall. Cornish representation at Westminster was reduced to 12, the Duchy of Cornwall was abolished as an administrative unit, and a County Committee ran Cornwall, mindful that Parliament still considered that "Cornwall was cavileerish enough . . .".[113] Again reminiscent of 1549, many of the Cornish clergy were ejected from their livings after the Parliamentary victory — from parishes all across Cornwall, from areas as diverse as St Cleer, Warbstow, St Goran, St Keverne, and St Buryan. The Restoration in 1660, of course, undid much of this, but Cornwall's constitutional accommodation did not fully recover from the Cromwellian assault. The Duchy of Cornwall did not recover its old influence and prestige (nor did the Stannaries), and — as with the Spanish Wars and the colonisation of the Americas in the Elizabethan age — the Civil War and its aftermath had pulled Cornwall once more into the centre of English national affairs. Interestingly, the Cornish steered well clear of the Monmouth Rebellion in 1685, once again showing no inclination to make common cause with the Puritan enthusiasts of Devon and Somerset,[114] although in the veiled hint in 1688 that "twenty thousand Cornishmen"[115] might rise in protest at the imprisonment of Sir Jonathan Trelawny, we see perhaps a final spark of that old rebellious isolationism.[116]

The emergence from isolation, in particular the new role in colonising America, had also provided new economic opportunities for Cornwall (although Whetter considers that Cornwall did not make the most of the prospects of American trade[117]), opportunities that were enhanced by new ideas and new technologies — such as the introduction of seine fishing. Despite the political instability and upheavals of the seventeenth century, the Cornish economy continued to develop. Sea traffic increased during this period; the populations of fishing centres such as St Ives and Mevagissey grew markedly; and there were advances in corn production and export, in cloth manufacture and sheep farming, and a variety of other industries. The rapid development of Falmouth Haven led to the exploitation of hitherto latent resources — both on land and in the sea — in west and central Cornwall, and the development of agriculture was not accompanied by the distress and dislocation of "enclosure" experienced elsewhere, for much of Cornwall was already enclosed. Most notable, as Whetter has said, was that Cornwall ". . . had a near monopoly of both tin and pilchards in Britain, and indeed, in Western Europe . . . tin mining and pilchard fishing were geared almost entirely to overseas markets . . .".[118] The pilchards went, ironically enough, to the Catholic countries of Europe. But it was the development of tin mining which would prove to be of the greatest consequence for the future of Cornwall.

As Whetter wrote, by the second half of the seventeenth century ". . . tin mining, in parts of the centre and west, was monopolising resources of labour and capital to a degree not known before".[119] Earlier, the Duchy of Cornwall had maintained a tight control over the production of tin — through the Royal prerogative of pre-emption, the right of the Crown to purchase all metal produced by the tinners and to sell it as it saw fit. In practice, pre-emption was normally "farmed" out to London pewterers in contracts which allowed these "pre-emptors" to purchase all the tinners' metals at a fixed rate, normally for a period of seven years. Pre-emption was considered a means of preventing the exploitation of the tinners, giving them security when times were bad, but it also militated against the tinners when demand for tin was high and the price of tin-based commodities rose — here the tinners (unlike the pewterers) did not share in the increased revenue and wealth, a factor which certainly helped to retard the development of the tin industry in the first half of the seventeenth century. However, the victory of Parliament in the Civil War brushed aside the Duchy and its administrations, and pre-emption was discarded along with all the other practices. The effect was dramatic, leading to tin price rises, an expansion of output, and the general development of the tin industry; so much so that attempts to introduce pre-emption at the Restoration were doomed to failure. As Whetter concluded, by the end of the century ". . . tin mining had become the dynamic element in the economy, the main force for prosperity — or for depression, as the case might be".[120]

Despite the general expansion of the Cornish economy, then, tin had nevertheless emerged as the central, crucial feature of Cornish economic activity, a main determinant of prosperity or depression in Cornwall — as it was to be for the next two centuries or more. Copper mining, too, re-emerged in Cornwall in the latter part of the seventeenth century, developing at an enormous rate in the eighteenth, and for much of the nineteenth being more important than tin. Together, copper and tin came to dominate Cornwall, and with this domination we see the final creation of those conditions which not only spelled the end of "Older Peripheralism" but ushered in the era of industrialisation and with it Cornwall's "Second Peripheralism".

To conclude, Cornwall's "Older Peripheralism of territorial and cultural isolation" had grown out of the Athelstan settlement in the tenth century, which had created the territorial unit of Cornwall and had allowed its "accommodation" — which in turn led to the emergence of the Duchy and Stannaries, affording a certain degree of constitutional independence and enhancing other features of Cornish "difference". This Cornwall was Celtic-speaking, looking towards Brittany for kinship, and psychologically and physically remote from England. However, the emergence of the centralism and expansionism of Tudor England broke this isolation, a process against which the Cornish reacted — in 1497, in 1549, and again in the Civil War — but nevertheless proved inexorable, dragging the Cornish into the frontline of the wars with Spain and into the colonisation of America. The Cornish economy also reacted to these conditions, with tin emerging as a major export commodity and with the tin industry — having lost the yoke of pre-emption — assuming its dominant position.

Elements of this "Older Peripheralism" did survive, however, to influence the ensuing period. These "constants of peripherality" included a continuing geographical distance from the centres of economic and political power (augmented now by distance from the centres of coal production), along with vestiges of Cornwall's constitutional "accommodation" — the Duchy, Stannaries, and 44 MPs. Nor was the Cornish language yet deceased, and the Cornish sense of independence and individualism endured — embedded in the settlement pattern and the landscape, enshrined in the economic activities of the small tenant farmers in an environment all but devoid of the influence of squire and parson, enshrined too in the practices of the mining industry with its "tribute" and "tutwork" systems of employment, and given renewed vigour in the eighteenth and nineteenth centuries through the rise of Methodism and political Liberalism. Smuggling and "wrecking", too, were echoes of the independence and lawlessness of earlier times. But peripherality is a dynamic condition, and the "Second Peripheralism" that emerged was in many respects strikingly different to that which had gone before, not least in the development of an assertive Cornish identity based upon technological advance and industrial prowess.

Notes and References

1. Michael Wood, *In Search of the Dark Ages*, British Broadcasting Corporation, London, 1983, p126, (quoting a list of relics given by Athelstan to the Church of St Peter in Exeter).
2. Ibid., p133, (quoting the "Altitonantis" charter, 964).
3. For example, Roy E.H. Mellor, *Nation, State, and Territory: A Political Geography*, Routledge, London, 1989, pp76-77, notes that "Marcher lordships were established against the Welsh and the unruly north of England as a means of consolidating Norman power".
4. Charles Thomas, *The Importance of Being Cornish in Cornwall: An Inaugural Lecture*, Institute of Cornish Studies, Redruth, 1973, p5.
5. Susan M. Pearce, *The Kingdom of Dumnonia: Studies in History and Tradition in South Western Britain, AD 350–1150*, Lodenek Press, Padstow, 1978.

6. G.H. Doble, *The Saints of Cornwall*, Parts 1-5, Dean and Chapter of Truro, Truro, 1960–1970; E.G. Bowen, *Saints, Seaways and Settlements in the Celtic Lands*, University of Wales Press, Cardiff, 1969, 2nd edition 1977; Barry Cunliffe, *The Celtic World*, Bodley Head, London, 1979, pp186-193; Catherine Rachel John, *The Saints of Cornwall*, Lodenek Press/Dyllansow Truran, Padstow/Redruth, 1981; Ada Alvey, *In Search of St James: Cornwall to Compestella — A Mediaeval Pilgrimage*, Dyllansow Truran, Redruth, 1989.

7. Peter Berresford Ellis, *Celtic Inheritance*, Muller, London, 1985, comes close to this position; see especially pp150-156.

8. Kenneth H. Jackson, *Language and History in Early Britain*, Edinburgh University Press, Edinburgh, 1953; Martyn F. Wakelin, *Language and History in Cornwall*, Leicester University Press, Leicester, 1975; J. Markale, *Celtic Civilization*, Gordon & Cremonesi, London, especially chapter 10 "The Britons and the Bretons", pp192-222; Pearce, op. cit.; N.K. Chadwick, "The Colonization of Brittany From Celtic Britain", Sir John Rhys Memorial Lecture, 1965, *Proceedings of The British Academy*, Vol. L1; N.K. Chadwick, *Early Brittany*, University of Wales Press, Cardiff, 1969.

9. W.G. Hoskins, *The Westward Expansion of Wessex*, Department of English Local History Occasional Paper No 13, Leicester University Press, Leicester, 1960, 2nd edition, 1970, p4.

10. Ibid., pp20-21; Malcolm Todd, *The South West to AD 1000*, Longman, London, 1987, pp270-275. Todd's account of this period is the most comprehensive and most recent contribution.

11. Orjan Svensson, *Saxon Place Names in East Cornwall*, Lund University Press, Lund, 1987; O.J. Padel, *A Popular Dictionary of Cornish Place-Names*, Alison Hodge, Penzance, 1988, pp7-9; Wakelin, op. cit., p55.

12. Hoskins, op. cit., pp21-22; Todd, op. cit., pp274-275, p289.

13. W.G.Hoskins, "Celt, Saxon and Norman in the Rame Peninsula", lecture at Millbrook 16/3/62, in unpublished manuscripts *Essays and Notes on Rame Peninsula*, Torpoint Public Library, Cornwall; Todd, op. cit., p289.

14. G.S.P. Freeman-Grenville, *Atlas of British History From Prehistoric Times Unil 1978*, Collings, London, 1979, Map 29 (for example).

15. Caroline and Frank Thorne (eds.), *Domesday Book-Cornwall*, Phillimore, Chichester, 1979, p152, consider that ". . . the 1086 boundary is conjectural", although Werrington (west of the Tamar but north of the Ottery) appears in the Exon book. Both Werrington and North Petherwin were later formalised as part of Devonshire, but were re-incorporated into Cornwall as recently as 1965 (see A.L. Dennis (ed.), *Cornwall County Council, 1889-1989: A History of 100 Years of County Government*, Cornwall County Council, Truro, 1989, p97.).

16. Pearce, op. cit., pp115-116; Todd, op. cit., p289.

17. The Duchy of Cornwall, *Preliminary Statement Showing the Grounds on which is founded the Right of The Duchy of Cornwall to the Tidal Estuaries, Foreshore, and Under-Sea Minerals within and around The Coast of The County of Cornwall*, Duchy of Cornwall, London, 1855, p9, asserted that the constitutional independence of the Duchy was greater than that of the Earldom:

". . . by the Third Charter, the Crown appears to have entirely denuded itself of every remnant of seignory and territorial dominion, which it could otherwise have enjoyed within the County or Duchy of Cornwall, and this made the rights of the Duchy, so far as such seignory and territorial dominion were concerned, more extensive even than had ever been enjoyed by the Earls . . .".

18. Geoffrey of Monmouth, (Lewis Thorpe, ed.), *The History of The Kings of Britain*, Guild Publishing, London, 1982.
19. Charles Thomas, *Celtic Britain*, Thames & Hudson, London, 1986, pp64-78.
20. The Duchy of Cornwall, *The Tidal Estuaries, Foreshore, and Under-Sea Minerals within and around The Coast of The County of Cornwall*, Duchy of Cornwall, London, 1857, p58, (quoting Charter Roll 11, Edward III, n55), Appendix L.
21. A.L. Rowse, *The Little Land of Cornwall*, Alan Sutton, Gloucester, 1986, p40; Crispin Gill (ed.), *The Duchy of Cornwall*, David & Charles, Newton Abbot, 1987, p14.
22. The Duchy of Cornwall, 1855, op. cit., p9.
23. Ibid., p11.
24. Richard Pearse, *The Land Beside The Celtic Sea: Aspects of Cornwall's Past*, Dyllansow Truran, Redruth, 1983, p51.
25. Julian Cornwall, *Revolt of The Peasantry 1549*, Routledge & Kegan Paul, London, 1977, p42.
26. Mary Coate, *Cornwall in the Great Civil War and Interregnum 1642–1660*, 1933, republished, D. Bradford Barton, Truro, 1963, p10.
27. The Duchy of Cornwall, 1855, op. cit., p3.
28. Ibid., p7.
29. Rowse, op. cit., p41.
30. The Duchy of Cornwall, 1855, p14.
31. John Hatcher, *Rural Economy and Society in the Duchy of Cornwall 1300–1500*, Cambridge University Press, Cambridge, 1970, p258.
32. Ibid., p43.
33. Ibid., p52.
34. Ibid.
35. Ibid., p52, pp60-61, p70, p220.
36. Cornwall, op. cit., pp42-43; Rowse, op. cit., p53; Henry Pelling, *Social Geography of British Elections 1885–1810*, Macmillan, London, 1962, p160.
37. Hatcher, op. cit., p29, p34, p220, p222.
38. Robert R. Pennington, *Stannary Law: A History of The Mining Law of Cornwall and Devon*, David & Charles, Newton Abbot, 1973, p13.
39. John Rowe, *Cornwall in the Age of the Industrial Revolution*, Liverpool University Press, Liverpool, 1953, p13.
40. G.R. Lewis, *The Stannaries: A Study of The Medieval Tin Miners of Cornwall and Devon*, 1908, republished D. Bradford Barton, Truro, 1965, p127.
41. Ibid., p39.
42. Duchy of Cornwall, 1857, op. cit., Part II, Supplementary Appendix, p16, (quoting Charter of Black Prince, 21 Edward II): ". . . the Stannary unquestionably extended over the whole County, it is manifest that the term Duchy was used in an equally extensive sense".
43. Pennington, op. cit., p19.
44. Lewis, op. cit., p126.
45. Ibid., pp98-99, p103.
46. Ibid., p126.
47. Pennington, op. cit., p20.
48. The Duchy of Cornwall, 1855, op. cit., p3; Henry Jenner, *A Handbook of The Cornish Language*, David Nutt, London, 1904, pxii.
49. Graham Haslam in Crispin Gill, op. cit., p43.
50. Roger Burt (ed.), *Cornish Mining: Essays on The Organisation of Cornish Mines and*

the Cornish Mining Economy, David & Charles, Newton Abbot, 1969, especially pp9-13 and pp111-206.

51. W.G.V. Balchin, *The Cornish Landscape*, Hodder & Stoughton, London, 1983, pp23-24. The intrinsic link between the "open" field system and Anglo-Saxon practice has been questioned of late, and one view asserts that strip fields appeared in Cornwall in medieval times as a result of pressure on land use (see H.S.A. Fox, "A Geographical Study of the Field Systems of Devon and Cornwall", University of Cambridge unpublished PhD, 1971).

52. Richard Muir, *Reading the Celtic Landscapes*, Guild Publishing, London, 1985, p88.

53. Balchin, Ibid., p120.

54. Ibid., p122.

55. James Whetter, "The English in Kernow in the Thirteenth Century", *Cornish Banner*, February 1988.

56. Arthur G. Langdon, *Old Cornish Crosses*, 1896; reprinted Cornwall Books, Exeter, 1988; A. Lane-Davies, *Holy Wells of Cornwall*, Federation of Old Cornwall Societies, Truro, 1970. E.W.F. Tomlin, *In Search of St Piran: An Account of his Monastic Foundation at Perranzubuloe, Cornwall, and its Place in the Western or Celtic Church and Society*, Lodenek Press, Padstow, 1982.

57. Catherine Rachel John, op. cit.

58. Muir, op. cit., p91.

59. James Whetter, *The History of Glasney College*, Tabb House, Padstow, 1988.

60. These works have survived into modern times. For example, William Jordan's 1611 version of Greans an Bys is available in Unified Cornish: E.G.R. Hooper (ed.), *Gwryans an Bys or The Creation of the World*, Dyllansow Truran, Redruth, 1985. Beunans Meriasek is available in an English translation: Myrna Combellack, *The Camborne Play*, Dyllansow Truran, Redruth, 1988.

61. Wakelyn, op. cit., is, however, less sympathetic in his modern assessment of language and history in Cornwall. A vigorous corrective is offered by Peter Berresford Ellis, *The Story of The Cornish Language*, Tor Mark Press, Truro, 1970; Peter Berresford Ellis, *The Cornish Language and Its Literature*, Routledge & Kegan Paul, London, 1974; P.A.S. Pool, *The Death of Cornish*, Cornish Language Board, Penzance, 1975; Crysten Fudge, The Life of Cornish, Dyllansow Truran, Redruth, 1982.

62. Wakelyn, op. cit., pp88-89.

63. Berresford Ellis, 1974, op. cit., p49.

64. Fudge, op. cit., p26.

65. James Whetter, *Old Cornwall*, Spring 1962; James Whetter, *The History of Gorran Haven, Part I 0-1800 AD*, Lyfrow Trelyspen, St Austell, 1991, p11 and pp15-16.

66. Wakelyn, op. cit., p89.

67. Fudge, op. cit., p25.

68. Wakelyn, op. cit., p99.

69. Cornwall, op. cit., p42; A.L. Rowse, *Tudor Cornwall*, Cape, London, 1941, republished, Dyllansow Truran, Redruth, 1990, p49.

70. G. Pawley White, *A Handbook of Cornish Surnames*, White, Truro, 1972, pp18, 33, 51.

71. F.E. Halliday, *A History of Cornwall*, Duckworth, London, 1959, p82.

72. Rowse, 1941, op. cit., pp101-113. Hugh Kearney, *The British Isles: A History of Four Nations*, Cambridge University Press, Cambridge, 1989, p105.

73. Rowse, 1986, op. cit., pp178-190; James Whetter, *The Bodrugans: A Study of a Cornish Medieval Knightly Family*, forthcoming.

74. Coate, op. cit., p2.
75. Cornwall, op. cit., p42.
76. Richard Carew, (F.E. Halliday, ed.), *The Survey of Cornwall, 1602*, Melrose, London, 1953, p139.
77. Coate, op. cit., p139.
78. Carew, op. cit.
79. Hatcher, op. cit., p1.
80. Ibid.
81. Ibid., p2.
82. Christopher Bice, *A Stamp For Cornwall*, MK Publications, Redruth, 1974, p6.
83. Ibid.
84. Coate, op. cit., p162.
85. Rowse, 1941, op. cit., p20.
86. Ibid., p9.
87. A.L. Rowse, *The Expansion of Elizabethan England*, 1955, Cardinal, London, 1973, p15.
88. Ibid., p6.
89. Ivan Roots, *The Monmouth Rebellion: Aspects of the 1685 Rebellion in the West Country*, Devon Books, Exeter, 1986, p9; J.A. Buckley, *Tudor Tin Bounds: West Penwith*, Dyllansow Truran, Redruth, 1987, pp8-9.
90. Cornwall, op. cit., pp44-46 and Rowse, 1941/1990, op. cit., pp114-140, detail the 1497 rebellions.
91. Cornwall, op. cit., p49.
92. Ibid., p47.
93. The events of the "Prayer Book Rebellion" are detailed at length in Rowse, 1941/1990, op. cit., pp253-290; Cornwall, op. cit., pp49-241; and John Sturt, *Revolt in The West: The Western Rebellion of 1549*, Devon Books, Exeter, 1987.
94. Cornwall, op. cit., p57.
95. Ibid.
96. Rowse, 1955, op. cit., p47.
97. The decline of the language is documented in P.A.S. Pool, op. cit.
98. John Boson, *Nebbaz Gerriau dro tho Carnoack*, 1700, quoted in Berresford Ellis, 1970, p18.
99. Rowse, 1955, op. cit., pp49-51.
100. Ibid., p51.
101. Ibid., p51; see also A.L. Rowse, *Sir Richard Grenville of The 'Revenge'*, Cape, London, 1937.
102. Cornwall, op. cit., p46.
103. Halliday, op. cit., p221; Coate, op. cit., pp70, 102, 139, 351.
104. Coate, op. cit., p351.
105. Ibid.
106. John Stucley, *Sir Bevill Grenvile and His Times*, Phillimore, Chichester, 1983.
107. Coate, op. cit., p89.
108. Ibid., p100.
109. Amos C. Miller, *Sir Richard Grenville of The Civil War*, Phillimore, Chichester, 1979.
110. Coate, op. cit., p147.
111. Ibid., p199.
112. Ibid., p197.
113. Ibid., p290.

114. Roots, op. cit., demonstrates that the Monmouth rebellion was Puritan in influence and centred upon Somerset and Devon and their neighbouring counties to the east. W. Macdonald Wigfield, *The Monmouth Rebels*, Sutton, Gloucester, 1985, p202, shows only one single, solitary rebel from Cornwall.
115. Immortalised in R.S. Hawker's famous ballad:
     "And have they fixed the where and when?
       And shall Trelawny die?
     Here's twenty thousand Cornish men
       Will know the reason why!"
   (see A.L. Rowse, *A Cornish Anthology*, Alison Hodge, Penzance, 1982, p5).
116. There is, however, no mention of this in M.G. Smith, *Fighting Joshua: A Study of the Career of Sir Jonathan Trelawny, bart, 1650–1721, Bishop of Bristol, Exeter and Winchester*, Dyllansow Truran, Redruth, 1985.
117. James Whetter, *Cornwall in the Seventeenth Century: An Economic Survey of Kernow*, Lodenek Press, Padstow, 1974, p175.
118. Ibid., p176.
119. Ibid., p172.
120. Ibid., p173.

Part Three

Second Peripheralism — The Impact Of Industrial Change

"Great as are the advantages which this nation in general enjoys from the invention of the steam engine, and the successive improvements which it has received; there is, perhaps, no place in particular, where those advantages have been greater, or more evident, than in Cornwall. The very existence of its deepest, most extensive, and most productive mines, is owing, not merely to the invention of the steam engine, but to the state of great perfection to which that machine has been brought in that county . . . the improvements which the engine has, for many years, received, are due to native engineers; whose skill and watchful care, maintain it in its present state, or add continually still further improvements . . .".

> *Thomas Lean, 1839.*
> (Thomas Lean,
> *On The Steam Engines in Cornwall,*
> facsimile edition, D. Bradford Barton,
> Truro, 1969, p1).

"The Cornish are remarkable for their sanguine temperament, their indomitable perseverance, their ardent hope in adventure, and their desire for discovery and novelty; hence their wide distribution all over the world, in the most remote corners of which they are to be found amongst the pioneers; and to this very cause has science to boast of so many brilliant ornaments who claim Cornwall as their birthplace."

> *George Henwood, 1859.*
> (Roger Burt [ed.]
> *Cornwall's Mines and Miners,*
> D. Bradford Barton, Truro, 1972, p232).

"There was a time when Gwennap was alive with the clang of stamps, and thousands of tons of copper ore went down the Carnon Valley to Devoran for shipment; when the Perran and St Agnes districts were busy hives of industry, and East Wheal Rose was a name to conjure by. Where are they now? . . . gone to the limbo of forgotten things."

> *West Briton*, 8 November 1894

"Cornwall was no longer isolated . . . Even so, Cornwall retained a sense of 'difference'. Its attraction for English painters, particularly for Stanhope Forbes and his friends at the end of the century, can be compared with the enthusiasm of French artists for Brittany during that same period . . . Cornwall served a similar purpose in England: it had to remain remote yet accessible in its remoteness."

Kieth Robbins,
Nineteenth-Century Britain: England, Scotland, and Wales — The Making of a Nation, Oxford University Press, Oxford, 1989, p25.

CHAPTER FOUR

Cornubia Triumphant?

The condition of "Older Peripheralism", in which Cornwall had been conquered but accommodated — her regional identity tolerated and to an extent enhanced — was by degrees eroded, succumbing to the centralisation of the Tudor and Cromwellian States and disintegrating in the face of economic and political change which saw Cornwall assume a newfound strategic importance. These changes, however, wideranging though they were, led not to the integration of Cornwall with the English "centre" (to which she had become so suddenly important), but rather to new manifestations of peripherality. The growing importance of Cornwall as a tin mining centre (with a near monopoly of world production) emphasised her unique attributes and served to sharpen the differences between the Cornish and English economies, differences that would be further exacerbated by the subsequent development of copper and other metaliferous mining in Cornwall. This development was dependent upon technological advance and the industrialisation of the Cornish economy, but — for reasons that will be discussed — such industrialisation was imperfect and incomplete, at once both a product of *and* a perpetuating factor in Cornwall's inherent peripheral status. This, then, was the condition of "Second Peripheralism" — in which the "constants" of Cornish peripherality, increasingly shorn of the "Older" Medieval accommodation, were now augmented by a "Second" set of peripheral attributes associated with the process of industrialisation.

Cornwall in the period 1700 to 1850 does not appear at first glance to have been a region suffering the disadvantages and marginalisation of social and economic peripherality. The Cornish economy was amongst the first to industrialise, the early and successful application of steam power facilitating the development of deep mining and achieving for Cornwall a place in the forefront of technological innovation.[1] Paradoxically, it was the expansion of copper rather than tin which gave the initial impetus to technological advance, the 1680s witnessing the rise of several important copper-producers in the environs of Redruth.[2] By 1720 some 6,000 tons of copper ore were being raised in Cornwall annually, with many of the subsequently far-famed mines already well established — among them Wheal Busy, Roskear, Dolcoath, and Cook's Kitchen. The increasing depths of these ventures prompted experimentation with steam power (for pumping) and the development of drainage technology, the "Great County Adit" being commenced in 1748 as the device by which Poldice (and ultimately many other mines) could be kept efficiently and economically free of water inundation. The discovery of extensive copper deposits in Anglesey in 1768 threatened Cornwall's monopoly, but these were all but worked out by the 1790s, ushering in a new period of Cornish expansion. In 1809 a tramway was opened, linking the major mines of Scorrier and St Day — Wheal Buller, Wheal Basset, Caharrack, Ting Tang, and others — to Portreath on the north coast (facilitating the export of ore), and in 1824 a similar railroad was constructed from the Gwennap mines to the port of Devoran on the Fal.[3] By then the parish of Gwennap alone was responsible for more than a third of the total world production of copper ore. As Morrison has written, ". . . mining in Cornwall was technically the most advanced in the world."[4]

From 1810 onwards the Cornish copper industry began to expand its horizons, moving out of its Gwennap and Camborne-Redruth heartland to new areas — eastwards to the district around St Austell Bay (the celebrated mines of Crinnis, Fowey Consols, and Lanescot) and westwards to St Just-in-Penwith where Levant was soon established as a major producer. And in 1836 came the spectacular discoveries at Caradon Hill, on the southern fringe of Bodmin Moor, leading to the rapid development of the St Cleer mining district and shifting the balance of copper production away from west to east Cornwall. Further discoveries, in the neighbourhood of Gunnislake, confirmed this shift of importance — and in 1844 there was a significant discovery of copper at what was to become Devon Great Consols. Although situated on the Devon bank of the Tamar, Great Consols was fully integrated into the Cornish mining industry — worked by Cornish methods and indeed employing many Cornish miners — and was considered as part of the Cornish scene by contemporary observers. Again, technological advances assisted the development of these new areas, involving (for example) the opening of the Liskeard and Caradon railway in 1844 and the growth of Tamar river traffic associated with new quays such as that at Morwellham.[5]

Despite the rapid development of tin in the second half of the seventeenth century, with its important consequences for the nature of the Cornish economy, it was in the eighteenth century a less dynamic influence than copper upon the process of industrialisation.[6] The market was increasingly controlled by merchants and smelters, who excercised a retarding influence, and what Barton has termed "the fetters of coinage"[7] also served to discourage the expansion of tin production in the decades before 1838. The East India Company, however, emerged as an important purchaser of Cornish tin in the latter part of the eighteenth century, and by 1800 the demand for tin-plate in the British domestic market was beginning to increase rapidly. By 1810 a veritable boom was underway, leading to the working of Wheal Vor and a string of other mines around Helston and Marazion and in other parts of Cornwall, this expansion benefitting from the technological advance that had already attended the rise of copper. Although tin was to play second fiddle to copper throughout most of the nineteenth century, with the deleterious effects of Straits competition being felt as early as 1813, there was nonetheless a continuing high demand for tin-plate. The abolition of "coinage" in 1838 assisted the expansion of Cornish tin mining (allowing it to ride the depression of the 1840s more easily than it might otherwise have done) and in the period 1850 to 1864 there was vigorous activity as demand surged from the Welsh tin-plate works and as many Cornish mines turned from copper to tin. Wheal Vor was in the forefront of this activity, but Dolcoath had assumed a new importance as a tin producer, having turned from copper to tin as early as 1838 on the discovering of rich tin lodes at depth — a change that many other Camborne-Redruth mines were to emulate as copper became less profitable. A further tin boom in 1870-72 accelerated this process, leading to the rise of mines such as Wheal Owles, South Frances, and North Levant.

In the latter part of the nineteenth century the relative position of Cornwall in the mining world declined considerably, as first copper and then tin were plunged into crisis, but tin mining did survive (largely as a result of continuing technological innovation, such as the introduction of rock drills and improvements in explosives) while there was some diversification into arsenic mining and, of course, clay quarrying. Indeed, in the period 1850 to 1909 Cornwall was still responsible for half of the total United Kingdom non-ferrous metal production, while there were no fewer than 1500 separate Cornish mining ventures between 1845 and 1913.[8] Lead, too, featured in the production of Cornish minerals, along with silver, zinc, wolfram and smaller quantities of other metals.

The technological innovation which accompanied Cornwall's mining pre-eminence in the eighteenth and nineteenth centuries not only facilitated rapid industrialisation but led to the emergence of Cornwall as a principal centre of engineering expertise. This, in turn, as Barton has shown, was tied inextricably to the development of the Cornish beam engine — for pumping, winding, ore-crushing, and the operation of man-engines so that ". . . by 1850 Cornishmen had more experience of deep mining, and with it deep pumping, than the rest of the world together".[9] By 1716 at least one Newcomen engine was in use in Cornwall (probably at Wheal Vor or neighbouring Godolphin Ball) and this was followed by others in the 1720s[10] and — by the 1770s — the more economical Watt engines. Watt's determined defence of all aspects of his patent lapsed in 1800, precipitating in Cornwall a great era of experimentation. Cornish engineers competed with one another in their attempts to perfect the beam engine, and considerable rivalry existed between the different mines as they strove to improve the efficiency of their engines. This competitive spirit was echoed in the pages of Lean's *Engine Reporter*, a journal founded in 1810 to report and record the "duty" achieved by the principal engines at work in Cornwall, "duty" being defined as the number of pounds of water raised one foot high by the consumption of one bushel of coal.[11]

Arthur Woolf, a Cornish-born engineer, returned home to Cornwall in 1811 after a period of absence, bringing with him his new engine designs,[12] and in 1812 the celebrated Richard Trevithick successfully introduced his high pressure engine at Wheal Prosper in Gwithian parish. William Sims, yet another Cornish inventor, in 1816 introduced numerous improvements to his engines at Wheal Chance, in Gwennap, and at Wheal Hope in Gwinear parish emerged one of the greatest practical engineers of the day, Samuel Grose. The period 1825 to 1850 witnessed a continuing improvement of the "duty" figures, great feats of efficiency being achieved, for example, by Grose's 80 inch engine at Wheal Towan in the early 1830s or by the famed "Ale and Cakes" 85 inch engine at United Mines — where in 1840 the best "duty" ever reported by Lean was recorded. The 1850s saw the pinnacle of the Cornish beam engine's performance, in terms of technical perfection but also in respect of standards of maintenance and the degree of ingenuity demonstrated by Cornish engineers.[13] Along with Woolf, Trevithick, Sims and Grose (and the Cornish-adopted Hornblower family, originally from the Midlands) were other well known Cornish innovators who achieved British and in some cases international recognition, among them John Hocking, Michael Loam, William West, and the incredible Michell dynasty whose activities spanned from the late eighteenth to early twentieth centuries — almost the entire period of Cornish steam engineering.[14]

Associated with the rise of the Cornish beam engine was the establishment of numerous Cornish engineering foundries. Many were modest affairs, such as the Charlestown Foundry or Hodge's of St Austell, but amongst the giants were Harvey & Co of Hayle and the Perran Foundry at Perranarworthal.[15] By 1800 Harvey was already employing 50 hands, and the foundry grew rapidly in the first half the nineteenth century, responding to demand for its engines and components from both home and abroad, and playing a leading role in the development of Hayle as an industrial port. Perran's hey-day ran from 1820 to 1860, with Perran-built engines finding their ways to destinations as diverse as the Real del Monte mines in Mexico, Burra Burra and Wallaroo in South Australia, and Kimberley in South Africa. The international importance of Cornish engineering was also demonstrated in the rise of Holman Brothers of Camborne, which by the end of the nineteenth century was exporting pneumatic rock drills and other mining appliances to districts as far-flung as the silver-lead-zinc mines of Broken Hill in New South Wales and the goldfields of the Rand. Although (despite the efforts of the Cornish Copper Co at Hayle[16]) there was little development of copper smelting in Cornwall, the growth of the Cornish engineering foundries was also reflected in the success of local tin smelting activities. Modern smelters, using the reverberatory furnace and employing coal as fuel, gradually replaced the ancient, charcoal-fired "blowing-houses", and by 1800 a number of smelting houses had been established in the environs of Truro and Penzance, with smaller smelting works scattered across other parts of Cornwall.

Complementary to the process of industrialisation was an improvement in transport and communications. Cornwall's links with the rest of the world continued to be by sea, reflected in the fact that the Royal Albert Bridge — and with it the railway across the Tamar — was not opened until 1859, but the tramways and railroads constructed *within* Cornwall to link the mines with ports and quays were amongst the earliest built in the United Kingdom. Many of these were later amalgamated into the routes of grander railways and incorporated into the British network, and indeed between 1809 and 1908 no less than 350 miles of railway were laid. New ports were also established — Portreath, Par, Pentewan, Hayle, Newquay, Charlestown, Trevaunance, Bude, and others — while long-established harbours such as Fowey, Looe and Saltash were equipped for the export of minerals and the import of coal, timber and other necessities for the mining industry.[17]

A special "breed" of Cornish industrialist emerged during the industrial expansion and technological innovation of the eighteenth and nineteenth centuries, demonstrating a single-mindedness and determination which reflected the traditional independence of Cornishmen in earlier centuries but which also embraced the "new culture" of industrialisation with great enthusiasm. To the distinguished ranks of the mining engineers should be added the names of the great entrepreneurial families and individuals who derived their wealth from the mineral deposits exploited in their lands — the Bassets of Tehidy (who made so much from Dolcoath), the Fox family of Falmouth (associated with Tresavean, North Downs, and United Mines), the Lemons, the Williams family — and the Cornish capitalists who took their investments outside of Cornwall: John Vivian who became involved in the Welsh copper-smelting industry, and William Praed of Trevethow — the banker who built the Grand Union Canal between London and Birmingham. The fame and significance of many of these Cornishmen, indeed, spread far beyond the confines of Cornwall — Sir Humphry Davy (inventor of the "safety lamp", and a President of the Royal Society) achieved lasting international stature, while Francis Trevithick won prominence as the first Mechanical Engineer of the London and North Western Railway. J.T. Treffry found fame as the renowned "King of Mid-Cornwall" for his development of mines, ports and mineral railways around St Austell and Fowey, and perhaps the greatest of these technocrats was Davies Gilbert — the "Cornish philosopher" as he was known throughout Britain in the early part of the nineteenth century.[18] As Member of Parliament, President of the Royal Society, and chairman of numerous Parliamentary committees, Gilbert used his influence and energy to promote many "improving" causes — technical education, the application of steam power, agricultural reform, road construction, and Poor Law reform — his enthusiasm mirroring the self-confidence and optimism of Cornish society at that time.

But this industrial prowess, the Cornish capacity for invention and progress, disguised the underlying characteristics of industrialisation in Cornwall. That great, pervasive constant of peripherality — geographical isolation and distance from the seats of economic and political power — to a considerable degree moulded the process of industrialisation, ensuring that it would be imperfect, incomplete and over-specialised, itself peripheral in quality. Greatest of the geographical constraints placed upon Cornwall was her lack of coal deposits — there were coal mines in Gloucestershire and Somerset, but in the days before rail communications these were more remote and less accessible than those in South Wales, which could be reached from Cornwall by sea. A trading cycle was thus established with South Wales, in which ships carrying coal for Cornwall returned to Welsh ports with copper ore destined for Welsh smelters, a cycle which itself served to retard smelting and other industrial diversification in Cornwall. As Burt has written,

> The greatest *deficiency* in Cornwall's mineral wealth was without doubt its lack of *coal*. This proved to be a near fatal flaw in terms of the

county's general industrialisation and long-term economic welfare. The smelting and manufacture of its metallic minerals was generally forced outside of the region to areas where fuel was plentiful and cheap. The secondary industries which developed within the county related only to primary mining and quarrying activity. With the long-term decline of these activities — which now (1987) amount only to the rump of a tin mining industry and large-scale quarrying confined to the St Austell area — there has been a progressive contraction of the industrial base on which to build a new future.[19]

As Rowe observed, the chief characteristics of the Cornish copper industry had been established between 1689 and 1740, the most significant of which was the dependence upon the South Wales (and, to a lesser extent, Bristol) smelting interests. Even then, says Rowe, the Cornish were aware of the danger of exploitation, but the early failure of an attempt to establish smelting at Polrudden (Pentewan) re-emphasised the difficulties of creating a competitive industry in Cornwall.[20] In 1725 the uniquely Cornish "ticketing" system was introduced for the sale of copper. "Ticketing" was an echo of the long-established "tribute" system of employment (in which a miner bid, as in an auction, for the area of ground he was to work) in that potential purchasers of copper were required to submit "tickets" (bids) for the lots in which they were interested. In an industry where the potential purchasers (and hence the likely nature of their bids) were all well known to one another, "ticketing" tended to have the effect of keeping prices down — to the detriment of Cornish interests.

Ironically, the Cornish had at first approved of "ticketing" (it reflected the sturdy independence of "tributing") but by 1755 there was general agreement in Cornwall that there was an unjustified disparity between the low prices paid for copper ore and the high prices asked for manufactured copper goods. In that year the Cornish Copper Co smelting works was opened at Hayle; although successful, its output was tiny by Welsh standards and did not have a significant effect. In 1785 a Cornish Metal Co was set up in Truro, a marketing organisation dedicated to raising the price of copper and dismantling the "ticketing" system. It had little success, however, for the Anglesey mines had contributed to the problem of low prices through over-production, and the Cornish Metal Co found its activities confined to managing the orderly closure of some Cornish mines and subsequent compensation of adventurers (shareholders). By 1791, indeed, the Company itself was dead. Birmingham brass and copper manufacturers tried to help the Cornish mines (but also secure *their* control of the industry) by setting up a co-operative arrangement involving mining, smelting and manufacturing interests, but in the end the Cornish adopted the old maxim of "if you can't beat them, join them" by penetrating the Welsh smelting industry. In 1803 Pascoe Grenfell went into partnership with Thomas WIlliams to open a smelting works at Swansea, while John Vivian commenced operations at Penclawdd. In 1809 Vivian leased the much larger Hafod works, near Landore, while the Morfa works were taken over by the Williams family from Scorrier! For the Cornish capitalists themselves, this strategy was a considerable success — but for the broader Cornish economy there was little change in the relationship between mining and smelting, and still little scope for diversification.[21]

Another financial and managerial eccentricity born of Cornish isolation and independence was the so-called "cost-book" system, which prevailed in Cornwall's mining industry until the 1890s. Under the "cost-book" system, each of the adventurers coming together to open a mine would hold a share and contribute accordingly. Adventurers' meetings were held regularly (usually at two-monthly intervals) at which the mine's progress would be reviewed. If the mine was still at an embryonic stage, with much developmental work still in hand, then "calls" could be levied on each shareholder at a level determined by the meeting. But if the mine was already profitable, then dividends would be declared and paid out. Often, an ailing mine would need repeated financial support through a series of "calls", a situation which might lead individual adventurers to their own financial embarrassment or even bankruptcy. Shares might be subdivided to bring in additional cash, while an adventurer might be forced to relinquish (or sell — if he could find a buyer) his share. Response to a "call" was obligatory, and an adventurer unable or unwilling to pay was liable to forfeiture. Although such unlimited liability might lead an individual to ruin, the "cost-book" system was nonetheless popular in Cornwall for it also held the prospect of immense gains for those adventurers who had invested in profitable mines. For example, as Morrison noted, between 1834 and 1845 the adventurers of East Pool mine received no less than £32,256 in dividends on an outlay of £640.[22]

As an accounting device the "cost-book" was unique. As Morrison wrote,

It represented a single fund which received all income from calls, ore sales and other sources, and disbursed all cash for labour, materials, dividends and — an important point — all capital expenditure on plant, construction and development. Thus capital expenditure appears as an operating cost and was financed from calls or profits.[23]

Despite these curious features, the "cost-book" system proved flexible in operation and equal to the task of financing even the biggest of mines in the hey-day of Cornish mining: in the 1830s, for example, Consolidated and United involved capital investment of tens of thousands of pounds and were amongst the largest enterprises in the world.[24]

However, the "cost-book" system did have its disadvantages. The legal requirement that all profits should be distributed as dividends at each adventurers' meeting led to the dispersal of funds which might more properly have been re-invested in the mines. And adventurers were often more interested in short-term profit maximisation than long-term development, leading to dubious practices ("picking the eyes" out of a mine by plundering its best reserves, irrespective of market prices or other considerations; or sinking crooked — and ultimately inefficient — shafts to follow lodes so that ore might be produced while sinking) and an unwillingness to re-invest profits in long-term capital-intensive projects. The mine companies themselves were unable to make efficient use of "spare" monies by, for example, purchasing shares in other mining ventures or even lending funds to earn interest.

These disadvantages led in many cases to the long-term underdevelopment of many Cornish mines, a situation exacerbated by the relations between the indigeneous Cornish adventurers and those from outside. In the eighteenth and early nineteenth centuries, shares in Cornish mines were largely in the hands of individual Cornishmen (indeed this was still partially true as late as 1870, when mine ownership was still vested in individuals or small groups), and there was a general hostility towards outside interests — capitalists from across the Tamar (with the remarkable exception of Norfolk-born John Taylor, who thoroughly understood mining[25]) were dismissed as "foreigners" or, more cynically, "the wise men of the east". However, the rising power of the City of London became irresistable — Cornish mines needed ever-greater investment, and the prospect of vast profits tempted the speculators of the metropolis. These latter, however, were wary of the unlimited liability of the "cost-book" and pressed for the adoption of an alternative system of limited liability. This, in turn, was met with resentment in Cornwall — with the result that the concept of limited liability was opposed west of the Tamar while the "cost-book" was discredited among English investors. This had the effect of diverting much-needed City capital away from Cornwall to the new mining fields overseas, aggravating the already significant problem of underdevelopment. Unhappily, those English capitalists who did take an interest in Cornwall were often drawn into the net of sharp sharedealing (which developed in the mid nineteenth century) and which helped further to bring Cornish mining into disrepute and to widen the rift between Cornish and "foreign" adventurers.[26]

Like "ticketing", then, the thoroughly Cornish "cost-book" system did not always operate in the long-term interests of the Cornish mining industry, especially when that industry was exposed to the pressures of outside interests. Cornish adventurers, however, seemed only dimly aware of this, with the desire for spectacular riches (in reality reserved for only the lucky few) leading them to prop up ailing mines for many years in the hope of striking better lodes. All too often a far-famed but marginal concern was allowed to continue for the occasional patches of rich ore that it produced, consuming as it did vast quantities of capital, while a potentially more promising but obscure prospect was examined briefly and then abandoned. Burt, indeed, has argued that it is probable that the overall sale of ore from Cornish mines never did repay the total investment in the industry, a significant factor in the explanation of the Cornish economy's failure to expand or diversify as mining became less important.[27] Rowe states the case quite plainly, asserting that the Cornish expended their efforts and finances for too long in shoring-up their mining industry, with the result that ". . . the industrialization of the textile manufacturers in northern England left it too late in the day to promote spinning, knitting, and lace-making in Cornwall":[28] while the Cornish had tarried with their mines, other regions of Britain (many with the additional advantage of local coal deposits) had already turned their hands to new industries, leaving the Cornish with few opportunities of their own and with Cornwall's experience of industrialisation cut short — imperfect and incomplete.

The Cornish determination to support mining, and the consequent reluctance and eventual inability to diversify into new industries, lends a fascinating insight into the psychology and culture of Cornish society in the eighteenth and especially nineteenth centuries. The Cornish were aware and intensely proud of their mining heritage, their engineers elevated to the level of supermen, the reputation and significance of Cornwall's pre-eminence acknowledged and understood across the world. Mining became a central plank of the Cornish identity, the raison d'etre of Cornwall and Cornishmen, and the great entrepreneurial families, adventurers, practical miners and engineers alike could think of little else. Mining *was* Cornwall, and *Cornwall* was mining; and at its height the industry employed directly one-third of the Cornish working population, with many more working in support enterprises.[29] Geographically, as well as socially and economically, mining was a unifying force in Cornwall: even the most far-flung districts could boast their Cornish mines — such as Wheal Morwenna in Morwenstow parish, Wheal Tamar at Saltash, and Wheal Carew near Torpoint. In such an atmosphere and environment, it was hardly surprising that the society's institutions should reflect this all-encompassing passion for mining affairs. There was, for example, as Burt says, a ". . . distinctive Cornish hue . . ."[30] in the many mutual-improvement and educational bodies that had grown up by the 1850s: organisations such as the Liskeard Institution, the St Austell Literacy Society, the Launceston Pilosophical Society, and — of course — the Camborne School of Mines itself. As Burt explained

> The most noticeable "Cornish" sector of the educational system were the non-vocational institutions: "Non-vocational" in the sense that they had no specific commitment to providing instruction in basic literacy or for any particular profession, but highly "Cornish" in that their programs reflected the district's consuming interest in mining affairs and related subjects.[31]

Within such an educational system Cornish skills became highly specialised but also limited, encouraging the movement of Cornish technology into ever more specialist and specific avenues. Although advantageous during the years of mining expansion, it left Cornwall's resources of skilled manpower and technological expertise dangerously narrow and unbalanced in times of decline. The Cornish beam engine was a case in point: in the hey-day of the *Engine Reporter* the specialist concentration on the development of the Cornish engine seemed all to the good, but by the 1850s the engine had reached the practical limit of its technological refinement, while overseas markets such as Australia were already setting up home-grown foundries to produce their own engines — to the detriment of the Cornish industry. Once again, the Cornish economy was left with little opportunity for diversification in the face of industrial change.

A combination of factors, then, geographical and economic but also cultural and psychological, served to determine the peripheral characteristics of Cornwall's industrialisation, ensuring that it would indeed be imperfect, incomplete and over-specialised. However, the inherent flaws in the Cornish industrial base were to a degree camouflaged by Cornish prominence in the worlds of mining and engineering. Ironically, the "Great Migration" of Cornish folk — which gained momentum in the 1830s and ran strongly until the Great War — was hailed in Cornwall as the pinnacle of Cornish achievement, with the might and glory of Cornwall writ large across the world as her sons took their unrivalled expertise to new lands thirsting for knowledge and labour.[32] The reality, of course, was rather different — for while the new lands did indeed benefit from Cornish skills, the "Great Migration" was itself a symptom of Cornwall's predicament and the means by which Cornwall was shorn of her most able and energetic inhabitants. Nonetheless, the "Great Migration" did create a certain Cornish international identity — in which Cornwall was the hub with spokes radiating outwards to North America, South Africa, Australia — with the Cornish confident and assured in their status as world leaders.[33] This further enhanced the new pride in "Cornishness" which had accompanied the growth of industrial prowess, and which found its ultimate expression in the ". . . astonishing stream of Cornish patriotism . . ."[34] (as Rowse called it) unleashed by the creation of the Cornish diocese in 1877 and the building of Truro Cathedral.

The Cathedral and diocese were in some respects a renewed "accommodation" of Cornwall, a response to the assertive Cornish identity born of industrial modernity, and the development of prestigious and august bodies such as the Royal Geological Society of Cornwall, the Royal Cornwall Polytechnic Society, and the Royal Institution of Cornwall, was in part an expression of the new "Cornishness". Against this background, the more ancient and already faltering symbols of "accommodation" — most notably the Duchy and the Stannaries — became less relevant. The Duchy, indeed, was increasingly the subject of scorn and criticism in Cornwall, especially in the early nineteenth century when the retarding effect of "coinage" (duty payable to the Duchy) upon the tin industry was much attacked. The *West Briton* newspaper, often radical and always vociferous in its defence of Cornish interests, asked rhetorically: "Surely the tin mines are not to be sacrificed in order to supply a revenue for the Heir Apparent?"[35] As a result of such criticism, the "coinage" arrangements were at first made more flexible, and then in October 1838 they were abolished altogether. Compensation for the loss of "coinage" was still payable to the Duchy, however, and this was augmented by the not inconsiderable income from mines owned directly by the Duchy and, more importantly, by the rents and royalties from metal mines and quarries on Duchy land. In this way, income from Cornish mining provided a large proportion of Duchy revenues in the nineteenth century. But, as Burt has shown, little of this revenue was re-invested in Cornwall — the Duchy was ". . . quick to extract its royalties and taxes but slow to re-invest in infrastructural development; content to take out tens of thousands of pounds each year but laggardly in assisting the wealth-creating activities of entrepreneurs and miners".[36]

This failure to take a constructive interest in Cornish mining was symptomatic of a wider Ducal indifference to Cornwall. During the reigns of George IV and William IV events moved from bad to worse so that, as Haslam has written,

By the third decade of the nineteenth century the Duchy was again at a low point. In retreat on all fronts, its political influence in disrepute, the Duchy's income had long been stagnant. The reputation of Prince George Augustus and his inability to live within his means starkly highlighted the shortcomings of the unreformed Duchy.[37]

In Cornwall and elsewhere the Duchy was seen increasingly as a discredited remnant of the ancien regime, a brake on the forces of progress and improvement. In response to this feeling Albert, the Prince Consort, was appointed Lord Warden of the Stannaries in 1842 with a wideranging brief to investigate and reform the organs of the Duchy of Cornwall. He approached the task with his usual energy and thoroughness and succeeded in transforming the Duchy into a highly efficient managerial unit, the new mechanisms of which were enshrined in the Duchy of Cornwall Management Act of 1863.[38] In so doing, however, Prince Albert effectively redefined the Duchy as an essentially commercial organisation, to some extent distanced from the territorial entity of Cornwall and certainly divorced from the civil administration of the County.[39] The Duchy's raison d'etre was now commercial rather than constitutional (a change in emphasis that was not opposed in Cornwall) and in the Local Government Act of 1888 Cornwall was defined as a County equal in status in every way with those of England and Wales, and with no mention of a special constitutional position afforded by the Duchy. The estrangement of Duchy from County was now almost complete, and with the rise of the Duchy's commercial image its "accommodating" function all but disappeared.

Inevitably, the decline, reform and redefinition of the Duchy of Cornwall was reflected in the changing fortunes of the Stannary organisation. During the eighteenth century the Stannary system had become less important as a means by which Cornwall might be "accommodated" by the State but was increasingly significant as a vehicle through which the interests of local mining capitalists could be pursued. The extremely broad definition of "tinner" lent by the Stannary Legislation had invited the involvement in Stannary affairs of the entrepreneurial families and adventurers, who in time came to dominate the Convocation (or Stannary Parliament) at the expense of the ordinary working miner.[40] These capitalist Stannators used the system to safeguard the peculiar attributes of Cornish mining — "cost-books", "tributing", and all the rest — and to strengthen their hold on the industry. Not surprisingly, the Stannary system was thus supported by most Cornish "notables", both Whig and Tory, its apologists ranging from the arch-conservative Sir Richard Vyvyan to the radical E.W.W. Pendarves.[41] Equally, the Stannary organisation was reviled by outside capitalists who, as Rowe has argued, saw it as part of the fettering traditions of a feudal and archaic past, on a par with other discredited features of the Duchy.[42] At first this caused little concern in Cornwall (indeed, it may even have been welcomed — it kept the "wise men of the east" at bay) but, as outside capital was increasingly required and sought, so objections to the Stannary system became more significant. The Parliament itself had last met in 1752, and in the reforming spirit of the Great

Reform Act of 1832 it was unlikely that such an apparently archaic constitutional idiosyncracy should ever be allowed to convene again. Nevertheless, there was an influential body of Cornish Whigs which did indeed press for a revival of the Parliament in 1835,[43] while the system of Stannary legislation remained vibrant and intact — the last case to be tried according to Stannary Law was heard in 1896.[44] Be that as it may, however, the Stannary system — as a means of determining and controlling the features of the Cornish mining industry — became progressively less important during the course of the nineteenth century. By 1900 it was all but irrelevant and, like the Duchy itself, had long since ceased to be a meaningful factor of constitutional "accommodation".

Just as the Great Reform Act of 1832 had served to inhibit whatever remaining constitutional independence the Stannary Parliament might have enjoyed, so it brought to an end another remnant of Cornwall's old "accommodation" — the unique situation in which Cornwall sent 44 MPs to the Westminster Parliament, only one fewer than those sent by the entire nation of Scotland! But, as with the Stannary system, the nature and function of the 44 MPs had been changing long before the impact of 1832. Before the Civil War, as Coate has shown, the MPs were more or less genuinely "Cornish" — they were born in Cornwall or were of Cornish descent, they had married into Cornish families or held land in Cornwall — and perceived themselves as such.[45] By the end of the seventeenth century this was becoming less true (Bishop Trelawny pointed to the increasing number of what he called "foreigners" amongst Cornish MPs[46]) and, in contrast to the earlier bands of independent Cornishmen, the Parliament of 1702–5 contained a docile group of Cornish "Churchmen" supportive of Queen Ann's policies and unlikely to offer its own opinions, let alone dissent. As George Granville wrote approvingly at the time, Cornwall ". . . never sent up an honester set of gentlemen than now, for out of the four and forty there are but two exceptionable persons".[47] Men such as Sidney Godolphin (who owned Godolphin Ball tin mine[48] and was Lord High Treasurer under Ann) had, with the rise of tin, acquired economic and therefore political influence, facilitating their search for "place" in government.

This docility (but not the search for "place") disappeared, however, as the eighteenth century progressed. A feature of the Hanoverian era was the Royal propensity for quarrelling — George I was at daggers drawn with Prince George, George II fell out with Prince Frederick Louis, and a scandalous and embarrassingly public rift developed between George III and Prince George Augustus. The Princes, as Dukes of Cornwall, had a reservoir of political patronage which they could mobilise in disputes with the Kings. Plumb noted that in the reign of George I ". . . the Prince disposed of a considerable amount of private patronage — and also, as Duke of Cornwall, he could influence a number of parliamentary elections".[49] In this way the 44 Cornish MPs became embroiled in the arguments between Sovereign and Heir, and during the reign of George III became a significant component of the "Opposition" party which grew up around Prince George Augustus. Calder has described the activities of a "Cornish mafia which played a large role in the politics of Walpole's England . . .";[50] and Plumb commented:

Nor was the Prince's power negligible. He exercised considerable influence over the Parliamentary elections in Cornwall, which was his Duchy, and, of course, he could offer future prospects to the young. They clustered around him so eagerly that Walpole dubbed his party the "Patriot Boys".[51]

Such politicking, of course, had little to do with the pursuit of the real interests of Cornwall, and the 44 MPs could hardly be said to be representative of Cornish opinion. For, in addition to the powerful Ducal influence in many Cornish seats, were the notorious Cornish "rotton boroughs" and "pocket boroughs" in which the franchise was severely restricted and votes were bought or sold. In the climate of the "Reforming Thirties" such a system was difficult to defend, and Cornish radicals argued that the 44 MPs ". . . represented the Cornish no more than the man in the moon . . .".[52] 1832 reduced the number of Cornish MPs drastically to 12, removing once and for all Cornwall's special representation at Westminster, and to some extent increasing the franchise at the same time as abolishing the worst excesses of the "rotten" and "pocket" boroughs. There was, however, a somewhat ambivalent and paradoxical attitude to this reform in certain areas of Cornish opinion (Davies Gilbert expressed misgivings) for, whilst reform itself was welcome, there was also a feeling that Cornwall — and to an extent, too, Britain and the Empire — would be the worse for the loss of so many Cornish MPs. In short, the passing of this remnant of "accommodation" was, for Cornwall, despite everything, tinged with a momentary regret.[53]

The decline of these old symbols and mechanisms of "accommodation" — the Duchy, Stannaries, and 44 MPs — reflected the changing nature of Cornish peripherality. To some extent they were replaced by new institutions of "accommodation" — the newly-created Cornish diocese of 1877, the County Council set up in 1888 (which recognised, re-affirmed and perpetuated the traditional boundaries and territorial extent of Cornwall and allowed a measure of self-government), and perhaps even the widespread deference and respect in Britain for Cornish learned societies. But the Cornwall of the era of industrialisation was not in need of widespread "accommodation", for it was confident of its status and of the (as it thought) unassailable strength of its own "Cornishness", based as it was on industrial prowess. The "accommodation" so central to the fabric of "Older Peripheralism" had been rendered redundant by the new conditions of modernity associated with the rise of "Second Peripheralism".

In the same way, this modernity swept aside other facets of Cornish society which had survived from earlier times, and as the nineteenth century progressed so Cornwall became less deserving of its unflattering reputation as "West Barbary". In the eighteenth century Cornwall was still perceived as a rough and lawless country, its tinners and farmers notorious for their parochialism, violence and hostility to outsiders. Even as late as 1850, according to Hamilton Jenkin, miners in the more remote, westerly parts of Cornwall — especially the wild districts of Breage and Sithney[54] — could scarcely venture outside their own parishes for fear of being assaulted, while local rivalries such as those between Camborne and

Redruth or Padstow and Wadebridge would spill over often into violent confrontations. Smuggling, too, was at its zenith in the eighteenth century — a veritable way of life for the inhabitants of certain especially notorious stretches of coast, such as Cawsand Bay and Mount's Bay — and "wrecking" reached its apogee during the same period. Unlike the "commercial organisations" of Dunkirk and elsewhere which had dominated smuggling in the eastern Channel, smuggling in Cornwall was largely a result of individual enterprise, relying upon the use of small, individually owned cutters or fishing boats and dependent upon personal "contacts" with Brittany and the Channel Islands.[55] "Wrecking" was even less organised, often no more than the almost spontanious reaction of local folk to news that a vessel had come to grief on their shores, providing an opportunity for spoil and plunder. Both smuggling and "wrecking", however, reflected the Cornishman's view of the sea (a "harvest-field"[56] which offered opportunities for livelihood and support) and his capacity for individualistic enterprise, as well as his readiness to act beyond the law. Robert Hunt, writing in 1871, drew a telling if unsavoury picture of life in Cornwall ". . . about a hundred years since . . ."[57] in his report of "The Faction Fight at Cury Great Tree". Impressionistic and perhaps apocryphal, it nevertheless provides an insight into the reputation that Cornwall had acquired:

> A wreck took place near the Lizard, and the Breage-men being nearest, were soon upon the spot to appropriate whatever flotsam and jetsam might come in their way. Returning laden with their spoils, they were encountered at the Great Tree by the Wendron-men bound on a similar errand, and a fight, as a matter of course, ensued, which was prolonged till the following day. The contest is said to have been a terrible one, each party being armed with staves . . . These fights between parishes were so common in those days that any death occuring in the fray was quietly passed over as a thing of course, and soon forgotten.[58]

Likewise, "food riots" were an almost commonplace part of life in eighteenth century Cornwall, seen by both contemporary observers and modern scholars in the same light as smuggling and "wrecking", and indeed remaining a significant feature until at least May 1847 when hungry and angry miners forced "fair prices" for corn at Callington market and miners and clayworkers looted shops in St Austell, and echoed in part at the end of the nineteenth century in the Camborne and Newlyn riots. Hobsbawm and Rude have noted that ". . . Cornwall was one of the chief centres of food rioting in the country"[59] and that ". . . the tinners were regarded as almost beyond the pale of civilization,"[60] pointing to their widespread outrages in 1709, 1727-9, 1748, 1757, 1766, 1773, 1795–9, 1810–13, 1831 and 1847. Paradoxically, however, Cornwall (unlike neighbouring Devon and Dorset) did not become involved in the "Captain Swing" disturbances which swept southern Britain in 1830. The Swing outrages occurred in rural areas where population growth had not been accompanied by industrialisation, whereas in

Cornwall the expansion of mining and industry had absorbed the increase in population.[61]

Savagery and smuggling, "wrecking" and riot, reflected the inheritance from Cornwall's "Older Peripheralism", epitomising both the independence of action and frequent lawlessness of the individualistic Cornish. But, like the institutions of "accommodation", these features of Cornish life came increasingly under attack as the conditions of "Second Peripheralism" took root. The most significant of these was Methodism, part of the "new culture" of industrialisation, which — though strong in the industrial Midlands and North of England — was especially successful in Wales (in its "Calvinistic" guise) and Cornwall where local conditions favoured its growth. The Methodists, of course, advocated an orderly and sober life, and "riot" as a means of achieving ends (however desirable those ends might be) was opposed by Wesley and his followers. Although Cornish smugglers sought to reconcile their traditional pursuit with the demands of their new religion by describing the import of contraband as "Free Trade"[62] (something liberal-minded Methodists might be expected to support), Wesley himself described smuggling as an "abomination".[63] In July 1753, for example, he rebuked members of the St Ives Methodist Society for endulging in the practice and warned that they must cease forthwith or ". . . see my face no more".[64] Similarly, the Methodists were horrified by the barbarity of "wrecking" and did much to create a new attitude of mind in Cornwall in which the emphasis was on helping those in peril on the sea: "The reforming influence of Wesley and the Methodists had its effect . . . and so gradually the Cornish, for centuries feared because of their wrecking propensities, began to win a more creditable reputation for the saving of ships and lives in danger around their coasts".[65]

In this way, the Methodists were able to effect a considerable transformation in Cornish society, "West Barbary" giving way at length to "Delectable Duchy", the new Cornwall marked by its "God-fearing" and increasingly "civilised" and "educated" qualities. The Methodists, indeed, played no small role in the creation and promotion of the self-improvement and educational institutions that emerged in nineteenth century Cornwall, the Methodist commitment to improvement and self-help permeating so many aspects of Cornish life. By 1781, John Wesley, then 78 years of age, could attract a crowd of 20,000 when he preached at Gwennap Pit; by 1851 only 27 per cent of Cornish people remained Anglicans — 60 per cent were Methodists, while the rest were mostly Nonconformists of other denominations.[66] Even in 1899, after the creation of the new Cornish diocese, Bishop Benson had still to admit that "The land is theirs at the moment."[67]

Paradoxically, although Methodism had served to eradicate many of the attributes (albeit unpalatable ones) of Cornish individualism, the basic causes and tenets of that individualism remained. These were, as argued in Chapter 3, essentially socio-economic — the lack of local gentry or squirearchy, the preponderence of small tenant farmers living in isolated and scattered settlements, the independent tinners with their "tribute" and "tutwork" system of employment. Although these features had emerged in the Medieval period they survived as "constants of peripherality" into the era of industrialisation. Todd, in describing the social conditions of nineteenth century Cornwall, wrote that there were "No great families in the English[68] sense" and that ". . . differences between social groups were never as clearly marked as elsewhere",[69] the tenant farmers in particular sporting a long tradition of independence as a result of the relative weakness of the manorial system in Cornwall. Pelling, too, has noted the significance of these factors in moulding the character of nineteenth century Cornish society, while others have shown that the nineteenth century was the great hey-day of the "tribute" and "tutwork" system — not only did it operate in virtually every mine in Cornwall, but also it was significant abroad in those areas where there had been a major Cornish impact, most notably in California and South Australia.[70] "Tributing" and "tutwork" set the standard and tone of a independence and individualism amongst the working people of Cornwall, its influence reflecting the central position of mining in Cornish society and economy.

The mechanics of "tributing" were quite simple. It was essentially a form of contracting in which the miner performed part of the entrepreneurial function himself. Individual sections of a mine ("pitches") were contracted out to individual miners or — more commonly — small groups of miners ("pares") as a result of open bidding on "survey day". Prior to this bidding, each pitch was inspected by a mine agent ("captain") to ascertain the value of the ore that it contained. Each pitch would then be offered at "captain's prices" — for a rich section of ground the "captain's price" might be as low as a few shillings in the pound, so that for each pounds-worth of ore raised the "tributer" or "pare" received only a couple of shillings, but for lower-grade pitches the "captain's price" might be considerably higher — an incentive for a "tributer" or "pare" to work indifferent ground. It was unusual, in fact, for tribute pitches to be let at "captain's prices" — more often there was considerable competitive, downward bidding between rival "pares", especially for attractive sections of ground. A pitch was awarded to the lowest bidder, at a figure often well below "captain's prices", and the tributers — being in a sense self-employed — were also expected to provide their own candles, powder and other materials. Tributing was thus something of a gamble. An apparently rich rection of ground might suddenly fail, leaving the tributer with little remuneration for his toil, but — equally — indifferent ground might suddenly yield pockets of high-grade ore ("sturts"), affording a tributer vast earnings during that particular "take" or contract period.[71]

Tributing lent the miner a certain independence and gave him an opportunity to profit directly from his enterprise, energy and expertise. Although one effect of tributing was to set miner against miner in bids for pitches offered to the lowest bidder, the system was generally well liked in the nineteenth century and its widespread adoption in Cornwall served to enhance the miner's reputation and disposition as an "individualist". The effect of "tutwork" was identical, although here the contracts were concerned with the amount of ground mined rather than the value of ore won — contracts reserved usually for the sinking of shafts or driving of levels, and tending perhaps to attract the less skilled or less enterprising miner.

The organisation of the fishing industry, too, both reflected and encouraged the individualistic strain in Cornish society. In the absence of large commercial groups, Cornish fishing was in the hands of small men who owned their vessels or, more typically, of the small co-operative companies ("seines") which had emerged: by the beginning of the nineteenth century almost every Cornish cove and harbour had its "seine" — such as the "Trusty" of St Mawes or the "Dolphin" of Mevagissey.[72] Like the tributing "pares", the "seines" might encourage co-operation between small groups of workers (often family-related) who were prepared to pool their resources, but their principal effect was to encourage individual enterprise and action. This was also an echo of the farming industry in Cornwall, with its small-holdings and tenant farmers, and isolated families on their isolated farmsteads. Interestingly, the pattern of scattered land settlement was only partially disturbed by the spread of mining. Given the sporadic and random nature of mining activity, the establishment of mining villages often emulated the earlier scattered pattern — as in St Cleer parish where the settlements of Darite, Tremar, Tremar Coombe and Common Moor re-emphasised the nature of Cornish land settlement. Even the apparent "conurbation" of Camborne-Redruth was in reality a curious partly-urban, partly-rural mix — a strange coalescence of individual settlements such as Blowinghouse, Scorrier, Barncoose, Pool, Illogan Highway, Tuckingmill, Roskear, Brea, Beacon, Troon, and so on. Elsewhere in Cornwall a similar "ribbon development" could be found in localities (such as Fraddon-Indian Queens and Delabole) where there was also considerable extractive activity. In this way, the social structure and behaviour dependent in part upon settlement pattern was in certain respects enhanced by the developments of the industrial period.

It was against this background of individualism and independence — in farming, mining and fishing — that Methodism took root in Cornwall. In the absence of nucleated villages, many folk lived isolated from the remote "churchtowns" — physically insulated from the influence of Church and Vicar — and with few figures of squire-like stature or authority to encourage their conformity. The Anglican Church itself was rather weak in Cornwall, perhaps never having fully recovered from the trauma of 1549, the remoteness from the episcopal centre at Exeter making supervision of the often lacklustre Cornish incumbents difficult if not impossible. Pelling has noted the ". . . failure of ecclesiastical adaption that gave a special stimulus to the growth of Nonconformity in the region",[73] while Pearce has argued that "The Wesleys and their itinerants restored heart religion in Cornwall . . . The Cornish were moved as they had not been moved for centuries".[74] And in the rapidly expanding mining towns, with the social problems and poverty associated with their burgeoning populations, the Methodists found fertile ground in which to plant their ideas. Their emphasis upon self-help and individual improvement provided constructive and practical support, while the preoccupation with the "next world" helped to alleviate some of the despair in this. Rule has also identified the simplicity of Methodist theology as an important factor in explaining the popularity of the movement in Cornwall, asserting that the especially un-sophisticated Bible Christian sect owed much of its vigour to the superstitious frailties of the Cornish people.[75] Be that as it may, Methodism certainly found itself attuned to Cornish society and emerged in the nineteenth century as a principal strand of the Cornish identity, a "popular religion" of enormous power and influence.[76]

Methodism, of course, was much concerned with the individual and his betterment, leading to the emergence of all manner of temperence, educational, literary and "improving" societies, and even prompting the development of a rudimentary welfare system ("club and doctor" funds) in the larger mines. Similarly, it influenced the development of a liberal philanthropy in nineteenth century Cornwall, manifested — for example — in the generosity of emigrant Cornishmen who had "done well" "up country" or abroad and were moved to make substantial charitable contributions to Cornish institutions. J. Passmore Edwards — whose liberality allowed the construction of hospitals, institutes and public libraries throughout Cornwall[77] — was perhaps the greatest of these but there were others, notably Sir John Langdon Bonython in South Australia.[78]

Methodism also displayed an egalitarian strand, reflecting the general lack of class consciousness in Cornwall and pursuing a theology which taught compassion, concern for the needy, the equality of men before God, a contempt for riches. Although Wesley and his early followers were politically conservative (they opposed expressions of political dissent and were hostile to the Chartist cause, advocating instead a passive and philosophical acceptance of one's lot in life) Methodism did become linked with political radicalism, political action seen by many as merely the practical extension of their Christian convictions.[79] Although the Wesleyans tried to remain independent of political debate, other factions within the Methodist movement were less inhibited. Being in part a reaction to what was seen as the staid practices and attitudes of the Anglicans, Wesleyan Methodism — once it had become established and "set in its ways" — itself experienced dissension and reaction, resulting in the formation of various breakaway denominations. The story of factionalism and reunion in Cornwall is a complicated one, but three principal denominations emerged — the "original" Wesleyans, the Primitive Methodists, and the Bible Christians.[80]

The Primitive Methodists had their origins in the English Midlands, and became an essentially working-class movement associated with social and political radicalism. The "Prims", as they were known, argued that they alone had remained true to the original style and teaching of John Wesley and they found a ready appeal in the mining districts of Cornwall — their chapels springing up in areas as diverse as Redruth and St Cleer. Associated more exclusively with Cornwall were the Bible Christians, a denomination founded by William Bryant (or O'Bryan) from Luxulyan and established initially in the North Cornwall parishes of Launcells and Week St Mary and across the Devon border at Shebbear.[81] From there the Bible Christians spread eastwards through the south-western peninsula, but their greatest impact was in Cornwall itself — in the mining districts but also in the countryside. Again, a distinct working-class identity can be discerned, and Shaw has argued that although "Politically, Cornish Methodists have tended to be Liberals . . .",[82] the Bible Christians especially ". . . were radicals of the old Liberal school".[83]

Todd notes that by the 1830s ". . . radicalism was becoming a force to be contended with in Cornwall",[84] and there was some Chartist activity in the late

30s and 1840s. Lovatt, one of the Chartists' leaders, was a Cornishman from Newlyn, Bryant noting the activities of ". . . radical members of Parliament, dissenting ministers and Irish and Cornish orators."[85] Most especially, there developed an important link between Cornwall and the emerging Liberal Party, and between Cornish Methodism and Cornish Liberalism, with Cornish MPs such as John Trelawny declaring their support for civil and religious liberty (Jenkins notes that ". . . the Trelawnys were typical examples of the Cornish tradition of lesser aristocratic families with radical leanings . . .".[86]). Methodism, with its anti-Anglican attitudes, represented a kind of social or religious radicalism of some considerable strength (the creation of the Cornish diocese in 1876 was in certain respects a counter-attack, mounted with almost missionary fervour), and as political radicalism emerged so Methodists were attracted to its ranks. Of the 25 Methodists elected to the first Cornwall County Council in 1889, 18 were Liberals, three independent Radicals, and only four Conservative.[87] In the same way, local Methodist organisations in Cornwall made it their business to influence political affairs, as in June 1908, for example, when the ministers and lay representatives of the Kilkhampton Bible Christian Circuit in North Cornwall added their voices to the widespread Liberal and Nonconformist opposition to the Conservative Government's Education Bill, at the same time expressing their hostility to Tory and Anglican forces at a more theoretical level: "The members of our churches and congregations prize and stand by the privileges of civil and religious liberty won for them by their forefathers at a great cost and handed down not simply to enjoy, but to establish and extend".[88]

As Pelling observed, Cornish socio-economic conditions in the nineteenth century — ". . . the strength of Nonconformity, the weakness of the large landowners, the generally small scale of farming, and the paucity of nucleated villages . . ."[89] would lead one to expect a Liberal, " . . . indeed a Radical, predominance . . ."[90] in Cornish politics. Certainly, between 1885 and 1910 each of the Cornish Parliamentary constituencies (with the exception of tiny Penryn) returned Liberal or Liberal Unionist candidates at every election, including by-elections.[91] Often seats were contested not by opposing parties but by Liberals of different hues, as in the ". . . intense and bitter . . . contest between Whig and Radical in 1885 . . ."[92] when the radical Independent Liberal, C.A.V. Conybeare, defeated the official Liberal candidate, A. Pendarves Vivian, in the Camborne constiuency. Liberalism was very much in tune with the individualistic strain in Cornish society, imbued with Benthamite concern for the individual and his freedom of action, and Rowse had commented on ". . . the democratic Cornish — monarchy and aristocracy meant little to them, unlike the more conservative English".[93] Rowse, indeed, recalls that in the early years of this century "In an independent clay village, I never heard anyone say Sir to anybody . . . The bulk of our people lived in independent villages, like the china clay area, or Redruth and Camborne. They are all of them democratically inclined, everybody equal with everybody else".[94]

The triumph of Methodism and of Liberalism in Cornwall seems ironic when set against the earlier Cornish determination to fight for the Catholic religion and to eschew the "Good Old Cause" of Cromwell and Monmouth. But the paradox can be resolved, for the Cornish fighters of 1549 and the Civil War were demonstrating a regional difference born of peripherality — as were the Cornish Methodists and Liberals of the nineteenth century. The culture of these Methodists and Liberals, indeed, owed much to the spirit of individualism and independence inherited from those earlier times, although, again paradoxically, it was also a product of the modernity of industrialisation. Methodism and Liberalism were part of the "new culture" of industrialism and, although not specifically or exclusively Cornish, nonetheless there developed in Cornwall (as in Wales) a way of life of which they were integral and indispensible components. They were, indeed, a vital aspect of Cornish culture in the era of "Second Peripheralism', reflecting both an inherited constant from the "Older Peripheralism" *and* the particular conditions of the new age.

A similar process was observable in other features of Cornish culture in the nineteenth century, a reconciliation of elements of the "new culture" of industrialism with remnants of earlier identity. The widespread formation of brass and silver bands, although also found in other regions (most notably the North East of England), was associated very much with the mining districts of Cornwall — as were the many male-voice choirs (a phenomenon shared with industrial Wales) and the peculiarly Cornish "Cornish Carols" produced by Thomas Merritt and other local composers.[95] These musical activities were perceived as "Cornish" because they were products of the mining communities, inextricably entwined in the sense of "Cornishness" based upon industrial prowess. This sense of identity generated a considerable pride, sometimes a feeling of superiority, in being Cornish, which — although born of the eighteenth and nineteenth centuries — was in many respects in keeping with the earlier Cornish identity based upon geographical isolation, political accommodation, and Celtic culture.

The Cornish language itself was still in decline in this period — Dolly Pentreath, described variously as the last monoglot speaker or the last native speaker with a comprehensive knowledge of the tongue, died in 1777, although she was certainly survived by others with at least some grasp of the language. John Davey of Boswednack in the parish of Zennor, who died in 1891, was reputed to have had a considerable understanding of Cornish, and elsewhere odd phrases and the ability to count in the language survived until perhaps as late as the 1920s.[96] Essentially, however, Bannister was correct in his assessment when he wrote in 1871 that "The close of the 18th Century witnessed the final extinction, as a spoken language, of the old Celtic vernacular of Cornwall".[97] The concept of "Cornish nationality" did not die, however, and (for example) in 1875 that very phrase was employed by the Moonta Mines Directors in South Australia (a prosaic and sober group of men not given to exaggeration or misrepresentation), while the sayings "Cornwall, near England" and "into Cornwall, out of England" were in common use.[98] The description of a non-Cornish person as a "foreigner" continued to be standard practice in Cornwall.

Observers from east of the Tamar were still careful to depict Cornwall as a land of "difference". Wilkie Collins, the novelist, visited Cornwall in the middle of the last century and reminded his readers that this was,

92

. . . a county where, it must be remembered, a stranger is doubly a stranger, in relation to provincial sympathies; where the national feeling is almost entirely merged in the local feeling; where a man speaks of himself as Cornish in much the same way that a Welshman speaks of himself as Welsh.[99]

Likewise, an issue of the popular *Chambers Journal* in 1861 described Cornwall as ". . . one of the most un-English of English counties . . .",[100] while George Henwood — a frequent contributer to the *Mining Journal* in the 1850s and an astute observer of the Cornish miners and their habits — wrote that Cornish folk were " . . . particularly proud of their parentage, to a degree almost rivalling that of the Welsh, and refer to King Arthur and Trelawney as demigods and patterns of virtue and patriotism".[101] Even at the turn of the century, W.H. Hudson, the naturalist, felt moved to describe ". . . the remote and most un-English county of Cornwall . . ."[102] and hinted that there were few ". . . Englishmen in Cornwall who do not experience that antipathy or sense of separation in mind from the people they live with, and are not looked at as foreigners".[103] Interestingly, Hudson concluded that "The Cornish people, I take it, are Celts with less alien blood in their veins than any other branch of their race in the British Isles".[104]

The Cornish themselves, despite the often disapproving influence of Methodism, retained many of their ancient customs and superstitions — belief in the mystical qualities of holy wells, the practice of Cornish wrestling and hurling, the Padstow Hobby Horse and Helston Furry Dance, the celebration of Midsummer's Eve and St Piran's Day, the reverence of Cornish saints and the observance of their feasts.[105] The Cornish sense of identity, often held quite unselfconsciously, was perhaps best captured and expressed in Hamilton Jenkin's delightful account of an incident in a nineteenth century dame-school. A pupil, asked to describe Cornwall's geographic and political status, declared that ". . . he's kidged to a furren country from the top hand".[106] This answer was ". . . heard by the whole school with much approval, including old Peggy (the school-dame) herself".[107] The "furren country" to which Cornwall was "kidged" (joined) was, of course, England, the pupil's response indicative of a developed sense of identity — of the sort so noticeable to Collins, Henwood and other writers — which was widespread in Cornwall. It was, as argued above, an identity given self-confidence and vigour — and indeed new content and meaning — by Cornwall's supremacy in the realms of mining and engineering but it had also, as shown here, inherited the lingering remnants and fading attributes of an earlier Celtic culture.

A complex and often paradoxical picture emerges, then, of Cornwall and its economy and society in the eighteeenth and nineteenth centuries. It was an era of urgent, rapid change, witnessing the swift decline of ancient institutions on the one hand and the arrival of new ideas and technologies on the other, but with change tempered and sometimes moulded by conditions surviving from earlier times. Widespread industrialisation had altered the face of Cornwall, thrusting the Cornish economy into the forefront of technological advance, and yet that industrialisation was itself imperfect, incomplete, and over-specialised. It had, however, led to the rise of a new assertive "Cornishness" which perpetuated Cornwall's distinct sense of identity, despite the decline in this era of the traditional symbols and mechanisms of "accommodation" such as the Duchy and Stannary system. Part of the "new culture" of industrialism which grew up in Cornwall was Methodism, a religious movement which did much to reform the nature of Cornish society and yet which owned its very success to the deeply-rooted independence and individualism of the Cornish people. Methodism and individualism combined to create a political atmosphere in Cornwall receptive to the Liberal Party as it emerged in the last century, the success of Methodism and Liberalism reflecting not only the triumph of new ideas and imperatives but also the enduring impact of older influences, a blend also observable in other facets of Cornish society and culture.

The explanation for this sometimes bewildering mixture of processes lies, as has been argued, in the changing nature of Cornish peripherality. The demise of Cornwall's "Older Peripheralism" saw her emerge from her long-enjoyed isolation, where geo-political distance and a separate culture had held her cocooned by an array of "accommodating" devices from the influence of the English "centre", into a new condition in which she was suddenly of strategic and economic importance to the "centre". The decline and ultimate destruction of this "Older Peripheralism" was never a speedy or straightforward, let alone systematic, process — and it was survived by elements of both its causes and effects, which were in turn to have an important impact in the following era. But this new era, that of "Second Peripheralism", was profoundly different from that which had gone before. Worldwide economic importance and a place in the forefront of technology were new phenomena, as was Cornwall's recruitment into the ranks of religious dissent, and the new standards of "civilisation", "education" and "improvement" saw Cornwall's reputation increasingly removed from the image of "West Barbary". "Second Peripheralism", however, involved not only the rise in mining and engineering prowess and the attendent changes in society — the subject of this chapter — but also encompassed the consequences of Cornwall's imperfect experience of industrialisation. A consideration of these consequences, indeed, is crucial in elucidating the full extent and nature of "Second Peripheralism", and forms the subject of the following three chapters.

Notes and References

1. The breadth and diversity of this experience is demonstrated clearly in D.B. Barton, *Essays in Cornish Mining History: Volume I*, Bradford Barton, Truro, 1968, and D.B. Barton, *Essays in Cornish Mining History: Volume II*, Bradford Barton, Truro, 1970. See also Roger Burt and Peter Waite, *Bibliography of the History of British Metal Mining*, University of Exeter, Exeter, 1988, pp106-145.
2. Details of the Cornish copper industry are drawn principally from D.B. Barton, *A History of Copper Mining in Cornwall and Devon*, Bradford Barton, Truro, 1961, revised ed. 1968.
3. D.B. Barton, *The Redruth and Chasewater Railway, 1824–1915*, Bradford Barton, Truro, 1961, 3rd ed. 1978.

4. T.A. Morrison, *Cornwall's Central Mines: The Northern District, 1810–1895*, Alison Hodge, Penzance, 1980, p11.

5. C.F.D. Whetmath et al, *Railways of Looe and Caradon*, Forge Books, Bracknell, 1974; Amber Patrick, "The Evolution of Morwellham: A Tamar River Port", unpublished M. Phil thesis, CNAA (Plymouth Polytechnic), 1980.

6. Details of the Cornish tin industry are drawn principally from D.B. Barton, *A History of Tin Mining and Smelting in Cornwall*, Bradford Barton, Truro, 1967, republished Cornwall Books, Exeter, 1989.

7. Ibid., p17.

8. Roger Burt et al, *Cornish Mines: Metalliferous and Associated Minerals, 1845–1913*, University of Exeter, Exeter, 1987, ppix-x.

9. D.B. Barton, *The Cornish Beam Engine*, Bradford Barton, Truro, 1965, republished Cornwall Books, Exeter, 1989, p252.

10. K.H. Rogers, *The Newcomen Engine in the West of England*, Moonraker, Bradford-on-Avon, 1976, pp16-27.

11. Barton, 1965, op. cit., p28; see also Thomas Lean, *On The Steam Engines in Cornwall*, 1839, republished Bradford Barton, Truro, 1969.

12. The biography by T.R. Harris, *Arther Woolf, 1766-1837: Cornish Engineer*, Bradford Barton, Truro, 1966, lends a fascinating insight into this period.

13. Barton, 1965, op. cit., p58.

14. Ibid., pp137-147; A.C. Todd and Peter Laws, *Industrial Archaeology of Cornwall*, David & Charles, Newton Abbot, 1972, p12.

15. Todd and Laws, Ibid., p47.

16. W.H. Pascoe, *The History of the Cornish Copper Company*, Dyllansow Truran, Redruth, 1981.

17. Todd and Laws, op. cit., p12.

18. Ibid.; John Keast, *The King of Mid-Cornwall: The Life of Joseph Thomas Treffry, 1782–1850*, Dyllansow Truran, Redruth, 1982; A.C. Todd, *Beyond the Blaze: A Biography of Davies Gilbert*, Bradford Barton, Truro, 1967.

19. Burt, 1987, op. cit., pxxxiii.

20. John Rowe, *Cornwall in the Age of the Industrial Revolution*, Liverpool University Press, Liverpool, 1953, pp19-20.

21. Barton, 1961/68, op. cit., pp37-39.

22. Morrison, op. cit., p40.

23. Ibid.

24. Burt, 1987, op. cit., pxviii.

25. Roger Burt, *John Taylor: Mining Entrepreneur and Engineer, 1779–1863*, Moorland, Buxton, 1977.

26. Morrison, op. cit., pp16-17, p41.

27. Roger Burt and Michael Atkinson in Crispin Gill, ed., *The Duchy of Cornwall*, David & Charles, Newton Abbot, 1987, p206.

28. Rowe, op. cit., p90.

29. An insight into all this is provided in contemporary accounts of Cornish mining; for example, Lean, op. cit.; J.R. Leifchield, *Cornwall — Its Mines and Miners*, 1857, republished Frank Graham, Newcastle-on-Tyne, 1968; Roger Burt, (ed.) *Cornwall's Miners and Miners*, Bradford Barton, Truro, 1972 (being a collection of articles written by George Henwood in the 1850s and reprinted from the *Mining Journal*).

30. Roger Burt, *The British Lead Mining Industry*, Dyllansow Truran, Redruth, 1984, p123.

31. Ibid. The full flavour of this flowering of Cornish educational scientific genius can be gleaned from: Laurence Piper, "The Development of Technical Education in Cornwall from the Early Nineteenth Century until 1902", unpublished M Ed thesis, University of Leicester, 1977; Sally Freeborn, "The Royal Institution of Cornwall and its Role in Adult Education during the Nineteenth Century", unpublished M Phil thesis, CNAA (Cornwall College), 1986; and Denise A. Crook, "The Early History of the Royal Geological Society of Cornwall", unpublished PhD thesis, Open University, 1990.

32. Burt, 1984, op. cit., p232; John Pearce, *The Wesleys in Cornwall*, Bradford Barton, Truro, 1964, p27.

33. Philip Payton, *The Cornish Miner in Australia: Cousin Jack Down Under*, Dyllansow Truran, Redruth, 1984, p198.

34. A.L.Rowse, *The Little Land of Cornwall*, Alan Sutton, Gloucester, 1986, p278.

35. *West Briton*, 7 September 1832.

36. Burt and Atkinson in Gill, op. cit., p215.

37. Graham Haslam in Gill, ibid., p48.

38. Ibid., p57.

39. The Duchy itself, however, fought a rearguard action against the consequences of this process when in 1855-57 it attempted to assert its rights over the tidal estuaries, foreshores, and under-sea minerals within and around the coasts of Cornwall by claiming its dominion over the whole territorial extent of Cornwall. The issue was compromised and the constitutional implications avoided by Act of Parliament in 1858.

40. G.R. Lewis, *The Stannaries: A Study of The Medieval Tin Miners of Cornwall and Devon*, 1908, republished Bradford Barton, Truro, 1965, p128.

41. Rowe, op. cit., pp193-194.

42. Ibid., p193.

43. Ibid., p195.

44. Robert R. Pennington, *Stannary Law: A History of the Mining Law of Cornwall and Devon*, David & Charles, Newton Abbot, 1973, p70.

45. Mary Coate, *Cornwall in the Great Civil War and Interregnum, 1642–1660*, 1933, republished Bradford Barton, Truro, 1963, p19.

46. Keith Feiling, *A History of the Tory Party 1640–1714*, 1925, republished Oxford University Press, Oxford, 1950, p205.

47. Ibid., p366.

48. The importance of Godolphin Ball was noted in James Whetter, *Cornwall in the Seventeenth Century: An Economic Survey of Kernow*, Lodenek Press, Padstow, 1974, pp72-73.

49. J.H. Plumb, *The First Four Georges*, Batsford, London, 1956, p55.

50. Angus Calder, *Revolutionary Empire: The Rise of the English-speaking Empires from the Fifteenth Century to the 1780s*, Jonathan Cape, London, 1981, p476.

51. Plumb, op. cit., p83.

52. Todd, op. cit., p267.

53. Ibid., p268.

54. A.K. Hamilton Jenkin, *The Cornish Miner*, 1927, republished David & Charles, Newton Abbot, 1972, p284.

55. Cyril Noall, *Smuggling in Cornwall*, Bradford Barton, Truro, 1971.

56. The phrase "harvest-field" was employed in this context by A.K. Hamilton Jenkin, *Cornwall and Its People*, 1932-34, republished David & Charles, Newton Abbot, 1983, p2.

57. Robert Hunt, *Popular Romances of the West of England*, 1871, republished in part as *Cornish Customs and Superstitions*, Tor Mark Press, Truro, n.d. c1971, p18.

58. Ibid., pp18-19.

59. E.J. Hobsbawm and George Rude, *Captain Swing*, Penguin, London, 1973, p98.

60. Ibid., p106.

61. John Stevenson, *Popular Disturbances in England, 1700–1800*, Longman, London, 1979, p237.

62. Noall, op. cit., p12.

63. Ibid.

64. Ibid.

65. John Vivian, *Tales of the Cornish Wreckers*, Tor Mark Press, Truro, n.d. c1971, p4.

66. Ian Soulsby, *A History of Cornwall*, Phillimore, Chichester, 1986, p106.

67. Henry Pelling, *Social Geography of British Elections, 1885–1910*, Macmillan, London, 1962, p161.

68. Todd, op. cit., p12.

69. Ibid., p13.

70. Pelling, op. cit., p162; Payton, op. cit., pp94-95, 97, 100-103; A.C. Todd, *The Cornish Miner in America*, Bradford Barton, Truro, 1967, p24.

71. Payton, op. cit., pp90-91.

72. Cyril Noall, *Cornish Seines and Seiners: A History of the Pilchard Fishing Industry*, Bradford Barton, Truro, 1972.

73. Pelling, op. cit., p160.

74. Pearce, op. cit., pp24-25.

75. J.G. Rule, "The Labouring Miner in Cornwall c1740-1870: A Study in Social History", unpublished PhD thesis, University of Warwick, 1971, p258.

76. D.H. Luker, "Cornish Methodism, revivalism and popular belief, c1780–1870", unpublished D Phil thesis, University of Oxford, 1987.

77. R.S. Best, *The Life and Good Works of John Passmore Edwards*, Dyllansow Truran, Redruth, 1981.

78. Fred. Jones, *The Honourable Sir Langdon Bonython KCMG: An Eminent South Australian*, Royal Cornwall Polytechnic Society, Camborne, 1931.

79. Peter Hayden, "Culture, Creed and Conflict: Methodism and Politics in Cornwall, c1832-1979", unpublished PhD thesis, University of Liverpool, 1982.

80. Thomas Shaw, *A History of Cornish Methodism*, Bradford Barton, Truro, 1967; Thomas Shaw, *The Bible Christians*, Epworth Press, London, 1965.

81. Michael J.L. Wickes, *The Westcountry Preachers: A History of the Bible Christians, 1815–1907*, Wickes, Bideford, 1987.

82. Shaw, 1967, op. cit., p100.

83. Shaw, 1965, op. cit., p101.

84. Todd, 1967, op. cit., p201.

85. Arthur Bryant, *Protestant Island*, Collins, London, 1967, p255. An insight into Cornish Radical politics of the era is glimpsed in Alison Adburgham, *A Radical Aristocrat: Sir William Molesworth of Pencarrow*, Tabb House, Padstow, 1990.

86. T.A. Jenkins (ed.), *The Parliamentary Diaries of Sir John Trelawny, 1858–1865*, Camden Fourth Series, Volume 40, Royal Historical Society, London, 1990, p3.

87. Shaw, 1967, op. cit., p114.

88. Cornwall Record Office, DDX 384.3, *Kilkhampton Bible Christian Circuit Minute Books 1891–1910*, 19 June 1902, Resolution 11.

89. Pelling, op. cit., p162.

90. Ibid.
91. F.W.S. Craig, *British Parliamentary Election Results 1885–1918*, Macmillan, London, 1974, pp242-345.
92. L.L. Price, "West Barbary", 1895, reprinted in Burt (ed.), 1969, op. cit., p130.
93. A.L. Rowse, *The Cornish in America*, Macmillan, London, 1969, p17.
94. A.L. Rowse, "The Essence of Cornishness", *Cornish Banner*, November 1987.
95. Leonard H. Truran, *Thomas Merritt: Twelve Cornish Carols*, Dyllansow Truran, Redruth, n.d. c1980; Kenneth Pelmear, *Carols of Cornwall*, Dyllansow Truran, Recruth, 1982; Philip Payton, *Cornish Carols From Australia*, Dyllansow Truran, Redruth, 1984.
96. P. Berresford Ellis, *The Cornish Language and Its Literature*, Routledge, London 1974, pp115-131.
97. John Bannister, *A Glossary of Cornish Names*, Williams and Norgate, London, 1871, quoted in Ellis, ibid., p146.
98. Payton, *Miner*, op. cit., pp7, 74, 99.
99. Wilkie Collins, *Rambles Beyond Railways, or Notes in Cornwall taken a-foot*, Richard Bentley, London, 1851, p124.
100. *Chambers Journal*, 17 February 1861.
101. George Henwood, in Burt (ed.), 1972, op. cit., p220.
102. W.H. Hudson, *The Land's End: A Naturalist's Impressions of West Cornwall*, 1908, republished, Wildwood, London, 1981, p34.
103. Ibid., p142.
104. Ibid., p175.
105. Hunt, op. cit.; William Bottrell, *Traditions and Hearthside Stories of West Cornwall*, 1870, republished Frank Graham, Newcastle-on-Tyne, 1970. See also A. Ivan Rabey, *Hurling at St Columb and in Cornwall*, Lodenek Press, Padstow, 1972; Donald R. Rawe, *Padstow's Obby Oss and May Day Festivities; A Study in Folklore and Tradition*, Lodenek Press, Padstow, 1971.
106. Hamilton Jenkin, op. cit., p274.
107. Ibid.

CHAPTER FIVE

Decline And Diaspora

Tucked away in the midst of Maxine Berg's monumental discussion of *The Age of Manufacturers* is a breathtaking generalisation which asserts that in Cornwall ". . . in the middle of the nineteenth century mining suddenly declined and the region was rapidly transformed into a holiday resort".[1] It comes as a surprise that Berg's recent work — conceived as a major and fresh re-appraisal of the industrial revolution, with a fierce insistence that a full understanding of industrial change can come only through a ". . . reconciliation of social and economic history . . ."[2] — can dismiss (indeed ignore) the complexities of the Cornish experience in such a glib and simplistic fashion. It reflects, however, a psychological response to peripherality (Cornwall was a "sideshow" and need not feature in any discussion of mainstream industrial change in Britain) shared by academics and general public alike, and gives no hint of the reality and extent of the crisis in nineteenth century Cornwall. This was a crisis born of the imperfect, incomplete and over-specialised industrialisation that Cornwall had experienced and which culminated in social and economic marginalisation; the condition of "Second Peripheralism".

The descent into crisis has been described in the several narrative histories of Cornish mining, illustrating the collapse of copper and later decline of tin in the face of changing economic conditions.[3] Although the 1850s had witnessed the peak of Cornish copper production, the warning signs of dangerous days ahead were already there for those who cared to see them. The mines were becoming ever-deeper (and therefore more costly to work) and many were proving increasingly less rich at depth, the optimistic production figures of the 1850s being in a sense "artificially" boosted by the mines of Caradon and the Tamar Valley whose spectacular riches tended to conceal the declining performance of their West Cornwall counterparts. Equally important was the emergence of overseas competition — from the United States, from Chile and Cuba, and from South Australia. In each of these cases the costs of the production and marketing of copper were lower than in Cornwall, which was dangerous for the Cornish industry when copper prices were high and disastrous when they were low. Even distant South Australia, where there were important copper discoveries in the 1840s, 1850s and 1860s, could compete successfully with the Cornish industry. As the Royal Geological Society of Cornwall noted, South Australia was a wool-exporting colony, with the effect that,

> . . . the wool-ships on account of the lightness of the cargo are obliged
> to take in a large quantity of ballast, and they are therefore glad to
> take in the lead and copper ore at a merely nominal rate of freight; — at
> the time in question about eight or ten shillings per ton. That
> circumstance was considered as bringing their mines, as it were, actually
> into Europe, or at all events as placing them upon equal footing with
> European mines . . .[4].

To make matters worse, the Cornish firm of John Williams arranged (ironically
enough) for the sale of South Australian copper ore at the Swansea ticketings.

After 1856 there was a marked decline in the output of Cornish copper,
culminating in the great crash of 1866 in which the industry was one of the victims
of the financial crisis precipitated by the collapse of the Overend-Guerney Bank.[5]
Richer, shallower and less costly overseas mines — like those of Moonta and
Wallaroo in South Australia — could survive the ensuing period of low copper
prices but the ancient mines of Cornwall could not. Many famous names — Fowey
Consols, St Day United — faded from the scene, and by 1871 each one of the
Gwennap mines was closed. The East Cornwall mines struggled on towards the
end of the century but to all intents and purposes the Cornish copper mining
industry was at an end. Copper prices did revive strongly in the early part of the
twentieth century, but by then — with the demise of the old Cornish cost-book
system — the remnants of the Cornish industry had been fully integrated into the
international mining economy, with financial control vested very strongly in the
City. (The Cornish banking system was subsumed into the English — Bolitho's,
for example, becoming part of the Barclays empire.) As Burt has written, "British
mining capital was henceforth determinedly channelled abroad, to the new areas
of production and the mines of the future rather than the past".[6]

A number of the old copper-producing mines were able to prolong their existence
by turning to tin (which many had fortuitously struck at depth), the tin industry
outliving its copper counterpart and indeed appearing for a time in the early 1870s
to be the saviour of the otherwise faltering Cornish economy. But from the 1860s
onwards the tin industry in Cornwall was dominated by the triple concerns of cost
of production, the market price of tin, and the effect of overseas competition.[7] The
latter had been felt as early as 1815, when tin from the Malay Straits had started
to make an impact upon the tin market, and the abolition by Peel in 1845 of duty
on imported tin brought depression to the Cornish industry. In the mid-1860s the
price of tin fell as a result of the American Civil War, the demand for tin-plate
having fallen off in the United States, and in the general gloom of 1866 many
Cornish tin mines were also abandoned.

There was something of an upturn in 1869, however, the revival in tin prices
aided by the civil disturbances in the Malay States which had had the effect of
disrupting Straits production (the British were forced to intervene militarily in the
crisis in 1874), and the early 1870s witnessed a considerable tin mining boom in
Cornwall. It was short-lived, however, the discovery of vast deposits of tin at

Mount Bischoff in the Australian colony of Tasmania providing an ominous new source of competition. Even in 1873 tin prices were starting to fall, but 1874 was far worse. There was panic in the ranks of mining investors, attempts at wage cuts and a return to the "five week month", and the inevitable closure of mines — no fewer than 47 in 1874, 48 in 1875, and 37 in 1876. By dint of continuing technological innovation, the Cornish tin industry survived the traumas of the 1870s (albeit in much leaner form) but the 1880s — a time of international economic downturn — were no better. Straits production doubled between 1887 and 1894, "Bimetalism" making Straits tin increasingly attractive on the world market and the development of Malay alluvial deposits boosting supply. Bolivian tin was also increasingly important, and by 1896 the Cornish industry was facing extinction with only nine mines in production, somehow struggling on until the outbreak of war in 1914 dealt further blows.

The decline of copper and tin mining in Cornwall was accompanied by the fall from grace of the Cornish beam engine, which had reached its zenith in the 1850s but declined therafter.[8] By the 1860s, as mines began to close, many second-hand engines were offered for sale. Some went overseas (although increasingly overseas foundries were able to meet local demand) with many more going to other mining districts in Britain. The trade in surplus engines became thus an economic activity of considerable importance, increasingly more important than the manufacture of new ones, and in the Cornish mines themselves cheap (as opposed to economical) working became the order of the day. Engineers were no longer concerned to improve their engine's duty but were anxious to reduce overheads and running costs. Standards of maintenance and performance fell, and certain mines became notorious for their antiquated engines and equipment.[9] By the 1890s even the market in second-hand engines had collapsed. A few found new homes in china-clay pits but the majority of Cornish beam engines were broken up for scrap. In 1895 only seven engines were reported in Lean's *Engine Reporter*; by 1903 the number had fallen to only four and in 1909 that once august and world renowned journal ceased publication altogether.

The demise of the Cornish beam engine had obvious deleterious effects upon the engineering and manufacturing industries in Cornwall, as had the general collapse in copper and tin mining — an inevitable consequence of the over-specialisation of Cornish industry. Not only was there falling demand for all kinds of goods and services, forcing the closure of many establishments, but that demand which remained was for increasingly specialist and technologically advanced equipment for deployment in the unequal struggle to prevent the total collapse of the remaining rump of the mining industry. That industry, of course, quite apart from the problems of overseas competition and international prices, had to contend with the pressure upon viability exerted by the fact that Cornish mines were becoming extremely deep and increasingly difficult to work, with "payable" resources of ore constantly declining. The Cornish experience was exactly in tune with an explanation, offered by an American survey in the 1930s, of the inherent disabilities of mining economies:

... the history of mineral exploitation is a record of a struggle against increasing natural difficulties. It is commonplace that the richer and more accessible of the known deposits are attacked first. As these are exhausted, operations proceed to the poorer and less accessible deposits, and the physical conditions become progressively more difficult.[10]

In Cornwall's case, such increasingly difficult conditions were matched by ever-more sophisticated technological innovation, and — in a truly paradoxical vicious circle — as the mining industry became progressively less competitive and less viable, so it demanded more and more complex technology. At the same time that the industry became ever more economically precarious, it became increasingly advanced and specialised, so that those establishments which had survived the general fall in engineering demand found that their remaining market was now extremely narrow but also extremely advanced. In these conditions, Cornish industry became even more specialised than it had been hitherto, precluding even further the possibility of industrial diversification.

As Schmitz has observed, there was in this experience a relationship between technological change and capital formation of considerable importance.[11] Before the post-1860s decline there had been a steady rise in capital formation in Cornwall, as mines were opened and devleoped, but thereafter there was a steady fall as properties were abandoned and assets depreciated or stripped. Schmitz agrees, however, that the Cornish industry,

> ... had to pursue ores of diminishing value to greater depths as the nineteenth century progressed. The capital requirements of such a mining field, with limited opportunities for discovery of fresh deposits near surface, would reflect the need for more extensive programmes of exploration and underground development to stock up larger quantities of low-grade ores. At the same time deeper mining would require more efficient and higher capacity pumping equipment; more complex or leaner ores would require more advanced and capital-intensive forms of milling and concentrating equipment at surface.[12]

Schmitz adds that "By the last quarter of the nineteenth century technological change in south-west metal mining was running at a significant level",[13] echoing the words of the mining economist L.L. Price who wrote of the Cornish industry in 1891: "Metallic mining is no longer . . . the hap-hazard pursuit of signs and tokens — deceptive or otherwise — that it once was . . . mere rule of thumb is being replaced by a body of scientific experience".[14] This contrasts, perhaps, with the image of the more ramshackle and run down Cornish mines, and yet it is certainly true that at the handful of larger mines (which constituted the principal part of the industry at the end of the century) there were numerous attempts to translate scientific theory into practical engineering — for example, the general introduction of compressed air drills in the 1880s and the use of compressed air winches. Set against the inexorable decline of the industry, this served to perpetuate the sorry cycle of diminishing viability and declining capital formation on the one hand and ever more specialised technological change on the other. Inevitably, therefore, the final collapse of Cornish mining would leave the Cornish industrial base fatally exposed and quite unable to marshall its highly specialised attributes to any other form of production. And, as Rowe says, the end of the industry in practical terms ('though the Cornish were loathed to accept, let alone act upon, it) had already occurred by the early 1900s: "A long historic past, during which many myths and traditions had developed, delayed recognition of the fact that, early in the twentieth century, Cornish mining had so drastically declined that in realistic economic terms it was only of minor significance".[15]

The social and economic effects of the decline of mining were exacerbated by periods of general depression: most notably the "Hungry Forties", the agricultural crisis of the 1870s, and the international downturn of the 1880s. Agricultural development had to some extent been dependent upon mining development, the increasing population in the mining districts in the first half of the nineteenth century stimulating the demand for wheat. Indeed, arable farming was still the dominant feature of Cornish agriculture as late as 1840, with an increasing emphasis in some areas upon the potato. Learning from the Irish experience, Cornish farmers found that potatoes were a useful preparatory crop for barley on heath or bog land, and potatoes were of course an important addition to the local diet.[16] As early as 1801 up to 25 per cent of the cultivated land in the Penwith peninsula was devoted to potatoes — an important contribution to the food supply for the mining districts of Marazion, St Just and St Ives.[17]

Although Cornish agriculture was in some respects well-suited to the peculiar characteristics of the land — the prevalence of the "outfield" system[18] (in common with other areas of Celtic and highland Britain) in land adjacent to moors and wastral allowed for the cultivation of "bonus" crops in good years without having to reduce the area devoted to livestock, and the predominance of ley-rotation[19] farming with its temporary grassland made good use of the mild, wet climate — the dependent link with mining was dangerous. It was understandable, given the levels of demand, that Cornish farmers were tempted to concentrate upon wheat and other arable crops (in 1808 Worgan wrote of Cornish farmers that as ". . . there is nothing like corn sacks for making money, they are very fond of the plough . . ."[20]). But Cornwall, with its shallow acidic soils and heavy rainfall was in fact not well-suited to the cultivation of wheat and similar crops, especially when compared to the more suitable soils and climate of the Midlands and East Anglia or, indeed, North America and South Australia. Cornwall made the best of things by treating its soils with sea-sand and manures such as seaweed and even rotten pilchards (all materials that were near at hand) but in the longer term the inappropriate concentration upon arable crops would have telling consequences.[21]

In the first place, the rapid expansion of population associated with the development of mining had subsided by the 1840s — that decade witnessing the first major stirrings of the "Great Migration" and pointing the way ahead to the second half of the century with its massive emigration, depopulation and collapse of mining. This, of course, removed the principal local demand or Cornish wheat at precisely the same time that the repeal of the Corn Laws opened the way for the penetration of British markets by overseas produce. The North American prairies were swiftly developed, and by the early 1850s South Australia had already emerged as "The Granary of Australia".[22] Added to this was the growth of central and eastern England as wheat producers, whose farmers could grow corn far more efficiently and economically than their Cornish counterparts. Their local market having collapsed, Cornish farmers were unable to compete against these superior producers in wider markets and learned the hard way the shortcomings of their earlier policy of dependence upon the mining communities. To take a broader perspective, the over-specialisation of Cornish industry forced by the overriding dominance of mining had forced a similar over-specialisation in Cornish agriculture — and with similar consequences to boot, reinforcing the peripheral nature of the Cornish economy in this era "Second Peripheralism". By the 1850s Cornish farming was in deep depression as a direct result of its over-dependence on corn.[23]

Likewise, the experiment with potatoes had disastrous consequences in the 1840s (the "Hungry Forties") when the dreaded potato blight struck in Cornwall as it had elsewhere in the British Isles, particularly Ireland and the Scottish Highlands. West Cornwall, in particular, became a sort of microcosm of the Irish experience, the Cornish crop failing in 1845 and again in 1846,[24] one result being the first movement en masse of mining (and also agricultural) workers to new destinations overseas. Cornish farming was already of a generally subsistence character,[25] with an inability to produce large surpluses (partly as a result of the inappropriate concentration on wheat, and partly because farms were small and the standard of management low) and the "Hungry Forties" were therefore especially damaging. Although, in the mining districts, there did emerge certain notable farmers who became "mechanically-minded" as a result of the proximity of the mines,[26] economic conditions generally precluded mechanisation and technological innovation in Cornish agriculture. This was partly because so many farms were marginal and their surpluses so small, but also because the distinctive characteristics of Cornish farming did not lend themselves to the introduction of the specialised equipment developed elsewhere. Instead, there was a range of relatively modest innovations of purely local application (eg "Cornish ploughs"); distinctly Cornish implements for distinctly Cornish forms of agriculture. As Jewell has noted, "Adoption of those technical inventions which promoted English lowland farming from the early eighteenth century fully penetrated only a few districts inside the Devon border".[27] West of the Exe, and most especially west of the Tamar, agriculture remained immune from the developments further east, with — as noted above — the influence of mining further exaggerating the differences between farming in Cornwall and that which obtained in the bulk of England, and with the predominant characteristics of "small farming" reinforced.

At length, in the wake of mining's collapse and the strength of competition, Cornish farmers did abandon their reliance upon corn. As the mining populations emigrated and the mines went into terminal decline, Cornish agriculture began to adapt to the new conditions. In particular, the depression years of the 1870s and

1880s resulted in much land in Cornwall being switched from the production of wheat to mixed farming and permanent pasture.[28] There was a move to dairy farming and, aided by the arrival of the railway in 1859, to horticulture in the Tamar Valley and in West Cornwall. By 1880 there were twice as many cattle on cultivated land in Cornwall than was the average per acre in England and Wales, and there were eight sheep for every seven elsewhere and three pigs for every two.[29] The 1870s, of course, had been a time of agricultural depression throughout the United Kingdom. Competition from North American produce had reached acute proportions, the situation made worse by a series of poor harvests and by outbreaks of swine fever and foot-and-mouth disease. The United Kingdom alone, of all the major European powers, was reluctant — due to its ideological commitment to Free Trade — to protect its agricultural industry, and as a result there were declining wages and agrarian poverty throughout Britain and Ireland. A Royal Commission found Cornwall less badly hit than other parts, largely due to the timely movement away from wheat to stock farming.[30] We might conclude, therefore, that Cornish farming had at last been successful in recovering from the over-specialised and inappropriate concentration upon corn, but it is nonetheless interesting to note that the "new" forms of agriculture that emerged served still to mark Cornwall off from the experience east of the Tamar. Paradoxically, at the very time that Cornwall was abandoning corn in favour of cattle, so lowland England was redoubling its concentration upon arable farming and in particular the production of wheat. Cornwall remained thus out of step with the broad patterns of farming development and was still unable to make much use of the rapid technological advance (harvesters and the like) that was occurring elsewhere. To the outsider, Cornish farms still seemed remarkably small and extremely under-capitalised — as indeed they were.

The economic crisis in the second half of the nineteenth century was made still worse by the changes that affected fishing, the third of Cornwall's staple industries. In many respects, the fortunes of Cornish fishing resembled those of tin and copper, with an early near-monopoly of pilchards (Whetter notes that such a monopoly existed in the seventeenth century[31]) leading to an over-specialised concentration upon pilchard seining which, in the long run, would prove dangerous. The reliance upon pilchards was all right so long as the shoals continued to appear off the Cornish coast, and the reliance upon seining was all right so long as it was not made redundant by new technologies and new practices. The demand for pilchards remained fairly constant in the nineteenth century, coming — as it had done traditionally — from the Catholic countries of Europe but also from the plantation communities in the West Indies. Pilchard oil was also much in demand from the Royal Navy. But the behavioural patterns of the pilchard shoals began to change (possibly as a result of changes in the Gulf Stream direction), so that their annual arrival in Cornish waters could no longer be guaranteed. In the 1830s, for example, they made no appearance for several successive seasons, although as late as 1871 there was a bumper catch when a record 46,000 hogsheads were exported. The general pattern, however, was one of gradual decline with the pilchards increasingly deserting the inshore waters. By 1872 they had disappeared from the entire stretch of coast between Cawsand and Mevagissey, leaving the rump of the seining fishery in the western districts around St Ives and Newlyn.[32]

Some blame was also attached to the "foreign" drifters from the southern and eastern coasts of England who were increasingly fishing the waters off Cornwall and who, it was claimed, were dispersing the pilchard shoals before they had had an opportunity to come inshore. Some Cornish operators converted to the use of drifters themselves, but most seining companies were little more than extended-family co-operatives and lacked the necessary financial wherewithal to make the change from seining to drifting. With the pilchards becoming increasingly un-predictable, many seiners switched their attention to mackerel — especially after the arrival of the railway in 1859 facilitated the penetration of the London market by fresh Cornish fish. However, the mackerel were also sought by the "foreign" drifters and, in the closing decades of the century, by East Coast stream trawlers. These vessels had greater flexibility, range and endurance than their Cornish seining counterparts, and — ironically — could also take advantage of the new railway connections. The Cornish boats were thus outclassed, the *West Briton* newspaper lamenting in 1891 that ". . . this is probably the first year in which not a single seine has been put into the water".[33] In fact, seining struggled on into the early years of this century but the advantage had been won by the East Coast men and their superior technology, the decline in Cornish seining reflected in a consequent decline in Cornish boat and ship building.[34] The Cornish blamed the East Coast men (the "Yorkies", as they were known in Cornwall) for the demise of both pilchards and seining, and a hostility grew up between the two groups of fishermen. The Cornish rationalised and articulated their resentment by pointing to the habitual "Sabbath-breaking" of the East Coast "Yorkies". As the *West Briton* explained in May 1877,

> The Cornish fishermen suspend work on Sundays, but the east country fishermen, who come to St Ives in the season have no such scruples. Last year there was a disturbance, and this year the St Ives men have again prevented the others from landing at the St Ives pier fish caught on Saturday night or Sunday.[35]

Such disturbances continued to characterise the relationship between the Cornish and the "Yorkies". The Cornish were aware that the fiercely Catholic Irish and fiercely Presbyterian Scots had successfully prevented "Yorkie Sabbath-breaking" in their respective fisheries, and were determined to do likewise in Cornish waters. The situation came to a head at Newlyn in May 1896 in an extraordinary paroxysm of violence in which the Cornish destroyed the catch (some 100,000 mackerel) landed by the Lowestoft boats. This incident, described by Noall and more recently and in greater detail by Corin, led to serious rioting and to the deployment by the Government of 350 soldiers and no less than three Naval gunboats in the Mount's Bay area.[36] The situation was smoothed over, but a lingering resentment remained — reflecting the continued demise of the Cornish fishing fleet and the success of the East Coast trawlers.

The failure of the Cornish fishing industry was a result of its over-specialisation upon pilchards and seining and its inability to modernise (with a few exceptions) in the face of new conditions and new competition. The reaction of the Cornish fishermen to the "Yorkies" reflected this but also afforded an insight into the strength of Cornish individualism and identity, as well as the power of Methodism. As such, the experience of Cornish fishing was largely in tune with that of wider Cornish society and economy in this era of "Second Peripheralism" and, rather like farming, fishing found itself in a state of considerable flux at precisely the same time that mining was undergoing its great decline. Thus, like Cornish farming, Cornish fishing was in no position to step into the economic vacuum left by mining — indeed, it could never have been for it was itself susceptible to the same kind of forces that had brought such difficulties to the mining industry. Together, the parlous condition of the Cornish "staples" — mining, farming and fishing — created a profile of economic marginalisation which served to mark Cornwall off in a most striking way from the experience elsewhere in the United Kingdom.

The economic marginalisation that progressively characterised Cornwall as the nineteenth century developed was mirrored in a consequent social marginalisation, the most significant feature of which was the process known as the "Great Migration". A full analysis of what was an extremely complex phenomenon has yet to be undertaken, but one estimate has suggested that some 230,000 people left Cornwall during the nineteenth century,[37] while Todd asserts that "It seems reasonable to suppose that Cornwall lost at least one third of its population . . .".[38] Indeed, Baines has demonstrated that between 1861 and 1900 Cornwall lost no less than 10.5 per cent of its male population overseas and 7.0 per cent to other counties (far and away the greatest percentage loss of any county), with a corresponding loss of 5.3 per cent of the female population overseas and 7.1 per cent to other counties.[39] This amounted to some 118,500 people, with Baines concluding that, as a percentage of the population, "This is not as high as from the famous regions of Italy . . . but it must be remembered that mass emigration from Italy lasted not much more than twenty years. Cornwall was probably an emigration region comparable with any in Europe".[40]

This picture was complicated by the oft-repeated process of emigration, counter-migration, and renewed emigration where individuals or even families might leave Cornwall for a destination overseas, return home after a number of years abroad, and then later still migrate again. Equally, this pattern was made all the more complex by the Cornish "international mobility" that emerged, with many Cornish folk (especially the miners) spending their lives roaming within and between the continents of the World.[41] The most obvious impact upon Cornwall itself of this "Great Migration" was of course the very visible depopulation that occurred — the population of Breage and Germoe fell by 27 per cent between 1841 and 1851, that of Tywardreath by 29 per cent between 1861 and 1871, and that of St Just-in-Penwith by 27 per cent between 1871 and 1881. Perranzabuloe lost 22 per cent between 1871 and 1881, and St Cleer lost 25 per cent of its population during the same decade and a further 22 per cent between 1891 and 1901.[42] But depopulation was only one effect, for emigration robbed Cornwall of the more skilled, more energetic and younger elements of its inhabitants. Between 1861 and 1900 44.8 per cent of the Cornish male population aged 15 to 24 left for overseas, with a further 29.7 per cent leaving for other counties. Over the same period and in the same age group, 26.2 per cent of Cornish females went overseas while 35.5 per cent went to other counties.[43] At the same time something of a "dependency culture" was created within Cornwall. Although many Cornish emigrants went overseas as "proper colonists" (especially to British possessions such as Australia, New Zealand or Canada), taking their families with them and settling permanently, others (normally males, and very often miners) went as individuals on a temporary basis — leaving behind spouses, children and perhaps other dependent relatives.[44] Even "proper colonists" might leave dependent relatives (elderly parents, perhaps) who, like all the other dependents, would rely upon the regular receipt at home in Cornwall of monies sent back by their kinfolk abroad. In this way, the welfare of large sections of the community was dependent upon the support of the Cornish overseas.

The "Great Migration" is popularly associated with the emigration of Cornish miners, as first copper and then tin declined, and that this identification is to a considerable degree correct is evidenced by contemporary newspaper reports such as that in the *West Briton* in May 1867 which noted that in the previous twelve months some 7,380 miners had left Cornwall.[45] Another, in the *Royal Cornwall Gazette*, recorded in January 1868 that "Eight thousand miners have recently left Cornwall . . .",[46] while Bradford Barton has written that "The resoundingly Cornish names of these captains appended to their reports in the *Mining Journal* in the period from 1850 to 1880 give chapter and verse . . ."[47] to this migration of miners: a Roskrow at Huelva in Spain; a Holman at the Salisbury Plain Mine, Jamaica; a Rickard at Pontgibard in France's Massif Central; a Champion at the St John del Rey Mining Co. in Brazil, and very many more in Portugal, Angola, Italy, Turkey, Algeria, and elsewhere. Not all Cornish emigrants were miners, however, and amongst the other migrating occupations were fishermen who sailed their little boats to new homes as near as Guernsey or as far as Victoria in Australia. There were Delabole slate men who were able to pursue their specialist occupation in destinations as far removed as the United States and South Australia, and Cornish farmers who — with considerable experience as arable farmers trying to wrest a living from marginal country at home — were well suited to the pioneer life on the wheat frontiers of North America and South Australia: in the latter colony, indeed, a major Cornish impact can be discerned in the expansion of the agricultural frontier in the last century.[48] In areas of Cornish concentration — such as Grass Valley in California or Moonta in South Australia — the Cornish settled into a variety of occupations. In Grass Valley, for example, where in the 1880s three daily and two weekly newspapers were edited by Cornishmen, it was said in 1884 that "The Cornishmen here are not engaged exclusively in mining. The signs over almost all the stores bear Cornish names, and several of the business men hold responsible positions in the county and State".[49]

The fortunes of mining, however, largely determined the ebb and flow of emigration, reflecting the overwhelming importance of the mining industry within

Cornwall. This, of course, was the "push" element in the "Great Migration" but equally important were the "pull" components — principally the various mineral bonanzas overseas, but also other considerations such as the planned expansion of South Australia's wheat frontier in the 1870s (when a Cornishman, James Penn Boucaut, was Premier of the colony) or the civil and religious liberty and socio-economic mobility offered by destinations such as the United States and South Australia's "Paradise of Dissent".[50] Overseas mining companies, of course, were well aware that Cornwall was the centre of mining technological innovation and were therefore understandably keen to recruit Cornish miners — especially the skilled captains and tributers — to their workings. North America, Australia and South Africa emerged as the principal destinations of these emigrant Cornish folk — but as the pages of the *West Briton* attest[51] — very many found their way to destinations as diverse as New Zealand, Cuba, Nicaragua, Brittany and Brazil.

Migration associated with economic change in Cornwall was at first an internal phenomenon, involving in the early part of the nineteenth century a small but discernable movement of population from the more easterly, more agricultural districts — such as the parish of Poundstock in North Cornwall — to add to the rapidly expanding populations of the copper parishes in the west. In this way, for example, the population of Gwennap rose from 4,594 in 1801 to 10,794 in 1841, and that of Redruth from 4,924 to 11,504 between 1801 and 1861.[52] This movement was sufficient to meet the expanding demand for labour, and consequently Cornwall did not experience mass immigration from outside (unlike the comparable district of South Wales, where there was an influx from western England and from Ireland), the overwhelmingly "Cornish" nature of the population accounting in part for the homogeneity, cohesion and sense of identity in nineteenth century Cornwall where all Cornish folk were almost literally cousins, "Cousin Jacks" as they were to be known in mining camps across the world. Later in the century, this geographical movement was reversed, with miners from the western districts moving — often with their families — to the new copper mining areas in the east: to St Austell, to St Cleer and the Caradon district, and to the Tamar Valley around Gunnislake and Calstock, some spilling across the border to the neighbourhood of Tavistock. This was itself a complex process, involving often a progressively eastwards shift by individuals or whole families from one area to another as the various mines rose and fell and as new ones were discovered (and as china clay quarrying was developed in mid-Cornwall) — movement that has been analysed in some depth by Deacon.[53] A considerable proportion of western miners moving to the Caradon district in the 1840s were from the Breage area (where the population dropped so alarmingly in that period as a result of local tin mine closures), this movement to East Cornwall being associated therefore with the first stirrings of decline in the western mines. It was thus migration in response to the first hints of the process of de-industrialisation that was to characterise Cornwall, and a precursor of the imminent mass "Great Migration".

There had, of course, been some Cornish movement to America in earlier times (in the seventeenth and eighteenth centuries there had been Cornish settlers in New

England and the Old South) and as early as 1778 copper miners from Redruth were sent to open up the copper deposits along Lake Superior. In 1817 Richard Trevithick was in South America erecting pump engines, and in 1825 a party of miners hired by the Anglo-Mexican Mining Association set out for the New World.[54] These early emigrants, however, were for the most part adventurers anxious to try their luck or apply their skills abroad, not driven by economic necessity in the sense that the later mass migrants were. By the 1830s the rate of emigration from Cornwall was starting to increase, however, escapees from agrarian poverty in the north-eastern parishes soon complemented by the first significant movement from the western mining parishes during the "Hungry Forties". Thereafter, the "Great Migration" continued virtually unabated until the Great War.

In the 1840s the Real del Monte silver mines in Mexico were an important magnet,[55] and in the same decade Cornishmen were employed in the iron mines on the shores of Lake Huron in Canada. In the United States,[56] the Wisconsin lead mines attracted many Cornish during the 1840s and by 1850 there were perhaps as many as 9,000 Cornish folk in the district of Mineral Point. The United States aimed to become self-sufficient in copper as well as lead, and in the early 1840s began a deliberate expansion of the Lake Superior mines. Cornish miners flocked to the Lakes from both Wisconsin and Cornwall, the Keweenaw peninsula soon earning a reputation as an American "Little Cornwall". In 1849 Cornish newspapers were full of news of the Californian gold discoveries and soon Cousin Jacks from all over Cornwall and North America were clamouring to become "Forty-Niners". At first, individual diggers working on their own had easy pickings but soon quartz gold was discovered at depth — which required heavy capitalisation *and* the expertise of Cornish miners. Consequently, as Rowse has said, "It is probable that there are more Cornish people in California than in any other state in the Union".[57]

The first important discoveries of quartz gold were in Nevada (at first a county of California, but soon to become a State in its own right) and by 1870 Grass Valley could boast 1,000 Cornish settlers. Rowse has shown that ". . . Grass Valley and Nevada City became predominantly Cornish towns",[58] with their Cornish Carols and pasties and wrestling matches. The discovery of the celebrated "Comstock Lode" ensured a continuing Cornish presence in Nevada in the 1870s and 1880s, but Cornish migrants also found their way to other parts of the Union: to Colorado where they were a significant part of the population of Gilpin County and the appropriately-named Leadville in the 1880s, and from North Carolina in the 1850s to Utah in the 1860s and New Mexico in the 1870s and Arizona in the 1880s. One especially important area of Cornish concentration was Butte, Montana, where many were attracted to the copper mines in the 1880s. In all these mining areas the Cornish were noted, according to the contemporary American journalist Wells Drury, for their ". . . religious fervour . . . independence, thrift, geniality, excitability, contempt for familiar dangers . . .".[59] He added, with a hint of admiration, "And with what zest they can sing their fellowship song 'One and All', and their old patriotic ballad, 'And Shall Trelawny Die' . . .".[60]

The Cornish experience in Australia was similar, their principal impact occurring in the mining districts and with their influence extending to the creation of religious, cultural and social patterns reminiscent of those that they had known at home. Although there had been some limited transportation and emigration to the Penal Colonies from Cornwall, the first major movement of Cornish people to the Antipodes did not occur until the foundation of South Australia in 1836. The discovery of copper — at Kapunda and Burra Burra in the mid-1840s and at Wallaroo and Moonta ("Australia's Little Cornwall") in 1859-60 — enticed many to South Australia, with further encouragement afforded by the colony's liberal immigration and assisted passage schemes. Indeed, between 1836 and 1886 as many as 16,000 Cornish settled in South Australia, some 8 per cent of all emigrants to the colony. Elsewhere in Australia the Cornish impact was also strong (as evidenced by the *West Briton's* comment in September 1875 that 10,576 people had left Cornwall for Australia during the first six months of that year[61]), the Victorian Gold Rush establishing sizeable Cornish communities in Ballarat and (especially) Bendigo during the 1850s. As in California, the development of deep quartz mining led — in the 1870s — to increased capitalisation in Victoria and to an era in which the skilled Cornish hard-rock miners came into their own. The Cornish were similarly important in the development of the Broken Hill silver-lead-zinc fields in the 1880s, and at the Coolgardie and Kalgoorlie gold mines in Western Australia in the 1890s. In Queensland they mined copper at Peak Downs and gold at Mount Morgan, and in Tasmania in the 1870s they were a crucial element in the exploitation of the tin deposits which, ironically, posed such a threat to the Cornish tin industry.[62]

In South Africa the first major Cornish influx was in the 1850s, to the Namaqualand copper mines in the northern Cape. Even more important was the discovery, in the mid-1880s, of the Kimberley diamond fields. By 1889 there was a vibrant "Cornish Association" active in the district, one manifestation of a deep Cornish influence that was further enhanced by Cornish involvement in the Eastern Transvaal gold rush in the 1870s and the celebrated Witwatersrand rush in the mid-1880s. Johannesburg had its own "Cousin Jacks' Corner", where the Cornish would meet to exchange news from home, and the Ferreira Deep was said to be manned almost entirely by old Dolcoath miners. In 1895 over 2,000 people left Cornwall for South Africa, but the Boer War created a lull in emigration between 1899 and 1902. Thereafter, there was a resurgence but in the years before the First World War there was a growing disillusion with South Africa, partly as a result of the realisation of the frightening extent of the disabilities amongst Cornish miners caused by phthisis contracted out there and partly because of growing industrial unrest in the South African mines.[63] By 1913 there was a steady stream of Cornish miners returning home from South Africa but by then — as the *Cornish Post* had remarked in December 1906 — the situation had already existed for many years whereby:

When the button is pressed in Africa, the bell rings in Cornwall . . . a change in thought and action in South Africa affects the little western

county which has contributed so much of the labour and enterprise to
. . . the land of gold and diamonds.[64]

Although the main thrust of the "Great Migration" was overseas, it is important
to note that many emigrant Cornishmen found employment (and their families,
homes) in other areas of the United Kingdom. Many, of course, worked the copper
mines of Devon (in so many respects to be considered an eastwards extension of
the Cornish industry) but others roamed further afield — to the silver mines of
West Somerset and the lead mines of the Mendips, to the collieries of South Wales
(where St Just, St Ives and Calstock men were noted at work in 1866), in the
Wicklow Mountains and the south-west of Ireland, and in Scottish coal and iron
mines (where 300 Cornish miners had gone in 1866). Many others went to the
North of England — to the Pennines lead mines, to the Lake District and Furness
metal mines, and even to the Settle and Carlisle Railway where in 1871 they were
employed to drive the Bleamoor tunnel.[65] In times of unemployment and shortage
they could also be induced to assume the roles of strike-breakers, as in 1873 when
900 men left Cornwall to make "Burnley a village of Cornish miners",[66] with local
observers noting that "The departures from St Cleer, Pensilva, and Linkinhorne
have been so numerous that there are scores of houses tenantless . . .".[67] Similarly,
in October 1877 over 100 strike-breaking miners left Cornwall for the Sunderland
coal fields.[68]

The vast panorama of the "Great Migration" is one of the great themes of
Cornish history, and in the latter part of the nineteenth century it dominated
Cornish life. Few individuals or institutions in Cornwall were not touched by its
effects, and the Cornish sense of identity expanded to insist, for example, that "If
you haven't been to Moonta, you haven't travelled"[69] or that those born of Cornish
parents overseas were equally as "Cornish" as those born in Cornwall itself — "If
a cat has kittens in the oven this doesn't make them into pasties".[70] There was,
indeed, a discernable Cornish "international identity" that emerged towards the
end of the century, one that was voiced in many parts of the globe through the
insistent declarations of loyalty to Cornwall from "Cornish Associations" such as
those in Broken Hill or the Transvaal, and which was exhibited at many levels —
most notably in the press. Not only did newspapers in Cornwall carry frequent
reports from Cornish communities overseas, but those communities themselves
carried regular "news from Cornwall" items in their papers and also reported the
activities of the other communities. Thus, for example, we find reprinted in South
Australian newspapers such as the *Wallaroo Times* and *Yorke's Peninsula
Advertiser* articles from the press in Cornwall reporting upon Cornish activities in
South Africa![71] This "international identity" was, of course, an expansion of the
Cornish sense of identity based upon industrial prowess, expressing an extraordinary Cornish pride in the achievement that had facilitated the mining
development of America, Australia, South Africa and elsewhere. There was also a
missionary and evangelical tinge to all this, for the Cornish were proud not only
of their technological contribution to the world but also their religious contribution
— especially in the field of Methodism. The Bible Christian Missionary Society,

for example, was in no doubt about its role in the "Great Migration" and many Cornish Methodists held the view, expressed by John Pearce, that if ". . . the Great Emigration is the crown of Cornish accomplishment, then John Wesley is seen to be its brightest jewel".[72]

In a sense, therefore, the "Great Migration" represented the highpoint of Cornish achievement as it was perceived in nineteenth century Cornwall — a view that was tragically ironic because in reality the "Great Migration" was (as intimated in Chapter 4) both a symptom of and a perpetuating factor in Cornwall's peripheral condition. The imperfect and incomplete nature of Cornish industrialisation had led not only to an over-specialised industrial base but also to an over-specialised workforce which had no alternative but to emigrate and apply its skills anew elsewhere as the Cornish economy fell into decline. To a considerable degree, indeed, the Cornish miners were pawns in the hands of what had become (as Burke has argued[73]) an international mining labour market, part of the international mining economy that had emerged in which market forces sped the "Cousin Jacks" from one area to the next as the relative fortunes of the different mines and different countries waxed and waned. Cornish economic and social marginalisation had, quite literally, world-wide effects, for as mining investment in Cornwall declined and British mining capital was increasingly directed overseas, so the Cornish miner was himself correspondingly directed abroad.

Given that Cornish expertise and energy abroad had to a considerable extent been responsible for the overseas competition in copper, tin, and even wheat, that had quickened the process of industrial decline in Cornwall, the Cornish pride in the "Great Migration" was all the more ironic. And by accelerating this decline the process of emigration also hastened the emergence of the "dependency culture" in which the continued dispersal of Cornwall's miners was seen as advantageous — not only because it removed "surplus" population but because it provided what was almost an informal welfare system for the support of dependents. In 1863 the *West Briton* admitted that the scale of emigration ". . . is becoming a matter of grave consideration . . . (for) . . . those who go abroad are the very bone and sinew of the country"[74] but went on to declare that:

> It is, however, highly gratifying to learn that wherever the Cornish miner goes, he is generally well received, and rarely fails not only to benefit himself, but those of his friends remaining at home, by the welcome remittances which arrive by almost every mail.[75]

In June 1866 the same newspaper considered that "The unprecedented exodus . . . is relieving us to a very beneficial extent of the surplus population of our mining districts . . ."[76] but with the *Royal Cornwall Gazette* noting eighteen months later that the recent departure of 8,000 miners had left ". . . 20,000 persons dependent upon their energies elsewhere".[77] The theme of dependency became more important as the century wore on, and as the industrial base began to contract. In January 1879 the *West Briton* perceived changes in the nature of emigration, with fewer families leaving as "proper colonists" but with more individuals departing as itinerent workers in the world's mining fields. "Thousands of people in Cornwall are supported . . ."[78] by these emigrants, claimed the newspaper, for the Cornish miner ". . . leaves the women, the children, and the old people behind — not on the parish, be it said to his honour".[79] By the end of the century the situation had become even more stark, the arrival of the "African Mail" a major calendar event in Camborne-Redruth and the other depressed mining districts. In September 1898, for example, the *West Briton* noted that,

> Saturday morning last saw the arrival of the African mail — the main delivery for the month from Johannesburg, Kimberley &C. The heavy mail was promptly dispatched from the post-office, and it was not long before the banks of the town were busy cashing drafts. With such an influx of money into the town a busy Saturday market was an assured thing, and so it turned out.[80]

As the Cornish mining industry all but expired there developed, as Richard Dawe has shown in his valuable study, a relationship between Cornwall and South Africa that was almost unique. There was, as Rowse observed, ". . . something very pathetic and moving in that close connection between our Cornish villages and South Africa".[81] The *Cornubian* newspaper in January 1902 summed up the situation succinctly: "We are living on South Africa".[82] In 1905 it was estimated that there were 7,000 Cornish miners on the Rand, earning per annum something like £300 each — if the cost of living accounted for perhaps half their wages, then as much as one million pounds per year could have been sent home to Cornwall.[83] Dawe concludes that there is little doubt that Cornwall did live off the Rand and that "The gold industry of South Africa cushioned Cornwall as its own tin and copper industries died a slow death, and families in Cornwall certainly benefitted from the high wages earned in South Africa".[84]

The Cornwall of the early 1900s, dependent so pathetically upon the energy of her emigres in distant South Africa, was a far cry from that vibrant, self-confident, innovative land that existed only a half century or so before. But that half century had witnessed the virtual destruction of the mining industry in Cornwall, involving not only closure of the mines themselves but the demise of the financial system (the cost book) that had supported it, along with the creation of an integrated international mining economy and labour market where British capital and Cornish miners were drawn to new destinations abroad. This, indeed, was the direct consequence of the imperfect, incomplete and over-specialised industrialisation that Cornwall had experienced, ushering in the social and economic marginalisation of this era of "Second Peripheralism" of which the "Great Migration" was the most visible attribute. And yet the full characteristics of "Second Peripheralism" in its matured manifestations went deeper still, bringing to the Cornish economy and society a certain paraylsis or "fossilisation" which would endure until after the Second World War, and which continued to set the Cornish experience apart in a most fundamental way from that elsewhere.

Notes and References

1. Maxine Berg, *The Age of Manufacturers 1700–1820*, Fontana, London, 1985, p125.
2. Ibid., p319.
3. D.B. Barton, *A History of Tin Mining and Smelting in Cornwall*, Bradford Barton, Truro, 1967, republished Cornwall Books, Exeter, 1989; D.B. Barton, *A History of Copper Mining in Cornwall and Devon*, Bradford Barton, Truro, 1961, revised 1968.
4. Seymour Tremenheere, "Notice respecting the Lead and Copper ores of Glen Osmond Mines, three miles from Adelaide, South Australia", *Transactions of The Royal Geological Society of Cornwall*, Vol. VI, 1841-46.
5. John Rowe, "The Declining Years of Cornish Tin Mining", in Jeffrey Porter, *Education and Labour in The South West*, Exeter Papers in Economic History No 10, University of Exeter, Exeter, 1975, p59.
6. Roger Burt, *Diversification as a Response to Decline in the Mining Industry; Arsenic and South-Western Metal Production 1850–1914*, University of Exeter, Exeter, 1984.
7. Rowe, op. cit., p59.
8. D.B. Barton, *The Cornish Beam Engine*, Bradford Barton, Truro, 1965, republished Cornwall Books, Exeter, 1989.
9. John H. Trounson, *Historic Cornish Mining Scenes at Surface*, Bradford Barton, Truro, 1968, p35.
10. F.G. Tyron and Margaret H. Schoenfeld, "Mineral and Power Resources" in *Recent Social Trends in the United States*, McGraw-Hill, New York, 1933, p64.
11. Christopher Schmitz, "Capital Formation and Technological Change in South-West England Metal Mining in the Nineteenth Century", in Walter Minchinton (ed.), *Capital Formation in South-West England*, Exeter Papers in Economic History No 9, University of Exeter, Exeter, 1978, p52.
12. Ibid., pp52-53.
13. Ibid., p53.
14. L.L. Price, "West Barbary", 1891, in Roger Burt (ed.), *Cornish Mining: Essays on the Organisation of Cornish Mines and the Cornish Mining Economy*, David & Charles, Newton Abbot, 1969, p187.
15. Rowe, op. cit., p59.
16. John Rowe, *Cornwall in the Age of the Industrial Revolution*, Liverpool University Press, Liverpool 1953, p231.
17. Mark Overton, "The 1801 Crop Returns For Cornwall", in Michael Havinden (ed.), *Husbandry and Marketing in The South West 1500–1800*, Exeter Papers in Economic History No 8, University of Exeter, Exeter, 1973, p56.
18. Harold S.A. Fox, "Outfield cultivation in Devon and Cornwall: a reinterpretation", in Havinden, ibid.
19. Andrew Jewell, "Some Cultivation Techniques in the South-West of England", in Walter Minchinton (ed.), *Agricultural Improvement: Medieval and Modern*, Exeter Papers in Economic History, University of Exeter, Exeter, 1981.
20. G.B. Worgan, *General view of the Agriculture of the County of Cornwall*, London, 1811, p53, cited in Overton, op. cit., p47.
21. Overton, ibid., pp47-48.
22. R.M. Gibbs, *A History of South Australia*, Balara Books, Adelaide, 1969, p65.
23. Rowe, 1953, op. cit., p249.
24. *West Briton*, 17 July 1846.

25. A.H. Shorter, W.L.D. Ravenhill, K.J. Gregory, *Southwest England*, Nelson, London, 1969, p139.
26. Rowe, 1953, op. cit., p252.
27. Jewell, op. cit., p106.
28. Shorter et al, op. cit., pp139-148.
29. Rowe, 1953, op. cit., pp258-259.
30. S. Daniell, *Old Cornwall: Life in Cornwall About a Century Ago*, Tor Mark Press, Truro n.d. c1969, pp18-21.
31. James Whetter, *Cornwall in the Seventeenth Century: An Economic Survey of Kernow*, Lodenek Press, Padstow, 1974, p176.
32. Cyril Noall, *Cornish Seiners and Seiners: A History of the Pilchard Fishing Industry*, Bradford Barton, Truro, 1972, details the fortunes of the fisheries.
33. *West Briton*, 8 January 1891.
34. J. Herman Gilligan, "The Rural Labour Process: A Case Study of a Cornish Town", in T. Bradley and P. Lowe (eds.), *Locality and Rurality; Economy and Society in Rural Regions*, Geo Books, Norfolk, 1984.
35. *West Briton*, 14 May 1877.
36. Cyril Noall, *Tales of the Cornish Fishermen*, Tor Mark Press, Truro, 1970, pp16-26; John Corin, *Fishermen's Conflict*, David & Charles, Newton Abbot, 1988.
37. Leonard Courtney in 1897, cited in A.C. Todd, *The Cornish Miner in America*, Bradford Barton, Truro, 1967, p19.
38. Ibid.
39. Dudley Baines, *Migration in a Mature Economy: Emigration and Internal Migration in England and Wales, 1861–1900*, Cambridge University Press, Cambridge, 1985, p232.
40. Ibid., pp157-159.
41. This complexity is apparent in the analyses of family histories in Keith Skues, *Cornish Heritage*, Werner Shaw, London, 1983; Henry Cecil Blackwell, *From A Dark Stream: The Story of Cornwall's Amazing People and their Impact on the World*, Dyllansow Truran, Redruth, 1987.
42. John C.C. Probert, *The Sociology of Cornish Methodism*, Cornish Methodist Historical Association, Truro?, 1971, p61.
43. Baines, op. cit., p230-231.
44. John Rowe, *Cornish Methodists and Emigrants*, Cornish Methodist Historical Association, Truro 1967, p19.
45. *West Briton*, 17 May 1867.
46. *Royal Cornwall Gazette*, 2 January 1868.
47. D.B. Barton, *Essays in Cornish Mining History, Vol 1*, Bradford Barton, Truro, 1968, pp20-21.
48. Philip Payton, *The Cornish Farmer in Australia*, Dyllansow Truran, Redruth, 1987.
49. *West Briton*, 13 September 1984.
50. Payton, op. cit., pp3-9, p42, pp45-47; Philip Payton, *The Cornish Miner in Australia: Cousin Jack Down Under*, Dyllansow Truran, Redruth, 1984, p15, p92; A.C. Todd, op. cit., p20; A.C.Todd with David James, *Ever Westward The Land*, University of Exeter, Exeter, 1986, pp4-11.
51. For example, *West Briton*, 20 February 1857 (Brazil), 12 April 1877 (Venezuela), 11 March 1886 (Spain, Colombia, India), 24 August 1893 (Chile).
52. Probert, op. cit., p61.

53. Bernard Deacon, *Migration and the Mining Industry in East Cornwall in the Mid-Nineteenth Century*, University of Exeter, Exeter, 1985.
54. A.K. Hamilton Jenkin, *The Cornish Miner*, 1927, republished David & Charles, Newton Abbot, 1972, pp323-324.
55. A.C. Todd, *The Search For Silver: Cornish Miners in Mexico, 1824–1947*, Lodenek Press, Padstow, 1977.
56. Todd, 1967, op. cit.; A.L. Rowse, *The Cornish in America*, Macmillan, London, 1969, republished, Dyllansow Truran, Redruth, 1991; John Rowe, *The Hard-Rock Men: Cornish Immigrants and the North American Mining Frontier*, Liverpool University Press, Liverpool, 1974.
57. Rowse, op. cit., p241.
58. Ibid., p246.
59. Ibid., pp295-6.
60. Ibid.
61. *West Briton*, 27 September 1875.
62. Payton, 1984, op. cit.; Oswald Pryor, *Australia's Little Cornwall*, Rigby, Adelaide, 1962; Jim Faull, *The Cornish in Australia*, AE Press, Melbourne, 1983; Ruth Hopkins, *Where Now Cousin Jack?*, Bendigo Bicentennial Committee, Bendigo, 1988.
63. Graham B. Dickason, *Cornish Immigrants to South Africa*, Balkema, Cape Town, 1978; Brian Kennedy, *A Tale of Two Mining Cities: Johannesburg and Broken Hill 1885–1925*, Melbourne University Press, Melbourne,1984; A.L. Rowse, *The Controversial Colensos*, Dyllansow Truran, Redruth, 1989; Richard D. Dawe, "The Role and Influence of the Cornish in South Africa 1886-1925", unpublished MA thesis, Middlesex Polytechnic, 1986.
64. *Cornish Post*, 20 December 1906.
65. For example, *West Briton*, 31 August 1866 (South Wales), 2 November 1866 (Scotland), 15 June 1871 (Bleamoor).
66. *West Briton*, 20 October 1873.
67. *West Briton*, 18 September 1873.
68. *West Briton*, 11 October, 1877.
69. Pryor, op. cit., p148.
70. Charles Thomas, *The Importance of Being Cornish in Cornwall*, Institute of Cornish Studies, Redruth, 1973, p12.
71. Payton, 1984, op. cit., p198.
72. John Pearce, *The Wesleys in Cornwall*, Bradford Barton, Truro, 1964, p27.
73. Gillian Burke, "The Cornish Miner and the Cornish Mining Industry 1870–1921", unpublished PhD thesis, University of London, 1981; Gillian Burke "The Cornish Diaspora of the Nineteenth Century", in Shula Marks and Peter Richardson, (eds.), *International Labour Migration: Historical Perspectives*, Temple Smith, London, 1984.
74. *West Briton*, 23 October 1863.
75. Ibid.
76. *West Briton*, 15 June 1866.
77. *Royal Cornwall Gazette*, 21 January 1868.
78. *West Briton*, 23 January 1879
79. Ibid.
80. *West Briton*, 1 September 1898.
81. A.L. Rowse, *A Cornish Childhood*, Cape, London, 1942, p34.

82. *Cornubian*, 31 January 1902.
83. Richard D. Dawe, "The Effect Chinese Labour Had on the Cornish Miner in South Africa", unpublished paper, Middlesex Polytechnic, 1984, p23.
84. Dawe, 1986, op. cit., p108.

CHAPTER SIX

The Great Paralysis

The parlous condition of the Cornish economy at the end of the nineteenth century, in particular the collapse of its industrial base, was — as has been argued — a function of Cornwall's peripheral position within the United Kingdom. That same peripherality was to ensure that Cornwall would be powerless to react to the new situation in which she found herself. The creation of an international mining economy had, through emigration, deprived Cornwall of her native expertise and allocated her an inferior and generally indifferent position in the international mining labour market. Financial control of mining had passed to the City, whose interest was set firmly abroad, depriving Cornwall of her last vestiges of local control and ensuring that Cornwall would attract little mining and associated industrial investment. Cornwall was thus not only starved of resources — especially expert labour and industrial investment — but was also denied the means to make amends. At the mercy of the internationalised character of the mining industry, and with little indigenous financial wherewithal, Cornwall experienced an economic near-paralysis. This paralysis, indeed, had arisen in the closing decades of the last century and was to characterise the Cornish economy until after the Second World War. It was accompanied by an attendent paralysis, a "fossilisation" in Cornish society and culture, and represented the matured manifestation of "Second Peripheralism", the inevitable consequence of the imperfect, incomplete and over-specialised experience of industrialisation described in Chapters 4 and 5.

This era of Cornish paralysis co-incided, of course, with two great international cataclysms — the First World War, and the "Great Depression" of the inter-war years — which affected Cornwall as they affected other areas and which served to exacerbate Cornish problems. But, despite this shared international experience, the Cornish condition remained highly individual. A survey by the University of Exeter, published in 1947 but drawing largely upon the Census for 1931, concluded that the Cornish economy was ". . . highly differentiated from that of the country as a whole".[1] Proportionately higher numbers were engaged in service industries and in agriculture but, in remarkable contrast to the situation that had obtained less than a century before, there were ". . . fewer in manufacture and mining".[2] Similarly, the population density of Cornwall in 1931 was an average of 234 persons per square mile, while for England and Wales as a whole it was 685. This in part reflected the legacy of the "Great Migration" (since 1861 Cornwall had registered a decrease in population for each decade except that of 1901–11) and

119

what the survey termed Cornwall's ". . . unfavourable . . . demographic situation . . .".[3] Between 1901 and 1911, it was noted, the population of England and Wales had grown by 10.9 per cent. In that same period, however, Cornwall's population had fallen by 0.1 per cent, in marked contrast even to neighbouring Devon where the population had risen by 5.7 per cent. Similarly, between 1911 and 1921 the population of England and Wales had risen by 4.9 per cent whereas the rise in Cornwall had been only 1.8 per cent, and between 1921 and 1931 the Cornish population had fallen by 0.9 per cent while the rise for England and Wales had been 5.5 per cent. For the remaining years of the inter-war era, the population of Cornwall had decreased by 2.5 per cent compared with an increase of 3.2 per cent in Great Britain as a whole and an increase in Devon of 1.2 per cent. In making its comparative judgments, the survey emphasised that the demographic problem ". . . was more serious in Cornwall than in Devon."[4]

The contrast between Cornwall and Devon on the one hand, and between Cornwall and England on the other, was even more apparent in the statistics for unemployment where Cornwall (despite its declining population) was especially badly placed. Commenting upon the decade 1929-38, the University's survey concluded that:

> Whereas, over the period, Devon's average unemployment experience was less severe than that of the country as a whole, that of Cornwall was more severe. The annual average unemployment in Devon was but 12.3 per cent, that of Cornwall 17.7 per cent, and that of England 14.8 per cent. The greatest differences between the yearly figures occurred during 1930–33; then Devon's average percentage unemployment was 14.4 per cent, while that for England was 18.8 per cent, and that of Cornwall was 21.6 per cent. As these were the years of world depression, Devon escaped more lightly than the country, but Cornwall was affected more acutely. While the general trend of the figures is similar in each of the three areas, recovery after the ending of the depression was both more complete and faster in Devon than in Cornwall. Indeed, the persistence of high unemployment in Cornwall suggests a post-world war depression problem more chronic than in either England or Devon.[5]

This "problem", of course, was the underlying paralysis of the Cornish economy: even the awesome and international effects of the "Great Depression" could not, as the survey showed, disguise the highly individual and long-term nature of the Cornish paralysis.

In further consideration of the contrasts between Cornwall and Devon in this period, the survey noted that "The contrast between the (unemployment) figures for Cornish and Devonian areas is also marked; not only are those in Cornwall higher in general than in Devon, but the range between the extremes is greater".[6] In the decade 1929-38, for example, the annual average percentage unemployment in Newquay was as low as 7.4 per cent, reflecting the development of service industries there, but contrasting with St Austell (15.8 per cent) and Liskeard (17.4 per cent) where the decline in china clay had important effects, and quite unlike the disastrous situation in the old mining and engineering districts of Redruth (32.9 per cent), Camborne (22.0 per cent) and Hayle (28.4 per cent). Acknowledging Cornwall's by now markedly below average performance in industrial production and manufacture, the survey listed the obvious features of Cornwall's geographic peripherality — the lack of coal (with a note that ". . . by 1931 the partial compensation provided by the electricity grid system had not fully developed"[7]), the limited and modest nature of local markets and the distance from ". . . the great markets of the country . . .",[8] the indifferent nature of the local transport and communications systems, the paucity of industrial services and training, and the fact that "No one industry possessed locational advantages pronounced enough to foster large-scale growth, and in consequence the rise of subsidiary industries which might have grown around it was inhibited".[9] But the analysis hinted at a deeper appreciation of the nature of the Cornish paralysis when it added that "Lastly, deficient industrial enterprise and industrial inertia must not be overlooked".[10] There was, however, no attempt to identify the causes of such deficiency and inertia.

A fuller understanding of the nature of Cornwall's industrial experience might have led to the conclusion that in this era of paralysis it was no surprise that the Cornish response was one of fatalism and resignation, but always with a blinkered and rather vain hope that tin mining might yet revive and regain its old glory. In the decades before the Second World War there was certainly a reluctance to accept that Cornish mining was now only of marginal economic importance — to Cornwall and to Britain — and one of the ironies of the paralysis is that such energy and resources that there were, were channelled into forlorn attempts to revive the mining corpse.[11] A supposed recovery in the industry in 1906–7, for example, aroused some optimism — particularly with press reports that the number of miners employed in Cornwall had risen to over 8,500 (although as recently as the mid-1870s three times that number had been employed, while in the hey-day of the mid-nineteenth century the figure had been five times as large). The recovery was shortlived, however, with the press soon lamenting the high levels of unemployment in the Tamar Valley and recording the disastrous effects upon the Truro district of the closure of Wheal Jane. Dolcoath struggled on as the flagship of Cornish mining (sinking a new 300 fathom-deep shaft as an act of faith in the future) and with technological developments advocated by the Camborne School of Mines being embraced enthusiastically by the very small handful of Cornish mines that could afford to apply them.[12] The outbreak of war in 1914 led to renewed demands upon young, trained manpower in Cornwall — those with mining and engineering backgrounds, in particular, finding their way into the Cornwall Fortress Royal Engineers and the Royal Navy, and with many others drawn into the ranks of the Duke of Cornwall's Light Infantry. Inevitably, many of these were destined never to return.

Although tin, as a strategic metal, remained in demand throughout the war, the Government's policy was one where ". . . the Cornish tin mines had been exploited

121

rather than developed".[13] The price of tin had been pegged at an artificially low level, mainly as part of a deal with the U.S.A. to secure strategic supplies of copper, and developmental work in the mines had been neglected at the expense of the short-term policy of "picking the eyes" out to secure maximum output from easily accessible deposits. This was against a background of constantly rising wage bills, exacerbated at the end of the war by rising material and coal costs. After 1918, too, the demand for tin declined, leading to a fall in tin prices. In 1919 mine owners and labour unions together lobbied the government for support, but without political muscle and influence their pleas had little effect: " . . . assistance was long in coming, so long that when at length loans were advanced to help some Cornish mining concerns to modernize themselves, on almost cast-iron security, it was too late to save many mines that had been forced to close down".[14] As Rowe adds, "Early in 1919 talk of a total cessation of Cornish mining became more prevalent . . .".[15] The railway strike in the September brought fresh problems, and in October the dreadful Levant mine disaster seemed to cast a shadow of despair upon the whole industry. The abandonment of Wheal Grenville in the early months of 1920 heralded what was to be the deepest crisis in Cornish mining, and soon emigration (especially to the gold mines of Canada, which had conducted a recruiting campaign in Cornwall) was once again a feature of Cornish life. Rowe recalls that,

> Harrowing tales have been told of the distress prevalent in Cornish mining districts during 1921 and 1922. Relief funds were organized, and associated with them was the organization of a Miners' Choir which after giving a number of concerts in the less fortunate towns and villages of the home county went up-country to London, Bournemouth, Taunton, Cardiff . . . . Further money for relief came back from Cornish emigrants in Canada, Australia, the Transvaal, and the United States. Camborne police station was transformed into an emergency centre for clothing, and one estimate reckoned that 3,800 folk had received clothes with a further four thousand still in need.[16]

Although a brief upturn in tin prices warranted some expansion during 1926, the crash of the 1930s badly affected Cornish mining (at its lowest ebb there were only 426 employed in the industry) and on the eve of the Second World War there were but three mines in operation: Geevor, South Crofty, and East Pool and Agar.

The production of "minor" minerals assisted this lingering survival, most notably arsenic which was of importance around the turn of the century. Although the large-scale production of arsenic came too late to prolong the life of Cornish copper (though several former copper mines did survive as arsenic mines) it nevertheless was important in ensuring the continuation of tin operations at several major tin mines.[17] Of longer-term significance was the china clay industry, not "mining" in the underground, hard-rock sense that the Cornish understood it but an extractive industry nonetheless and one which could harness existing technology within Cornwall. Tentative development work by potters from outside Cornwall in the late eighteenth century paved the way for Cornish adventurers to take control of the industry in the 1820s. Its development was erratic, however, reflecting poor organistaion and periodic crises of over-production. Compared to copper and tin mining it was never a major employer (even in 1881 there were no more than 1600 men engaged in it), and of course it was geographically concentrated upon the district north of St Austell.[18]

Despite these limitations there was a hope in the early years of this century that the production of china clay and china stone might expand to fill the vacuum left by the decline of mining proper. Indeed, the annual output of china clay between 1900 and 1916 never failed to exceed half a million tons, a peak of over 860,000 tons being achieved in 1912. The First World War had disastrous effects, however, as export markets closed. Profits turned to losses, costs rose alarmingly, and production in 1917 was halved. After the war the depressed state of the industry was not easily remedied, and in 1921 and 1922 there was fearful hardship in the little villages of the china clay country. By 1923 the export trade with the United States was reviving and the industry almost returned to its pre-war condition. However, the American slump of 1929 and the "Great Depression" of 1932 precipitated a renewed decline. By the end of 1932 output had fallen by 40 per cent since 1929 and the price of china clay by more than 30 per cent. The clay industry reacted by forming a Producers' Federation, which had some success in dealing with the external problems of the industry, and the amalgamations which created the large English Clays Lovering Pochin & Co Ltd allowed for various economies of scale until the Second World War threw the industry once again into turmoil.[19]

The china clay industry, therefore, was at no time in a position strong enough or stable enough to stir Cornwall from its economic paralysis. But even with strength and stability it is doubtful whether it could have achieved the industrial renewal and diversification that was needed. Although a versatile product with an enormous range of industrial and commercial applications, china clay received little more than initial processing in Cornwall. The Cornish industry was essentially extractive, with the applications of its products being carried out elsewhere in Britain and overseas. As such, it suffered problems of over-specialisation and under-diversification in tune with the general Cornish experience, a further manifestation of Cornwall's peripheral and marginalised economy and certainly not the type of enterprise from which might spring broader renewal and diversity.

The periods of expansion in clay output had been facilitated by the development of ports such as Par and Charlestown, but the railway had also played a part. The railway had arrived too late, however, to play a wider role in industrial development in Cornwall. By the time the Royal Albert Bridge at Saltash was opened in 1859, linking Cornwall by rail with the rest of Britain, copper was on the eve of its terminal decline and with the peripheral characteristics of Cornwall's industrialisation already firmly and irretrievably established. The railway brought with it the "telegraph" and improved postal services, as well as encouraging Cornish authorities to switch at last from local to Greenwich time, but it was slow to develop both passenger and goods traffic. David St John Thomas has explained that,

Even today Cornwall is Britain's most individual county, but differences from the 'mainland' are nothing to what they were before the opening of the Royal Albert Bridge in 1859. The bridge was supposed to let in the Devil. What in fact trickled in were all kinds of national unifying influences — to the true Cornishman, of course, these were the very Devil. But the older order disintegrated only slowly, and it was largely for this reason that the Cornwall Railway was so poor a proposition financially. For instance, Cornishmen were reluctant to accept mass-produced Midland goods, while only a few were persuaded to venture as far afield in their own country as even Plymouth — though many had gone straight from Cornwall to seek employment in mines all over the world.[20]

The lacklustre performance of the Cornwall Railway[21] was not at all the exciting economic consequence of "opening up Cornwall" that its promoters had anticipated, but Thomas' explanation is only part of the story. At root was the inability of the Cornish economy to escape from the effects of its experience of industrialisation, with its (in 1859) impending economic marginalisation and paralysis. The railway did create employment in its own right, of course, and elsewhere it did encourage certain specific economic activities — spring flowers from the Isles of Scilly, broccoli and "new potatoes", milk, and of course fresh fish, could be transported swiftly to the London markets with relative ease. The rates charged by the railway for the conveyance of such perishables were habitually criticised as punitive in Cornwall, however, and the economic activities encouraged by the railway were not always in Cornwall's best interests: as noted earlier, penetration of the London markets stimulated "Yorkie" competition at the expense of the Cornish fishermen, while the creation of new up-country markets for the higher-priced varieties of fish discouraged the catching of the cheaper sorts that had formed the staple diet for many Cornish poor.[22]

Cornish fishing, indeed, participated in the general paralysis of the Cornish economy in the years after the turn of the century. Unable to participate in the new, vigorous expansion of the deep-sea fisheries of the Arctic and North Sea (partly as a result of Cornwall's geographic situation, but also because of the failure to produce large, deep-sea vessels), the Cornish fleet consisted of small inshore boats. In the years after 1918 there had been as many as 13 first-class steam trawlers registered in the ports of Cornwall and Devon. Incredibly, by 1938 the number had dropped to just two, of which one had not been employed since 1925. Of the motor fleets, the 150 first-class vessels of 1919 had reduced to 91 by 1938, with the number of sailing boats declining even more alarmingly. The total number of first-class vessels of varying types registered in Cornwall and Devon fell drastically from 306 in 1919 to 99 in 1938. This decay was reflected in the declining weight and value of fish landed at Cornish ports, the culmination of the much longer period of decline consequent upon the industry's structural problems inherited from the nineteenth century.[23]

The problems of Cornish agriculture in this period of paralysis were less marked than those of fishing or mining or china clay, but there was little innovation or advance. Improvements in grasslands, which would have raised the standards of stock, milk and beef cattle and sheep, had not occurred, and there were great inadequacies in both buildings and water supplies on many Cornish farms. Many farmers were ignorant of good stock management and modern techniques, and the small numbers of cattle per holding on many Cornish farms made milk production an uneconomic undertaking. In 1939 of the 12,881 holdings in Cornwall no less than 2,116 were sized between one and five acres, while only two were in the range 500 to 700 acres, and none was larger than that. To ensure viability in such conditions, a high standard of farming and a high degree of specialisation were seen to be necessary, but both were exhibited only rarely on Cornish farms. In the face of such apparent stagnation, the Exeter report hinted darkly that the "collectivisation" of Cornish farms might be a solution.[24]

Farming, then, like the other Cornish staples, experienced the economic paralysis that emerged in the wake of the industrial crisis of the nineteenth century. This paralysis was an inevitable function of the nineteenth century experience and an integral part of the era of "Second Peripheralism". Having reaped the consequences of imperfect, incomplete and over-specialised industrialisation, there was little or no opportunity for the Cornish economy to diversify. The railway arrived too late to be of any real value in this respect, and instead the period from the end of the century until the Second World War was, for Cornwall, one of paralysis in which there could be no response to the crisis. Mining and fishing continued their sorry decline, china clay was by its very nature unable to offer an alternative future, and farming slipped into an indolent stagnation. The First World War, the indifferent economic conditions generally of the 1920s, and the worldwide "Great Depression" of the 1930s, were, of course, further economic nails in the Cornish industrial coffin.

An apparent paradox in all this was the emergence of tourism, at first sight the one area of economic activity that did hint at industrial renewal and diversification, at odds — apparently — with the general thesis of paralysis. Certainly, the closing years of the nineteenth century and the opening decades of the twentieth witnessed a vigorous expansion of tourism, associated with the imaginative marketing techniques of the Great Western Railway (which had subsumed the old Cornwall Railway) and its rival, the London and South Western. However, a closer analysis of the tourist phenomenon reveals that, far from running counter to the general Cornish experience, it was in fact a natural and rational response to the process of de-industrialistaion. The development of tourism in Cornwall, indeed, was a conscious and calculated reaction, an attempt to construct a post-industrial economy. The railway accepted that its belated arrival on the Cornish scene precluded the possibility of industrial diversification, and some local businessmen and literati accepted (albeit reluctantly, perhaps) that Cornwall's industrial decline could not be reversed. Tourism, therefore, was a manifestation par excellence of the peripheral condition, an integral part of Cornwall's experience in the era of "Second Peripheralism". Its rise heralded not the arrival of a new industrial age, but confirmed instead the death throes of existing industrialisation. Tourism, in brief, represented the makings of a post-industrial economy.

1900 marked a turning point, coinciding with the Great Western's determination to make the most of its recently converted (in 1892, from broad gauge) mainline to Cornwall. Passenger traffic increased every year thereafter in the period up the the Great War, and the biggest increase was in 1904 (68.4 per cent) with the introduction of the superbly-named "Cornish Riviera Express".[25] The concept of the Cornish Riviera was a great coup, with its connotations of palm trees, balminess and Mediterranean sunshine.[26] Comparisons were made with the south of France and Italy, with Great Western posters imploring tourists to "See Your Own Country First"[27] but promising in Cornwall something both continental and foreign. Later, publications written by the inimitable S.P.B. Mais[28] and published by the Great Western hinted at a western land of Celtic mysticism and romance, whilst even the railway's locomotives sported tantalising and evocative names: "Tre, Pol and Pen", "City of Truro", "One and All", "Trelawney", "Trevithick", and later "Tintagel Castle", "Earl of Mount Edgcumbe" and "County of Cornwall". Branch lines took holiday makers to both north and south coasts, to Looe, Fowey, Falmouth, St Ives, Perranporth, Newquay and elsewhere, with the "Riviera" on offer not only to the privileged minority who might otherwise holiday in the real Mediterranean but also to anyone who could afford the price of a third class ticket from Paddington. For those unable to afford the substantial hotels of Penzance, there were always the serviceable camping-coaches at Marazion. The South Western Railway (after 1922, the Southern), not to be out done, made the North Cornwall district between Bude and Padstow its special preserve — putting such places as Tintagel and Boscastle on the tourist map, and again appealing to popular sentiment through the allocation of appropriate Arthurian names for the locomotives that worked its expresses out of Waterloo: "Merlin", "Lyonesse", "Iseult", "Sir Cador of Cornwall", "Sir Constantine". Here was the curious case of centre-based commercial organisations stressing (as an economic strategy) the cultural distinctiveness of the periphery (or at least their perceived version of it, based as it was on the images of Stanhope Forbes and the Newlyn School painters). As Robbins has commented, for the interests of commercial tourism, Cornwall ". . . had to remain remote yet also become accessible in its remoteness".[29]

Incredibly, this propaganda reached its apogee in the 1920s and 1930s, the image of romantic and carefree holidays contrasting ironically with the reality of industrial decline and dereliction, continuing emigration and hardship. A remarkable credibility gap had appeared between the Cornwall of popular fancy and the reality of socio-economic deprivation, a dichotomy that would continue to dog interpretations of Cornwall in the future. Tourism did, of course, create some employment, contributing to the general switch to the service sector which helped, for example, to protect certain areas such as Newquay from the worst ravages of unemployment in the 1920s and 1930s. Between 1920 and 1938 there was, indeed, a ". . . striking expansion of the tourist industry".[30] This was reflected in the rise of numbers employed in hotels, boarding houses and laundries in Cornwall and Devon by 80 per cent, as against 53.9 per cent for England and

Wales, and in the fact that between 1926 and 1939 the number of hotels of all kinds increased by 92.9 per cent while the number of boarding houses expanded by no less than 125.2 per cent. However, although the expansion of tourism was able to absorb some of the labour shed from mining, fishing, and agriculture, much of this new employment was of an inherently short-term and seasonal nature: hardly a long-term or stable alternative to industrial employment. The Exeter survey concluded that ". . . unemployment was more seasonal in Devon and Cornwall",[31] compared to the country as a whole, and that "Of the two counties, Cornwall's unemployment was distinctly more seasonal than that of Devon".[32] Between 1929 and 1938 employment in Cornwall habitually sank to its lowest ebb in January and reached its peak in June, the difference between the extremes being some 7.2 per cent or about 3,300 persons.

Nonetheless, tourism was perceived as being at least some alternative to industrial decline, and was accepted by some as an appropriate reaction to the process of de-industrialisation, a means of building within Cornwall some form of post-industrial economy. Sir Arthur Quiller-Couch encouraged debate on this issue in the pages of his *Cornish Magazine* and as early as 1898, at the very start of this era, stated his own position quite clearly:

> On the one hand I see Cornwall impoverished by the evil days on which mining and (to a lesser degree) agriculture have fallen. I see her population diminishing and her able-bodied sons forced to emigrate by the thousand, the ruined engine-house, the roofless cottage, the cold hearthstone are not cheerful sights to one who would fain to see a race so passionately attached to home as ours is still drawing vigour from its soil. In the presence of destitution and actual famine (for in the mining district it came even to this, a little while ago) one is bound, if he cares for his countrymen, to consider any cure thoughtfully suggested.
>
> The suggestion is that Cornwall should turn her natural beauty to account, and by making it more widely known, at once benefit thousands and honestly enrich herself.[33]

Although he advanced this view with conviction and determination, we see in an afterthought Quiller-Couch's reservation or at least resignation: "Well then, since we must cater for the stranger, let us do it well and honestly. Let us respect him and our native land as well".[34]

In fact, the rise of tourism was not so much the creation of a new era as a consequence of what had gone before, an integral part of the economic marginalisation of "second peripheralism" and consistent with the paralysis of the late nineteenth and twentieth centuries. Quiller-Couch, perhaps, realised at least some of this in his "heart of hearts", but he was determined to rise to the challenge of de-industrialisation. The promotion of tourism was the economic response to de-industrialisation, but there was an equally powerful social and cultural response. For, just as de-industrialisation had led to a certain economic paralysis, so too it had caused a parallel and attendent social-cultural paralysis. As detailed in earlier chapters, the fabric of Cornish society and the strength of the Cornish identity had in the eighteenth and nineteenth centuries been built around mining and its associated industrial activities. Cornwall and mining were inseparable, synonomous almost, every societal activity — from religion to education — shot through with the myriad influence of mining, the assertive characteristics of an almost aggressive Cornish sense of identity centred on Cornwall's unsurpassed industrial prowess. When, in a comparatively short period of time, Cornwall was stripped of that prowess and her mining industry almost obliterated, the effects upon Cornish society and its culture were inevitably traumatic.

In effect, economic paralysis was reflected in social and cultural paralysis, as the driving force of Cornwall's mining-Methodist culture lost its momentum. As the mines closed, so Cornwall's ablest and most articulate sons and daughters (whose skills had facilitated industrial advance, whose leadership qualities had made them local preachers, class leaders, Sunday school teachers) had emigrated, leaving their communities dispirited and often dependent on overseas support, the once vibrant chapels now facing declining attendance and sometimes even closure. As Deacon has put it, "The classical popular Methodist culture began to weaken and the debris of a shattered economy became the site of a fossilised culture as the popular culture ceased to change and develop".[35] At first the Cornish indulged in self-deception to try to shield themselves from the enormity of the situation in which they found themselves. The "Great Migration" was interpreted, not as a symptom of industrial collapse, but as the triumph of Cornish genius. Certainly, the process had created a briefly significant international Cornish culture and had provided the Cornish with an experience very different from that of their English neighbours, thus heightening a sense of "difference", but it was nonetheless an integral part of the process of de-industrialisation. The Cornish, too, as described above, were loathed to accept that Cornish mining had passed its zenith and could never regain its old glory, clinging on to a vain hope that perhaps the current impasse was only temporary and that the great days of Cornwall would come again. Now and then something of the old pride and assertiveness was rekindled, as in the heady days of 1908 when the triumphant Cornwall Rugby Football team went from victory to victory to secure the County Championship, when Camborne, Redruth and the other mining districts briefly rediscovered their old passion and exuberance.[36] But for the most part Cornish society sunk into a fatalism and resignation, a certain paralysis, mirroring the economic inertia that the Exeter survey was to identify.

However, just as a handful of Cornish were prepared to rise above economic paralysis and to advocate consciously a post-industrial economy (based upon tourism), so a similar (indeed, sometimes congruent) minority proposed to abandon social and cultural paralysis by a conscious attempt to "rebuild" Cornish culture through an appeal to Cornwall's pre-industrial Celtic past. Quiller-Couch embraced such an appeal as a deliberate response to the social and cultural consequences of de-industrialisation, but the phenomenon was most especially identified with Henry Jenner and the so-called "Cornish Revivalists". However, just as the advocacy of tourism was a delusion (insofar as it was in reality a function of the process of industrial decline rather than an alternative to it), so the attempts to "rebuild" Cornwall's Celtic culture must be considered within and as a part of the social and cultural crisis that Cornwall was experiencing. Indeed, the advocacy of tourism and the "Cornish Revival" at times went hand-in-hand, their aims at certain points coincidental, appealing together to a "Celtic culture" in the face of de-industrialisation — the one attempting to construct a post-industrial economy, the other a pre-industrial culture! Both, nevertheless, were consequences of the Cornish industrial experience, further matured manifestations of the condition of "Second Peripheralism".

The antecedents of the "Cornish Revival" can be found in the nineteenth century, most notably in the person of Robert Stephen Hawker, the eccentric vicar of Morewenstow from 1824 to 1874, whose ballads — often romantic, sometimes sentimental — recalled the earlier days of pre-industrial Cornwall: "The Ringers of Launcells Tower", "Sir Bevil — The Gate Song of Stowe", and of course "Trelawny" — "The Song of the Western Men" which became a sort of unofficial Cornish national anthem. An Anglo-Catholic, Hawker found himself out of step with the utilitarian, technological, Nonconformist character of nineteenth century Cornwall: "Who is there to come down with succour? What angel could arrive with duties to perform for that large Blaspheming Smithery, once a great Nation, now a Forge for Railways?".[37] And although "Trelawny" was taken quickly into the hearts of the Cornish people, Hawker's High Church, anti-industrial sentiments found little support and struck few chords in Cornwall at the height of its mining and engineering prowess. There was a spirit of "scientific" antiquarianism in nineteenth century Cornwall but it was hardly "Revivalist" and regarded the remains of earlier times as little more than curios. Davies Gilbert, the "Cornish Philosopher", was the archetypal Cornishman of the industrial age, a great defender of Cornish interests and indefatigable proponent of Cornish causes.[38] He took an antiquarian interest in times past and in 1826 published a version of the Cornish language passion poem "Pascon agan Arluth" (Passion of Our Lord). In his introduction to the work, however, Gilbert stressed that "No one more sincerely rejoices than does the editor of this ancient mystery that the Cornish dialect of the Celtic or Gaelic languages has ceased altogether from being used by the inhabitants of Cornwall".[39] Cornish, of course, would have been an obstacle to progress and advancement, an impediment in an English-speaking industrial world, an irrelevant relic from less enlightened days. Even Matthew Arnold, Cornish on his mother's side (she was a Penrose from Constantine),[40] favoured the decline of Celtic languages on such Gilbertian grounds, despite his romantic affection for Celtic literature and insistence upon its intrinsic value.[41]

It was Gilbert, therefore, and not Hawker, who most accurately expressed the prevailing social and economic ideology of nineteenth century Cornwall. The early "Revivalists" and their precursors such as Hawker, then, found themselves out of favour with the robust and hard-headed engineers and technocrats of the industrial age, men who had little time for whimsical or romantic notions of "Celtic Twilight" and had indeed welcomed the demise of the Cornish language as the triumph of progress. This gulf was important because it served to heighten the social and cultural crisis that Cornwall was to experience, contributing to the conflict and paradoxes that produced paralysis. For, as Cornwall fell into the mode of rapid de-industrialisation, so the Cornish "intelligentsia" — the educated middle-classes — found themselves pulled simultaneously in opposite directions. On the one hand, a refusal to accept that the industrial decline was real or permanent demanded continued loyalty to the Gilbertian culture of progress, but on the other the evidence of de-industrialisation that lay all around them gave credence to the "Revivalists'" calls for return to a pre-industrial culture and for the creation of a post-industrial economy.

One of the more pertinent ironies of this situation was that this ideological clash (for such it was) precluded any serious analysis of the condition in which Cornwall had found itself. A compromise or accommodation was sought, perhaps, in the work of A.K. Hamilton Jenkin whose "folksy" and sometimes sentimental treatment of nineteenth century Cornwall at least fitted the romantic mould of the "Revivalists". But when his *The Cornish Miner*[42] was published in 1927 the hey-day of Cornish mining was already passed long-since, the ruined and ivy-clad engine houses already romantic landmarks upon the burgeoning tourist trail. Thus, for the "Revivalists" and those that they influenced, nineteenth century Cornwall could at best be little more than an increasingly romanticised appendage to the grander and more ancient themes that they had chosen to explore. Outside their ranks, of course, there was still an alternative camp which continued to nurture its passion for Cornish mining and engineering.[43] Its devotees were not, however, social or economic historians attempting to explain the experience of Cornish industrialisation but rather practical men and commercial optimists who lobbied and planned for their much-vaunted rebirth of the tin industry. They had little in common with the "Revivalists", but equally they had little capacity or inclination to understand the reality of Cornwall's industrial experience. In the aftermath of Cornwall's industrial decline, therefore, there was no attempt to appreciate the significance of the industrial period in Cornwall's history. Those who did not accept Cornwall's industrial decline had, quite logically, no motivation to study it; the "Revivalists" were not interested in it anyway and looked to pre-industrial Cornwall for their inspiration and for their models for the future. There was a marked failure, then, by the "Revivalists" to address the problems of modern Cornwall. In a sense they contributed to the very paralysis from which they were attempting to escape!

As Berresford Ellis has noted, the emergence of the "Cornish Revival" should also be seen in the context of what was happening elsewhere.[44] In late Victorian and Edwardian Britain there was indeed a growing anti-industrialism,[45] with which the "Revivalists" could identify, and in the same period there was a new romanticism in which the sentimental enthusiasm for "other-worldly" Celtic mysticism and the Arthurian cycles aided the "Revivalists'" cause. More especially, the "Cornish Revival" was part of a wider "Celtic Revival", led by outstanding literary figures of international repute such as Sir Walter Scott and (later) William Butler Yeats, and given academic expression and credibility through the efforts of

Celticists such as Professor John Stuart Blackie.[46] There is no doubt whatsoever that the Cornish "Revivalists" looked to the other Celtic lands (especially Wales and Brittany) — for inspiration, for reassurance, for institutions to copy, for models to follow. Equally, the emergence of "Celtic Studies" as a respectable subject at British and Continental universities afforded the "Revivalists" much encouragement. However, in comparing the Cornish experience with that of the other Celtic lands, it is important to note that the causes, conditions and aspirations of the "Revivals" in these lands were not identical. In Ireland, for example, the motivation was primarily political, strengthening the cultural arm of the nationalist movement,[47] while in Scotland it was part of a post-Union, post-Jacobite attempt at nation-building: the rehabilitation of the Highlands and the bridging of the Highland-Lowland gap by the creation of a "Celtic Scotland" identity.[48] In Brittany it was a regionalist response (the "First Emsav", as it came to be known) to defend the still-living Breton language from the homogenising and assimilatory policies of the determinedly centralist French Government.

In Wales, the process of "Revival" was even more complex. As in Cornwall, so in Wales "In the sixteenth century the native culture bound up with Catholicism largely disappeared . . .",[49] to be replaced — again as in Cornwall — with an increasingly urbanised, industrial culture centred on Calvinistic Methodism. However, it is a mistake to draw too close a parallel between the Cornish and Welsh experiences in this period. To begin with, Welsh industry had in the main not yet experienced the de-industrialisation that had already so affected Cornwall (relative industrial decline in North Wales was more than off-set by the continuing vigour of South Welsh expansion) and the Welsh language was still a strong and essential feature of Welsh life. The Welsh language, indeed, had become an integral part of the popular, Methodist culture (in stark contrast to the Cornish experience), its very survival a springboard from which Welsh "Revivalists" in the nineteenth century could launch their attempts to relink modern Welsh culture with the earlier culture of pre-industrial Wales. In contrast to Cornwall it was the survival rather than death of a language which was an impetus to "Revival", and it was a "Revival" that grew out of economic and cultural vigour rather than economic and cultural paralysis. It was a "Revival", therefore, that was more accessible and more acceptable to the general Welsh populace than was the Cornish "Revival" to the Cornish. The Welsh "Revival" engendered widespread popular support to an extent that was not possible in Cornwall. Ironically, some of the outward and visible signs of Welsh "Revival" — especially the "invented" symbolism of the Gorsedd, the daffodil, the "national dress", the Red Dragon flag — were not dissimilar to some of the manifestations of the Cornish "Revival". It is also instructive to note that in the middle and latter parts of the twentieth century (when the Welsh industrial experience has come in several respects to resemble that of Cornwall) the renewed Welsh "Revival" has — as Dai Smith has argued[50] — been as much a result of pressure from a "Cymricizing" tourist industry as from the re-emergence of national sentiment, with Wales busy "reinventing" the past to serve the needs of the present, an experience reminiscent of that of Cornwall half a century before.

In further contrast to the "Revivalists" in Wales, who managed to address their aspirations to the Methodist majority, the "Revival" in Cornwall was from its beginning associated with Anglo-Catholic sentiment. This, of course, reflected the Hawker inheritance but it was also consistent with the appeal to a pre-industrial Cornish culture which was not only Celtic but also Catholic. The Cornish Rebellion of 1549, inevitably, assumed a new significance in the eyes of the "Revivalists" (had it not been in defence of both the Cornish language and the Catholic religion?), as did the pre-Reformation links with Brittany. Renewed Breton contacts were thus of particular importance to the "Revivalists", for they helped to reconstruct Cornwall's pre-industrial cultural contacts as well as practically assisting the mechanics of "Revival". This, in turn, was further encouragement to the Anglo-Catholic strand of the "Revival", for Brittany had remained loyal to the Catholic faith and was the repository for both the material relics and literary Lives of the Celtic saints. Brittany, indeed, had not experienced industrial development on a scale anything like that of Cornwall, and — with its continuing devotion to the Catholic faith and the widespread survival of the Breton language (so close in form to Cornish) — Brittany appeared for the Cornish "Revivalists" the perfect model in their quest to rebuild a pre-industrial Celtic-Catholic culture in Cornwall.[51]

The scholarship of Canon Doble rediscovered the multiplicity of Breton-Cornish religious connections, provoking in Cornwall a new enthusiasm for the Lives of the Saints, for Celtic crosses and other physical remains, and for the Medieval Miracle Plays (these in the Cornish language, to boot), an enthusiasm with connotations more significant than mere antiquarianism.[52] For some, this enthusiasm was an opportunity to awaken Cornwall from a perceived religious paralysis (suffered, it was alleged, by both the Anglican and Methodist Churches) that had accompanied the general socio-economic paralysis of industrial decline. Bernard Walke, who was Curate at Polruan in the early years of this century and who subsequently rose to fame as the Anglo-Catholic Vicar of St Hilary, wrote of the lacklustre churches of the 1920s and 30s:

> There was nothing here to kindle the faith that gave to Cornwall so many saints or to light again the fire that burnt so fiercely in the day of John Wesley. Only the worship of the Mass, where time and space have ceased to be the supreme realities, and where bread and wine have become the Body, Soul and Divinity of our Lord and Saviour, to be adored and to be offered by man as the all-prevailing sacrifice for the sins of the world, only the Mass could ever hope to win back man to the reality of God's love.[53]

The completion of Truro Cathedral (with its deliberate Breton ambience) had also encouraged the Anglo-Catholic strand of the "Cornish Revival", and in the decades before the Second World War the Anglo-Catholic movement grew in influence.[54] By 1933 the Anglican Church in Cornwall, for example, had accommodated the liturgical observance of the principal Celtic-Cornish saints.[55] In addition to the Breton connection, Walke and others like him were aware of a

Celtic-Catholic link with Ireland and ". . . when Ireland lay under the terror of the Black and Tans . . . we became involved in holding meetings for prayer in different parts of Cornwall on behalf of this distressed country".[56] In contrast to the apparent indifference of the broader "Cornish Revival", the Anglo-Catholic movement did demonstrate a concern for the condition of modern Cornwall, with Walke and colleagues during the 1920s attempting (albeit unsuccessfully) to launch a political and social movement to alleviate the distress caused by unemployment amongst the tin miners.[57]

Paradoxically, the Anglo-Catholic movement was the one part of the "Revival" to provoke actual antipathy and opposition. In 1929 one critic wrote that "The steady rise of the Anglo-Catholic movement has inevitably tended to harden denominational distinctions".[58] In particular, it was objected that "When incense is burnt in Truro Cathedral and confessions are heard there, and in many parish churches; when the validity of the sacraments is made to depend on episcopal ordination and apostolic succession, then, by implication . . . the Methodists and all Free Churchmen are unchurched".[59] A.K. Hamilton Jenkin added that there was ". . . a definite change in the doctrine of the Church itself, and one which has unhappily caused a widening of the rift between it and the chapels".[60] The issue came to a head in 1932 when a Kensitite mob (mainly from outside Cornwall, but encouraged from within) raided St Hilary and laid waste to the church, smashing its candles and pictures and carrying off its statues.[61] Shortly after, when Bishop W.H. Frere — who had acquired a reputation as an "Anglo-Catholic socialist"[62] — left Truro, the Low Church J.W. Hunkin (a former Methodist) was sent down as Bishop to temper the Anglo-Catholic influence.[63]

The broader "Cornish Revival" also experienced certain difficulties in appealing to the mass of Cornish people. To some degree this was because many of its leaders were "exiles", middle-class professionals who had been drawn to cities such as Plymouth, Bristol and London or emigrants overseas who had become prominent in colonial affairs. Prestigious "Cornish Associations" sprang up (London's was formed in 1886, South Australia's in 1890, Kimberley's in 1889), important vehicles for the "Revivalists'" interpretation of Cornish culture. For many "exiles", especially those abroad, the view of Cornwall had become evermore affectionate with the passing of the years, as the reality of emigration from destitution had become an ever dimmer memory. Inevitably, their interpretations of Cornwall became increasingly nostalgic and romantic, their concern for Cornwall sentimental, with little real attempt to understand the crisis of modern Cornwall. If there were calls for financial support for the deserving in Cornwall, then of course they would dip their hands in their pockets, but their main concern was for "Cornish evenings" with pasty suppers, humourous dialect recitations, lantern slides of Cornish beauty spots and antiquities, and lectures on Cornwall in the days of old.[64] Whilst all of this was very interesting, it could make but little contribution to the redemption of Cornwall from its paralysis.

In Cornwall itself the emergence of the "Cornish Revival" in earnest was signalled by the foundation in 1901 of a movement entitled Cowethas Kelto-Kernuak (the Cornish Celtic Society), formed by the Cornish language enthusiasts

L.C. Duncombe Jewell (another noted Anglo-Catholic) and Henry Jenner, and attracting distinguished supporters such as Sir Arthur Quiller-Couch.[65] It was unashamedly romantic in its attitude (Deacon, in a scathing assessment of the early "Revivalists", asserts that "The Cornish Revivalists, more than their Celtic colleagues, positively wallowed in the un-reason of Romanticism"[66]) and appealed directly to Cornwall's pre-industrial culture. The movement's principal aims were to revive Cornish as a spoken language and to establish a Cornish Gorsedd on the lines of the Welsh Gorsedd (which had been "re-established" in 1792) and the Breton Gorsedd which was being set up in that year.[67] There were, predictably, no corresponding political or economic aims (although Quiller-Couch had by now made public his views on tourism) and no attempt to address the problems of industrial decline. There was, however, a concern to acquire the symbols appropriate to the status of Celtic nationhood and amongst the movement's innovations was the "reintroduction" of the kilt in Cornwall. Later, the "Revivalists" also adopted the black and white cross of St Piran which Davies Gilbert had in 1838 described as formerly the banner of St Perran and the standard of Cornwall[68] and which had been depicted in the "Trevithick Window" in Westminster Abbey as early as 1888. In seeking recognition from the other Celtic countries, Henry Jenner in 1904 addressed the Celtic Congress on the subject of "Cornwall: A Celtic Nation"[69] and secured successfully Cornwall's membership of the Congress. In the same year Jenner's *A Handbook of the Cornish Language* was published.[70] Jenner had emerged as the principal scholar in the Cornish language but shortly he was to be joined by the equally talented and energetic Robert Morton Nance, who set about the full-scale reconstruction of the Cornish language with a new "Unified" orthography and grammar.

Inevitably, the First World War cut short the work of the "Revivalists", but after the war Jenner and Nance decided to replace the by now defunct Cowethas Kelto-Kernuak with a network of Old Cornwall Societies. The first Old Cornwall Society was formed at St Ives in 1920 and by 1924 there were enough Societies spread across Cornwall for a Federation to be formed, its journal *Old Cornwall* appearing for the first time during 1925. The foundation of the Old Cornwall Societies was a genuine attempt to bring the "Cornish Revival" closer to ordinary Cornish people but it was only partially successful in that respect.[71] The 1920s, of course, had witnessed the greatest crisis in the tin industry, and although the Old Cornwall Societies' appeal to pre-industrial Cornish culture was a response to industrial decline, their crusade to revive the Cornish language seemed hardly relevant amongst the destitution and depression of economic reality. Nonetheless, the number of Societies continued to grow, with A.S.D. Smith — a Sussex-born newcomer to the "Revival" — commenting that "An intense local patriotism was at the root of the Old Cornwall Movement . . . together with consciousness of our affinity with the other Celtic nations".[72]

In 1928 one long-term aim of the "Revivalists" was at last realised, the creation of a Cornish Gorsedd, affiliated to its Welsh and Breton sister institutions, a College of Bards who had been each admitted to the Gorsedd on account of some outstanding contribution to Cornwall. The blue-robed Bards met annually at the

Gorsedd to conduct their ceremony in the Cornish language, and the Gorsedd tried to cultivate an image of academic excellence and Celtic scholarship, producing language experts such as the celebrated E.G.R. Hooper. It gained recognition in Cornwall but slowly, however, and in 1937 one newspaper correspondent lamented that "If we are quite truthful we have to admit that the revival of the Gorsedd has scarcely touched the lives of the common people in Cornwall".[72] There had been occasional breakthroughs, such as at St Cleer Primary School, where the headmaster (Edwin Chirgwin) — a Bard — had taught his pupils the Lord's Prayer and Creed in Cornish,[74] but fundamentally the "Revival" had yet to pierce the Cornish paralysis.

In 1933, however, a new "Revivalist" organisation emerged entitled Tyr ha Tavas (Land and Language), composed mainly of young people and intent upon making a greater impact upon Cornwall.[75] It declared that it " . . . stands for the unity of persons of Cornish birth or descent who value their Cornish heritage, and who desire to maintain the outlook, individualism, culture, and idealism characteristic of their race".[76] It considered that its ". . . primary aim is to serve Cornwall and Cornish People . . ."[77] and was determined ". . . to show Cornish People what Cornishmen have done and what they still can do to help the World".[78] Tyr ha Tavas also pressured local MPs into giving greater consideration to specifically Cornish problems, the first overtly political action by the "Revivalists", but Tyr ha Tavas was at root not a political organisation and it failed to address itself to the crucial socio-economic issues of the day. It produced a magazine entitled *Kernow*, but it sold more copies outside of Cornwall than within.[79] Its contents were highly romantic, in tune with the general thrust of the "Revivalists", and bore no relation to the reality of economic despair in the Cornwall of the "Great Depression". Like the broader "Revivalist" movement, Tyr ha Tavas was ultimately unable to relate to the broad mass of Cornish people and their "fossilising" Methodist working class culture.

The relative failure of Tyr ha Tavas in the years before the Second World War reflected the continuing paralysis of Cornish society and economy. Appeals to a pre-industrial past and for a post-industrial economy had failed to alter the situation in any fundamental sense. The consequent rise of tourism was a function of de-industrialisation rather than an alternative to it. and the "Cornish Revival" had not been successful in lifting the majority of Cornish people from their social and cultural paralysis. The vague political posturing of Tyr ha Tavas, however, begs the question: why was greater political action not brought to bear in Cornwall in this period? The answer, as we shall see, is that Cornish politics too was in a state of paralysis as a result of its experience in this era of de-industrialisation, marginalised — like other facets of Cornish life — by the condition of "Second Peripheralism".

Notes and References

1. John Murray et al, *Devon and Cornwall: A Preliminary Survey*, Wheaton, Exeter, 1947, p175.

2. Ibid.
3. Ibid., p7.
4. Ibid.
5. Ibid., p239.
6. Ibid., p242.
7. Ibid., p191.
8. Ibid.
9. Ibid., p192.
10. Ibid.
11. John Rowe, "The Declining Years of Cornish Tin Mining", in Jeffrey Porter, *Education and Labour in the South West*, Exeter Papers in Economic History, No 10, University of Exeter, Exeter, 1975, p59.
12. Ibid., pp64-65.
13. Ibid., p66.
14. Ibid.
15. Ibid., p67.
16. John Rowe, "Cornish Mining Crisis in the 1920s", *Cornish Banner*, August 1986.
17. Roger Burt and Martin Timbrell, *Diversification as a Response to Decline in the Mining Industry: Arsenic and South Western Metal Production 1850–1914*, University of Exeter, Exeter, 1984.
18. R.M. Barton, *A History of the Cornish China Clay Industry*, Bradford Barton, Truro, 1966.
19. Murray, op. cit., pp96-99.
20. David St John Thomas, *A Regional History of The Railways of Great Britain, Vol. 1: The West Country*, David & Charles, Newton Abbot, 1960, 5th ed., 1981, pp135-136.
21. R.J. Woodfin, *The Cornwall Railway to Its Centenary in 1959*, Bradford Barton, Truro, 1960, republished 1972.
22. Jack Simmons, "The Railway in Cornwall, 1835-1914", in *Back-track: Recording Britain's Railway History*, Winter 1987, (first published in the *Journal of the Royal Institution of Cornwall*, 1962).
23. Murray, op. cit., pp113-119.
24. Ibid., pp159-172.
25. Simmons, op. cit.
26. R.B. Wilson, *Go Great Western: A History of GWR Publicity*, David & Charles, Newton Abbot, 1970, republished 1987.
27. P.B. Whitehouse, *Britain's Main-line Railways*, New English Library, London, 1977, pp202-203.
28. S.P.B. Mais, *The Cornish Riviera*, Great Western Railway, London, 1934. The Southern Railway attempted similar propaganda techniques; see: T.W.E. Roche, *The Withered Arm: Reminiscences of the Southern Lines West of Exeter*, Forge Books, Bracknell, 1967, republished 1977.
29. Keith Robbins, *Nineteenth-Century Britain: England, Scotland, and Wales — The Making of a Nation*, Oxford University Press, Oxford 1989, p25.
30. Murray, op. cit., p219.
31. Ibid., p240.
32. Ibid.
33. *Cornish Magazine*, Vol 1, 1895, p236.
34. Ibid.

35. Bernard Deacon, "Cornish Culture or the Culture of the Cornish?", *Cornish Banner*, November 1986.

36. Tom Salmon, *The First 100 Years: The Story of Rugby Football in Cornwall*, CRFU, Illogan, 1983.

37. Cited in A.L. Rowse, *The Little Land of Cornwall*, Alan Sutton, Gloucester, 1986, p264.

38. A.C. Todd, *Beyond the Blaze: A Biography of Davies Gilbert*, Bradford Barton, Truro, 1967.

39. Cited in P. Berresford Ellis, *The Cornish Language and Its Literature*, Routledge & Kegan Paul, London, 1974, p132.

40. A.L. Rowse, *Matthew Arnold: Poet and Prophet*, Thames & Hudson, London, 1976, pp12-16.

41. Victor Edward Durkacz, *The Decline of the Celtic Languages*, John Donald, Edinburgh, 1983, pp202-204.

42. A.K. Hamilton Jenkin, *The Cornish Miner*, 1927, republished David & Charles, Newton Abbot, 1972.

43. Something of the flavour of this continuing passion is enshrined in John H. Trounson, *The Cornish Mineral Industry: Past Performance and Future Prospect 1937–1951*, University of Exeter, Exeter, 1989.

44. Berresford Ellis, op. cit., pp147-152.

45. Martin J. Weiner, *English Culture and the Decline of the Industrial Spirit, 1850–1980*, Cambridge University Press, Cambridge, 1981.

46. Durkacz, op. cit., pp201-203.

47. John Hutchinson, *The Dynamics of Cultural Nationalism: The Gaelic Revival and the Creation of the Irish Nation State*, Allen & Unwin, London, 1987.

48. Some of these factors are discussed in Durkacz, op. cit., pp189-213.

49. Prys Morgan, "From a Death to a View: The Hunt for the Welsh Past in the Romantic Period", in Eric Hobsbawm and Terrence Ranger, *The Invention of Tradition*, Cambridge University Press, Cambridge, 1983, p44.

50. Dai Smith, *Wales! Wales?*, George Allen & Unwin, London, 1984.

51. For example, see Hugh Miners, *Gorseth Kernow: The First Fifty Years*, Gorseth Kernow, Penzance, 1978, p24. It was, perhaps, an experience not unlike that of Emile Bernard:
    "I returned a devout believer . . . Brittany has made a Catholic of me, capable of fighting for the Church. I was intoxicated by the incense, the organs, the prayers, the ancient stained glass windows, the hieratic tapestries, and I travelled back across the centuries, isolating myself increasingly from my contemporaries whose preoccupations with the modern industrial world inspired in me nothing but disgust. Bit by bit, I became a man of the Middle Ages, I had no love for anything save Brittany". (Quoted in A.D. Smith, *Ethnic Revival in the Modern World*, Cambridge University Press, Cambridge, 1981 pxi.)

52. Gilbert Hunter Doble (1880-1945) was for many years Vicar of Wendron and devoted his studies to the Lives of the Celtic Saints in Cornwall, the fruits of which appeared as *The Saints of Cornwall*, Parts 1-5, Dean and Chapter of Truro, Truro, 1960–1970.

53. Bernard Walke, *Twenty Years at St Hilary*, 1935, republished Anthony Mott, London, 1982, p33.

54. H. Miles Brown, *A Century For Cornwall: The Diocese of Truro, 1877–1977*, Oscar Blackford, Truro, 1976, pp1-54.

55. Ibid., p119.

56. Walke, op. cit., p180.
57. Ibid., pp203-213.
58. Superintendent of the Cornwall Wesleyan Circuit, cited in A.K. Hamilton Jenkin, *Cornwall and Its People*, 1932–34, republished David & Charles, Newton Abbot, 1983, p199.
59. Ibid., pp199-200.
60. Ibid., p200.
61. Walke, op. cit., pp292.
62. A.L. Rowse, *Quiller Couch: A Portrait of Q*, Methuen, London, 1988, p199.
63. Alan Dunstan and John S. Peart-Binns, *Cornish Bishop*, Epworth Press, London, 1977, pp84-85, pp90-106.
64. Philip Payton, *The Cornish Miner in Australia: Cousin Jack Down Under*, Dyllansow Truran, Redruth, 1984, p202.
65. Miners, op. cit., p12.
66. Bernard Deacon, "The Cornish Revival: An Analysis", unpublished paper, (in Redruth Cornish History Library), 1985, p8.
67. Miners, op. cit., p12.
68. Davies Gilbert, 1838, cited in Robert Hunt, *Popular Romances of the West of England*, 1871, p473.
69. Henry Jenner, "Cornwall: A Celtic Nation", *Celtic Review*, 16 January 1905.
70. Henry Jenner, *A Handbook of the Cornish Language*, David Nutt, London, 1904.
71. Deacon, 1985, op. cit., p22.
72. Cited in Miners, op. cit., p13.
73. Cited in ibid., p31.
74. Berresford Ellis, op. cit., p163.
75. Miners, op. cit., p27.
76. *Old Cornwall*, Summer 1933.
77. Ibid.
78. Ibid.
79. Deacon, 1985, op. cit., p24.

CHAPTER SEVEN

The Politics Of Paralysis

In the aftermath of Cornwall's industrial decline, Cornish society and economy had sunk into a paralysis, the fundamental characteristics of which remained virtually unchanged from the late nineteenth century until the Second World War — despite the creation of tourism and the emergence of a "Cornish Revival". This paralysis was compounded and complemented by a corresponding political inability in Cornwall to react to the new conditions. This led, on the one hand, to the features of Cornish politics becoming increasingly "fossilised" and out of step with developments elsewhere in Britain and, on the other, to the failure of Cornish politics to address the socio-economic problems of the era. It did, however, lend Cornwall an increasingly distinct political culture which, like the highly distinctive Cornish economy, served to emphasise the differences between Cornwall and England in this era of "Second Peripheralism".

Although her socio-economic problems were indeed highly distinctive, Cornwall's status as "just another county" amongst so many others served to disguise the distinctions and to dilute, even mute, any demands for special and separate attention. Cornwall was long-since shorn, of course, of her ancient vestiges of constitutional "accommodation", thus restricting Cornish opportunities to employ political means to seek redress or encourage new initiatives — no 44 MPs to lobby at the heart of Government, no politicised Duchy to trade the concerns of Cornwall, no Stannary Parliament to act as an institutional forum in which the interests of Cornwall might be articulated. As a mere "county", Cornwall's Local Government was affected by the distancing (described by Bulpitt) of local or "low" politics from the "high" politics of the centre, and was similarly restricted by the basic "depoliticisation" of the relationship between Local and Central Government in the United Kingdom.[1] Unlike, for example, the (in 1922) newly-created Province of Northern Ireland or, further afield, the State of South Australia (which in 1923 experienced a mining collapse reminiscent of the Cornish experience[2]), Cornwall had no recourse to mechanisms of constitutional accommodation in order to refashion her future.

This institutional inability to react was complemented by Cornwall's increasing political estrangement from the emerging pattern of British politics in the twentieth century. Again, this estrangement was a function of Cornwall's industrial decline and consequent paralysis. Specifically, the great age of Cornish industrial prowess already past, there was little incentive or opportunity for Cornish politics to realign in terms of the great Labour versus Capital (Conservative) divide that was emerging elsewhere. In industrial Wales, by way of contrast, which had hitherto exhibited many close comparisons with Cornwall, there were as yet few hints of de-industrialisation that might lie ahead and — in marked contrast to Cornwall — the industrial Welsh were early converts to the new creed of Labour. The South Wales Miners' Federation (the "Fed") had made its mark before the turn of the century, and in 1901 Keir Hardie made history when he was returned as Independent Labour MP for Merthyr. In the 1906 "Liberal Landslide" Election (when not a single Conservative Member was returned in Wales) Labour secured six Welsh seats as a result of its pact with the Liberals, and the decades that preceded the Second World War witnessed the inexorable replacement of the Liberals by Labour as the principal party of Wales. Although this appeared as a natural development of Welsh radicalism and served, perhaps, to enhance Welsh political culture through the creation of a thoroughly Welsh Labour Party, it nevertheless did not estrange Welsh politics from that of the rest of Britain (there were parallel developments in Scotland and industrial England) and did not prevent prominent Welsh public figures (such as Aneurin Bevan) from becoming involved intimately in politics at the British level.[3]

The traditional explanation for Cornwall's failure to produce its own version of the "Fed" and its attendant Labour movement has rested upon Hamilton Jenkin's (and later Barton's) assessment of the impact of individualism.[4] In this, the Cornish miner's individualistic predisposition was seen as an impediment to any collective action (such as trade unionism), a factor compounded by the tribute and tutwork system of employment which was not only a function of individualism but also an inhibitor of collective action. Tribute and tutwork, indeed, acted to force individual miners or groups of miners to compete against each other for pieces of work ("pitches"), these pitches being allocated to the lowest bidders; hardly the kind of industrial environment in which one might expect collective action to arise. However, whilst one must be careful not to underestimate the influence of individualism in general and tribute and tutwork in particular, it is important to note that critiques of this traditional explanation have emerged, most notably from Burke and Deacon.[5]

To begin with, Hamilton Jenkin's implied equation of "individualism" with "conservatism" (political or otherwise) does not bear closer scrutiny. Cornish individualism was in fact a dynamic and progressive force, manifested amongst other things in the Liberal Methodist radicalism that came to dominate nineteenth century Cornwall.[6] Similarly, Hobsbawm's contention that "Methodism in Cornwall produced an atmosphere of resignation and acceptance which worked against militancy"[7] will not do, for Cornish Methodism — based as it was upon Cornish individualism — was at the heart of the Cornish Liberal radicalism which embraced a number of reforming campaigns in the last century. The explanation for Cornwall's experience (and for its divergence from that of Wales) lies elsewhere, and is suggested in the important discussion offered by Deacon of attempts at combination by Cornish miners in the 1860s and 70s. Deacon has argued that

The historical divergence between Cornish metal miners and Welsh coal miners only became marked after the 1866–72 period. While coal mining continued to expand, copper and tin mining entered on a severe protracted slump characterised by large scale unemployment and emigration. Such conditions were hardly conducive to the formation of a permanent trade union.[8]

Elsewhere, Deacon has added that

If the development of industrial relations and trade unionism is viewed in a context that admits the experience of the Cornish communities overseas, then a very different model of the Cornish miner might emerge, one that finds a place for collective experience as well as heroic individuals.[9]

In terms of the argument presented here, the point is that the retardation of trade unionism and a wider Labour movement in Cornwall was not a specific result of Cornish individualism but rather a consequence of rapid de-industrialisation, a conclusion underscored by an examination of the collectivist behaviour of Cornish emigrants in mining fields overseas that were still undergoing expansion. Cornwall's failure to produce a "Fed" was, therefore, a reflection — indeed a part — of the social and economic paralysis that emerged swiftly in the closing years of the nineteenth century, an integral part of the era and process of "Second Peripheralism". Paralysis struck at precisely the time when the combination of Cornish miners might be expected to have happened (and when the Welsh miners were indeed organising), nipping in the bud early Cornish attempts at collective action at home but unable, of course, to inhibit Cornish behaviour overseas.

In the eighteenth and early nineteenth centuries, before the development of a fully fledged market economy and the extension of the suffrage, popular protest (economic and political) in Britain was in the form of the riot rather than the strike. Cornwall, indeed, as noted in Chapter 4, was especially notorious for its propensity to riot, with food riots remaining a feature of the Cornish way of life until the middle of the last century. Although a function of Cornish "savagery" and an expression of Cornish individualism, often without planning or co-ordination between individuals or districts, the riots were also in a sense "collective" — not only physically, in terms of the composition of the mobs, but also with regard to the common action and psychology of the "crowd". Rule has drawn parallels between the events of Cornish riots and the activities of the French Revolutionary crowds analysed by Rude.[10] Given that the riot was precursor of the strike in Britain as a whole, it is instructive to note that while the strike emerged relatively late in Cornwall, the riot survived rather longer than it did elsewhere — exhibited, for instance, in the Newlyn disturbances of 1896.

There had, however, been a number of attempts at industrial action by Cornish miners before the serious activity of the 1860s and 1870s. Barton admits that strikes in the Cornish mining industry were not as uncommon as was once supposed,[11] and amongst the earliest disturbances was a brief strike at Fowey Consols and Lanescot in February 1831 when the miners combined to try to force a rise in tribute rates. The strike was broken quickly, however, the leaders incarcerated in Bodmin Gaol and the men sent back to work, with no attempt or intention on the part of the workers to form a permanent miners' trade union. Similarly, there was a brief strike at the Consolidated Mines in Gwennap in 1842 over working hours and conditions of employment, when the men talked fleetingly and inconclusively of the possibility of unionisation, and during the 1840s Mining Association delegates from the North of England visited Cornwall to encourage solidarity with striking Durham miners and to discourage potential Cornish blacklegs from travelling North. In 1853 there was another brief strike at Bosweddan (near St Just-in-Penwith) over the alleged victimisation of men who had been involved in a food riot six years before, leading to more general disturbances at the neighbouring mines of Levant, Spearn Consols, Spearn Moor, and Boscean concerning tribute rates. In the same district, there were short and inconclusive strikes at Balleswidden in 1856, 1857 and 1859.[12]

The first determined attempt at organised trade unionism occurred in early 1866,[13] at the East Cornwall and Tamar Valley mines which had by now surpassed their western counterparts in terms of richness and economic importance. Dissatisfaction with various conditions of employment had been voiced in the mines during 1865, and the events of 1866 were precipitated by strike action at Wheal Trelawney lead mine (near Menheniot) in January when the miners demanded greater remuneration. Thereafter, the flood-gates opened, the workers from mines throughout the district holding meetings at Liskeard, Gunnislake, Callington, and Tavistock. Hundreds were reported joining a new Mining Association, whose leaders were Methodist local preachers and class leaders. This organisation was launched in February 1866 as the Miners' Mutual Benefit Association, its constitution surprisingly radical with rules such as those which proposed the setting up of workers' committees at the mines to determine whether the captains' prices for tribute and tutwork bargains were sufficient and what action was to be taken if they were not.

Deacon has suggested several reasons for this sudden upsurge of collectivist sentiment in the district, pointing to the influence and importance of the discussion that had attended Lord Kinnaird's Parliamentary Bill to improve the conditions in metal mines. The competitive spirit in negotiating tribute and tutwork bargains was also less noticeable in the district than in the older, more "traditionalist" mines of West Cornwall, with men at many of the eastern mines unwilling to engage in "downward bidding" to secure contracts. The copper mines in the area were, in addition, benefiting from the price rises (albeit temporary) of late 1865, with the miners feeling that this increased profitibility should be reflected in increased remuneration. Contacts with representatives of striking coal miners from Newcastle, who had come to Cornwall to try to prevent the recruitment of blackleg labour, heightened local interest in trade unionism. There was also an atmosphere of flexibility and change, men who had come from the western mines having experienced the effects of geographical uprooting and distancing from the traditional methods of the West.

Certainly, the mine employers perceived what was for them a new and dangerous phenomenon, acting quickly and in concert to meet the threat. At Drakewalls and other mines in the Gunnislake area the employers took pre-emptive action, "locking-out" Association members. Devon Great Consols (near Tavistock) feared an invasion from across the Tamar, with 150 soldiers from Plymouth and 131 special constables brought in to protect the mine if necessary (in the event, they were not needed). In the Caradon area, however, it was the Association which took the initiative. Strikes were declared at East Caradon and Marke Valley over insufficient prices for tribute and tutwork bargains, and a massive open-air meeting — reputedly attracting some four to five thousand miners — was held on Caradon Hill to articulate the workers' grievances. By now a clearly-defined, embryonic union was emerging, its ringleaders two prominent local preachers from St Cleer.

The Caradon action received a swift reposte from the employers, however, making clear that the more radical claims of the Association would never be accepted and (in an attempt to seize the initiative) proposing the foundation of an alternative Association representing both employers and employees. The Caradon strikes continued into March, nonetheless, but in the Tamar Valley mines the "lock-out" had already been successful in forcing men to drift back to work under the employers' conditions. This signalled the collapse of the industrial action and of the Association, and a little over three weeks after the initial Drakewalls "lock-out" the strike was over. Many had threatened that they would emigrate rather than bow to the employers, and many did just that — taking with them their new experiences of unionism and industrial action to destinations as diverse as the Isle of Man, the North of England, and South Australia.[14]

The failure of the adventure of 1866 mirrored the faltering fledgling steps of the Welsh miners in their unsuccessful action of 1863, and was attributable to financial weakness, poor organisation and a lack of co-ordination in the face of the sophisticated manoeverings of the employers. More particularly, the miners had chosen a poor time for their effort, for the price of copper was by now already dropping, the employers content to weather a period of inactivity at their mines and indeed happy to employ the "lock-out" weapon. Thereafter, things would not improve, the "Great Crash" of 1866 heralding the demise of Cornish copper mining, promoting the emigration of those very people who had taken the lead in the events of 1866. With the industry now in swift and terminal decline, and with so many of the community's natural leaders increasingly scattered abroad, there was little opportunity (unlike the Welsh experience) for the further development of trade unionism.

Tin, however, outlived Cornish copper and in the brief upturn in the fortunes of the tin industry in the early 1870s there was a correspondingly brief upsurge in renewed collective action amongst the Cornish miners.[15] The early 1870s were a time of economic boom in Britain as a whole, a period of renewed optimism and increased expectations which were reflected in strike action for better pay and conditions in industries throughout the United Kingdom. Cornwall shared in this experience, and as a supposed new era of tin mining prosperity was greeted with exuberance during 1871, so pressure for a "better deal" for the miners was exerted. Grievances centred around two main issues, the low levels of remuneration (it has been argued that employers kept their "captains' prices" artificially low at a time when the price of tin was rising) and the infrequent payment of wages. Traditionally, Cornish mines operated the system in which workers were paid "one month in hand", a system which had often forced miners to resort to the drawing of "subsist" (an advance on wages) to make ends meet. By the early 1870s, however, mines were increasingly reluctant to grant "subsist". This created some resentment, a grievance heightened by the employers' strict adherence to calendar months in determining pay periods. This led to "five week months" in which miners would receive no greater remuneration than during a shorter, "normal" month.

In December 1871 "several hundred miners" attended a meeting at St Blazey to protest against the "five week month", followed shortly by similar meetings in the Caradon and St Just districts. During that month there came the sudden announcement from Tincroft and Carn Brea mines that their "five week month" was to be abolished, an example followed speedily in other mines but which also provoked strike action (most notably at Wheal Basset, in Illogan) elsewhere when employers were tardy in their consideration of the issue. An emergency "County Mine Meeting" was held by the employers to debate the question, and as a result the "five week month" was systematically abandoned at most Cornish mines during February and March of 1872. At many mines this abolition was accompanied by a concessionary agreement on the part of the miners that they would no longer observe the traditional "Mazed Monday" holiday after pay periods, but in the St Just district men at several of the mines struck successfully for the retention of "Mazed Monday". The success of the miners' action promoted a spirit of confidence, encouraging other grievances to be aired elsewhere (such as a stoppage by bal-maidens and pickey-boys at the Caradon mines in pursuit of higher wages).

The speed and willingness with which the employers acceded to the miners' demands was a reflection of the relative strength of the workers' position. The mines could ill-afford periods of disruption at a time of increasing demand and higher tin prices, and years of emigration had led to a shortage of tributers and tutworkmen — they were much in demand in the upturn of 1871 and 1872 and a mine could not afford to alienate or lose its skilled labour. More subtly, the employers were happy to abolish the "five week month" because there were alternative means of controlling wages, not least the manipulation of "captains' prices". However, the economic climate deteriorated rapidly, leading to falling tin prices and the closure of numerous mines in the decade ahead. By 1873 the workers' strength was already eroded (there was an unsuccessful strike by surface workers at Tincroft in the October), and by early 1874 a number of mines had re-introduced the "five week month". A strike against re-introduction at Wheal Jane was defeated, although elsewhere — in the Camborne, Helston and St Just districts — re-introduction was opposed with some success. The struggle came to a head at Wheal Basset and South Condurrow in a strike where, in addition to the successful defeat

144

of re-introduction, there were movements towards the creation of a trade union structure.

A meeting in Camborne at the end of March 1874 announced the formation of a miners' trade union, the new enthusiasm for unionism undoubtably boosted by the events and successes of recent months (and also encouraged by visiting Burnley coal miners in late 1873 who had come to Cornwall to dissuade blacklegs). However, the successful resolution of the "five week month" left the potential trade unionists without an immediate cause upon which to focus their attention and mobilise their support. Equally, the position of the workers became increasingly less advantageous as the fortunes of the tin industry moved from bad to worse. Although there was sporadic industrial action in the 1880s and 1890s,[16] the Camborne trade union came to nothing, a victim of short-term organisational problems but also strangled by the longer-term economic crisis in Cornish mining. Indeed, the workforce in the Cornish tin industry was not effectively unionised until as late as 1917 (under wartime conditions) by which time — despite the strategic importance of tin during the war — mining was of marginal importance to the Cornish economy, geographically restricted to a few specific areas and employing relatively few people. As Burke has concluded, "The diminution of the Cornish industry during these years was most certainly one important factor in the delayed advent of Trade Union organisation on any scale in Cornwall . . . ".[17]

Effective trade unionism came to the mines too late to have any dynamic effect upon the Cornish workforce as a whole. There were brief strikes at several tin mines in 1918, 1919 and 1920,[18] but even in the relatively significant Transport and General Workers' Union strike at South Crofty in January 1939 (when there were clashes between strikers and police in Pool) only 234 men out of a total of 435 stopped work.19 Elsewhere in Cornwall, the only groups of workers to experience effective trade unionisation were the railwaymen and dock-workers (both of which were parts of larger union structures with a long history of organisation) and the china clay workers,[20] but even their efforts could not prevent the 1926 "General Strike" from being little more than a damp squib west of the Tamar.[21]

The experience of the china clay workers is interesting,[22] for it mirrors that of the miners. Although china clay did not undergo the cataclysmic decline of copper and later tin, the effects of that decline were felt nonetheless. Just as the clay industry was left as the isolated rump of extractive production in an otherwise de-industrialising economy, so the clay workers were increasingly isolated — both industrially and geographically. Inevitably, therefore, the unionisation of the clay workers was retarded. When, immediately prior to the Great War, a trade union structure did emerge, it had perforce to operate in an industrial environment with little experience of trade unionism. In earlier days, clay workers had been numbered in the ranks of food-rioting miners, and in the early and mid 1870s (during and in the aftermath of the tin miners' "five week month" strikes) the clay industry had seen some industrial action. In 1876, indeed, a China Clay Workers' Union had been formed, but the employers had reacted by attempting to weed out the unionists from their pits in order to ". . . scotch the serpent Union while it was still young and weak".[23] This, in turn, provoked a brief outburst of riot and strike, but the employers remained steadfast in their refusal to recognise the Union and by the end of the decade it was already a distant and almost forgotten memory. Thereafter there was little activity until 1911 when, as part of a general upsurge in trade unionism in Britain as a whole, the clay workers formed a branch of the Workers' Union. In July 1912 they demanded recognition, along with wage rises, an eight hour day, and other improvements in conditions of employment. With one or two notable exceptions, the employers refused to comply, setting the stage for a long and bitter ten week strike, characterised by violence and intimidation and the intervention of riot police brought in from Glamorgan and elsewhere. Finally, the strike collapsed, the workers forced back to work through economic necessity, their demands still refused by the employers.

There was little opportunity or likelihood, therefore, for any comprehensive and enduring unionisation of the Cornish workforce in the aftermath of the demise of copper and tin, a situation contributing still further to the general social and economic paralysis of Cornwall in the half-century or more before the Second World War. The emergence of tourism could do nothing to alter the situation, for its workers (many of them casual and seasonal) proved notoriously difficult to organise. The condition also contributed in a most significant way to the parallel political paraylsis, retarding development or a broader Labour Party and movement and "fossilising" the Liberal Party as the only credible radical alternative to the Conservatives in Cornwall, a position that was being eroded rapidly elsewhere in Britain. But before proceeding to an examination of that "fossilisation", it is important to trace the activities and impact of Cornish workers who emigrated abroad. The willingness and ability of the Cornish overseas to become involved in trade unionism demonstrates still further that their failure to combine successfully in Cornwall was a function of rapid de-industrialisation rather than the "inate" individualism of the Cornishman.

In the United States of America, for example, the Cornish formed a miners' league at Grass Valley in 1869 (which led to two serious strikes and a long period of industrial turbulence[24]) and later at the Butte copper mines and elsewhere the Cornish became — as Lingenfelter wrote — ". . . the leaders of the mining labor movement of the West".[25] Amongst their number was Richard F. Trevellick, described as ". . . one of the most important labor leaders in nineteenth century America . . .".[26] By 1864 he was President of the Detroit Trade's Assembly, and in the 1870s he was busy organising the anthracite miners of the East. Rowse considered that ". . . Trevellick must be regarded as the pioneer of the eight-hour day in the United States",[27] no mean achievement for an individual and a significant commentary upon the radical and trade unionist disposition of emigrant Cornishmen.

In South Africa, too, the Cornish emerged as prominent personalities in the developing trade union movement in the mines.[28] Tom Matthews from Newlyn, who had mined in Michigan and at Butte and had been President of the Miners' Union of Montana and in 1892 that State's only Labour member of its House of Representatives, was a central figure in the establishment of South Africa's Miners'

Association in 1902. Perhaps inevitably, the workers' struggle in South Africa became blurred by racial tensions, first with the issue of Chinese labour and then with the thorny question of the relationship between black and white miners. The Cornish presented themselves as a "labour aristocracy", as supervisors of the modern rock-drills operated by kaffir labour. Attempts by the employers at modifying this position were met in 1907 by stiff Cornish resistance in a disastrous strike which had the effect of encouraging blackleg Afrikaner labour into the mines. The general antipathy towards the Cornish strikers, and the corresponding Boer sympathy for the blacklegs, was epitomised in Prime Minister Botha's view that: "It is time South Africa began to raise her own skilled workers . . . in this vast, amply rich country with its army of imported artisans, with its perpetual stream of postal orders flowing to Cornwall".[29]

In contrast to the complex ethnic conflict of South Africa, the situation in the copper mines of South Australia was more clearly a transplantation and development of the Cornish experience, and it is in that colony that we can most successfully present the continuing growth of Cornish trade unionism in the period after the general collapse of mining in Cornwall.[30] As early as 1848 an intensely bitter strike interrupted production at the mighty Burra Burra, one hundred miles north of Adelaide, but it was an incoherent protest, hardly the advent of organised labour in the colony's mines, and did not lead to the formation of a miners' association. In 1864, however, almost on the eve of the significant trade union activity in East Cornwall, there was a more telling stoppage at South Australia's Moonta and Wallaroo copper mines, where effective action by the Cornish workers won various concessions from the employers. Ten years later, in 1874 (again coincident with industrial unrest in Cornwall's mines), an even more significant strike at Moonta and Wallaroo created a new era of unionism in which South Australia's Cornish miners organised themselves into a cohesive and effective Miners' Association. Its leaders were Methodist class-leaders and local preachers — Wesleyans, Primitives, and Bible Christians — and the Association formulated a broad policy of programme and action, ranging from tactics to deal with local industrial issues to a wider political view designed to influence the Adelaide Parliament.

In Cornwall, the industrial action of the 1870s came to nothing, as the collapse of tin eroded both the Cornish mining industry and the organisation of its workers, but in South Australia the continuing success of the copper mines facilitated the survival and indeed future development of the Cornish unions. Not only was trade unionism consolidated at Moonta and Wallaroo, but the Cornish influence was exported by migrating South Australian "Cousin Jacks" to the goldfields of Victoria and Western Australia and, most importantly, to the silver-lead mines of Broken Hill which were to emerge as one of the greatest centres of organised labour in the continent. As in Cornwall, the miners at Wallaroo and Moonta protested at the "five week month" and, later, at the abolition of "subsist" (an advance of earnings) for the long-term tribute and tutwork contracts. The practice of tribute and tutwork at Moonta and Wallaroo (and indeed many other Australian metal mines) lends further validity to comparisons with Cornwall. It is significant that tribute and tutwork, with all the implied individualism of the system, did not act as a long-term inhibitor of collective action in the South Australian copper mines. Equally, it is significant that once the South Australian union had reached a matured state of development, one of its principal objectives was the abolition or at least radical restructuring of tribute and tutwork contracting. As W.G. Spence, one of the early commentators on Australian trade unionism, wrote:

> The Cornish miner is generally a man who can do his share of grumbling, and frequently reckons he knows how to run a mine better than the manager, so when Unionism caught on they realised that many injustices might have been remedied years ago had they been organised and pulled together, instead of merely growling as individuals.[31]

During the 1880s there were periodic protests against tribute and tutwork at Moonta and Wallaroo, especially over the "percentage retained" system that had replaced "subsist", where a miner could be paid a weekly estimate of his likely earnings over a contract period but with a percentage of that amount retained by the company in case the full estimated earnings were not in fact realised at the end of the contract. When the percentage retained had reached 25 per cent the men struck successfully for its reduction to 12.5 per cent, and various other concessions were won. A major strike against contracting in 1891 ended in bitter defeat for the miners, however, although the employers did promise "substantial modifications" to the system in response to the return to work. There were, indeed, numerous adjustments during the 1890s, culminating in 1903 in the final abolition of "captains' prices" and their replacement by a "sliding scale" (based upon changes in the price of copper) in which the contractor participated directly in the company's profits. The union itself survived the trauma of 1891, emerging as a central feature of the industrial scene at Moonta and Wallaroo and an integral part of local community life, its myriad influence affecting areas as diverse as religion, education and welfare. It was an influence which lasted until the closure of the copper mines in 1923, and represented the survival and development in South Australia of a Cornish brand of trade unionism whose development in Cornwall had been cut short by the experience of rapid de-industrialisation.[32]

This Cornish experience of trade union activity overseas, of industrial radicalism, was mirrored in a corresponding political radicalism. Indeed, it was natural that political action should arise as part of a broader Labour movement. Todd notes that Cornish Methodist-Liberal radicalism, with its strongly individualistic strain, was tailor-made for the "American Dream": ". . . some openly talked of Cornwall as a 'land of bondage' and only desired to taste the liberty that . . . they presumed existed in America."[33] As Todd remarks, "Politically and socially they were already to some extent Americans even before their ships left Falmouth".[34] In the mining camps of North America this radicalism developed its collectivist hue, first through trade unionism and then through Labour politics as men like Tom Matthews stood for Office. Rowse singles out for attention the singular career of John Spargo, ". . . for some years a leading figure in the American Socialist Party . . . one of the most remarkable Cornishmen of this century . . .".[35] Born in Stithians in 1876, Spargo went to America in 1901. A Methodist by upbringing, Spargo had already earned a reputation as something of a Radical (he was a pro-Boer) and in the United States he found work as a journalist and writer, despite his earlier employment as a granite-cutter. In addition to his political activities, Spargo gained recognition as the first person to write a biography of Karl Marx in English.

Elsewhere overseas, individual Cornishmen made reputations as prominent Radicals. In South Africa, William Hosken emerged as an influential public figure, a champion of the civil rights of the Indian community and chairman of the "European Sympathisers" group which mediated between the Satyagrahis and the Government during Ghandi's 1908 campaign, while Bishop John Colenso was an indefatigable defender of blacks' rights.[36] In Victoria, John Quick from St Ives became a significant Liberal politician and a founding father of Australian Federation, while in South Australia James Penn Boucaut from Mylor was known for his "democratic sympathies".[37] The early Western Australian Labor movement included such figures as the celebrated Captain William Oates from St Just, Captain Samuel Mitchell (with a reputation for ". . . liberal and progressive activity . . ."[38]), and the ". . . liberal and democratic . . ."[39] journalist, F.C.B. Vosper from St Dominick.

More significantly, the political action that grew out of the miners' trade unions often bore a Cornish stamp, and in South Australia in particular the developing Miners' Association spawned a parallel United Labor Party. South Australia's first Labor MP (elected to the Adelaide Parliament in 1891 as the Member for Wallaroo) was a Cornish Methodist trade unionist, one Richard Hooper, and the State's first Labor Premier (in 1910) was John Verran — from Gwennap — who was likewise a Methodist and trade union activist from Moonta and Wallaroo. The United Labor Party itself was a largely South Australian phenomenon, fundamentally Nonconformist in its make-up and outlook and profoundly influenced by the Cornish miners, in many respects distinct from the Irish-Catholic influence in the Labor movement in Victoria and New South Wales. Its reputation was for moderation and pragmatism (". . . eminently practical rather than eloquently visionary . . .",[40] as Michael Davitt put it), and with chapel-oriented overtones. John Verran himself explained the United Labor Party's view of the inevitable and inextricable link between religion (Nonconformist, by definition) and politics:

> Religion is citizenship, and the relationship between religion and politics
> is very close . . . . When we come to justice and righteousness and
> truth . . . religion is not just a question of going to heaven. It is a
> question of living and making the world better for having been in
> it . . .[41].

Within the United Labor Party in South Australia there were obvious echoes of the Liberal Methodist movement in Cornwall, but the ULP claimed a "socialist" identity (despite its moderate image) and had its power base amongst a strong miners' union. These latter features served to distinguish it from the Liberal

Methodist movement at home, but rather than a repudiation of or deviation from the experience in Cornwall, the development of the United Labor Party in South Australia represented the maturing of Cornish radicalism in an environment where (unlike Cornwall) mining had survived and trade unionism had flourished. It represented, indeed, a model for what might have happened in Cornwall, had the Cornish experience of trade unionism not been cut short by rapid de-industrialisation and, consequently, the Cornish political environment "fossilised".

Certainly, in the period before the widespread collapse of mining and the ensuing paralysis of Cornish society, the Liberal Methodist movement in Cornwall had been a dynamic, progressive force. Although there had been little Methodist activity in Cornwall over the Reform Bill or Chartists, the Cornish Methodists proved heavily politicised on educational issues (they were anti-Anglican, and anti-Tory in this respect), on Catholic emancipation (which they opposed), and on slavery (which emerged as a major Cornish concern).[42] The Wesleyans tried to eschew formal party political identification but they did develop after 1832 what Hayden has termed "... a preference for the Liberal Party",[43] with the Primitive Methodists and Bible Christians pursuing the Methodist ideal of the "active citizen" through close association with Liberal politics. Temperence emerged as a unifying theme for the various Methodist factions in Cornwall and became, in turn, a Cornish political issue of some importance, culminating in the ill-starred "Cornwall Sunday Closing Bill" of the 1880s. In the 1880 General Election ten Liberals and only three Tories were returned for Cornish constituencies, with nine of these MPs supporting the temperence movement. As Hayden notes, "... the association of temperence with Liberalism was almost complete"[44] in Cornish politics: "In the last quarter of the century there was a clear link between Methodism and the Liberal Party through temperence. All the Methodist candidates in this period in Cornwall, mainly Liberals, were temperence supporters".[45]

The excitement caused by the industrial unrest of the 1870s had a certain — if temporary — radicalising effect, most notably in the Camborne constituency where in the General Election of 1885 (the first in the United Kingdom in which a majority of the adult male population was entitled to vote) the official Liberal candidate, Pendarves Vivian, was defeated by the Radical Liberal C.A.V. Conybeare (all the other Cornish seats were won by Liberals) who successfully mobilised many of the "new" votes. Pelling notes that the Camborne constituency "... was very Radical ..."[46] in the 1880s, but Rowe adds a telling insight when he remarks that an important contribution towards the Conybeare victory was the encouragement and moral support from Cornish miners in America.[47] Already the emigration of Cornwall's opinion leaders was having an effect, although increasingly that effect would (as described earlier) be felt abroad in the mining camps of North America, Australia and elsewhere, rather than in distant Cornwall. As mining further declined, with attempts at trade unionism proving unsuccessful and with still more of the community's ablest leaders emigrating overseas, the radicalising impulse was dulled. In other circumstances Conybeare's victory might have heralded a generally leftward shift from the Liberal Party, mirroring the experiences of South Wales or

South Australia, but Cornwall in the late 1880s and 1890s was already moving towards paralysis.

Indeed, the events of those decades suggested a shift in Cornwall away from the Liberal Party, not to the left but rather to the right — to the breakaway Liberal Unionists. It is tempting to interpret this shift as evidence of the collapse of Cornish radicalism (attendant upon the collapse in Cornish mining), with the Liberal Unionists becoming rapidly — as Soulsby has argued[48] — the backbone of a merged Conservative and Unionist Party in Cornwall. Closer analysis, however, reveals a different tale. Whilst radicalism of the Conybeare strand did ultimately come to little, the Liberal-Methodist movement was more enduring and the Cornish electorate more anti-Tory than the rise of the Liberal Unionists might suggest. The General Election of 1886 proved disastrous for the Liberals throughout the United Kingdom, with a net loss of some 144 seats, as Chamberlain's Liberal Unionists split from the Liberal camp over his opposition to Irish Home Rule. The Liberal Unionists fared well in Chamberlain's Birmingham, but elsewhere the chief areas of Liberal Unionist success in 1886 were rural Scotland, a sprinkling of English agricultural seats, and Cornwall[49] (which was dubbed "Chamberlain's Duchy"[50]). Significantly, none of these represented safe Conservative seats, for despite their Unionist alliance with the Liberal Unionists, local Conservative Associations in safe Tory constituencies rarely felt the need to nominate Liberal Unionist candidates in order to win seats. In areas of traditionally weak Conservative support, such as Cornwall, however, it was the Liberal Unionists who emerged as the dominant partners and election candidates.[51]

The weakness of real Conservatism in Cornwall in this period was reflected in the great difficulty experienced by the "grass-roots" Primrose League in establishing itself in Cornish constituencies. Elsewhere in Britain in the 1880s, the Primrose League brought a vibrant, popular Conservatism to bear which threatened the Liberals even in their areas of strength. "Only in some rural districts such as the Scottish Highlands and parts of Cornwall and Wales did the political culture prove hopelessly hostile to the league's form of Conservatism",[52] argues Pugh, and in Cornwall there were but three "Habitations" (league branches) of any strength — Bodmin (largely due to the energies of the Earl of Mount Edgcumbe), Truro (associated, perhaps, with Anglican revival), and traditionally Tory Penryn where the leader or "Ruling Councillor" in 1887 was a woman: ". . . we may surmise that male Conservatives, regarding the county as hopelessly radical, gladly gave the ladies full scope".[53] Despite an appeal to Cornish sentiment in the judicious selection of patriotic names for its "Habitations" ("Bevil Granville" at Stratton, "King Arthur's Round Table" at Camelford, "Tre, Pol and Pen" at Sheviock, and the archaic forms "Liskerret" and "Essa" for Liskeard and Saltash[54]), the Primrose League and with it the Conservative Party experienced severe difficulties in Cornwall, ". . . arising from the strength of Nonconformity, the prevalence of scattered, pastoral farms rather than nuclear villages, and the tendency towards small farms and comparatively few big landowners".[55] Even in neighbouring Devon and Somerset the League met with greater success, while the central southern England region — running from Dorset to Berkshire and Gloucestershire to

151

Hampshire — was, with its extensive aristocratic landownership and rapidly expanding residential areas, ". . . a pillar of Primrose League and Conservative strength".[56]

In Cornwall, then, the emergent Liberal Unionists were by no means a revamped or surrogate local Conservative Party but quite genuinely represented Liberalism with a Unionist face. As happened in certain other areas, the desertion en-bloc from Liberals to Liberal Unionists in Cornwall left the Liberal Party depleted and in some parts virtually leaderless.[57] Three seats fell to the Liberal Unionists in 1886, leaving the other three Cornish constituencies in the hands of the Liberals. Thereafter, the Liberal Unionists remained a significant force in Cornish politics until the 1906 "Liberal Landslide" and, indeed, resurfaced in 1910 as a factor to be reckoned with.[58] However, at times the Liberal Unionists in Cornwall were virtually indistinguishable from the Liberals themselves, save for their opposition to Irish Home Rule, as in St Ives constituency where the Liberal Unionist MP, T.R. Bolitho, who was elected unopposed in 1892 and again in 1895, was a well known Radical. Ironically, his programme included Radical Liberal demands such as shorter Parliaments, one man one vote, and the extreme temperence "Direct Veto". A further irony is that the Liberal who replaced him in 1906 was in fact also hostile to Home Rule, demonstrating the fluidity of party alignment in Cornwall and the ideological common ground of both Liberals and Liberal Unionists in Cornish politics.[59]

Elsewhere in Cornwall there was a fine balance between Liberals and Liberal Unionists in the period 1886-1906. Mid-Cornwall, the china clay country, was the strongest Liberal division (as it is today) but Truro ". . . was on balance more Unionist . . .",[60] with the tiny borough of Penryn and Falmouth uncertain and Bodmin a marginal seat. The thoroughly Nonconformist constituency of Launceston was more clearly Liberal. In all these areas, as Pelling notes, the attraction of the Liberal Unionists was not their pact with the Conservatives (far from it) but rather the fact that Cornish Liberal Unionists were opposed to Irish Home Rule while nonetheless remaining genuinely Liberal on domestic and Cornish issues. As Pelling himself concluded, ". . . representatives of the Unionist cause had fought as Liberal Unionists rather than as Conservatives; their success indicated the persistence of a body of opinion which, while radical on domestic questions, was conservative on Imperial matters."[61] The general Cornish concern on Imperial policy reflected the Cornish stake in the Empire in terms of the emigrant communities, but the specific Cornish hostility to Irish Home Rule is at first glance a surprise. Notwithstanding the anti-Irish outburst of the second "Camborne Riots" in 1882,[62] there were no sizeable Irish communities in Cornwall and no deep-seated evidence of anti-Irish sentiment. However, just as the Methodists had earlier opposed Catholic emancipation, so they feared the rising star of Popery in a Home Rule Ireland. They feared, especially, for the future of their fellow Nonconformists in a "Rome Rule" Ireland, and the geographic proximity of Cornwall made Irish Home Rule a strategic issue. Moreover, Cornish fishermen feared that a self-governing Ireland would exclude them from Irish waters — they were therefore persuaded to vote Liberal

Unionist, despite the fact that "The fishermen . . . were regarded as being strongly Radical".[63]

The rise of the Liberal Unionists in Cornwall, therefore, reflected not the demise of the Liberal Methodist movement but actually underscored the political importance of Cornish Nonconformity and the significance of Cornish issues. Although Imperial policy was hardly a domestic issue, Cornish perceptions of it were nonetheless distinctive and highly "local". The apparent flux of the period 1886 to 1906 in reality disguised a consistency in Cornish politics, with its continuing Liberal Methodist momentum and relative Conservative weakness. Cornish politics remained radical to a point, but strictly within the Liberal/Liberal Unionist framework. Significantly, where the radical impulse was renewed, it was — as in the days of Conybeare and his American supporters — a result of outside influences. Specifically, in the General Election of 1900 (when Cornwall returned three Liberal Unionists and three Liberals), the Camborne constituency once again recorded a swing to the left. In 1895 Conybeare had lost his seat, for the reasons summarised by Pelling:

> . . . the acute depression in the tin and copper industries in the middle 1890s demoralised the miners. Many of them lost the vote owing to dependence on poor relief; others emigrated; and still more were inclined to listen to the promises of a wealthy tin-merchant, A. Strauss, who, standing as a Liberal Unionist, advocated various nostrums including bimetallism, which would 'tend to raise the price of tin'. In an election which turned entirely on these local problems, Strauss secured the victory in 1895.[64]

However, Strauss' novel panaceas failed to deliver, and in the continuing crisis of the mining industry his local support was eroded rapidly. More particularly, the Boer War — a political issue throughout Britain, but with a peculiar significance and immediacy within Cornwall — emerged as a point of conflict in Camborne. Although it was alleged that Cornish miners had received rough treatment at the hands of the Boers in the Transvaal,[65] with many Cornish Liberal Unionists arguing for a vigorous Imperial policy in South Africa, there were also those who feared that war would dry up the flow of financial support to Cornwall. There was therefore a vocal anti-war (inevitably dubbed "pro-Boer") faction in Cornwall, and in the Election of 1900 its spokesman, W.S. Caine, defeated Strauss. As Dawe has noted, "On the political front Cornwall voted against the national tide when Liberal Unionist lost to the Liberal Radical, who was a pro-Boer".[66] Caine, like Conybeare before him, derived support from emigrant Cornishmen, claiming that ". . . out of 700 Cornish miners home from South Africa, at least 650 had voted for him".[67] Caine was not alone in his pro-Boer sympathies, others including Leonard Courtney — the MP for Bodmin (ironically a Liberal Unionist) — and J. Passmore Edwards (formerly Liberal MP for Salisbury), along with the Cornish-born Emily Hobhouse who drew British attention to conditions in the concentration camps.[68]

153

In the early 1900s Liberal Unionist support in Cornwall was further eroded as a result of Nonconformist hostility to the Conservatives' Education Bill, with the Liberal *West Briton* noting the return of some Liberal Unionists to the Liberal fold and expressing pleasure that ". . . Unionist Nonconformists have not sunk all their Nonconformity in their Unionism".[69] South Africa remained a principal political issue in Cornwall, however, perpetuated by the "Chinese Slavery" scare. Some 60,000 Chinese workers were to be brought in to South Africa in the four years after February 1904, in an effort to restore the production of the mines to pre-war levels, but they had a generally depressing effect on wages and conditions and were seen by many as unacceptable competitors for mining jobs. At first there was an ambivalent reaction in Cornwall, for while Cornish miners shared in the general hostility to the Chinese, the Cornish economy relied very much upon the restoration and success of South African mining. The *Mining Journal* noted that,

> . . . contrary to what might generally have been expected in a county which, taken by and wide, is essentially Liberal not to say Radical, as regards its political opinions, the proposition to employ Chinese labour in the Transvaal, instead of being opposed, is receiving active support, not only from the local Press, but from mining men generally.[70]

The actual arrival of the Chinese in South Africa galvanised Cornish opinion however, the fear that Chinese coolies would take Cornish jobs (and therefore Cornish wages destined otherwise for Cornwall) proving irresistable. This hostility was given a Christian and Radical tinge through the argument that the Chinese were to all intents and purposes being forced into "slavery", the victims of an exploitation which coerced them through unfair contracts to work for wages far below the economic level that the work demanded. The Liberal Party at UK level adopted opposition to "Chinese Slavery" as part of its political programme in the 1906 General Election campaign, and in Cornwall the issue was seen as more significant than many other important questions of the day, such as Tariff Reform. The *Cornubian* thundered: "Will you vote for a Government that has ruined South Africa for the Cornish miner? Will you vote for Chinese labour? If it be not a kind of slavery, what is it?"[71] In the ensuing "Liberal Landslide" election the Liberal Unionists (seen as supporters of the Government, and therefore of "slavery" — the curse which Cornish Methodists had fought to eradicate in the previous century) were trounced in Cornwall, each Cornish seat returning a Liberal member.[72] The re-assertion of the Liberal Methodist link proved crucial in achieving this result, the *West Briton* claiming in April 1906 that in the St Austell district " . . . nearly every Nonconformist chapel in this constituency was used as a Liberal committee room during the last election".[73] Similarly, the *Western Morning News* noted that at Launceston "The chapel, on the quiet roadside or in the secluded valley, is the governing factor in this division. It has been said that in these little Bethels, is preached the Radical shibboleth from January to December".[74] In the Lands End peninsula in 1906, Hudson found that "Fishermen and miners were almost to a man on the Liberal side, led by their ministers, who were eagerly looking to have their revenge on the Church . . .".[75]

The victorious Liberal Goverment did indeed put a stop to "Chinese Slavery", and in the General Election of January 1910 — when the Unionists regained many of the rural English seats that they had lost in 1906 — Cornwall remained solidly Liberal, although in the further Election in the December marginal Bodmin did fall to the Liberal Unionists.[76] The entire episode from 1885 until 1910 had demonstrated the underlying tenacity of the Liberal Methodist equation in Cornwall, the intervention of the Liberal Unionists demonstrating, paradoxically, the powerful political strength of Cornish Nonconformity. Liberal Unionists, indeed, were in many respects a different breed from their Unionist contemporaries across the Tamar, Radical on domestic issues and motivated by specifically Cornish considerations. The Liberal Party itself remained at root the party of Cornwall, although increasingly its radicalising impulse came from Cornish emigrants overseas — the shock when Pendarves Vivian lost Camborne in 1885, and the later influence of South African considerations. The shift of the radical influence abroad was, of course, consistent with the broader Cornish experience in this period, reflecting the success of Cornish trade unionism and radical politics overseas.

By 1910, then, the position of Cornwall as part of the "Liberal heartland" had been tested and confirmed, its Methodist input as crucial as ever, but with a local and distinctive style of politics — in which Cornish issues could assume great importance — also apparent. At the same time, however, the potential for further radicalisation of the Cornish electorate at home had diminished with the decline of mining, the failure of trade unionism, and continuing emigration. Cornwall might remain Liberal, but its propensity to embrace the new cause of Labour was inevitably limited.

By 1910 a broader picture in the United Kingdom as a whole was apparent in which, as Blake has said, ". . . the weakness of the Conservative party in northern England and the 'Celtic fringe' becomes clear enough".[77] The "Tory heartland" was central, southern and south-eastern England, with the Liberals (along with the infant Labour Party's contribution) dominant in the North and in Scotland, Wales, and Cornwall. On the eve of the First World War, therefore, British voting behaviour reflected the fundamental political and economic division between "centre" and "peripheries" — a prelude, indeed, to the "North-South" debate of the 1980s. Although Labour featured, albeit marginally, in this division, it was essentially a split between Liberal and Conservative.

After 1910 the basic division remained, although in the period to the Second World War the Liberals were progressively replaced by Labour as the principal radical alternatives to the Conservatives. Christopher Cook has termed this era "The Age of Alignment" in which British politics were transformed into a Labour versus Conservative contest.[78] Cook argues that between the General Elections of 1922 and October 1924 the party system changed irrevocably — the fatal point of Liberal downfall was reached in 1924, and by 1929 the Liberals had slipped too far back to be an effective force, their role by now usurped by Labour. Koss adds a further dimension to this approach by asserting that after 1918 Nonconformists in Britain became markedly less politicised: they faced declining membership of their Churches and disillusion with the Liberals, in the process losing their cohesion and their bonds with the Liberal Party. Koss concludes that by 1935 ". . . Radical Nonconformity, once a force to be reckoned with in national life, was not dormant but dead",[79] replaced by the secular socialism of Labour.

However, Koss admits that the Liberals were able to retain ". . . considerable loyalty among Nonconformists of particular persuasions in isolated areas . . .",[80] one of which was Cornwall. Cornwall, indeed, did not experience to the same degree as elsewhere the diluting of Nonconformist strength and remained, as Kinnear has shown, overtly Nonconformist in character when contrasted against comparable regions of England.[81] Even Devon was noticeably less Nonconformist than Cornwall, the only directly similar areas being parts of Durham and Northumberland. Politically, this was reflected in continuing support for the Liberal Party so that in Cornwall, as Smart has argued, " . . . the age of alignment was the age of consolidation".[82] Instead of participating in the new alignment of Labour versus Conservative, Cornish politics were consolidated into a Liberal against Conservative contest.

The ambivalence of the Liberal Unionist era having passed, the Cornish party system weathered the continuing internal splits within the Liberal Party, producing by the 1930s a clear political pattern of Liberal-Tory conflict. The fortunes of the Labour and Conservative Parties in Cornwall contributed to this state of affairs but most significant was the survival of Liberalism. This was linked to the surviving strength of Nonconformity, and both Liberalism and Nonconformity owed their perpetuation in Cornwall to the paralysis that had afflicted Cornish society and economy. In the absence of conditions in which a secular Labour movement might have arisen, the Liberal Methodist movement was "fossilised" as the only viable radical alternative to the Conservatives and, indeed, as the "party of Cornwall". This "fossilisation" was, in turn, a function of that rapid de-industrialisation that had precluded the development of a Labour movement and produced a late Labour electoral presence, a feature of the condition of "Second Peripheralism". It also served to mark the Cornish experience apart from that that obtained elsewhere, further emphasising and accentuating the distinctive nature of Cornish politics.

In the aftermath of the Great War, British politics were afflicted by much faction-fighting, reflected in Cornwall in the 1922 General Election in a bewildering result which saw the return to Parliament of two "Lloyd George Liberals", one "Asquith Liberal", and two Conservatives. In 1923 the Liberals recovered remarkably, capturing all five Cornish seats. But in the 1924 General election — which saw ". . . the virtual elimination of the Liberals"[83] at Parliamentary level, leaving them with only a handful of seats in rural Wales and northern Scotland — they held only Camborne (where their candidate stood as a "constitutionalist"), the rest of Cornwall falling to the Tories. Five years later, in 1929, there was a very limited Liberal revival in English rural areas and in parts of Scotland and Wales, but by then the Labour Party was not only consolidating its earlier successes but also making striking advances elsewhere: the "Age of Alignment" had arrived.

156

In Cornwall, however, the Liberal recovery was complete, the Party winning all five Cornish seats, an experience presenting Cornwall as a curious Liberal bastion — an anachronism, almost — in a wider political world now dominated by Labour-Conservative conflict.[84] In the remaining elections of the pre-war era — 1931 and 1935 — the Liberals' position in Britain as a whole became even more parlous, leaving them with merely a tiny collection of seats in the remnants of their traditional heartlands. Cornwall shared in the general swing to the Conservatives, in 1931 producing two Liberals, one National Liberal, and two Conservatives, and in 1935 returning one "Lloyd George Liberal", one National Liberal, and three Conservatives.[85] Labour, however, remained of only marginal importance in Cornwall, despite the events elsewhere.

The towering figure of Cornish Liberalism in this period was Isaac Foot. Although born in Plymouth, Foot identified with Cornwall and Cornish politics, living first at St Cleer and then at Callington, and as a Methodist preaching in many of the little chapels of East Cornwall. His granddaughter and biographer, Sarah Foot, declares that "He was a radical, uncompromising Liberal, a staunch Methodist of illuminating faith . . ."[86] and that "Isaac Foot's Liberalism and Methodism were closely linked".[87] He represented Bodmin for much of the period, monopolising the radical vote (Labour did not manage to save its deposit in Bodmin until 1945) and perpetuating the issues of classical Cornish Liberalism — such as Temperence — until the eve of the Second World War. As a Parliamentarian he won a reputation as an orator of great skill, and briefly in the 1930s he was Parliamentary Secretary for Mines in the National Goverment. He resigned, however, over his commitment to Free Trade, another of the great Liberal themes. To Koss, who has stressed the demise of Radical Nonconformity in the inter-war period, Isaac Foot — with his anti-drink, anti-betting, evangelical stance — appears an anachronistic enigma: ". . . surely the last of the great Nonconformist parliamentary careers".[88] In Cornwall, however, Foot was anything but that. He was revered as "Our Isaac" and "Sir Isaac", and it is said that at Looe even the fishermen's luggers were painted in Liberal colours in his honour.[89] Out of step with the broad thrust of British politics but closely attuned to the concerns of Cornwall, Isaac Foot personified the "fossilisation" of Cornish politics in this period of paralysis.

Against such vehement championship of traditional Cornish Liberalism it was especially difficult for Labour to make headway in Cornish constituencies in their attempt to pierce the Cornish paralysis. A.L. Rowse considers that "The prime task for Labour in Cornwall was to bring home the futility of going on being Liberal".[90] Rowse, in an assessment of the Cornish political climate in the 1920s, complains of ". . . backward Cornwall, smothered as it was in Nonconformist Liberal humbug . . .",[91] with Cornish Liberalism ". . . a fossilised survival: the political expression of Nonconformity".[92] In the St Austell area in particular, "The little chapels out in the china-clay district were virtually Liberal recruiting stations in my time".[93] Rowse, however, as a Labour candidate, carefully nurtured the Falmouth-Penryn constituency (preparing the ground for the Labour victory in Falmouth-Camborne in 1945), in Labour's debacle of 1931 keeping Labour's share of the vote steady and in 1935 putting Labour into second place with a very respectable 13,000 votes. The *Cornish Labour News* newspaper attempted to popularise Labour's image locally, with Jack Donovan — a local trade unionist — mobilising the Falmouth dockyard vote.[94]

Smart notes, too, that by the start of the 1930s Labour — on the evidence of the statistics — seemed to be making at least some headway. In the 1929 General Election, Labour obtained 17 per cent of the vote in St Ives (first contested by Labour in 1918, the very first Labour challenge in Cornwall), 25 per cent in Camborne, and 29 per cent in Falmouth-Penryn. As Smart comments, the ". . . Liberal victors in the Cornish seats must have reflected on how close Labour came to letting in the Conservatives".[95] However, as Smart has also argued, it is statistically difficult to make comparisons between the results of one election and another (not least because of the continually altering size of the electorate) and that, in the case of Cornwall, ". . . given the increase in the size of the electorate by 1929, Labour's regional performance at the end of the decade in vote share terms is no better than at the beginning".[96]

But if Labour was unable to make significant headway in Cornwall, the Conservatives in the inter-war period were able to make an impression upon Cornish politics in a way that had not been possible before. Whilst the position of the Liberals was not challenged seriously in terms of their status as the radical party of Cornwall, their overwhelming superiority and popularity was progressively eroded. Notwithstanding the Liberal triumphs of 1923 and 1929, the Liberal-Conservative conflict — as it developed in Cornwall — did become more finely balanced. Earlier in the century the contest had been between Liberals and Liberal Unionists, in some respects an academic distinction within Cornwall, but thereafter the Conservatives emerged as a genuinely alternative opposition. To some extent this was facilitated by an understanding with the National Liberal faction, epitomised (as Lee has noted) in St Ives constituency where ". . . the period since 1918 has seen an unusual relationship between Liberals and Conservatives. In 1931 and 1935 the National Liberal candidate was returned unopposed, and the National Liberal/Conservatives . . . candidates have held the seat ever since".[97] This understanding between the National Liberals and Conservatives reflected a common desire to ensure that a Labour candidate was not elected. This, in turn, reflected the tone of Liberal anti-Labour invective in Cornwall, where Liberal exhortations to the electorate not to vote "socialist" but to ensure instead an "anti-socialist" result played into the hands of the Conservatives. Taking up this theme, echoing and indeed absorbing the Liberal cry, ". . . the Conservatives in the south west succeeded in making the rhetoric of anti-socialism their own . . .".[98]

To this was added the rehabilitation of Conservatism in the United Kingdom as a whole under Baldwin. In 1906 the Conservatives had lost much of the middle ground of British politics and, as Blake has observed, "From 1906 to 1914 they had seemed too often to be the party of rich men reluctant to pay taxes, of Englishmen determined to retain control over the 'Celtic fringe' . . . The Conservatives seemed to lack compassion".[99] Under Baldwin, however, the Conservatives seemed to acquire a new awareness of social problems, of poverty

158

and unemployment, and the Conservatives — in offering stable government — appeared a reasonable alternative to the "inept" Labour Party and "strife-torn" Liberals.[100] They offered, too, a security against the "interfering" and "centralist" policies of Labour, an important consideration in independent and individualistic Cornwall where Labour aspirations were viewed with suspicion. To some extent, therefore, the progress of the Conservatives in Cornwall was a function of hostility towards the Labour Party and its policies, nonetheless contributing to the situation where Cornish politics was essentially a clash between Liberals and Conservatives. Labour had been kept out of Cornish politics, but at the expense of increasing Tory importance.

Of course, in the atmosphere of paralysis that characterised Cornish society in this period one would expect to find neither the rise of Labour nor the dynamic advocacy of Liberalism. Instead, the already "fossilising" Liberal Methodist movement was carried along by its own momentum but without radicalising injections for the future (despite the stature of Isaac Foot), the imperative of "fossilisation" being essentially conservative. Against a background of Labour failure to infiltrate Cornish politics, and of the cataclysmic failure of the Liberals in Britain as a whole, the relative success of the Conservatives in Cornwall is not at all a surprise.

However, it remains the case that the essential conflict in Cornish politics in the 1920s and 1930s was Liberal versus Conservative, a state of affairs which marked the Cornish political scene as "different" from that which obtained elsewhere but which had also the effect of marginalising Cornwall's impact upon Britain as a whole. Divorced from the increasingly dominant Labour-Conservative conflict that had emerged elsewhere, Cornwall was progressively unable to influence or participate in the wider political environment. As a mere "county" Cornwall had, in the era of duality between "low" provincial politics and "high" politics at the centre, only a minor voice in any case, but this minority was accentuated by the apparent irrelevance of Cornish politics. For those who sought the "Revival" of the Cornish language and Celtic identity, this political impotence might have been irksome, but Tyr ha Tavas was only marginally politicised and the wider "Revivalist" movement was if anything opposed to political nationalism. Certainly, Henry Jenner had written that,

> . . . every Cornishman knows well enough, proud as he may be of belonging to the British Empire, that he is no more an Englishman than a Caithness man is, that he has as much right to a separate local patriotism to his little motherland . . . as has a Scotsman, an Irishman, a Welshman, or even a Colonial; and that he is as much a Celt and as little of an Anglo-Saxon as any Gael, Cymro, Manxman or Breton.[101]

But, like the Liberal Unionists, Jenner was opposed to Irish Home Rule and the wider political expression of Celtic nationalism, a report on his address to the Truro Rotary Club in 1924 noting that:

After discussing what nationality amounts to, he said that Cornwall, by reason of its history, its position, and its individuality, had every bit as much right to call itself a nation as had Scotland, Wales, and England. In saying that he was not advocating Cornish independence, or even "Cornish Home Rule", nor did he wish to translate the Irish words Sinn Fein into Cornish — their version of them was "One and All", a better motto . . .[102].

In practice the day to day activities of the "Revivalists" had little bearing upon the conduct of politics in Cornwall. Whilst Cornish politics had, for the reasons discussed above, become increasingly distinct from those of England, there had been no attempt by the "Revivalists" to exploit that distinction. "Distinctiveness" was not yet a cue for political action but remained merely a feature of Cornwall's political "fossilisation", of the paralysis that characterised the matured manifestation of "Second Peripheralism".

Notes and References

1. Jim Bulpitt, *Territory and Power in the United Kingdom*, Manchester University Press, Manchester, 1983.
2. In contrast to Cornwall, there was a South Australian State Government able and willing to react to industrial decline through its ability to manipulate taxation, mobilise resources, attract investment and so on, so that "South Australia became the first of the Australian States, with the possible exception of Victoria, consciously to undertake the transformation of its economic structure by shifting its base from primary to secondary industry". (Neal Blewett and Dean Jaensh, *Playford to Dunstan: The Politics of Transition*, Cheshire, Melbourne, 1971, p2.)
3. A.H. Dodd, *A Short History of Wales*, Batsford, London, 1979, pp156-159, p164.
4. A.K. Hamilton Jenkin, *The Cornish Miner*, 1927, republished David & Charles, Newton Abbot, 1972; D.B. Barton, *Essays in Cornish Mining History*, Vol 1, Bradford Barton, Truro, 1968, especially pp46-47.
5. Gillian Burke, "The Cornish Miner and the Cornish Mining Industry, 1870–1921", unpublished PhD thesis, University of London, 1981; Bernard Deacon, "Attempts at Unionism by Cornish Metal Miners in 1866", in *Cornish Studies* 10, 1982; Bernard Deacon, "Heroic Individualists? The Cornish Miners and the Five-Week Month 1872-74", in *Cornish Studies* 14, 1986.
6. Peter Hayden, "Culture, Creed and Conflict: Methodism and Politics in Cornwall, c1832–1971", unpublished PhD thesis, University of Liverpool, 1983.
7. Eric Hobsbawm, *Labouring Men*, Weidenfeld & Nicolson, London, 1964, p9.
8. Deacon, 1982, op.cit.
9. Deacon, 1986, op. cit.
10. J.G. Rule, "The Labouring Miner in Cornwall c1740-1870", unpublished PhD thesis, University of Warwick, 1971, p393.
11. D.B. Barton, *A History of Tin Mining and Smelting in Cornwall*, Bradford Barton, Truro, 1967, republished Cornwall Books, Exeter, 1989, p148.

12. Ibid., pp148-149; Rule, op. cit., pp380-383; John Rowe, *Cornwall in the Age of the Industrial Revolution*, Liverpool University Press, Liverpool, 1953, p143.
13. Deacon, 1982, op. cit.
14. For example, see Philip Payton (ed.) and Cyril Noall, *Cornish Mine Disasters*, Dyllansow Truran, Redruth, 1989, p16.
15. Deacon, 1986; op. cit.
16. Barton, 1967/1989, op. cit., p196 and p199.
17. Burke, op. cit., p383.
18. Barton, 1967/1989, op. cit., pp259-60.
19. Ibid., p281; J.A. Buckley, *A History of South Crofty Mine*, Dyllansow Truran, Redruth, n.d. c1982, pp165-168; J.A. Buckley, *A Miner's Tale: The Story of Howard Mankee*, Penhellick Publications, Redruth, 1988, pp49-53.
20. Burke, op. cit., pp390-391.
21. Devon and Cornwall Development Bureau, *Engineering in Devon and Cornwall*, DCDB/Cambridge Consultants, Plymouth, 1988, p9.
22. Jack Ravensdale, "The China Clay Labourers' Union", *Historical Studies* 1, 1968; Jack Ravensdale, "The 1913 Clay Strike and the Workers' Union", in *Exeter Papers in Economic History No 6*, University of Exeter, Exeter, 1972, pp53-68; R.M. Barton, *A History of the Cornish China-Clay Industry*, Bradford Barton, Truro, 1966, pp130-131 and pp153-162.
23. *Royal Cornwall Gazette*, 22 January 1877.
24. A.L. Rowse, *The Cornish in America*, Macmillan, London, 1969, pp247-248, republished, Dyllansow Truran, Redruth, 1991.
25. Richard E. Lingenfelter, *The Hardrock Miners*, University of California Press, Berkeley, 1974, p6.
26. Rowse, op. cit., p149.
27. Ibid., p152.
28. Richard Dawe, "The Role and Influence of the Cornish in South Africa 1886–1925", unpublished MA thesis, Middlesex Polytechnic, 1986, p54, p64, pp75-76.
29. Ibid., p76.
30. Philip Payton, "The Cornish in South Australia: Their Influence and Experience from Immigration to Assimilation, 1836–1936", unpublished PhD thesis, University of Adelaide, 1978, especially Chapter 8; Philip Payton, *The Cornish Miner in Australia: Cousin Jack Down Under*, Dyllansow Truran, Redruth, 1984.
31. W.G. Spence, *Australia's Awakening: Thirty Years in the Life of an Australian Agitator*, Workers' Trustees, Sydney, 1909, p27.
32. Payton, 1978, op. cit.; Payton, 1984, op. cit.
33. A.C. Todd, *The Cornish Miner in America*, Bradford Barton, Truro, 1967, p20.
34. Ibid.
35. Rowse, op. cit., p411.
36. Dawe, op. cit., p95; A.L. Rowse, *The Controversial Colensos*, Dyllansow Truran, Redruth, 1989.
37. A contemporary description, cited in Payton, 1984, op. cit., p92.
38. As above, ibid., p186.
39. As above, ibid., p187.
40. Michael Davitt, *Life and Progress in Australasia*, Methuen, London, 1898, p53.
41. *People's Weekly* (Moonta, South Australia), 18 August 1917.
42. Hayden, op. cit.
43. Ibid., p125.

44. Ibid., p161.
45. Ibid., p238.
46. Henry Pelling, *Social Geography of British Elections 1885–1910*, Macmillan, London, 1962, p165.
47. John Rowe, *The Hard-Rock Men: Cornish Immigrants and the North American Mining Frontier*, Liverpool University Press, Liverpool, 1974, p292.
48. Ian Soulsby, *A History of Cornwall*, Phillimore, Chichester, 1986, p108.
49. Michael Kinnear, *The British Voter: An Atlas and Survey*, Batsford, London, 1981, pp18-19.
50. Soulsby, op. cit., p108.
51. Kinnear, op. cit., p98.
52. M. Pugh, *The Tories and the People 1880–1935*, Blackwell, Oxford, 1985, p136.
53. Ibid., p97.
54. Ibid., p216.
55. Ibid., p97.
56. Ibid., p99.
57. Kinnear, op. cit., p18.
58. Ibid., pp18-19, 23, 24, 26, 28, 33.
59. Pelling, op. cit., p163.
60. Ibid., p165.
61. Ibid., p173.
62. *West Briton*, 4 May 1882; Hamilton Jenkin, op. cit., p342.
63. Pelling, op. cit., p164.
64. Ibid., p165.
65. Payton, 1984, op. cit., p198.
66. Dawe, op. cit., p48.
67. *Cornish Post*, 27 September 1900.
68. Richard Dawe, "The Effect Chinese Labour Had on the Cornish Miner in South Africa", unpublished paper, Middlesex Polytechnic, 1984, pp15-16.
69. *West Briton*, 12 February 1903. See also Hayden, op. cit., pp261-265.
70. *Mining Journal*, 2 April 1904.
71. *Cornubian*, 20 January 1906.
72. Kinnear, op. cit., p28.
73. *West Briton*, 23 April 1906.
74. *Western Morning News*, 19 January 1906.
75. W.H. Hudson, *The Land's End: A Naturalist's Impression in West Cornwall*, 1908, republished Wildwood House, London, 1981, p102.
76. Kinnear, op. cit., pp33 and 35.
77. Robert Blake, *The Conservative Party From Peel to Churchill*, Eyre and Spottiswoode, London, 1970, p200.
78. Christopher Cook, *The Age of Alignment: Electoral Politics in Britain 1922–29*, Macmillan, London, 1975.
79. Stephen Koss, *Nonconformity in Modern British Politics*, Batsford, London, 1975, p11.
80. Ibid., pp8-9.
81. Kinnear, op. cit., p127.
82. N. Smart, "The Age of Consolidation: South West Electoral Change in the Age of Alignment", unpublished paper, Plymouth Polytechnic, 1988, p28.
83. Kinnear, op. cit., p47.

84. Ibid., p48.
85. Ibid., pp50-52.
86. Sarah Foot, *Isaac Foot: My Grandfather*, Bossiney Books, Bodmin, 1980, p6.
87. Ibid., p41.
88. Koss, op. cit., p161.
89. Foot, op. cit., p42.
90. A.L. Rowse, *A Man of the Thirties*, Weidenfeld & Nicolson, London, 1979, p91.
91. Ibid., p55.
92. Ibid.
93. Ibid., p56.
94. Ibid., p7 and pp89-90.
95. Smart, op. cit., p7.
96. Ibid., p15.
97. Adrian Lee, "How Cornwall Votes", unpublished paper, Plymouth Polytechnic, 1977, p15.
98. Smart, op cit., p22.
99. Blake, op. cit., p244.
100. Ibid., p245.
101. Henry Jenner, *A Handbook of the Cornish Language*, David Nutt, London, 1904, ppxi-xii.
102. *People's Weekly*, 23 August 1924.

Part Four

Third Peripheralism: The Dynamics of Post-war Change

"The visitors have come to Cornwall. 'Visitors', 'foreigners' we're called by the Cornish. We litter the cliffs with our houses. We litter the cliffs with our shacks. When I was a boy all this was open fields".

John Betjeman, from "One Man's County", in *Betjeman's Cornwall,* John Murray, London, 1984, p20.

". . . Cornwall's present inhabitants, native-born and newcomers alike, might still manage a wry smile of satisfaction at the opinion of a Plymouth correspondent to the *Western Morning News* that 'we may have built the Tamar Bridge between us but there is still something pretty odd at the western end of it'!".

Ian Soulsby, A History of Cornwall, Phillimore, Chichester, 1986, p114.

"Smaller minorities also have equally proud visions of themselves as irreducibly Welsh, Irish, Manx or Cornish. These identities are distinctly national in ways which proud people from Yorkshire, much less proud people from Berkshire, will never know. Any new constitutional settlement which ignores these factors will be built on uneven ground."

Guardian (editorial) 8 May 1990

CHAPTER EIGHT

Beyond The Golden Circle

By the eve of the Second World War the full impact of "Second Peripheralism" in its matured condition had been felt in Cornwall. A lengthy period of all-embracing "paralysis" — which had crucially affected the social, economic and political profiles of Cornwall — had grown out of the industrial decline of the latter part of the nineteenth century, this de-industrialisation in itself the inevitable consequence of the early features of "Second Peripheralism" which had ensured that Cornwall's industrial experience was imperfect, over-specialised and incomplete. Athough the advent of "Second Peripheralism" had put paid to many of the remnants of Celtic-Catholic Cornwall (including the Cornish language) and its "Older Peripheralism" of territorial and cultural isolation, a Cornish sense of identity had survived, though based now upon industrial prowess and the distinctive qualities of Cornish industrialisation. The demise of that prowess had led initially to an enhancement of identity, with the "Great Migration" seen as the pinnacle of Cornish accomplishment, but this could hardly be sustained in an era of de-industrialisation, unemployment and de-population and ushered in, therefore, a new period (the period of "paralysis") in which Cornish pride gave way to Cornish fatalism and indifference. Paradoxically, however, despite this superficially apparent threat to and potential weakening of the Cornish identity, Cornwall remained stubbornly "different". This was a difference born not from choice but from the very peripheral characteristics that affected Cornwall. Socially and economically, as the Exeter Survey was to show, Cornwall remained strikingly different not only from England but even from neighbouring Devon, while Cornish politics singularly failed to participate in the new "alignment" of Conservative versus Labour.

The dynamics of peripherality were the root cause of this paradox, of course, for while they ensured that the nature of Cornish peripherality changed dramatically over time, they also determined a continuing and inevitable "difference" between peripheral Cornwall and the English "core" or "centre". Given the unchanging geographical construction of the British Isles and of the "monocephalic", "territorial space" nature of the centralised British State, Cornwall remained remote from the centres of political and economic power. Indeed, with the decline of the mechanisms of "accommodation" and the new dominance of the City in an internationalised mining market, that "remoteness" had in one sense actually increased as a result of the experience of "Second Peripheralism". In the same way, there remained "constants of peripherality" which served to perpetuate Cornwall's "difference. Geographical constraints and the physical (and psychological) distances from the "centre" were obvious "constants", but more subtly there remained elements of "constancy" inherited not only from the early phases of "Second Peripheralism" but even from the era of "Older Peripheralism". As shown already, Cornwall remained a land of scattered settlements, of small-holdings and of small farmers immune from the influence of squire or Church, Nonconformist in religious leanings and Liberal in politics. Again, the experience of industrialisation had served to enhance these characteristics, with the rise of Methodism in Cornwall and the attendent emergence of Liberal popular politics. Despite the trauma of de-industrialisation, these characteristics survived as markers of Cornish "difference" and of a sustained Cornish individualism and independence.

The Second World War, however, did bring some changes to Cornwall, disturbing for a time the "paralysis" into which Cornish society had sunk, as the nature of the exertion of political and economic power within the State altered in response to wartime conditions. There was, for example, some immigration, with an inflow of evacuees, workers for key occupations, and — especially towards the end of the war and in its immediate aftermath — European refugees, some of whom were drawn to Cornwall (eg miners) as a result of their specialist skills. In this way, groups of Polish and Italian immigrants, particularly, established themselves in Cornwall. Statistically, however, such immigration was negligible and did not represent a significant counter-flow to the underlying trend of continuing emigration and relative depopulation. Economically, the war provided a boost to manufacturing in Cornwall, especially in the Truro district where there were noticeable increases in shipbuilding, engineering, metalwork, woodwork, and textiles as a result of war-induced demand. Loss of jobs in the china clay industry and in tourism and service industries was to some degree offset by these manufacturing increases, and recruitment to the Armed Forces and Civil Service siphoned-off surplus labour.[1] Such effects were tranistory, however, and the end of hostilities in 1945 led to a situation where by 1947 "Certain types of regional production which were inaugurated or expanded during the war will have been drastically restricted, or closed down".[2] There was a hope that the newly-expanded textile industry might retain some of its strength as a result of its export potential, and a belief that shipbuilding would survive at least in the short-term because of the need to make good wartime losses, but this was tempered by the realisation of an inevitable contraction in other areas of manufacture and engineering, together with the fact that "Firms evacuated to the region will return rather than stay . . .".[3] Although china clay production was able to recover from its wartime restrictions, "The prospects for employment in tin-mining are not roseate",[4] while in the hitherto busy Truro area "The stoppage of war contracts will appreciably curtail employment".[5] In an economic climate of austerity with continued rationing and restraint, an early tourist boom was also unlikely. The Exeter Survey considered that particular areas would be especially hit by post-war contraction, and that "One such district is Camborne-Redruth-Hayle . . . manifestly it would be hurt by the decay of tin-mining, by contraction in the export trade of mining engineering and reduced activities in textiles and other mineral working. Localised unemployment threatens there."[6] In general, Cornwall in the aftermath of war suffered a debilitating combination of declining countryside and urban decay.

As the temporary stimulus of wartime conditions began to dissipate, then, it seemed as though Cornwall was destined to return to her "paralysis". Commentators (remembering, perhaps, the contraction after the Great War) observed with alarm the loss of wartime "advantages" and feared that the populace would sink again into a morass of industrial decay, rural ignorance, and emigration, with many areas ". . . so thinly populated that it will be impossible to maintain any reasonable standard of social life."[7] The underlying characteristics of Cornwall (and of remote North and West Devon) seemed perversely unsuited, even opposed to the progressive forces of modernisation which sought in the late 1940s to embark upon the construction of a new Britain. The exasperated tone of the Exeter Survey revealed a thinly-disguised contempt for the condition of peripherality:

> . . . in the bleak, lonely areas . . . where the village nucleus may consist merely of an isolated church, with perhaps a few cottages; where the parish is less of a community than a widespread powdering over the landscape of scattered farms; where towns are few and small in size, distances between them great and communications poor — it is here that rural decadence, materially, mentally and spiritually is seen at its lowest depths.[8]

"Paralysis" thus interpreted was seen as evidence of a deep Cornish malaise, of a fundamental deficiency in social, cultural and economic life in the periphery:

> The "foreigner" from a northern city who comes in summer to taste, perhaps superficially, of the pleasant, unhurried life of Devon and Cornwall, may condemn its people for being stupid and backward, even while secretly he considers the peaceful, picturesque, isolated village as an ideal spot in which to end his days. But let him retire into that village permanently; let him live there for years, winter and summer, with little means of leaving it, and with no contact with urban life — and in time he will begin to understand from within himself that strange mentality of people in remote rural parts.[9]

From this perspective, drastic action was needed to rescue Cornwall from "paralysis", to allow the Cornish to benefit from post-war re-construction and the new order of the Welfare State. Here again the Exeter Survey was unequivocal in its views. It considered it essential that farming ". . . should be more scientifically organised . . .",[10] that ". . . housing conditions must be improved . . .",[11] and that

> . . . it is desirable to establish such industries as will offer alternative sources of employment for young people. On the one hand, maximum

industrial use should be made of all local products such as milk, meat, fruit and vegetables; but, as these industries employ mainly unskilled labour, a proportion of factories needing more highly-skilled operatives, and which are not pre-determined by unavoidable locational controls, should be introduced into country towns. A more balanced industrial structure will provide wider vocational opportunity within the region, and will serve to counteract the present tendency of those young workers with higher intelligence and more venturesome spirit to migrate from the region, and so leave behind them a community impoverished not only quantitively, but, more importantly, qualitively.[12]

The strategy for Cornwall's regeneration, then, it was argued, should be based upon appropriate industrial diversification which would both create economic activity in its own right and retard the emigration of the younger, more intelligent population. Allied to this was a conviction that an ". . . onward march of the tourist and holiday industry (is) destined . . ."[13] which, despite its attendant problem of "serious seasonal unemployment",[14] would act as an important stimulus to Cornwall's economic development. Cornwall's "paralysis", then, was seen purely and simply as a matter of isolation, of geographical remoteness and the backward, unscientific, untutored, materially poor and spiritually impoverished characteristics of the "decadent" Cornish people with their "strange mentality". Within this paradigm the antidote for such ills was equally simplistic (and prejudiced), with a generalised call for new industry and an act of faith in the panacea of tourism. Although lacking any developed analysis of the problem of peripherality, such a view became quickly the conventional wisdom — not only for those looking at Cornwall from outside (from the "centre") but also for those inside who seemed to need little convincing of their own inadequacies. The tone of Cornwall County Council's own survey of Cornish resources and prospects, published in 1952, was based squarely upon such an interpretation.[15] And, in its attempt to secure such Cornish regeneration (based apparently on the belief that the best brains had already crossed the Tamar, and that invigorating dynamism from outside was a must), the County Council in the 1950s developed the tendency of filling its key administrative posts with candidates from outside Cornwall. The elevation of parts of Cornwall to Development Area status by the Government in 1958, as part of its broader policy of Regional Development, also mirrored the conventional wisdom.[16]

However, by the early and mid 1960s there was in reality little improvement to report. Unemployment in the Camborne-Redruth district was still consistently two or three times the national average, while in early 1964 the percentage of people without a job in Falmouth had risen to nearly 20 per cent.[17] Moorhouse, in his study, detected little evidence of vigour or development, writing that " . . . Bodmin is not much more than a moorland village, Truro is a dozy little cathedral town, while the hybrid Redruth-Camborne is nobody's idea of a pulsating heart".[18] His impressions, indeed, reflected those expressed in the Exeter Survey a decade and a half earlier, and he noted similar socio-economic phenomena to that recorded in

170

the earlier report. Between 1952 and 1962 the population of England and Wales had gone up by six per cent, and yet (in stark contrast) that of Cornwall had risen by a mere 0.07 per cent, while "Between 1951 and 1962 Camelford, Launceston, Liskeard, and St Germans lost between 5 and 16 per cent of their populations; Lostwithiel, Padstow, St Just, and Penzance between 4 and 13 per cent".[19] Ominously, he added that "In the past three years 17 per cent of the people emerging from the Cornwall Technical College in Camborne have gone straight across the Tamar in search of jobs".[20]

Moorhouse concluded, in his disarmingly direct journalistic style, that "Unmistakably Cornwall is in a fix".[21] There were as yet no signs of Cornwall's emergence from her by now deeply-entrenched "paralysis", no indications that the plans of 1952 or the post-war revival of tourism would indeed rescue Cornwall from her plight. Moorhouse recognised, however, that Cornwall's problems were not merely ones of "remoteness" or "backwardness" but reflected a more deep-seated problem within the United Kingdom as a whole based on the dichotomy between "centre" and "periphery". He was one of the first commentators to describe a "North-South Divide" in socio-economic terms, and he identified an "Other England" which had not participated fully in the post-war advances and consumer boom: ". . . between 1952 and 1960 the London region, with 27 per cent of Great Britain's population — not England's — acquired 40 per cent of the new jobs created in Britain".[22] Cornwall was firmly excluded from this London-oriented "Golden Circle" (as Moorhouse called it) and this accounted, he argued, for its parlous socio-economic condition. "How many", he asked rhetorically, "are aware that by far and away the highest rate of unemployment in England is not to be found in the North-east or along Merseyside, but in Cornwall?"[23]

Moorhouse's analysis, then, with its emphasis upon the causal effects of a "core-periphery" relationship, was in fact a major departure from the conventional wisdom. However, this had little impact upon Governmental or quasi-official thinking, at least in the short-term, and certainly not in Cornwall, despite the nationalist and regionalist stirrings in far-flung parts of Britain (which would lead shortly to the Crowther-Kilbrandon Commission) and the first hints of disquiet in Ulster. Instead, the recipe for recovery in Cornwall and other parts of peripheral Britain continued to be expressed in conventional terms, with the need to overcome "remoteness" and "backwardness" through tourist development and the encouragement of industry and commerce by means of a selective Regional Development policy. Indeed, regional policy was brought to the forefront of the political agenda in the 1960s as first the Conservatives and, after 1964, the Labour Government viewed with dismay the poor economic performance and indifferent industrial growth of the United Kingdom, especially when set against the success of Britain's principal overseas competitors. Regional policy was seen as one method of improving economic performance in the United Kingdom as a whole, by attempting to bring peripheral Britain up to the same standard as the economically "over-heating" London and the South East (Moorhouse's "Golden Circle"). It was not, it should be noted, a response to any regional disquiet or protest, nor was it led by policy preferences expressed in the various regions themselves. Instead, it was essentially a centrally-devised policy, a macro-economic approach to a perceived macro-economic problem.

As Ward has argued, before the Second World War Government economic policy reflected little interest in or concern for a "regional problem", with State policies, if anything, actually exacerbating uneven development in the United Kingdom.[24] Rearmament, war and new macro-economic policies necessitated new approaches, however, and led — as Schonfield[25] has shown — to a remarkable political concensus where regional policy became an article of faith for both Conservatives and Labour, regardless of their other ideological and policy differences. The fundamental aim of such policy was to ". . . seek to reduce or eliminate disparities between different geographical areas in incomes, industrial growth, migration, and, above all, unemployment".[26] With this in mind, as Cable explained, "The strategy underlying UK regional policy has been to identify specific areas requiring assistance, primarily on the basis of above-average unemployment rates. Firms moving to these areas have then been offered various financial incentives . . .".[27] A limited Special Areas Act in 1934 introduced this notion but the policy was not pursued with vigour, commitment or consistency until the various Distribution of Industry Acts since 1945, the Local Employment Acts from 1960, the Industrial Act of 1972, and post-war Finance Acts. By the early 1980s it was possible to distinguish between four main types of area identified for special treatment. Broad "Development Areas", usually covering the whole or most of one of the "standard regions" of the United Kingdom, were introduced in 1966, while "Special Development Areas" were set up in 1967 to deal with areas where problems were especially acute. "Intermediate Areas" emerged in 1969 as locations where problems were not as profound as in "Development Areas" but where, nonetheless, some assistance was appropriate. Later, in 1980, "Enterprise Zones" were created — very small districts of decaying "inner-city" areas.

˙ Cornwall emerged from this mix as an area attracting considerable assistance through regional policy. For the greater part of the 1960s, 1970s and early 80s, the Falmouth-Camborne district was identified as a "Special Development Area" of acute problems, while virtually the whole of the rest of Cornwall was a "Development Area". Even after the severe re-assessment of assisted areas in 1984, when many areas lost their rights to assistance altogether, the Kerrier and Penwith District areas of West Cornwall were designated "Development Areas", while south-east and North Cornwall were "Intermediate Areas"[28]. This, then, was the central Government's reaction to Cornwall's "paralysis" (or at least its economic features), although — as noted above — it was a reaction prompted by wider macro-economic concerns and not a response to any peculiarly identified features of Cornwall's condition.

Be that as it may, there appeared to be positive and measurable responses in Cornwall to the application of these Regional Development policies. More than fifty new factories were constructed in Cornwall between the end of the war and the mid-1960s, while during the 1960s manufacturing employment grew by as much as fifty per cent.[29] The Wilson Government, in an echo of the French system of centrally-directed regionalism, set up a series of regional economic councils based on the "standard regions", one of which was the South West Economic Planning Council (SWEPC) which was based in Bristol and whose writ ran from Gloucestershire to Cornwall. In 1967 SWEPC published its planning document *A Region With A Future*, its optimistic tone reflecting the earlier stance of Cornwall County Council in 1952, but now with the existence of a vigorous Regional Development policy to give credence to its projections, together with an even bolder assessment of the future which foresaw not only economic development in Cornwall but also a significant expansion of the Cornish population.[30] Practical evidence of the impact of regional policy was manifested in the appearance of "Advanced Factory Units" (whose construction in Cornwall was made possible by the Local Employment Act of 1960) in areas as diverse as Camborne and Saltash, and after the Industrial Development Act of 1966 new industrial estates sprang up in the disparate parts of Cornwall: by 1984 there were no fewer than 49 such estates.[31] Spooner considered this ". . . a minor industrial revolution . . .",[32] with the expansion in manufacturing jobs matched by a surge in tourist and service industry employment. Between 1961 and 1971 employment in tourism in Cornwall rose by 3,300 (a rise of 28 per cent), while that in service industries increased by 4,200 (six per cent).[33] Spooner enthused over "This encouraging picture of industrial growth . . ."[34] and concluded that "The changes that are taking place do not appear to be temporary, but are creating a genuine long term transformation of the regional economy".[35]

There was even optimism in the tin mining industry. Despite the fears for the industry in the immediate post-war era, together with the closure of East Pool and Agar in 1956, South Crofty (at Camborne) and Geevor (near St Just-in-Penwith) had survived and appeared solid, stable concerns in the 1960s and 70s. An academic article on Cornish mining noted that in 1968 the industry's production of 1,540 tons of tin had saved the United Kingdom about £2,200,000 in foreign exchange, and that a number of firms were engaged in prospecting in different parts of Cornwall (which led subsequently to the opening of the Mount Wellington, Pendarves, and more successful Wheal Jane mines), although warning that the support afforded by limited tax concessions and the provisions of the Industrial Development Act would not be enough to secure widespread regeneration of the industry.[36] The Cornish Chamber of Mines foresaw a great future for the industry, however, explaining in 1977 that "Far from the possibilities of further expansion being exhausted, there are more than 20 areas in Cornwall where there appear to be good prospects of making additional discoveries of tin, tungsten, lead, zinc and, possibly, even of copper . . .".[37]

The experience of the late 1960s and early 1970s appeared, then, to suggest that the massive assistance afforded to peripheral Britain through the central Government's Regional Development policy had worked for Cornwall. Moorhouse's analysis seemed hardly relevant even less than a decade after the publication of his work, and Spooner's assessment pointed to a permanent reversal of Cornwall's economic condition. Cornwall's economic "paralysis", it seemed, was at last broken. However, the apparent success of regional policy in Cornwall had occurred against the background of economic development in the United Kingdom as a whole, with Cornwall sharing in this new growth. When, in the aftermath of the oil prices rises after the Yom Kippur war, the international and British economies fell into deep depression, new factors at work in Cornwall became apparent. Grafton and Bolton showed that even in the expansionist early 1970s, employment growth in Cornwall had not been matched by the reduction in the numbers of unemployed.[38] Thereafter, the situation had deteriorated steadily. A Department of Employment report *Unemployment in West Cornwall* noted in January 1979 that "Unemployment in West Cornwall has in recent years been much higher than that experienced in most other parts of the country. Since 1974 . . . the problem has worsened".[39] In Cornwall as a whole there was a net decline in manufacturing jobs between 1976 and 1982, with 4,000 lost and only 2,000 created. Between 1976 and 1981 there was a further loss of 1,000 jobs in extractive industries, principally china-clay.[40] In 1981 came the symbolic closure of the Rank Radio "Advanced Factory Unit" at Pool, near Camborne, the very first "AFU" to have been built in Cornwall, and the removal of the concern across the Tamar to Plymouth with the loss of Cornish jobs.[41]

To this reversal in employment and manufacture was added the fact that Cornwall had remained an area of extreme low pay. In 1985 Gregory argued that "Workers in the South West . . . are amongst the lowest paid in the country"[42] and that, specifically, ". . . Cornwall tops the low pay table . . .".[43] Gregory defined "low pay" as anything below £100 per week and went on to show that in Cornwall no fewer than 30 per cent of male manual workers were by this measure "low paid". Twenty-three per cent of male non-manuals were also "low paid", as were 58 per cent of females in the same category. No figures were available for female manual workers, although a figure of 81 per cent for Devon (where "low pay" was less of a problem in all other categories) was a frightening clue to the extent of the problem in Cornwall. All this was against a background of the fact that, as Gregory pointed out, the costs of living in Cornwall and the South West are ". . . second only to those of the South East".[44]

Gregory also showed that more than half of the "low paid" jobs were in the tourist and service industries, the two sectors that had hitherto experienced considerable growth in employment. Dunkerley and Faerden, also in 1985, investigated the tourist industry in Cornwall (and Devon), in particular examining the problem of seasonal employment and unemployment.[45] They introduced the concept of a dual labour market with "primary" and "secondary" sectors. The "primary" sector consisted of those with permanent, secure jobs with promotion and career prospects, along with favourable conditions of employment. The "secondary" sector, by way of contrast, consisted of those under-priviledged through low wages, low mobility potential, low promotional prospects, and lack of stability of employment. In the tourist industry, employers and managers might fall into the "primary" sector, but all too often — argued Dunkerley and Feardon — their employees belonged to the "secondary", especially those who were employed only seasonally. With 13 per cent of the total employment in Cornwall in the summer months occurring in tourism, and with much of this concentrated

174

in certain specific "tourist areas", the problem of the "secondary" sector was seen as widespread. The view that many of these seasonal jobs were taken by temporary visitors from outside Cornwall was exposed as fallacious, and instead it was shown that such vacancies were more likely to be taken by local people who, in turn, were mostly women, were skewed towards the younger/older age ranges, and had tended to have a long history of irregular employment. Dunkerley and Faerdon found low aspirations and low expectations amongst such people, a great sense of resignation and an indifference to their own plight. In a blistering critique of the tourist industry, Dunkerley and Faerden concluded that,

> There exists a large pool of available labour that can be tapped and untapped at will. This labour force is generally willing to work for low wages and with minimal security. Its low expectations and low collectivism make for a very malleable group who, if dissatisfied, can easily be replaced by others from the pool. What exists is a profile of seasonal workers who are dependent on this form of employment, who have few means of escape from their situation, whose resignation to the situation derives directly from the situation but which, equally, leads to them colluding in their own exploited position.[46]

Such a picture seemed uncannily like the "paralysis" from which Regional Development policies had supposedly rescued Cornwall, hinting that the expansion of the late 1960s and 1970s had been perhaps a temporary abberation in the Cornish experience, prompted by external factors such as Government macro-economic policies and the general performance of the British economy. However, a more detailed analysis emerged to suggest that what had happened in Cornwall was even more profound, and that the experience of the late 1960s and early 1970s had been a direct function of Cornwall's peripheral status. Far from eroding Cornwall's peripherality, Cornwall's experience in that period was both a function of her status and a perpetuating influence which served to exacerbate further certain peripheral features. Spooner in the early 1970s had hoped that "The South West may becoming part of South East England"[47] and that ". . . possibly Devon and Cornwall is (sic) incorrectly categorised as a peripheral area, and is becoming part of a constantly enlarging 'central' region of the country".[48] In fact, events were to show that Cornwall had remained obstinately "different" from the rest of the country, and, indeed, — as we shall see — aspects of that "difference" had actually been heightened as a result of the experiences of the 1960s and 1970s. Spooner's assessment (like that of other observers) may have been coloured by his erroneous assumption that Cornwall together with Devon formed a homogeneous and cohesive "South West", throughout which the same conditions and experience applied, but his analysis of the Cornish situation was surprisingly flawed. In contradiction of Spooner's conclusions and assumptions, the Plymouth Business School was able to show in 1989, in its assessment of the South West economies, that "The South West Region . . . is regarded as prosperous by UK standards . . . There are however great disparities within the region and one county in particular,

Cornwall, is one of the most economically depressed in the whole of the UK".[49] Having enthused over the success of Bristol, Swindon, Bournemouth, Exeter, and even Plymouth, the assessment added that "It is impossible to be as confident of the economic prospects of Cornwall,"[50] marshalling and displaying an array of ". . . sufficient indicators to show clearly the extent of intra regional disparities . . ."[51] in which "Cornwall not surprisingly perhaps comes last"[52].

Specifically, the Plymouth Business School was able to produce a summary table of 18 major economic indicators in which, for each indicator and overall, the counties of the South West Region were ranked in the order 1 to 7. As the School noted, the further westwards one travels in South West Britain the lower the levels of prosperity that are encountered. Significantly, however, it was felt important to emphasise that,

> . . . the table masks the extent of the disparities between Cornwall and the rest of the region. Typically . . . it is not just that Cornwall ranks seven for a particular variable but that it comes a very bad seventh. It should be emphasised, therefore, that although Devon scores closer to Cornwall than anywhere else in terms of overall rankings the performance of its economy is closer to that of the northern parts of the region.[53]

That Cornwall's economy remained highly differentiated from that of Devon and the rest of Britain was noted in 1988 by Lee, who concluded that:

> Cornwall remains an area of high unemployment; reliant industrially on extractive industries, branch factories and small-scale business; with an agricultural structure in which the small tenant farmer is the norm; and with high proportions of both private and public sector service employment. There are high rates of owner-occupation, correspondingly low rates of council-house occupation, and the county has the lowest average wage-rates in mainland Britain.[54]

Lee's selection of "branch factories" as a feature of importance in Cornwall's distinctive socio-economic profile was significant, for it echoed a more general concern among analysts of the real nature of economic change in Cornwall during the period of apparent growth and development. Perry noted that 60 per cent of manufacturing growth in Cornwall in the 1960s and 70s was of the "branch factory" type, where enterprises were merely local branches of much larger national or even international companies, component parts of wider organisations and reporting to head offices long distances away as well as being reliant upon external infrastructures. Perry went on to show that a further 50 per cent of manufacturing employment in Cornwall was brought under outside control over the same period, as a result of mergers and takeovers, and concluded that by the end of the 1970s a full three-quarters of Cornish manufacturing manpower was controlled from beyond the Tamar.[55] Even Holman's, the former flagship of Cornish mining

	Avon	C'wall	Devon	Dorset	Gloucs	Som'set	Wilts
% change in population 1981/86	7	2	5	1	6	3	4
average gross weekly M	1	7	6	4	2	5	3
earnings 1987 F	3	7	4	5	1	6	1
cars per 000 pop 1986	5	6	7	1	3	4	2
% change in car owner-ship 1980/86	2	6	4	5	3	7	1
Av rates paid 1987/88	1	7	5	2	3	6	4
% of households lacking inside WC 1981	2	7	4	1	6	5	3
% change in stock of dwellings 1982/86	7	4	5	1	6	2	2
% change in employees in employment 1981/84	3	1	4	5	7	6	2
male activity rate 1981	6	4	7	5	2	3	1
female activity rate 1981	1	7	6	5	2	4	3
unemployment rate 1988	5	7	6	2	3	4	1
% long term unemployed 1987	1	2	6	5	7	4	3
% of school leavers with A level 1985/86	1	7	4	3	2	5	5
GDP per head 1984	2	7	5	6	3	4	1
Net capital expenditure in manufacturing 1985	4	6	5	7	3	1	2
Gross value added in manufacturing 1985	2	7	3	5	6	4	1
Growth of new businesses 1979/86	3	7	6	5	4	2	1
TOTAL	56	101	92	63	69	75	40
Overall rank	2	7	6	3	4	5	1

Notes: 1 = highest

Summary Table: Major Economic Indicators
Cornwall and South West England
Source: P Gripaios et al, 1989, p47

engineering and symbol of Cornwall's lost industrial prowess, fell victim to this process, becoming part of an international corporation and losing in the process not only jobs but also local control. This trend in the private sector was mirrored in the public, with the demise of many Cornish-controlled utilities and the creation in their stead of "regional" bodies with head offices and managerial jobs situated east of the Tamar. The setting up of the Devon and Cornwall Constabulary and the South West Water Authority, both with headquarters in Exeter, was perhaps the most notable example of this.[56]

The overwhelming importance of the "branch factory" in Cornwall's manufacturing sector meant, as Grafton and Bolton argued, that during the 1960s and 1970s employment in Cornwall became more dependent on outside influences (rather than less) and, therefore, more dependent upon the economic performance of the "centre" or "core".[57] In times of economic difficulty, it was the "branch factories" which were the first to be closed or cut by large companies. Thus, as R. Payne showed, employment in new firms opened in Cornwall and Devon in the two decades before 1971 fell by 10 per cent in just one year (1979–80).[58] As Grafton and Bolton concluded,

> The decentralisation of branch, often routine processing plants to the rural periphery in search of cheaper land, low-cost, poorly unionised and often female labour does not remove the status of the periphery of a dependent, relatively weak regional economy.[59]

This analysis pointed, however, not only to the deleterious effects of the "branch factory" phenomenon, but also to the particular significance of the specific features of the "branch factory" economy — cheaper land, low wages, poorly unionised workers, and so on. This, in turn, echoed the work of Massey and others who saw in the "branch factory" economies of the peripheries a "spatial division of labour". According to this view, head offices, top jobs, specialist research facilities, decision-making loci, and resource allocation and control, were all based in the "centre", with more mundane functions dispersed to peripheral areas where average wages were lower, where workers were poorly organised and not militant, and where aspirations and standards of educational achievement were generally of a lower level. This, argued Massey and others, represented a "hierarchial organisation of production" (that hierarchy being based upon the "spatial division of labour"), with the growth of the "branch factory" economy (encouraged as it was by regional policy) representing a transition from regional specialisation to the new hierarchy.[60] Here, as several observers have noted, Massey — although addressing her analysis to peripheral regions in general — had caught the essence of the Cornish experience. Cornwall was, as has been shown here in some detail, a classic case of "regional specialisation" in its period of industrialisation.[61] But, with the passing of that industrial period, such specialisation gave way at length to "the hierarchical organisation of production" of the "branch factory" economy. In other words, the specialisation (or over-specialisation) which characterised Cornwall's industrial experience in the era of "Second Peripheralism" was replaced ultimately by a new form of peripherality, based upon the "branch factory" economy with its "spatial division of labour" and "hierarchical organisation of production". This, in turn, suggested strongly that Regional Development policy had after all disturbed Cornwall from her "paralysis", albeit not in the manner anticipated by the planners.

As part of a broader examination of peripheralisation and industrial change, Barta and Dingsdale compared the impacts of changes in industrial company organisation on selected peripheral regions in Hungary and the United Kingdom.[62] In seeking a quantative definition of economic peripherality, they identified the "economic potential surface for the United Kingdom" in 1984 by subdividing the 11 "standard regions" to create 19 regions. Economic activity in each of these was approximated by Gross Domestic Product, apportioned on the basis of population, while road mileage between major urban centres was used as the distance measure. With this information to hand, isolines were drawn on the map of the United Kingdom. Isolines were calibrated in percentage points of the highest values, and the regions classified as "central", "intermediate" or "peripheral". According to this analysis, Northern Ireland, Scotland, Wales and much of South Western Britain and Northern England were "peripheral" in varying degrees. Significantly, those areas identified as the most acutely "peripheral" were Northern Ireland outside the Belfast hinterland, the most northerly far-flung Highlands and Islands of Scotland, and all Cornwall west of the (roughly) Fowey-Camel line. East Cornwall was, by their analysis, shown to be marginally less "peripheral" and comparable to west Devon, rural west Wales, the Belfast area, and the greater part of central Scotland. Barta and Dingsdale noted, too, the significant increase in "branch factories" and external ownership in what they termed euphamistically "The Peripheral Far South West", concluding that the apparent increase in employment, infrastructure and standard of living ". . . has largely been achieved by the extension of a branch-plant network and not locally based initiative . . ."[63] while ". . . the demands of the dynamic core have tended to contribute to the decline and peripherialisation of other regions".[64]

This analysis hinted, too, at an apparently changing nature of peripherality (in Cornwall as in other regions), but it was also a direct critique of regional policy. In this Barta and Dingsdale reflected existing criticism, such as the Cornwall Industrial Development Association's disquiet (expressed as early as 1977[65]) about the deleterious effects of the "branch factory" economy, and Gripaios' comment that ". . . central and local government should change the focus of their location policies towards encouraging indigenous potential".[66] Perry, in arguing for such indigenous activity based upon an internally developed Cornish economic (and intellectual) infrastructure, had complained in 1982 that

. . . conventional regional policies, with their obsession for the short-term aim of mopping up pools of unemployment whenever and wherever they occur, rarely address themselves to ways of enhancing the long-term locational competitiveness of peripheral and rural areas.[67]

More forcefully, Grafton and Bolton concluded that ". . . regional policy has not been successful in breaking the core-periphery structure . . . The power relationship central to the core-periphery model remains, at a fundamental level, intact".[68]

By 1982, however, the basis of regional policy was in itself under review. In its attempts to reduce Government expenditure and to allow the free play of market forces without Government interference, the Thatcher administration re-defined (and therefore eroded) those areas qualifying for assistance. The review of 1982 represented a retreat from the high point of 1974 (when two thirds of the United Kingdom qualified for aid), and the erosion of 1984 led to the dilution of support for even the most far-flung peripheries, including Cornwall. In January 1988 a further review confirmed the extent and status of the areas earmarked for assistance in 1984, but ruled that in future grants for firms relocating in those areas would no longer be automatic but would be subject to scrutiny by the Department of Trade and Industry. These alterations were reflected in significant reductions in Government expenditure on regional aid. The figure had been halved between 1979 and 1986 (a cut of £1,000 million) and was halved again by 1989.[69]

With so much of the increase in manufacturing employment in the "boom" years being based upon "branch factories" fostered by regional aid, the reduction in Government expenditure further exacerbated the economic malaise of peripheral Britain, Cornwall included. In 1988 Champion and Green, in a discussion of *Local Prosperity and the North-South Divide*, contrasted "deprived areas" of the United Kingdom with "growth areas", identifying Cornwall as a "deprived area" and placing it in economic terms within the "North"[70]. This echoed Gamble's perspective, which alleged that the reduction in Government aid had accelerated industrial decline in both the "North" and "West" of Britain.[71] The notion that Cornwall was somehow in the "North" in the increasingly significant "North-South" divide and debate appeared geographically perverse, but the very nomenclature reflected a situation where the real problems of industrial decline and unemployment were popularly perceived as those of Merseyside, Tyneside, Clydeside and other "northern" regions. In this concern Cornwall was often overlooked, partly because of its relatively small size but also — as Shaw and Williams noted — because the popular image of Cornwall in the "core" or "centre" stressed a perceived high quality of life and did not recognise problems of decline and unemployment.[72] For Cornwall the real irony, however, was that just as regional policy had led to a significant increase in manufacturing employment, so it was regional policy that was contributing to its decline. Cornwall's "branch factory" economy had created a veneer, an illusion of prosperity during the period of economic "boom" and high levels of regional aid, but had displayed its seriously deleterious features in the ensuing era of recession and cuts in assistance.

The perception of a high quality of life and an illusion of prosperity had also been enhanced by the phenomenon of "counterurbanisation" experienced in Cornwall, where the population increased dramatically in the 1960s, 70s and 80s as a result of massive immigration ("in-migration") from across the Tamar[73]. Given the century-long era of emigration and de-population that had come to epitomise the Cornish experience, this population turnaround was both startling and unexpected. As Perry et al summarised:

At the beginning of the 1960s, after a hundred years of more or less uninterrupted decline, what had Cornwall to offer? Some valuable raw materials, almost unique as far as the UK was concerned, like tin and china-clay, together with potential for new energy sources — wave, wind, tide, geothermal — and a climate and terrain suitable for dairy-farming and horticulture. A strong sense of identity, a positive attitude to industrial redevelopment and a distinctive semi-urban settlement pattern with larger labour catchment areas than many other rural areas. On the other it lay at the end of a long and narrow peninsula, much farther away in travel-time and travel-cost than the rest of England or Wales, or indeed much of Scotland, from the main centres of industry and commerce. Unemployment was double the national rate, per capita incomes were 30 per cent below and earnings 20 per cent below the national level and employment both in the primary and in the manufacturing sector was falling. On balance it hardly seemed set for rapid expansion.[74]

And yet, despite this seemingly unpromising picture, Cornwall not only experienced the growth of a "branch factory" economy (in the manner described above) but also attracted a high level of "in-migration". Between 1961 and 1981 the population of Cornwall increased by an extraordinary 25 per cent, and during the 1970s the rate of expansion was twice that of Devon and the rest of the South West.[75] To Spooner, this population growth was a function of the new economic order, the "in-migration" occurring in response to the creation of jobs in the manufacturing and other sectors, as indeed SWEPC had forecast. As Bolton and Grafton noted, "According to this view, the core-periphery structure had been broken. The region could no longer be classified as a periphery, but rather had become part of the UK core with counterurbanisation the dominant force".[76]

However, just as Spooner's assessment of the nature of economic change in Cornwall was mistaken, so his view of the nature of "in-migration" and "counterurbanisation" was incorrect. In fact, far from removing Cornwall's peripheral characteristics, counterurbanisation was — like the creation of a "branch factory" economy — both a function of Cornwall's peripheral status and a feature of its perpetuation. There was, of course, a link of sorts between regional policy and counterubanisation. Not only, as we shall see, was "in-migration" encouraged by official policy, but the creation of a "branch factory" economy led to a situation in which key workers and managers were encouraged into Cornwall from outside. Perry et al asserted that there was " . . . strong evidence that migrants were taking many of the better jobs . . .",[77] and in 1982 a survey by Nelson and Potter found that over one third of skilled workers in Cornwall were "in-migrants".[78] Deacon interpreted this to mean that a "cultural division of labour" within Cornwall had been superimposed upon the "spatial division of labour"

181

identified by Massey, further emphasising the impact of peripherality upon the indigenous Cornish people.[79]

SWEPC, as an arm of central government Regional Development planning, considered that "in-migration" was a necessary accompaniment — indeed a complementary process — to the strategy of job creation.[80] New jobs would attract new workers from outside Cornwall, which would in turn generate further demand for goods and services and thus create still more economic activity. In this way, it was argued, a new dynamism could be injected into Cornish society and economy, the resultant growth rescuing Cornwall from her isolation, backwardness and general "paralysis". SWEPC encouraged "Overspill" schemes, in which the Greater London Council would co-operate with Cornish authorities in settling Londoners in Cornwall, but this approach was resisted strongly by Cornish public opinion (see Chapter 9). Instead, the emphasis was changed to encouraging voluntary "in-migration", a strategy that was evident in Cornwall County Council's *West Cornwall Study* in 1970 and in the document *Towards 2001* where Cornwall and Devon County Councils combined to make planning projections for the "Plymouth Sub-Region".[81] In 1974 this approach was re-emphasised in SWEPC's *Settlement Pattern*,[82] and by the time Cornwall County Council produced its *Structure Plan* in 1980 the view that "in-migration" was an essential component of economic and social revival in Cornwall had become deeply ingrained in the conventional wisdom of planning. The *Structure Plan* argued for a parallel and inter-dependent rise in both jobs and population, and predicted (conservatively, as it happened) that between 1976 and 1991 the population of Cornwall would have risen by some 46,300 people.[83]

However, at precisely the same time that the *Structure Plan* was elucidating its new-jobs/population-growth strategy, Cornwall's newly-created "branch factory" economy was already beginning to falter in the face of economic recession and would soon receive the further blow of cut-backs in Government support through regional policy. The rise in population was accompanied, therefore, not by increased job opportunities but by rising unemployment. In its *First Alteration* of the *Structure Plan*, published in 1988, Cornwall County Council admitted that "The underlying assumptions of the Approved Plan in relating population growth to employment opportunities has not held good".[84] And, amidst a storm of protest from organisations such as Cornish Alternatives to the Structure Plan and the Cornish Social and Economic Research Group (see Chapter 10), the *First Alteration* went on to articulate a revised strategy in which ". . . the approach . . . is much more based on housing and population factors rather than employment factors".[85] In other words, because the creation of enduring employment opportunities had not materialised, unlike the growth in population which had more than fulfilled the planners' expectations, the *First Alteration* concerned itself merely with the "accommodation" of population expansion, with the hope that this in itself would generate new jobs in the service sector.

The *First Alteration*, indeed, was tantamount to an admission that the post-war policy of expansion in Cornwall had been a failure, despite the clear and consistent articulation of its conventional wisdoms and policy aims since the Exeter Survey had first identified Cornwall as a "suitable case for treatment", and despite the support lent coincidently for much of the era by central government Regional Development policies. And yet, even if the policy had been a failure, it could not be denied that it had changed the economic and social face of Cornwall. A "branch factory" economy had been created and population turnaround through "in-migration" had led to a process of "counterurbanisation" which stood in stark contrast to the earlier Cornish experience of emigration. But, as Lee and Gripaios had noted, Cornwall was nonetheless still distinctively "different" in socio-economic terms, and with enduring problems such as low pay unaddressed or unresolved by the new conditions. Indeed, the Cornwall of "branch factories" and "counterurbanisation" was in several respects even more distinctly "different" from that which had gone before, setting the Cornish experience widely apart from that of most other areas of the United Kingdom.

As the work of Grafton and Bolton, Barta and Dingsdale, had hinted, the experience of Cornwall in the post-war era not only confirmed and reflected Cornwall's peripheral status but in fact pointed to the emergence of a new mode of peripherality. The "paralysis" that had characterised "Second Peripheralism" in its matured condition from the latter part of the nineteenth century until the Second World War and after, had indeed been disturbed by "branch factories" and "counterurbanisation". Such disturbance had not, however, heralded the end of Cornwall's peripheral status (as Spooner had supposed) but ushered in instead a new era of peripherality. In short, the era of "Second Peripheralism" associated with the nature and consequences of Cornwall's experience of industrialisation had given way in the face of new conditions to a "Third Peripheralism" based upon a "branch factory" economy and the process of "counterurbanisation". Those new conditions reflected the changing dynamics of the centre-periphery relationship, in particular the post-war development of central Government Regional Development policies.

The trauma associated with rapid change in Cornwall was in itself evidence that "paralysis" had been disturbed and the nature of peripherality altered radically. At the practical level, the rapid expansion in house prices in Cornwall during much of the 1980s, and particularly during 1987–88, not only reflected movements in the housing market in the United Kingdom as a whole but was also a function of acute demand resulting from "in-migration". Consequently, house prices in Cornwall rose to levels much higher than those in otherwise comparable peripheral regions. At the beginning of 1988 the average house price in Cornwall was estimated at £52,000, with this increasing by an average of £29 per day. With average male earnings then some 20 per cent below the British average (representing about £180 per week, and with females in Cornwall earning an average of only £124), it was not surprising that the estate agents Miller & Co should admit in December 1987 that local first time buyers were "almost getting squeezed out" of the Cornish housing market.[86] "In-migrants", however, many from London and the South East where house prices were also buoyant, were undaunted by Cornish house price rises and many were able to endulge in "equity stripping" as they moved to what was for them more moderately-priced housing in Cornwall. An advertisement in *Private Eye* in August 1987 expressed the situation succinctly: "For the price of a poky flat or a boring semi, you could move to Cornwall, buy one of these super properties AND have a fistful of change".[87]

Trauma was also experienced at the intellectual level. In the 1970s the Cornwall Industrial Development Association and the Cornwall Conservation Forum had sounded warnings of what lay ahead,[88] but it was not until as recently as 1986 that Perry et al rationalised and articulated increasing concern about the fate of Cornwall.[89] Perry undertook a detailed analysis of "counterurbanisation", confirming the link between "in-migration" and the "branch factory" economy, and acknowledging the impact of both local planning and central Government Regional Development policy. But he was also able to show that a considerable amount of "in-migration" had occurred in isolation of the stimulus provided by regional policy and local planning, explaining in the process how it was that massive "in-migration" continued even after the onset of recession in the 1970s. Extraneous factors were also at work, he argued, most especially the increasing desire to seek an improved quality of life. In moving to Cornwall, many "in-migrants" were deliberately seeking to escape the pressures and resist the pull of London and the South East (or similar areas such as Birmingham and its Midlands hinterland, and were hoping to find a more congenial environment and pace of life, considerable numbers participating in (and therefore encouraging and facilitating the growth in service and tertiary employment which had occurred alongside the emergence of "branch factory" manufacturing. Perry detected the influence of the "small is beautiful" and "intermediate technology" ethos, part of the "decline of the industrial spirit" noted by Wiener which reached its apogee in the 1970s, exhibited in ". . . antigrowth and antitechnology movements . . . from environmentalism to historical preservation to the Campaign for Real Ale . . .".[90] Associated with this, too, were the new attitudes to the "culture of technology" identified by Pacey, with their ". . . humanitarian stress on need-oriented values . . .".[91] Indeed, Perry identified traces of a hippy-culture amongst some of the "in-migrants", especially those who came to Cornwall in search of environment rather than jobs and contributed to what Perry called "imported unemployment". Many retirees from across the Tamar also sought peace, quiet and what they considered a saner way of life.

Generally, however, Perry found that the "in-migrants" were extremely active (perhaps surprisingly so, given their desire to escape the "rate race"), often middle-class and middle-aged folk who ". . . restore old properties, revive traditional arts and crafts, create tourist attractions, modernise school systems and set up planning committees for new developments".[92] In analysing the statistics of population growth in Cornwall, Perry discovered that the 30-39 age group had increased by over 40 per cent between 1971 and 1981, while the 10-19 group had increased by 30 per cent and the 70 plus group by 25 per cent over the same decade. This was not a result of any increase in birth rate, nor even a result of an arrest of emigration (in fact, the emigration of indigenous Cornish had continued, rising between 1966 and 1977 by one sixth compared with the early 60s) but was due overwhelmingly to the effect of "in-migration".[93] In examining the geographical distribution of "in-migrants" within Cornwall, Perry noted that the District Council areas of Kerrier, Carrick and Restormal had reached their peak population growth during the 1960s. Penwith, at the western extremity of Cornwall, had not experienced its growth until the 1970s, and North Cornwall presented an extremely complex picture, having remained static for most of the post-war era but suddenly in the period 1976-84 experiencing significant population expansion of a magnitude five times that experienced by Penwith over the same period. In the Caradon District of south east Cornwall, the population had increased by as much as 25 per cent during the 1970s but this also reflected the influence of Plymouth where a process of "mini-counterurbanisation" had — following the construction of the Tamar Bridge in 1960 — led many Plymouth commuters to settle in the hinterlands of Saltash, Torpoint, Callington and Liskeard.[94]

To further identify the socio-economic characteristics of "in-migrants", Perry conducted (by questionnaire) a "West Cornwall Study" of the Districts of Penwith, Kerrier, Carrick, and Restormal. In his analysis of "in-migrants" he distinguished between "new settlers" and "returned migrants" (ie returning Cornish), contrasting both groups with "locals". Not surprisingly, he found that in "attractive" areas such as the Lizard, Carbis Bay, and Feock there were many "new settlers" and few "locals", whilst in "unattractive" areas such as St Stephen-in-Brannel (in the china clay country) the reverse was true. Specifically, Perry was able to show that,

> The new settlers, who made up 43 per cent of our sample, had the highest proportion of retirees, of older working-age groups, of higher education categories, of top socio-economic occupations and of owner-occupiers. Locals, who accounted for 44 per cent of the sample, came bottom in all these respects. Return migrants, who represented 13 per cent of the sample, occupied the middle ground, forming a distinctive category of their own rather than simply an appendage of either the new settlers or the locals.[95]

The "West Cornwall Study" further emphasised the importance of both "pull" (attractive environment) and "push" (escape from "rat race") factors in causing "in-migration". For the "returned migrants" there was the additional consideration of "coming home", which helped to explain why they were more easily assimilated into existing communities than were the "new settlers". A fifth of the "new settlers" perceived some conflict with the "locals", perhaps not surprising when a full half of them did not acknowledge any distinctive Cornish cultural attributes. Some ten per cent of "new settlers" did, however, refer specifically to Cornwall's Celtic roots and the Cornish language, although Perry concluded that "Apart from a small number of Celtic revivalists, most of them repatriates, the incomers imported their own culture with them rather than immersing themselves in local traditions".[96] With more than a tinge of regret, Perry went on to report that the leisure interests of "in-migrants" tended to be ". . . middle-class, middle-brow and cosmopolitan — classical music, Gilbert and Sullivan, amateur productions of West End plays,

Morris Dancing, visits to stately homes".[97] With an air of resignation he concluded that,

> . . . the picture that emerges from our study is of a Cornwall swamped by a flood of middle-class, middle-aged, middle-browed city dwellers who effectively imposed their standards upon local society. Integration and assimilation was a one-way process — of "urbanisation" rather than "ruralisation".[98]

In a further study, in which he compared counterurbanisation in Cornwall with the population turnaround experienced over the same period in the geographically and historically similar Finistere region of western Brittany, Perry returned to these concerns. He contrasted the condition of Cornwall with what he saw as the happier experience of Finistere, where population turnaround — after decades of emigration and depopulation like that of Cornwall — had been achieved by stemming the loss of young Bretons and by securing economic stability through internally-generated and self-sustained growth. "In-migration" from outside Brittany had been less intense, and the local culture (including the Breton language) had proved better equipped to assimilate newcomers. The French Government had itself proved more responsive to the real needs of peripheral regions and had decentralised economic power more successfully. The result was, Perry concluded, that: "Instead of the Cornish tripartite structure of an English majority (sic), a large anglicised minority and a marginal group of Celtic or Cornish enthusiasts, the Breton consciousness of the Finistere population is likely to grow stronger".[99]

Empirically, it was difficult to fault Perry's findings or to question his methodology and broad analysis of the phenomenon of counterurbanisation. There was, however, an inconsistency in his conclusions. Although his analysis had served to destroy the Spooner interpretation of Cornwall's experience, and had shown instead that the Cornish condition was highly distinctive and a function of peripherality, Perry nonetheless seemed to agree with Spooner's assessment that "The South West may becoming part of South East England". In fact, as this chapter has argued, the opposite was the case. In some respects the era of the "branch factory" economy and of "counterurbanisation" had heightened the peripheral condition of Cornwall, breaking the erstwhile "paralysis" and unfolding a new era of "Third Peripheralism". Perry, it seems, had overlooked Grafton and Bolton's point that, fundamentally, the centre-periphery power relationship had not been broken. Equally, Perry had underestimated the enormous influence of peripherality in creating "difference". This "difference" from the centre or core was the root cause of identity in all its manifestations, a fact as true in the "Older Peripheralism" of Celtic-Catholic Cornwall in its territorial and cultural isolation as in the Cornish industrial experience of "Second Peripheralism". Perry may not have like the features of Cornwall's difference in this new era of "Third Peripheralism", but they served to perpetuate an identity based on difference which, as will be argued in subsequent chapters, had an important effect upon post-war Cornish life, most especially in the field of politics.

Perry's misgivings, however, voiced a wider paradox that had emerged in Cornwall during this period of vigorous post-war change, the new era of "Third Peripheralism". To observers outside of Cornwall, as Wight noted and as the commentaries of Lee and Rallings evidenced at length, the Cornwall of the late twentieth century was still noticeably "different" in terms of culture, society, economics and politics.[100] Indeed, such commentaries went further, to express a degree of surprise at the apparent strength and continuity of the Cornish identity in the face of post-war change. Interestingly, these "outsiders'" perceptions contrasted strongly with the view of writers inside Cornwall who, like Perry and Charles Thomas, felt that Cornwall and Cornishness were now under permanent threat as a result of the changes that had been wrought. Thomas, in his inaugural lecture as Professor of Cornish Studies, considered

> . . . that Cornwall is approaching some sort of internal social crisis. It is increasingly difficult to be Cornish. It is correspondingly important . . . for those who are Cornish, and presumably value their identity, to stand up and to be counted . . . If we do not succeed, this little land of ours will end up scarcely distinguishable from the Greater London Area, with undertones reminiscent of Blackpool or Skegness.[101]

Paradoxically, in expressing concern for the demise of the Cornish identity, Thomas was in fact demonstrating its survival and, equally as importantly, articulating a new feature of the post-war "Third Peripheralism": the concept that the Cornish people should resort to social and political action in defence of the Cornish identity.

Notes and References

1. John Murray et al, *Devon and Cornwall: A Preliminary Survey*, Wheaton, Exeter, 1947, pp248-271.
2. Ibid., p272.
3. Ibid., p273.
4. Ibid., p279.
5. Ibid.
6. Ibid., p289.
7. Ibid., p40
8. Ibid., p63.
9. Ibid.
10. Ibid., p40.
11. Ibid.
12. Ibid., p41.
13. Ibid., p291.
14. Ibid.
15. Cornwall County Council, *Development Plan 1952: Report of A Survey*, Cornwall County Council, Truro, 1952.

16. Geoffrey Moorhouse, *Britain in the Sixties: The Other England*, Penguin, London, 1964, p34.
17. Ibid., p44.
18. Ibid., p45.
19. Ibid., p35.
20. Ibid.
21. Ibid.
22. Ibid., p20.
23. Ibid. p18.
24. Stephen V. Ward, *The Geography of InterWar Britain: The State and Uneven Development*, Routledge, London, 1988.
25. Andrew Schonfield, "The Politics of the Mixed Economy in the International System of the 1970s", *International Affairs*, Vol 5, No 1, 1980. See also, Wayne Parsons, *The Political Economy of British Regional Policy*, Routledge, London, 1988.
26. J.R. Cable, "Industry", in A.R. Prest & D.J. Coppock, *The UK Economy: A Manual of Applied Economics* Wiedenfeld & Nicolson, London, 9th ed., 1982, p228.
27. Ibid., p230.
28. John Osmond, *The Divided Kingdom*, Constable, London, 1988, p57.
29. D. Grafton and N. Bolton, "Planning Policy and Economic Development in Devon and Cornwall 1945-84", in Peter Gripaios (ed.), *The Economy of Devon and Cornwall*, South West Papers in Geography, Plymouth Polytechnic, Plymouth, 1984, pp3-5; Bernard Deacon, Andrew George and Ronald Perry, *Cornwall at the Crossroads? Living Communities or Leisure Zone?*, Cornwall Social and Economic Research Group, Redruth, 1988, p48.
30. South West Economic Planning Council, *A Region With A Future: A Draft Strategy For the South West*, HMSO, London, 1967.
31. Andy C. Pratt, "Industrial Estates and Local Economic Development in Cornwall", in Peter Gripaios (ed.), *The South West Economy*, Plymouth Business School, Plymouth, 1985, pp88-89, p97.
32. D.J. Spooner, "Industrial Movement and the Rural Periphery: The Case of Devon and Cornwall", *Regional Studies* 6, 1971.
33. Grafton and Bolton, op. cit., p4.
34. D.J. Spooner, "Some Qualitive Aspects of Industrial Movement in a Problem Region of the UK", *Town Planning Review*, 45, 1974.
35. Ibid. See also D.J. Spooner, "Industrial Development in Devon and Cornwall 1939-67", unpublished PhD thesis, Unviersity of Cambridge, 1972.
36. J.R. Blunden, "The Redevelopment of the Cornish Tin Mining Industry: Its Problems and Prospects", in K.J. Gregory and W.L.D. Ravenhill, *Exeter Essays in Geography*, University of Exeter, Exeter, 1971.
37. Cornish Chamber of Mines, *Mining in Cornwall Today*, C.C.M., Truro, 1977, p33.
38. Grafton and Bolton, op. cit., p7.
39. R. McNabb, N. Woodward and J. Barry, *Unemployment in West Cornwall*, Department of Employment, London, 1979, pi.
40. C. Griffin, "Economic Change in Cornwall: An Overview", in Gareth Shaw and Allan M. Williams (eds.), *Economic Development and Policy in Cornwall: Proceedings of a Regional Studies Association — Institute of Cornish Studies Conference, Spring 1982*, South West Papers in Geography, Plymouth Polytechnic, Plymouth, 1982, pp3-4.
41. Pratt, op. cit., p92.

42. P. Gregory, "Low Pay in the South West", in Gripiaos, 1985, op. cit., p27.
43. Ibid., p35.
44. Ibid., p32.
45. David Dunkerley and Ingrid Faerden, "Aspects of Seasonal Employment in Devon and Cornwall", in Gripiaos, 1985, op. cit.
46. Ibid., p22. See also Ingrid Faerden, "The Social Impact of Seasonal Employment in Devon and Cornwall", unpublished PhD thesis, CNAA (Plymouth Polytechnic), 1986.
47. Spooner, 1972, op. cit., p8.
48. Spooner, 1971, op. cit.
49. Peter Gripaios and Consultancy South West, *The South West Economy: Trends and Prospects*, Plymouth Business School, Plymouth, 1989, p1.
50. Ibid.
51. Ibid., p46.
52. Ibid.
53. Ibid.
54. Adrian Lee, "The Persistence of Difference? Electoral Change in Cornwall", unpublished paper presented to PSA annual conference, Plymouth Polytechnic, 1988, p15.
55. Ronald Perry, "The Role of the Small Manufacturing Business in Cornwall's Economic Development", in Shaw and Williams (eds.), op. cit., p30.
56. Ronald Perry, with Ken Dean and Bryan Brown, and with the assistance of David Shaw, *Counterurbanisation: International Case Studies of Socio-Economic Change in the Rural Areas*, Geo Books, Norwich, 1986, p71.
57. Grafton and Bolton, op. cit., p9.
58. Cited in ibid., p7.
59. Ibid., p9.
60. Doreen Massey, "In What Sense a Regional Problem?", *Regional Studies*, 13, 2, 1979.
61. Bolton and Grafton, op. cit., p9; Perry et al, op. cit., p6.
62. Gyorgyi Barta and Alan Dingsdale, "Impacts of Changes in Industrial Company Organisation in Peripheral Regions: A Comparison of Hungary and the United Kingdom", in G.J.R. Linge (ed.), *Peripheralisation and Industrial Change: Impacts on Nations, Regions, Firms and People*, Croom Helm, London, 1988.
63. Ibid., pp181-182.
64. Ibid., p182.
65. Cornwall Industrial Development Association, *The Economy of Cornwall*, C.I.D.A., Truro?, 1977.
66. Peter Gripaios, *Manufacturing Industry in Devon and Cornwall: An Analysis of Decision Taking, Industrial Linkages and Locational Perceptions*, Plymouth Business School, Plymouth, 1984, pi.
67. Perry, op. cit., p30.
68. Bolton and Grafton, op. cit., pp9-10.
69. Osmond, op. cit., p56.
70. Tony Champion and Anne Green, *Local Prosperity and the North-South Divide*, Institute for Employment Research, University of Warwick, Warwick, 1988.
71. A. Gamble, "Thatcherism and The Politics of Inequality", unpublished paper presented to the Institute of British Geographers' Conference, Portsmouth, 1987, cited in Linge, op. cit., p169.
72. Gareth Shaw and Allan M. Williams (eds.), *Industrial Change in Cornwall: Pro-

ceedings of a Seminar on the Collection and Analysis of Data, South West Papers in Geography, Plymouth Polytechnic, Plymouth, 1981, pp10-11.

73. Perry et al, op. cit.; see also R.W. Perry, *The Impact of Counterurbanisation on Cornwall: A Preliminary Examination of Conceptual and Empirical Issues*, South West Papers in Geography, Plymouth Polytechnic, Plymouth, 1984.

74. Perry et al, op. cit., p42.

75. Ibid.

76. Bolton and Grafton, op. cit., p8.

77. Perry et al, op. cit., p63.

78. D. Nelson and D. Potter, *A Survey of Employees in the Manufacturing Sector in the South West*, Regional Research Series No 3, Department of Industry, London, 1982, cited in Perry et al, op. cit., p63.

79. Bernard Deacon, "Is Cornwall an Internal Colony?", in Cathal O'Luain, *For A Celtic Future*, Celtic League, Dublin, 1983, pp265-267.

80. SWEPC, op. cit.

81. Cornwall County Council, *West Cornwall Study*, Truro, 1970; Cornwall and Devon County Councils, *Towards 2001: The Future of the Plymouth Sub-Region*, Truro/ Exeter, 1975.

82. South West Economic Planning Council, *A Strategic Settlement Pattern For the South West*, SWEPC, Bristol, 1974.

83. Cornwall County Council, *Cornwall Structure Plan*, Truro, 1980; see also Deacon et al, 1988, p53.

84. Cornwall County Council, *Structure Plan: First Alteration*, Truro, 1988, 1.8; cited in Deacon et al, op. cit., p55.

85. Ibid.

86. Deacon et al, pp133-141.

87. *Private Eye* 670, 21 August 1987. Concern for the situation of the indigenous Cornish led to the publication of Andrew George et al, *Homes For Locals in Cornwall/Chyow Rag Genesygyon Yn Kernow*, Cornwall Rural Communicy Council, Truro, 1987, and Andrew George (ed.), *Planning: A Guide for Cornish People/Steeva: Gwerez lever rag Kernowyon*, Cornwall Rural Community Council and Cornwall Association of Parish and Town Councils, Truro, n.d. c1985.

88. Ian Wight, "Territory versus Function in Regional Development: The Case of Cornwall", unpublished paper, University of Aberdeen, 1981, pp15-23.

89. Perry et al, op. cit.

90. Martin J. Weiner, *English Culture and The Decline of The Industrial Spirit 1850–1980*, Cambridge University Press, Cambridge, 1981, p165.

91. Arnold Pacey, *The Culture of Technology*, Blackwell, Oxford, 1983, p178.

92. Perry et al, op. cit., p15.

93. Ibid., p43.

94. Ibid., pp52-56.

95. Ibid., p89.

96. Ibid., p101.

97. Ibid.

98. Ibid., p129.

99. Ronald Perry, *Population Turnaround in Cornwall and Finistere: Contrasting Models of Development in the Rural Periphery*, South West Papers in Geography, Plymouth Polytechnic, Plymouth, 1987, p65. The "English Majority" relates to Perry's assumption that "in-migrants" now — or soon will — outnumber the indigenous Cornish.

100. Wight, op. cit., p6 and p9; Lee, op. cit.; Colin S. Rallings and Adrian Lee, "Politics of the Periphery — The Case of Cornwall", unpublished paper presented to the Conference of the PSA work group on The Politics of the United Kingdom, Aberystwyth, 1977.

101. Charles Thomas, *The Importance of Being Cornish in Cornwall: An Inaugural Lecture*, Institute of Cornish Studies, Redruth, 1973, p13 and p16. The "outsiders" and "insiders" perception paradox is also noted in Andrew Griffiths, *Change in the Countryside: The Cornish Perspective*, Cornwall Rural Development Committee/ University of Exeter Enterprises, Exeter, 1989.

CHAPTER NINE

Kernow Resurgent?

The construction of a "branch factory" economy and the process of "counter-urbanisation" together had served to propel post-war Cornwall from the length period of socio-economic paralysis that it had experienced hitherto in the latter phases of "Second Peripheralism". They had not, however, dispelled the condition of peripherality but had instead ushered in a new era of "Third Peripheralism" in which, despite the emergence from paralysis, Cornwall remained obstinately and identifiably "different" when compared to the English "centre". Despite the hopes of Spooner and the fears of Perry, Cornwall had singularly failed to become like South East England. Thomas in 1986, in apparent surprise at this state of affairs, asked "Why is there still so much of this un-Englishness . . . ?",[1] and went on to express the view that ". . . it may well be another century more before native Cornish cease to think, subconsiously and automatically, in terms of 'Cornwall' and 'England' . . .",[2] pointing to ". . . an Us-and-Them syndrome sharpened by distance from central government and, recently, by post-war revivals of a Cornish national consciousness movement".[3]

Thomas' comments implied a political response to the condition of peripherality, involving a perception of remoteness from the seat of government and the mobilisation of national sentiment, a phenomenon that had indeed characterised the post-war period in Cornwall and was in sharp contrast to the pre-war era in which the "Revival" had been essentially apolitical and Cornish politics for the most part "fossilised". "Third Peripheralism", then, had witnessed not only an emergence from paralysis at the socio-economic level but had seen also an attendant movement in political activity. This movement was to some extent a reaction to the new socio-economic conditions associated with "Third Peripheralism", but it was also a response to new levels of sophistication within the Cornish "Revival" itself. In pre-war Cornwall the "Revival" had largely dissociated itself from the problems and imperatives of the industrial era, appealing instead to the Celtic-Catholic culture of pre-industrial Cornwall and selecting an essentially romantic image of Cornwall in preference to the reality of socio-economic decline. In the post-war era, however, the "Revivalists" proved readier to come to terms with Cornwall's more recent past and, consequently, more able to address the condition of modern Cornwall.

The "rehabilitation" of industrial Cornwall in the estimation of the "Revivalists" had been anticipated in Hamilton Jenkin's *The Cornish Miner*[4] in 1927 but after

1945, with bal-maidens and beam engines already acquiring the romantic glow of history, it continued apace with, for example, the Cornish Engines Preservation Society placing industrial archaeology firmly within the realms of Cornish Studies, and with the appearance of John Rowe's *Cornwall in the Age of the Industrial Revolution*[5] in 1953 marking the birth of academic interest in Cornwall's industrial era. Thereafter, the theme of industrial Cornwall was elaborated at length, most noticably in the many books published (and written) by D. Bradford Barton of Truro[6] and, later, in the various publications of the widely-respected Trevithick Society. In these the significance of Cornwall's industrial era was established beyond doubt or dispute, and with this arose an appreciation of the inherent "Cornishness" of the period. Students learnt of the unique qualities of the *Cornish* beam engine, of the activities of industrial concerns such as the *Cornish* Copper Company, of the social and religious importance of Methodist publications such as the Bible Christian *Cornish Banner*. In short, there emerged a new-found appreciation of the dynamnic nineteenth century Cornish identity based upon industrial prowess. "Revivalists" recognised that Cornish pumps and Cornish boilers could be placed legitimately alongside Celtic crosses and Cornish language miracle plays as integral parts of Cornish culture and determinants of Cornish identity. And with this recognition came a potential broadening of the "Revivalists" appeal, and of their concern for modern Cornwall.

This "rehabilitation" was reflected in Cornish literature as a whole, leading to detailed histories of the tin, copper and china-clay industries, to books on Cornish engineers and engineering, and, in time, to the documentation of the "Great Migration".[7] It became clear that the identity of modern Cornwall must rest to some considerable degree upon the legacy of this industrial era, a clarity which impressed the "Revivalists" but which would also lead commentators to insist that the nature of modern Cornwall must be examined in a framework which not only acknowledged a dim and distant Celtic-Catholic past but which also addressed the issues of industrialisation and de-industrialisation. And, despite continuance of a popular literature based upon images of a romantic "Vanishing Cornwall", this "rehabilitation" prompted a new Cornish literature based upon realism, epitomised in the realms of poetry and fiction in the works of Jack Clemo (the blind and deaf writer of the clay country) and Myrna Combellack and, in non-fiction, in the "travel books" of Donald Rawe (most notably *A Prospect of Cornwall*) where details of a Celtic past were tempered by consideration of current social, economic and ecological issues.[8]

The Cornish "Revival", then, developed in the post-war era as a more broadly-based phenomenon, with a potentially wider appeal for the broad mass of Cornish people and with a reformed ideology which had expanded to acknowledge the significance of Cornwall's industrial experience and which now expressed a concern for the condition of modern Cornwall. This, in turn, provoked political consequences. Exclusive concern for the Celtic-Catholic culture of pre-industrial Cornwall was essentially apolitical, but the new-found concern for the condition of modern Cornwall inevitably begged questions of a political nature. Increasingly, therefore, the "Revivalists" interpreted their objectives in political terms, with an emerging political strategy which sought to defend and promote the ethnic identity of Cornwall and the Cornish. In this, of course, the Cornish "Revivalists" were mirroring events that were occurring or had already occurred in Wales and Scotland, in European regions such as Catalonia, Brittany, and Flanders, and increasingly too in "Third World" countries, where — as A.D. Smith has shown — similarly politicised elites were leading "ethnic revival".[9]

As a direct result of this process, Mebyon Kernow was founded in 1951.[10] Although conceived as a pressure group rather than a party, it was nonetheless overtly political in purpose. The *New Cornwall* magazine explained that Mebyon Kernow existed to foster the Cornish identity, to gain for Cornish people a "square deal", and to ensure the proper use of Cornish resources for the benefit of Cornish people.[11] Emerging in the wake of the Scottish Covenant of 1948, when hundreds of thousands of Scots had declared their support for a Scottish Parliament within the framework of the United Kingdom, Mebyon Kernow moved quickly to assert its claim that Cornwall too should achieve self-government.[12] At a time when the activities of nationalists in many parts of the Empire were bringing independence to many former colonies and accelerating the transformation to Commonwealth, Mebyon Kernow felt confident to claim that ". . . Cornish people are no less intelligent than Maltese or Jamaicans and so are equally capable of running their own affairs".[13] According to one interpretation, "This would be a form of self-government within Great Britain — a system that already works well in the Isle of Man, the Channel Isles and Northern Ireland",[14] while Mebyon Kernow's own literature asserted that its principal aim was "To maintain the Celtic character of Cornwall and its right to self-government in domestic affairs",[15] but with a qualification that ". . . Cornwall should have the greatest possible autonomy, while not wishing to sever itself from the United Kingdom."[16]

In marked contrast to the "Revivalists" of the inter-war period, Mebyon Kernow expressed an interest in economic issues, culminating in the publication in 1968 of its economic strategy *What Cornishmen Can Do*.[17] Generally, Mebyon Kernow proposed "To study local conditions and attempt to remedy any that may be prejudicial to the best interests of Cornwall . . ."[18] and, perhaps more controversially, it argued that ". . . Cornish men and women should have preference in appointments to Cornish jobs, other factors being equal".[19] Mebyon Kernow warned that "A Regional government, based on Bristol or Plymouth will not improve matters for Cornwall".[20] In other fields, it declared its support for Cornish language, literature, culture, history and sport, and in particular for their advancement in schools, and by the late 1960s Mebyon Kernow had already prepared numerous policy documents on issues as diverse as transport, a university for Cornwall, fishing, local government reform, mining, and broadcasting.[21] By 1970 Mebyon Kernow boasted 21 branches spread throughout Cornwall, with a total membership of well over 3,000. The Launceston branch alone was one hundred strong, and in the Falmouth-Camborne constituency Mebyon Kernow claimed to have some 1,000 members.[22]

Throughout the 1950s and into the 60s Mebyon Kernow had carefully maintained its pressure group, non-party, identity. It successfully manipulated the various political parties and actively encouraged a policy of "dual membership" in which Mebyon Kernow activists could also declare themselves active in political parties, and vice versa. In this way, the Liberal MPs John Pardoe and Peter Bessell and the Conservative David Mudd were able to join Mebyon Kernow, while Harold Hayman (Labour), John Nott (Conservative) and David Penhaligon (Liberal) were all able to express broad support for MK policies.[23] Reflecting the success of this arrangement, Mebyon Kernow did not formally abandon its "dual membership" policy until as late as 1976, a number of years after having recast itself as a political party.[24] The pressure group role, however, was progressively eroded in the late 1960s, most especially by the decision to field official Mebyon Kernow candidates in local elections. Although the strong Independent tradition in local government in Cornwall meant that Mebyon Kernow candidates were unlikely to be involved in direct fights with Liberal, Labour or Conservative candidates at that time, the decision was nonetheless a highly political one. In April 1966 four Mebyon Kernow local election candidates protested that "Mebyon Kernow is not . . . a political party. It represents no sectional interests at all and . . . comprises a very respectable cross section of the public",[25] but this argument seemed to wear thin when in the following year an official Mebyon Kernow candidate, Colin Murley, won the St Day seat on Cornwall County Council with an anti-Overspill "Keep Cornwall Cornish" campaign.[26] In 1969 Mebyon Kernow won two further local council seats, with its journal *Cornish Nation* anticipating the birth of a new era in which Mebyon Kernow might move more openly onto the political offensive.[27]

The "Overspill" schemes, as noted in Chapter 8, heralded the emergence of "counterurbanisation". Mebyon Kernow's growth in reaction to "Overspill" was therefore a function of the new socio-economic conditions of "Third Peripheralism" as well as a result of the new politicisation of the "Revivalists". Certainly, "Overspill" proved a successful political issue for Mebyon Kernow. In 1968 its Bodmin Branch secured 1400 signatures on an anti-Overspill petition, and MK agitation contributed significantly to the defeat of "Overspill" schemes at Camborne, Redruth, St Day, and Liskeard.[28] Coming at a time of important nationalist advances in both Scotland and Wales, Mebyon Kernow considered that its "Overspill" successes were an indication that it should follow more closely the examples of Plaid Cymru and the Scottish National Party. Accordingly, at the beginning of 1969 Mebyon Kernow announced that it would fight the Parliamentary seat of Falmouth-Camborne in the next General Election.[29]

This decision had far-reaching consequences, ranging from Mebyon Kernow's intermittent and desultory intervention in elections at various levels over several years, to the inevitable narrowing of its support base and the consequent fragmentation of the nationalist movement. In the first place, Mebyon Kernow's intervention in the 1970 General Election attracted less than 1,000 votes in the Falmouth-Camborne constituency, although the seat was won for the Conservatives by a Mebyon Kernow member, David Mudd. Undeterred, Mebyon Kernow persisted with its "vote-catching" anti-Overspill strategy, with *Cornish Nation* in March 1971 voicing opposition to the *West Cornwall Study* and its

"Overspill" connotations.[30] A year later a contributer to the same journal was complaining that although "Overspill" had been defeated, many people were nonetheless moving to Cornwall as private individuals.[31] Although *Cornish Nation* had called for the assimilation of newcomers into the Cornish way of life, by September 1973 it was hardening its line with the view that ". . . the influx into the land of English people is giving rise to considerable anti-English feeling among ordinary Cornish people".[32] Mebyon Kernow entered the General Election year of 1974, therefore, with an image that was more overtly nationalist than that which had existed hitherto and with a message that was increasingly aggressive and uncompromising.

Surprisingly, Mebyon Kernow failed to capitalise upon its earlier intervention and apparent latent strength in Falmouth-Camborne, and concentrated its efforts instead upon neighbouring Truro, a reflection of its fundamental inability to devise an electoral strategy. In the March Election it secured 850 votes, but in the October Mebyon Kernow's vote slumped to 384 as nationalist supporters switched their support to David Penhaligon. In contrast to this poor performance, the elections of 1974 had witnessed spectacular nationalist advances in Scotland and a credible nationalist performance in Wales. The mid-1970s, therefore, were dominated by the "Devolution Debate" and in this Mebyon Kernow benefited from the apparent new-found credibility of Celtic nationalism. In the General Election of 1979 Mebyon Kernow contested Falmouth-Camborne, St Ives, and Bodmin, with an aggregate vote of 4155 (leaving the recently-formed Cornish Nationalist Party to face up to the formidable Penhaligon machine in Truro: CNP won 227 votes). With the failure of Devolution in Scotland and Wales, however, Mebyon Kernow shared too in the declining fortunes of the nationalist parties and, in the General Election of 1983, was able to achieve just over 500 votes apiece in the constituencies of Falmouth-Camborne and St Ives. Deciding not to oppose Penhaligon again, the CNP moved "out of the frying pan and into the fire" as it shifted its attentions to the Tory-Liberal marginal of North Cornwall, where it achieved 364 votes.[33] In the 1987 General Election neither Mebyon Kernow nor the Cornish Nationalist Party fielded candidates in any of the Cornish constituencies, the first time since Mebyon Kernow's decision to "go political" in 1969 that the nationalist cause had not been represented.

The failure of Mebyon Kernow to make a significant intervention in Parliamentary Elections was partly a function of electoral appeal and credibility, exacerbated by its failure to develop a coherent and consistent electoral strategy, a shortcoming not helped by the appearance of the Cornish Nationalist Party. The emergence of the "Penhaligon factor" and the electorally marginal nature of several Cornish constituencies were also inhibiting factors. More generally, as Deacon noted:

> When contesting Westminster elections Cornish nationalists suffer from the same factors as all minor parties in the UK. An electoral system that positively encourages tactical voting, lack of access to the media, in particular television, the adversarial structuring of General Election

campaigns by the Press, lack of financial resources all make electioneering an uphill task for the nationalists.[34]

In elections at other levels, however, Mebyon Kernow's performance was broadly more successful and rather more consistent. Although the St Day seat on Cornwall County Council was lost in the aftermath of the "Overspill" campaign, when that particular threat had apparently been averted, Mebyon Kernow continued to target specific County seats. In 1977, for example, the party contested seven County seats (winning an average of 17.06 of the vote) and in 1981 it contested nine seats, with 16.63 per cent of the vote. In 1985, at the nadir of its fortunes, Mebyon Kernow managed to contest only three County seats although, paradoxically, it won one of these (Colin Lawry in Penzance South) and came a close second in another (St Just-in-Penwith, with 40.3 of the vote). It is, incidentally, interesting to note here that in contesting local elections under its own party label Mebyon Kernow was in fact assisting the erosion of the Independent (ie non-party-party political) tradition in Cornish council politics. Equally, it should be recognised that a number of Councillors elected at County or District level as "Independents" were in fact Mebyon Kernow members or sympathisers.[35]

At District level, Mebyon Kernow contested five seats in 1976 (winning one), four in 1977–78, and a significant 19 (ie 8.3 per cent of all seats) in 1979 when the party achieved an aggregate of 10,421 votes and secured two seats. In the Penwith District Council election of May 1982 Mebyon Kernow won Penzance Central and came second in St Just (where it forced the SDP-Liberal Alliance into last place), and in a similar performance in 1986 MK held Penzance Central and came a very close second in Penzance East. In 1983, in Cornwall as a whole, MK contested seven seats of which it secured one. At Parish level, Mebyon Kernow was similarly interventionist during this period, securing representation on Parish and Town Councils in areas as diverse as Porthleven, Truro and Liskeard.[36]

Although hardly more than patchy, Mebyon Kernow's performance in local council elections at least demonstrated a certain ability to develop an electoral strategy at that level (most notably and successfully in Penzance where Colin Lawry proved an able "grass roots" politican and constructed a local MK power base) and the potential to attract sizeable electoral support in particular geographic areas where MK had been able to develop a local organisation. This potential to mobilise support under certain circumstances was demonstrated most convincingly, however, in the European Parliamentary Election of 1979. In 1978 (as we shall see in Chapter 10) Cornish local government bodies and many other organisations had voiced opposition to the proposed Cornwall and Plymouth European Parliamentary Constituency, demanding instead a Cornwall-only Constituency. When these objections were overruled there was considerable dissatisfaction within Cornwall, manifested, for example, in support for the Mebyon Kernow candidate (Richard Jenkin) in the European Election. As Butler and Marquand noted in their survey of the election, "A notable minor party vote was Mebyon Kernow's 5.9 per cent in Cornwall and Plymouth . . .".[37] In fact, MK's 10,205 votes represented some ten per cent of the vote in Cornwall (assuming, as Butler and Marquand put it, that ". . . a Cornish nationalist had no appeal in Plymouth . . ."[38]), a result that compared more than favourably with the performance of Plaid Cymru in the predominantly English-speaking parts of Wales (eg 7.9 per cent in Wales South and 7.3 per cent in Wales South East) and led *Cornish Nation* to conclude that " . . . 1979 has proved to be . . . a superb start to MK's first serious attempt to achieve multi-level representation from Parish Councils to the European Parliament".[39]

However, 1979 proved to be not the start but rather the high point of Mebyon Kernow's electoral performance, the 1980s witnessing decline at the Westminster level and a failure on Mebyon Kernow's part to contest the European Parliamentary Election in 1984 — despite the fact that it had been instrumental in forcing a Boundary Commission Inquiry into the Cornwall and Plymouth EPC in the preceding November. Such decline and failure was, as noted above, to some extent a function of the failure of Devolution in Scotland and Wales and the consequent decline in that period of the Scottish National Party and Plaid Cymru, with Celtic nationalism no longer enjoying the limelight of British political debate and media coverage. Locally, however, it was also a result of severe organisational difficulties encountered by Mebyon Kernow. These related to the broad inability to develop a proper electoral strategy, along with attendant financial constraints, but they also resulted from an increasing confusion and turmoil within the nationalist community itself.

Uncertainty in the nationalist camp had been evident as early as 1970, at the time of Mebyon Kernow's initial decision to intervene in Parliamentary elections. Most obviously, those local MPs who had earlier joined MK, approving of its pressure group role and seeing it as a useful basis for developing their own "localist" or "Cornish" image, had been placed in a rather ambivalent position. Peter Bessell offered to resign from MK, but David Mudd actually joined the movement at this time — in the process stealing much of the nationalist thunder in the Falmouth-Camborne constituency he was intent upon contesting as a Conservative. Mebyon Kernow's position was similarly ambivalent. On the one hand it had hoped to retain its old pressure group identity, appealing across party-lines to a broad spectrum of "patriotic" opinion in Cornwall (a tactic that had already won it considerable credibility) but on the other adopting a vigorous and overtly nationalist stance, directly opposing and competing with the London-based parties and claiming common cause with Plaid Cymru and the Scottish National Party. These two approaches were by no means compatible, and while Mebyon Kernow alienated many of its former supporters through its new, increasingly aggressive party-political style of nationalism, so it failed to satisfy some of its more radical members who had hoped to shed completely the pressure group image.

As early as January 1969 G. Harris, the Vice-Chairman of the Liberal Party Association in Redruth and Camborne, had resigned from Mebyon Kernow over its increasing "politicisation".[40] But for others MK's "politicisation" did not go far enough, and at the 1969 Annual General Meeting of Mebyon Kernow there was criticism from "A small minority determined to impose its so-called 'Progressive'

198

views . . ."[41] on the movement. This led directly to the establishment of the short-lived Cornish National Party (not to be confused with the later Cornish Nationalist Party) by a group of former Mebyon Kernow members who were determined to seek "Commonwealth member status" for Cornwall. This, as they explained in their policy document *Cornwall — Forward with Confidence*, would mean constitutional independence on the lines of that sought for Scotland by the Scottish National Party, a more extreme demand than Mebyon Kernow's "self-government in domestic affairs".[42] Although the Cornish National Party proved unable to command much support and disappeared quickly from the active political scene, with any distinctive features that it may have enjoyed being swiftly usurped by Mebyon Kernow's increasingly aggressive stance, a dangerous precedent had been set. In the years ahead, as Mebyon Kernow faltered in the development of its electoral strategy and as tension between the older "pressure group" wing and the more "politicised" radicals grew, so the propensity for the creation of dissident, break-away groups was enhanced.

For some, the Cornish Branch of the Celtic League was an alternative channel for their energies. Formed in 1961 with the intention of co-ordinating Celtic nationalism in the British, Irish and French States, and pursuing a Pan-Celtic ideology (which was outlined by P. Berresford Ellis in his *The Creed of the Celtic Revolution*[43]), the League formed branches in each of the Celtic countries and in Cornwall encouraged nationalists to see the Cornish situation in an inter-Celtic context. Others, however, sought a more distinctly Cornish approach and a number, uncertain of the benefits of Mebyon Kernow having moved from pressure group to political party and disappointed by its incoherent electoral strategy, considered that a more imaginative campaign would bring greater rewards. Accordingly, in 1974 a group of activists sought to restore Cornwall's ancient Stannary (or Tinners') Parliament. Although the Parliament had not met since the eighteenth century, its not inconsiderable powers still existed, at least in theory, and those supporting its restoration argued that the Stannary afforded Cornwall significant independence from Westminster. Their case was stated somewhat less than plainly in pseudo-legal language in the first issue of the *Cornish Stannary Gazette* in January 1975, published by these latter-day "Stannators" who — in the face of official disinterest — decided to reconvene the Stannary Parliament unilaterally.[44] This new Stannary movement created considerable interest and curiosity within Cornwall, but it was not successful in winning any general credibility or widespread support. It was, however, to prove a considerable thorn in the side of the Nirex organisation in its exploration of an abandoned quarry site in Cornwall, invoking ancient Stannary Law to "bound" the land in question. Equally, it formed a significant focus for anti-Community Charge activists in Cornwall in 1989 and 1990, arguing variously that the "Poll Tax" was contrary to Stannary Law and therefore illegal in Cornwall or that "Cornish tinners" (however defined) were exempt from such taxation.[45]

A perhaps more significant event was the formation in 1975 of the Cornish Nationalist Party by a group of disaffected Mebyon Kernow members under the leadership of Dr James Whetter. As editor of *Cornish Nation* Dr Whetter had attempted the further "politicisation" of Mebyon Kernow, in particular advocating the extension of the party's policy on self-government to embrace ". . . the formation of a Celtic Federation of Nations, of Eire, Scotland, Wales, Kernow, Isle of Man, Brittany"[46] and drawing comparisons between other Celtic countries and conditions that obtained in Cornwall. His militant, party-political nationalism was resisted by elements of the Mebyon Kernow leadership, however, and Dr Whetter was dismayed by the failure in 1974 to build upon the earlier intervention in Falmouth-Camborne. Having fought two solitary and rather fruitless battles in Truro during the 1974 General Election, Dr Whetter and his supporters broke away, a statement in the Cornish Nationalist Party's journal *Cornish Banner* in June 1975 declaring that Mebyon Kernow was ". . . not equipped to become a positive nationalist movement . . .".[47] Although promising at first a more clearly political approach and an all-embracing electoral strategy, the behaviour of the Cornish Nationalist Party in the 1970s and 80s in fact resembled that of Mebyon Kernow to a remarkable degree. This included ad hoc and unsuccessful interventions in elections at the Parliamentary, County and District levels, together with an intervention in the Cornwall and Plymouth EPC in 1984 when the Cornish Nationalist Party achieved 1,892 votes. The one area of policy where the CNP did vary noticably from MK was in the field of European relations, where the CNP from its beginning proved a vigorously pro-European organisation, affiliating itself with the European Federalist Party and forging links with like-minded nationalist and regionalist groups in Europe. As the *Cornish Banner* explained in November 1988:

> . . . from an early date we saw that one of the objectives of the CNP should be the attainment of regional status for Cornwall both within the British system and the European organisation in the future . . . The operation of the single European Act in 1992 may well present the European regions with a great opportunity for progress.[48]

This fragmentation of the Cornish national movement into several competing but electorally relatively insignificant groupings had a number of consequences. One response was an attempt at "bridge building" in a bid to bring the disparate elements of the movement together to at least agree a common set of objectives. A short-lived Cornish Congress ended in acrimony, but in 1979 there was a more serious and enduring attempt (encouraged initially by the *Cornish Guardian* newspaper) at the creation of a Cornish Assembly which not only brought together MK and the CNP but appealed to a wide range of other organisations and individuals, including members of other political parties. The Cornish Assembly styled itself "A non-party political forum and organisation, founded . . . for the protection of Cornwall and Cornish character and identity".[49] And — as well as providing that forum and bringing together as many Cornish groups as possible — the Assembly considered that its fundamental aim was ". . . to retain within Cornwall all existing powers and to campaign for the return of powers of administration and decision which would be better exercised from within

Cornwall".[50] However, despite its initial promise, the Cornish Assembly proved an unwieldy and sometimes grudging alliance of disparate interest groups, without an effective organisational base to turn resolutions into action and without the means to gain the continuing attention and confidence of the Cornish population. Although the Assembly survived, it was as a small and ineffectual body — adding to rather than overcoming the fragmentation of the Cornish national movement.

A more successful strategy was that of the more loosely defined and loosely structured Cowethas Flamank group. Cowethas Flamank emerged during the debate that attended the publication of the Maud Report in 1970 which recommended, amongst other things, the removal of part of South East Cornwall from the control of Cornwall County Council and its placement instead in an expanded Plymouth authority. John Fleet, a founding member, expressed the hope that Cowethas Flamank could provide a support service to Mebyon Kernow in its opposition to the Maud Report and in other areas as ". . . a kind of Mebyon Kernow Bow Group or Fabian Society . . .",[51] able to undertake sophisticated research and produce new ideas as well as providing secretarial and organisational support. As Fleet explained, "The Group is bound by the rules of Mebyon Kernow and is subject to the general direction of its executive".[52] By 1971, having "felt its feet" in the successful Cornish opposition to Maud, Cowethas Flamank announced that it was ". . . anxious to inaugurate a series of comprehensive economic, social and environmental studies for the whole of Cornwall . . ."[53] and in February 1972 it launched its own magazine, *Kevren*. However, by this time Cowethas Flamank was already voicing serious misgivings about the effectiveness of Mebyon Kernow as a political organisation, with *Kevren* detecting within MK ". . . an unhappy malaise . . . a general lack of confidence . . ."[54] and, later, complaining that "Unfortunately, our offers and suggestions have so far either been ignored or dismissed out of hand . . .".[55]

There was thereafter a subtle but very definite attempt by Cowethas Flamank to distance itself from its parent body. Increasingly, Cowethas Flamank described itself not as an integral part of MK but rather as an independent group which believed that ". . . Cornwall stands in need of a strong popular movement such as Mebyon Kernow".[56] In time even that explanation was dropped from *Kevren* and other Cowethas Flamank publications, and by the early 1980s Cowethas Flamank had successfully dissociated itself from Mebyon Kernow. This lent an even greater freedom of action to the group, and from this emerged Cowethas Flamank's central role in the establishment of the standing Conference on Cornwall which, following its successful inauguration at Perranporth in May 1983, developed as an independent Cornish institution in its own right. As a biannual conference, the Conference on Cornwall proved a far more successful forum for the discussion of Cornish affairs than the Cornish Assembly had ever been. More particularly, it developed a genius for the spawning of action groups which — having been formed at the Conference — would go away to pursue their particular fields of endeavour and then report their progress to future meetings of the Conference. In this way, the Conference set up working parties on issues as disparate as devolution and education (the latter leading to the publication of a book *Cornish Studies For Schools*[57]), while new bodies such as Skeusow (the Cornish film and television group), the Cornish Music Guild, the Cornish Literary Guild, Cornish Alternatives to the Structure Plan, the Cornish Bureau of European Relations, the Campaign For A Cornish (Euro) Constituency, and Tyr-Gwyr-Gweryn (Land-Truth-People) were all born from Conference activity. Within this diversity of activity the Conference had also secured the participation and co-operation of the various fragments of the Cornish national movement, and had been successful in bringing that movement to a wider public.[58]

A less constructive and rather sinister reaction to the electoral failure and fragmentation of the nationalist movement was the emergence of the shadowy "An Gof" group which was allegedly responsible for two bomb explosions in Cornwall in the early 1980s, and which may or may not have been responsible for the spate of "An Gof" daubings on railway bridges and the like. Frustration at the apparent powerlessness of constitutional nationalism was apparent in the foundation of the tiny Free Cornwall organisation, which saw itself as the vanguard of the Cornish movement and intended by a policy of criticism and prodding to "ginger-up" the existing parties. Its cynical, satirical and sometimes waspish magazine, also entitled *Free Cornwall*, was itself a manifestation of another element of the fragmentation, the plethora of "underground" fringe journals (mostly shortlived) such as *An Weryn*, *Gwyn ha Du*, *An Kenethlor*, *Cornish Voice*, and at least two called *Kernow*, along with the more successful all-Cornish language *An Gannas* (the organ of Cowethas an Yeth Kernewek, the Cornish Language Fellowship).

In the face of such fragmentation, Mebyon Kernow in the late 1970s and early 1980s attempted to re-assert its leadership of the Cornish national movement, and this may also help to explain its surprisingly high profile in the various elections of 1979. Be that as it may, Mebyon Kernow reacted to the fragmentation by adopting an even more decidedly "politicised" posture, its policy discussion booklet in 1976 offering a vigorously nationalist critique of the:

> . . . spurious doctrine of English regionalism that would include us as a part of a South-West English region . . . (which) represents not decentralisation and a recognition of national rights for Cornwall but an attempt to retain central power by a minimum dispersal to its agents into powerful regional strongpoints . . . On every issue we are told that we are an English County, a part of an English Region, and the answer always means more English exploitation and even less Cornish well-being . . . Cornwall was a Country, it is a Country and will be a Country as long as there are Cornish people who assert their historic nationhood.[59]

Nonetheless, there continued to be those who sought to establish a yet more overtly political stance, with Mebyon Kernow shorn finally of its pressure group image and with a nationalist ideology and programme clearly and unequivocally articulated. This debate was resolved at length with the production of a new constitution — in which MK's party political role was enshrined — with Wight in 1981 concluding that "It seems clear that MK is only now completing the transition from a pressure group to a political party".[60] Inevitably, the less ideologically-committed felt compromised within such an arrangement and, as *Gwyn ha Du* (MK's new political journal) admitted in 1980, ". . . out of the confusion has emerged a slimmer, battered and partly discredited party".[61] It was, however, a ". . . party . . . poised on the edge of its best opportunity for years . . . a chance to adopt a set of policies and tactics (for) . . . uniting and politicising the party".[62]

In fact, Mebyon Kernow was in 1980 entering a period of decline. Critics in *Gwyn ha Du* and *Cornish Nation* continued to protest that Mebyon Kernow's decision to forsake its pressure group role and embrace instead the faction-fighting of party politics had been a crucial error of strategy.[63] But opponents of this view responded with the argument that the relative failure of Mebyon Kernow was not so much a function of strategic error but rather a reflection of the fact that Cornish nationalism had failed to establish and elucidate a clear and genuinely nationalist philosophy. According to this view, the apparent vaccilations and contradictions in Mebyon Kernow's behaviour had resulted from the fact that its activists had been "patriots" rather than true nationalists, their ideology too narrow and too ill-formed to construct successfully a fully developed nationalist paradigm and an attendant, intellectually coherent political programme. Deacon summarised this approach with the argument that ". . . although adopting the terminology of nationalism, especially in the late 60s and partly under the influence of Scotland and Wales, the Cornish movement has not actually evolved a coherent vision of Cornish nationalism . . .".[64]

Deacon's conclusion appeared a damning indictment of the Cornish national movement, a movement which despite twenty or more years of increasing "politicisation" still lacked a core of politically-aware and ideologically-committed nationalists, a movement still unsure of its strategy and objectives, poorly organised, and habitually gauche and naive in its attempts to enter the arena of political activity. Indeed, much of this criticism was justified — as is demonstrated above — but such stark judgement failed to recognise the real extent of the "politicisation" of the Cornish "Revival" in the years after the Second World War. Moreover, such a view did not acknowledge or appreciate that the most profound influence of this "politicisation" lay outside the confines of the activities and electoral performance of Mebyon Kernow, the Cornish Nationalist Party and the other groups.

Of course, the most extraordinary feature of the emergence and influence of Mebyon Kernow (and the others) was the very fact that it had happened at all. This, as Lee noted, was in itself enough to mark the political experience of Cornwall off from that of English counties and to suggest the existence of an autonomous political culture in which the articulation of separate identity and a sense of anti-metropolitanism was of underlying significance.[65] This too, as Thomas had noted,[66] was a specific feature of the post-war era, hinting at the emergence of Cornish politics from its pre-war "fossilisation" and indicating a re-assessment within the Cornish "Revival" which had led to a re-interpretation in political terms of its broad objectives. That re-assessment and re-interpretation had been faci i-tated, as argued earlier, by the "rehabilitation" of industrial Cornwall within the ideology of the "Revival" — prompting a new-found concern for the condition of modern Cornwall — but it was also precipitated and popularised by the socio-economic changes of the post-war era. The planned "Overspill" schemes of the 1960s were the heralds of "branch factory" regional planning and of "counterurbanisation", and the emergence of Cornish nationalism was therefore a response to (indeed, a part of) the condition of "Third Peripheralism".

However, the appearance of Cornish nationalism was but one feature of the emergence of Cornish politics from its earlier "fossilisation" and of the new "politicisation" of the Cornish "Revival". Both these phenomena had wide-ranging effects upon Cornish political culture and activity, reaching beyond the bounds of the nationalist parties, and it is therefore misleading to attempt to judge the extent of their influence and impact by examining the fortunes of the nationalists in isolation. Instead, to ty to achieve a more balanced and more comprehensive understanding of the effects of these phenomena, it is important to examine the nature of political change in Cornwall as a whole in the post-war era and to identify the extent that it was "different" from that which obtained in England.

Notes and References

1. Charles Thomas, *Celtic Britain*, Thames and Hudson, London, 1986, p13.
2. Ibid., p65.
3. Ibid.
4. A.K. Hamilton Jenkin, *The Cornish Miner*, 1927, republished David and Charles, Newton Abbot, 1972.
5. John Rowe, *Cornwall in the Age of the Industrial Revolution*, Liverpool University Press, Liverpool, 1953.
6. Epitomised, perhaps, in D.B. Barton, *The Cornish Beam Engine*, Bradford Barton, Truro, 1965, republished Cornwall Books, Exeter, 1989.
7. The flowering of Cornish publishing was led in the 1960s and 1970s by D. Bradford Barton of Truro, and in the 1980s and 1990s by Dyllansow Truran of Redruth.
8. Jack Clemo, in *Penguin Modern Poets 6*, Penguin, London, 1964; Myrna Combellack, *The Playing Place*, Dyllansow Truran, Redruth, 1989; Donald R. Rawe, *A Prospect of Cornwall*, Robert Hale, London, 1986.
9. Anthony D. Smith, *Ethnic Revival in The Modern World*, Cambridge Unviersity Press, Cambridge, 1981.
10. Adrian Lee, "Cornwall: Aspects of Regionalism and Nationalism", unpublished paper presented to Workshop of Nationalist and Regionalist movements in Western Europe, University of Strathclyde, 1978, p10.
11. *New Cornwall*, Vol I, No 1, 1952.
12. George Thayer, *The British Political Fringe: A Profile*, Anthony Blond, London, 1965, p185.
13. Richard and Ann Jenkin, *Cornwall: The Hidden Land*, West Country Publications, Bracknell, 1965, p27.
14. Ibid.
15. Mebyon Kernow policy leaflet and membership form, c1969.

16. Ibid.
17. Mebyon Kernow, *What Cornishmen Can Do*, MK Publications, Redruth, 1969.
18. MK policy leaflet, c1969, op. cit.
19. Ibid.
20. Ibid.
21. Ibid.
22. *Cornish Nation*, January-February 1969; September 1970.
23. Lee, op. cit., p13.
24. Bernard Deacon, "The Prospects for Cornish Politics — Constructing an Ethnic Politics", unpublished paper, Redruth, 1984, p8.
25. Ibid.; see also *Cornish Guardian* 28 April 1966.
26. *Cornish Nation*, November 1968.
27. *Cornish Nation*, June-July 1969.
28. *Cornish Nation*, November 1969.
29. *Cornish Nation*, January-February 1969.
30. *Cornish Nation*, March 1971.
31. *Cornish Nation*, December 1972.
32. *Cornish Nation*, September 1973.
33. Statistical details of nationalist interventions are shown in Bernard Deacon, "The Electoral Impact of Cornish Nationalism", in Cathal O'Luain, *For A Celtic Future*, Celtic League, Dublin, 1983.
34. Ibid., p244.
35. Interesting analyses of nationalist interventions at local levels appear in the Cowethas Flamank journal *Kevren*, No 29 Gwaf 1979, No 36 Kynaf 1982, No 38 Haf 1983, No 41 Haf 1985, No 44 Haf 1986.
36. Ibid.
37. David Butler and David Marquand, *European Elections and British Politics*, Longman, London, 1981, p133.
38. Ibid.
39. *Cornish Nation*, Summer 1979.
40. *Cornish Nation*, January-February 1969.
41. *Cornish Nation*, June-July 1969.
42. Cornish National Party, *Cornwall — Forward With Confidence*, Liskeard, c1969.
43. P. Berresford Ellis, *The Creed of the Celtic Revolution*, Medusa, London, 1969.
44. *Cornish Stannary Gazette*, January 1975.
45. *Western Morning News*, 25 November 1988, 14 June 1989.
46. *Cornish Nation*, March 1972.
47. *Cornish Banner*, June 1975.
48. *Cornish Banner*, November 1988.
49. Cornish Assembly policy leaflet and membership form, c1980.
50. Ibid., see also *Cornish Nation*, Summer 1979.
51. *Cornish Nation*, September 1970.
52. Ibid.
53. John Fleet in *Celtic League Annual*, Dublin, 1971.
54. *Kevren* No 1, February 1972.
55. *Kevren* No 5, August 1973.
56. Ian Wight, "Territory Versus Function in Regional Development: The Case of Cornwall", unpublished paper, University of Aberdeen, 1981, p40.

57. Cornwall County Council and Institute of Cornish Studies, *Cornish Studies For Schools*, Cornwall County Council, Truro, 1987.

58. The relationship between Cowethas Flamank, the Conference on Cornwall, and its various working parties was outlined by John Fleet, "Cowethas Flamank and the Conference on Cornwall", unpublished memorandum, Camborne, 1986.

59. Leonard Truran, *For Cornwall — A Future!*, MK Publications, Redruth, 1976, p4.

60. Wight, op. cit., p30.

61. *Gwyn ha Dhu*, No 1, 1980.

62. Ibid.

63. *Gwyn ha Dhu*, Summer 1982; *Cornish Nation*, No 44, 1982.

64. Deacon, 1984, op. cit., p1.

65. Lee, op. cit., p1.

66. Thomas, op. cit., p65.

CHAPTER TEN

The New Politics of The Periphery

At first glance, the relative electoral failure of Mebyon Kernow and the Cornish Nationalist Party, along with their apparent inability to construct a comprehensive nationalist philosophy, might suggest that their impact upon the Cornish political scene was only marginal and that the "politicisation" of the "Revival" — from which the nationalists had sprung — had had only a minimal effect upon Cornish political activity. Further examination, however, reveals that the reality is quite the reverse. In fact, the "politicisation" of the Cornish "Revival" had been the precipitating impetus which — in response to the new conditions of "Third Peripheralism" — had forced Cornish politics out of its earlier "fossilisation". This had led not only to the preoccupations and electoral invervention of the nationalist groups, but was manifested too in a much broader range of political activity in Cornwall. Stemming directly from the "Revivalists" reinterpretation of their objectives in political terms, with its emphasis upon the defence and promotion of ethnic identity, was a new concern for the political "accommodation" of Cornwall. This was a concern which not only motivated the nationalist groups but which came, in various circumstances, to affect the whole spectrum of political opinion and activity in Cornwall and which, on specific occasions, dominated political debate. Added to this was an increasingly sophisticated and incisive critique of those policies that had led to the creation of the "branch factory" economy and "counterurbanisation", voiced initially by the nationalist groups but soon embraced by a series of highly articulate and well-informed pressure groups. And, lastly, there was the impact of all this upon the existing political party structure in Cornwall in which an already distinctive Cornish political culture was enhanced as it responded to the new conditions of "Third Peripheralism".

In the era of "Second Peripheralism", when Cornwall enjoyed a self-confident sense of identity based upon the strength of its industrial prowess, the symbols of Cornwall's political "accommodation" (most notably the Duchy and the Stannary) were seen as outmoded and unnecessary and were allowed, even encouraged to decline or metamorphose. Although the creation of Cornwall County Council and the new diocese of Truro were in some respects new symbols of political "accommodation" (although they did not lend an identity in any way distinctive from that of an English county), the passing of industrial prowess had left Cornwall largely bereft of any symbolic means of expressing or asserting its sense of identity. In the inter-war period the "Revivalists" had reacted to this situation in their appeal to the pre-industrial culture of Celtic-Catholic Cornwall. This had meant reviving the Cornish language, promoting the use of the Cornish flag, and emphasising the specifically "Celtic" aspects of the Cornish inheritance (such as Celtic haiography). It had also required the "invention" of tradition (a la Hobsbawm and Ranger[1]) in those areas where nothing suitable existed already in the genuinely authentic historical baggage. In this way a Gorsedd, complete with Bardic ceremony, was "revived"; and the kilt was "reintroduced" on the basis that it was a Celtic form of dress and therefore appropriate to Cornwall. Even the revival of the language was subject to a similar process, with Robert Morton Nance pooling the elements from surviving Cornish sources to construct a vocabulary, orthography and grammar in a Unified form, employing in the process various assumptions and accretions and loans from Breton and Welsh decided at his discretion.

In the post-war era this search for cultural symbolism continued apace. A Cornish National Tartan was introduced to complement the kilt, organisations such as the Celtic Congress and Kernow Pan-Celtic strove to rebuild Cornwall's links with the Celtic world (securing, for example, Cornwall's participation in Celtic festivals such as those in Killarney in Ireland and Lorient in Brittany, as well as the establishment of Cornwall's own Lowender Peran), Cornish towns and villages clamoured to "twin" with similar communities in Brittany, and folk dance and music enthusiasts formed groups such as Cam Kernewek with a distinctly "Celtic" flavour. Cornish wrestling (a genuine survival from ancient times) was also put on an "inter-Celtic" footing as Cornish-Breton contests were arranged. Most importantly, in the wake of fierce criticism of Nance's Unified Cornish (condemned by Price as a mutant "Cornic"[2]), language enthusiasts were at pains to modify revived Cornish in a manner that would make it more academically acceptable. The Cornish Language Board (set up in 1967 to administer the language revival[3]) in 1986 adopted Ken George's revised "phonemic" or "common" Cornish, a more internally consistent and academically rigorous system than Nance's but with an orthography which was also "invented".[4] Slavish adherence to the system's "phonemic" rules threw up some unusual results, however, such as the recasting of the familiar Cornish word chy (a house) as "tji" and the obscure respelling of otherwise familiar Cornish placenames. Other Cornish speakers, therefore, were attracted to the alternative "Traditional" or "Late" or "Modern" Cornish expounded by Richard Gendall in which the language was spelt and constructed in a form closely resembling that in which it had last been spoken naturally.[5] Although this version was not approved by the Language Board, it nonetheless found support in academic circles.[6] Unified supporters, however, not to be out-manoeuvred, formed the Agan Tavas ("Our Language") group to defend the Nancean inheritance, with Rod Lyon arguing for the development of Unified Cornish along "Traditional" lines.

Disconcerting though this confusion was to those who actually wished to study or learn the language, the important fact was that there was a language revival at all. Once again, rather like the plain fact of the existence of Mebyon Kernow, it was — as the "politicised" "Revivalists" had intended it to be — a powerful symbol of "difference". It was, for example, a passport to Cornwall's inclusion in books detailing the "minorities" of Western Europe, and it afforded Cornwall a place on the European Bureau For Lesser Used Languages.[7] In a balanced assessment of the significance of language revival, Thomas commented that:

> . . . Revived Cornish, as to its spelling, an increasing part of its vocabulary, and most of its pronounciation, cannot be regarded as genuine, and this is why it is viewed with such suspicion and reserve by almost all Celticists . . . . This does not amount to failure . . . the achievement of Henry Jenner, Robert Morton Nance, and their contemporaries, was the establishment of a sense of Cornishness, of national consciousness . . . had this overall Cornish Revival not been attempted, and accomplished, it would by now be quite impossible to construct the particular platform on which the linguistic, cultural, nationalistic, and environmental movements in Cornwall all perform.[8]

Indeed, amongst its consequences could be counted the Institute of Cornish Studies (funded jointly by Cornwall County Council and the University of Exeter), which was founded in 1972 with Thomas as its first Director.

As Thomas intimated, it was but a short step from the symbols of cultural "accommodation" to those of political "accommodation". This too was recognised by the post-war "Revivalists" and an important tactic was to press for the use of the Cornish language on public road signs, such as "welcome" notices at the entrances to towns. The Gorsedd had already successfully arranged for the erection of bi-lingual "Cornwall-Kernow" signs at the border, and in a test case in 1988-89 the Liskeard Chamber of Commerce was able to force the Department of Transport to acknowledge officially the legitimate use of the Cornish language on road signs.[9] This to some degree involved "governmental recognition" of the language and was therefore "accommodation" of Cornwall's "difference". Likewise, a campaign to achieve official status for the Cornish flag came to fruition in 1985 when Cornwall County Council decided that it should be flown alongside the Union flag at County Hall in Truro.[10] In similar fashion, the celebration of St Piran's Day (March 5th) as "Cornwall's National Day" received increasing recognition, albeit at unofficial levels while "Trelawny" continued to be regarded as the "Cornish National Anthem" — a status which was still further enhanced by its presentation and use as such by Cornwall Rugby Football Union in 1989 and again in 1991 and 1992 during Cornwall's progress to the County Championship Final at Twickenham.[11]

Having effected the "rehabilitation" of industrial Cornwall within their ideology, the post-war "Revivalists" were aware that it was necessary to construct a bridge between the somewhat exclusive "Celtic" culture that they had embraced hitherto and the more widespread popular culture based on Methodism, Rugby Football, male voice choirs, brass bands and the like. Not only would this broaden the potential appeal of the "Revival" but also it would create the necessary credibility and momentum to win political "accommodation". That the "Revivalists" had achieved some success in this endeavour was evident by 1989, when the third "Eisteddfod" aroused considerable enthusiasm throughout Cornwall and proved to be an amicable alliance of "Celtic" and "popular" Cornish culture, with events ranging from the Gorsedd's Bardic ceremony and Cornish language recitations to brass band and choir competitions, a mix also observable to some extent in Camborne's "Trevithick Day" celebrations. Most noticeably it was manifested in the behaviour of the enormous Cornish crowd ("Trelawny's Army", as it was dubbed by the press) of some 25,000 at Twickenham at the RFU Final in April 1989. The *Independent* newspaper considered that "Twenty thousand Cornishmen used the great ground for a statement, if not of Celtic nationhood, then at least of their distinct identity"[12] and admitted that ". . . the 20,000 had been an astonishing sight, flourishing the Cornish flag . . . and bedecked in Cornish rugby's black and amber".[13] The *Guardian* explained that "Like the Welsh, the Cornish take the view that rugby and community are the same thing",[14] with the opinion that if the Final " . . . proved anything, it was that the lusty spirit of national independence is alive and flourishing in the undeclared Republic of Cornwall".[15] Continuing such political allusions, the *Cornish Times* felt that the occasion was ". . . more reminiscent of an international . . . ".[16] Demonstrating that this was not a "one off" event, there was a repeat performance in even more spectacular style by the tens of thousands of Cornish folk who journeyed to Twickenham in April 1991 to witness the defeat of Yorkshire.

The distinction between the symbols of cultural "accommodation" and those of political "accommodation" was similarly blurred in the campaign, which was at its height in the later 1960s and early 1970s, to achieve a postage stamp for Cornwall. Following the introduction of regional issues by the Post Office of stamps for England, Wales, Scotland and Northern Ireland (and against the background of the existence of separate stamps for the various Channel Islands and the Isle of Man), John Nott attempted unsuccessfully to press for a Cornish stamp when in March 1967 he asked the Postmaster General in Parliament if ". . . he will give consideration to the production of a Cornish stamp, Cornwall being the only Celtic country in the United Kingdom which is without its own postage stamp".[17] Subsequently, Mebyon Kernow produced its own booklet entitled *A Stamp For Cornwall* in which the case for Cornwall was expounded at some length, although without avail.[18]

The postage stamp question was at root a constitutional issue with political implications of some considerable importance, reflecting a determination to secure a form of political "accommodation" for Cornwall which would confirm a constitutional identity distinct from that of just another English county. This explained in part the brief enthusiasm in the mid-1970s for the attempts to revive the ancient Cornish Stannary Parliament, a somewhat bizarre event which nonetheless did much to highlight Cornwall's unusual constitutional history and the fact that Stannary law remained intact as an integral part of the British Constitution. A more considered attempt at elucidating Cornwall's constitutional heritage in the interests of effecting renewed political "accommodation" was the Cowethas Flamank report *The Detectable Duchy*, published in 1986, which argued that historically the government of Cornwall was vested in the Duchy of Cornwall and that the distinction between County and Duchy — today taken so much for granted — was in fact a result of a nineteenth century reinterpretation of the Duchy's role.[19] Indeed, the Kilbrandon Commission on the Constitution addressed itself to the position of the Duchy, and in its recommendations stated that:

> The creation of the Duchy of Cornwall . . . established a special and enduring relationship between Cornwall and the Crown. Use of the designation on all appropriate occasions would serve to recognise both this special relationship and the territorial integrity of Cornwall . . .[20].

The Kilbrandon recommendations did not extend as far as the advocacy for Cornwall of a Devolutionary assembly on the lines of those proposed for Scotland and Wales, but nonetheless they had recognised the existence of a special Cornish constitutional identity and had indeed proposed that more emphasis be placed upon it. The Kilbrandon Commission had also proved an important opportunity for Cornish groups to state their case for Cornwall's political "accommodation". Both the Cornish Branch of the Celtic League and the Cornish National Party submitted evidence to the Commission, and in a lengthy memorandum Mebyon Kernow sought ". . . a re-definition of Cornwall's constitutional status in such a way as to set Cornwall apart from the English counties and provide a basis for differential treatment".[21] Following the publication of the Kilbrandon recommendations, with their proposals for Scotland and Wales and their limited but encouraging words on Cornwall, articulation of the Cornish case was perpetuated by Cowethas Flamank (then still associated with Mebyon Kernow) with the publication in 1974 of its report *Towards Self-Government* in which it explained that "The Kilbrandon Report controversy provides us with a heaven-sent opportunity to press the claim of Cornwall"[22] and concluded that ". . . Cornwall should demand her own devolutionary Cornish Parliament with administrative, legislative and executive powers at least equal to those already proposed for Scotland".[23]

Significantly, the case for the political "accommodation" of Cornwall submitted to Kilbrandon included not only the nationalist demand for decentralisation and devolution but also a concern for the territorial integrity of Cornwall. This was recognised and acknowledged by the Commission's Report, noting with some sympathy the concern of Cornwall that ". . . its traditional boundaries shall be respected".[24] The concern for the territorial integrity of Cornwall had various facets, including hostility to units of administration or planning (such as the South West Economic Planning Council) which merged Cornwall in a larger South West and were managed in Bristol or other centres east of the Tamar, opposition to the creation of entities such as the Devon and Cornwall Constabulary or South West Water in which previously existing Cornish bodies lost their identities, and criticism of the activities of public utilities whose sub-regions exhibited "border blurring" or encouraged a "Devonwall" mentality in that they cut across or did not recognise the Tamar boundary.[25] At the time of Kilbrandon, however, the fundamental preoccupation was with the perceived expansionist designs of Plymouth and their apparent threat to the integrity of Cornwall County Council, an issue that had dominated the local debate on local government re-organisation in the wake of the Redcliffe-Maud Report in 1969.

In fact, the Redcliffe-Maud debate had been anticipated more than two decades earlier with the publication of the Abercrombie Report in 1943 (a blueprint for the reconstruction of Plymouth) which in 1946 led Plymouth City Council to propose to the Local Government Boundary Commission that it take over a significant section of South East Cornwall. As Cornwall County Council's centenary history has put it, the result was that "The battle to keep the invader at bay and preserve intact the County of Cornwall has been waged since the Second World War".[26] Under the determined leadership of Colonel Sir Edward Bolitho, Cornwall defeated the proposal, only to find it re-emerge twenty years later as part of the Redcliffe-Maud proposals for local government reform. Amongst these proposals was the creation of Plymouth as a "unitary authority", composed of the city itself along with acquisitions from both South West Devon and South East Cornwall. Once again, Cornwall opposed the move. Not only did Mebyon Kernow mount its own campaign, accusing the Redcliffe-Maud Commission of "Disregarding Cornwall's identity as a Celtic nation . . .",[27] but the County Council — this time under the singleminded leadership of Alderman K.G. Foster — fought the proposals as a fundamental matter of principle. Indeed, as a fundamental matter of principle the concern to preserve the territorial integrity of Cornwall — the most basic level of political "accommodation" — won widespread support across Cornwall, an indication that such sentiment was by no means confined to the nationalist groups and a demonstration of the extent to which the "politicised" objective to defend and promote the Cornish identity had permeated Cornish society. According to one objector to the proposals:

> . . . the Tamar has come to acquire a symbolic, almost mystical significance for Cornishmen . . . for countless thousands of them it has stood — and stands — as the place of parting or return, the end or the beginning of home . . . It is Celtic land that is at stake.[28]

The then Labour Government accepted the Redcliffe-Maud proposals and indicated its intention to introduce legislation to reorganise local government in the fashion advocated by the Report. However, after the General Election of 1970 the incoming Conservatives carried out their own review of local government, which offered conclusions significally different from those of Redcliffe-Maud. The result was that the Cornish border was to be preserved at the Tamar. Plymouth responded to this change of plan with its own "Tamarside" proposals, in which Plymouth would become focus of a new "Tamarside" county with, as before, some component territory drawn from Cornwall. Although these "Tamarside" proposals were not adopted for the Bill at its second reading, the Department of the Environment nevertheless capitulated to renewed Plymouth demands for further "Tamarside" discussions. In the words of the Council itself, "Cornwall County Council countered by mobilizing again all interests in the threatened parts of Cornwall and indeed from the whole of Cornwall . . . K.G. Foster . . . never ceased

212

to lead strenuously the defence of Cornwall . . .".[29] Convinced of the strength and unanimity of Cornish opinion, the Government finally rejected "Tamarside" and by the summer of 1972 Cornwall's territorial integrity was assured. Nonetheless, the Council later reflected upon the ensuing legislation which did rob many counties of their territory or identities, and with some relief observed that "Cornwall has been luckier, thanks largely to the stubbornness and determination of Cornishmen past, and still retains most of the Tamar as the barrier to invasion from England".[30] Significantly, in another of its publications the Council could also reflect that ". . . Cornwall is administratively 'in' England, but is not 'of' England. Culturally the River Tamar is a national boundary . . .".[31]

In similar spirit, there was a move within Cornwall County Council in 1987 for Cornwall to seek its own Secretary of State on the lines of those admitted already for Scotland, Wales, and Northern Ireland. Fearing that what it considered to be a unique mix of Cornish socio-economic problems was not recognised sufficiently at Westminster, and mindful of apparent threats to the Cornish identity, the Council's Planning and Employment Committee passed a recommendation to the full Council that it should demand a Minister for Cornwall.[32] The full Council, however, declined to proceed with the suggestion, and what would have been a controversial and almost revolutionary demand for political "accommodation" within the British State was shelved almost as soon as it had been proposed. But, once again, the significant feature was not that the scheme should have failed to come to fruition, but rather that the idea had arisen at all and received serious consideration at official levels.

A more sustained campaign for Cornwall's political "accommodation", but this time within the structure of the European Community rather than the British State, was the demand that Cornwall should constitute a European Parliamentary Constituency (EPC) in its own right in elections for the European Parliament. In preparation for the first direct elections to the European Parliament in 1979, the several Boundary Commissions within the United Kingdom had been tasked with the creation of EPCs, the size and shape of which were to be determined fundamentally by a concern for electoral parity between constituencies. The electorate of Cornwall was deemed too small, therefore, for Cornwall to exist as an EPC in its own right, and consequently its numbers were boosted by the addition of Plymouth and the creation of a joint constituency. In the aftermath of the Redcliffe-Maud battles, this decision seemed strangely perverse within Cornwall, and the objections to the Boundary Commission for England's recommendations were dominated by those from Cornwall. These objections were led, as in the case of Redcliffe-Maud, by Cornwall County Council and once again there was a general mobilisation of Cornish opinion. All six Cornish District Councils objected to the recommendations, as did a majority of Cornish MPs, with David Penhaligon making an impassioned speech in the Commons in defence of the Tamar border and the demand for a Cornish EPC. Incredibly, in England a mere 18 Parish Councils objected to the recommendations, while in Cornwall alone there were objections to the proposed Cornwall and Plymouth EPC from no less than 76 Parish/Town Councils.[33]

Despite the strength of the Cornish objections, the Cornwall and Plymouth EPC was enshrined in the ensuing legislation. Dissatisfaction with this state of affairs was expressed to some extent in Mebyon Kernow's very credible performance in the following European Parliamentary Election in June 1979 (when it won some ten per cent of the Cornish vote[34]), and in 1983 when a petition of some 600 Cornish electors (organised by Mebyon Kernow) forced the Boundary Commission to hold a Public Inquiry into its proposed Cornwall and Plymouth EPC for the 1984 election. At that Inquiry, held in Plymouth in November 1983, a wide range of Cornish objectors argued that Cornwall alone should constitute an EPC by virtue of the fact that (under European legislation) the Cornish were one of the "Peoples" of Europe and should be represented therein, and that because (under British legislation) Cornwall attracted certain "special geographical considerations" it was possible to create a Cornish EPC with an electorate below the parity quota. The Assistant Commissioner who presided at the Inquiry rejected these submissions out of hand, however, thus perpetuating the joint EPC.[35] A somewhat dazed Mebyon Kernow failed even to field a candidate in the election in the following June.

In 1988 the debate was renewed with a vigour which outstripped even that of 1983, however, with formal objections to the Boundary Commission's proposals for the 1989 election coming from both North Cornwall District Council and a petition of almost 1,000 Cornish electors, and with the Commission once again forced to hold a Local Inquiry. This time a Campaign For A Cornish Constituency was set up to mobilise and co-ordinate Cornish opinion, and in a startling performance it won the support of Cornwall County Council, all the District authorities, a majority of Cornish MPs, and scores of Parish Councils and other Cornish organisations and individuals. At the same time, it initiated and sustained an unprecedented level of debate on the issue in the local press, most especially the *Western Morning News* newspaper. The Public Inquiry was held at Bodmin in July 1988 amidst widespread publicity, the *Telegraph* explaining that "Many Cornish detest the EEC constituency in which they live . . ."[36] and declaring that "Regionalist fervour will clash with Government plans . . . Cornwall . . . is demanding its own voice in Brussels".[37] It noted, too, that an Early Day Motion in Parliament — which had attracted the support of Cornish MPs, along with those from Plaid Cymru and the Scottish National Party — had also called for a Cornwall EPC.

Again it was argued at the Inquiry that the Cornish were one of the historic "Peoples" of Europe, but with rather more sophisticated evidence this time which showed that the British Government had already identified the constituent English, Welsh, Scottish, and Northern Irish as "Peoples" by allocating to each nation its own Boundary Commission and by ensuring that no EPC compromised any of their national borders. The Cornish, it was argued, should be allowed the same degree of "accommodation" as these other "Peoples". In addition, the Campaign For A Cornish Constituency and many other objectors made much of the European Parliamentary Act of 1978 which stated that "The electorate for any European constituency shall be as near the electoral quota as is reasonably practicable having regard, where appropriate, to special geographical considerations".[38] The electoral quota announced by the Boundary Commission in 1988 was 552,234. The combined Cornwall and Plymouth EPC produced an electorate of 542,471 — slightly smaller than the quota — while a Cornwall-only EPC would produce an electorate of 361,477, well below the quota. However, it was argued that such a Cornwall EPC would be directly comparable with the Highlands and Islands of Scotland EPC, which had approximately 310,000 electors and had been created as a result of "special geographical considerations", and with Northern Ireland which returned three Members of the European Parliament for a total electorate of about 1,080,000 (ie 360,000 electors per MEP). Once again the claim for the political "accommodation" of Cornwall was made against the background of similar treatment being afforded already to other components of the "Celtic fringe".[39]

In presenting the case for "special geographical considerations" relating to Cornwall, the Campaign For A Cornish Constituency and other objectors identified areas of physical, historical, economic, and political geography where they considered that the Cornish experience was unique. The joint EPC was seen as having had deleterious effects upon the Cornish economy as well as compromising Cornwall's territorial integrity, with funds which might otherwise have gone to Cornwall in their entirety being shared with an already relatively prosperous Plymouth, and with the view from Brussels of Cornwall's special socio-economic problems being fatally obscured by the link with Plymouth. It was argued, too, that as Cornwall had consistently opposed the joint EPC, and that as Cornwall was in 1988 the only area to force a Public Inquiry, the democratic will of the Cornish people was in itself a "special geographical consideration" of some importance.[40]

From the myriad evidence presented by the various bodies at the 1988 Public Inquiry emerged one re-occurring central strand; that Cornwall should be afforded political "accommodation" on the strength of its special identity. Feock Parish Council, for example, asserted that "Cornwall is not a part of England . . . It is separately identified in Royal Charters and on early maps. Like Scotland, Wales and Ireland, its early peoples are of Celtic origin and its ancient language is akin to Welsh and Breton".[41] North Cornwall District Council added that ". . . to travel to Cornwall brings one beyond the bounds of the commonplace into practically another country,"[42] and Kerrier District Council insisted that ". . . Cornish culture is distinct from the rest of England and in dire need of special treatment on the same basis as other national groups within the European Community . . .".[43] Cornwall County Council itself summarised this sentiment by explaining that:

> Such feelings of loyalty are of a very different order from most counties in England. Indeed, Cornwall is almost an island with natural boundaries fixed by the coastline. It is largely isolated from the rest of the country. It has a strong separate identity with its own history, traditions, customs, language and (to some degree) law and institutions. Many of these attributes are firmly rooted in its Celtic past. It seems

215

anomalous that such a community should not have its own separate voice in the European Parliament.[44]

The Assistant Commissioner who presided at this Inquiry, however, was also unconvinced by this and the attendant arguments and recommended that the Cornwall and Plymouth EPC be perpetuated.[45] Nonetheless, in marked contrast to his colleague's uncompromising stand in 1983, he did recognise that there were "special geographical considerations" in relation to Cornwall, even though he did not feel it "appropriate" to have regard to such "considerations" in reaching his judgement. He admitted that:

> It is to be recalled also that together with the County Council of Cornwall, the views from other democratically elected bodies were virtually unanimous in their opposition. In the result my view is that there is a strong likelihood that the sentiments expressed at the Inquiry upon matters of history, culture, language, and other emblems of "separateness" would be shared by enough people in Cornwall to make this "geographical consideration", a consideration of weight.[46]

Similarly, the Assistant Commissioner acknowledged a ". . . de facto (if not de jure) joinder with England",[47] a phrase which served to suggest that in his view Cornwall was fundamentally not a part of England and that, in theory at least, a degree of Cornish constitutional independence still obtained. Thus although he was unable to recommend Cornwall's political "accommodation" within Europe as an EPC in its own right, his judgement nonetheless contained "accommodating" observations of considerable significance, a point not lost on the Campaign For A Cornish Constituency (which published a detailed critique of the Assistant Commissioner's Report, highlighting the alleged inconsistencies of its conclusions[48]) or on Matthew Taylor (Penhaligon's successor) who fought a spirited rearguard action on the issue in Parliament.[49]

The demand for a Cornwall-only EPC in many ways epitomised the Cornish experience of "accommodation" in the post-war era. The demand was by no means confined to the nationalist groups and was a genuine expression of widespread Cornish opinion with, as in other issues, the support of Cornwall County Council. Although it was not successful in achieving any major "accommodating" innovation it had nonetheless, like other campaigns, identified a general concern for the territorial integrity and identity of Cornwall, and — as in the Kilbrandon debate — had won at least some "official" recognition of a special constitutional position for Cornwall within the British State. This in itself represented a degree of political "accommodation", and the fact that the battle had been fought at all reflected the considerable success of the post-war "Revivalists" in projecting in political terms the defence and promotion of ethnic identity. The search for renewed political "accommodation", indeed, had emerged as a principal distinguishing feature of Cornish political activity as it arose from its earlier paralysis in this era of "Third peripheralism". When, in the late 1980s, Devolution re-emerged as an item on the

British political agenda, it was no accident or surprise when letters in the local press suggested that Cornwall might learn from Scotland's Govan by-election experience, or — for that matter — when the *Guardian* leader argued that,

> . . . devolution has become an issue once again, not because a bunch of bearded chaps in Hebden Bridge think it is a good idea, but because the regions (London as much as Cornwall or Tyneside) and nations (Northern Ireland as much as Scotland or Wales) of Britain are not properly enfranchised under the existing system.[50]

Nor was it surprising that concern for Cornish representation in the European Parliament should have broadened into a wider desire to link Cornwall directly with Europe, a Cornish Bureau for European Relations emerging to effect that link and — in a petition to the European Parliament — to call for European support for Cornish culture.[51]

In parallel with this concern for political "accommodation" was the growing criticism of the socio-economic policies and trends that had led to the new condition of "Third Peripheralism". These emerged initially in the guise of anti-Overspill campaigns, at first glance merely ethnic protest against immigration but — on closer analysis — critiques of socio-economic policy too. Mebyon Kernow, in 1971 through its journal *Cornish Nation*, for example, pointed to what it saw as the economic distinction between Cornwall and England, alleging too an ethnic division of labour and wealth within Cornwall itself:

> . . . the economic disparity of the 'Two Nations', Kernow and England, is likely to grow in the future. Wage levels are unlikely to catch up with those in England, more and more young Cornish will have to leave their land to find employment, the coastal areas will increasingly be bought up by the English, Cornish farms will be taken over by newcomers and the land exploited for short-term profits while the heavy work, the economic drudgery will continue to be done by Cornish people living in the interior in the poorer housing districts. Only when we have control of our own economy . . . will it be planned with local needs and requirements in mind and a proper balance of extractive, manufacturing and other industry achieved.[52]

In this analysis emerged issues — low wages, "counterurbanisation", exploitation, housing, "local needs" — which would characterise the debate on socio-economic policy as it developed. As early as June 1972, one contributer to *Cornish Nation* pointed to an alleged failure of central government regional planning policy in Cornwall, arguing that:

> Regional Planning . . . in relation to Cornwall, has been misguided and ineffectual in conception, organisation and achievement. It has done little to attack the underlying problems and many of the council's (ie

SWEPC's) assumptions have been positively dangerous in that they have posed threats to both the unity and character of Cornwall.[53]

Such criticism was not confined to the nationalists, however, and one significant commentary on the Cornish situation was that offered by the political economist J.C. Banks. Banks, in his *Federal Britain*, was in many respects ahead of his time. He was amongst the first to question the myth of the homogeneous state (the "Unionist Myth", as he termed it) in both political and economic terms, and he foresaw accurately both the Devolution Debate and the entry of Britain into the European Community with its wider implications for a "Europe of the Regions".[54] In all this, Banks argued that Cornwall had a special place in the analysis. Noting the wholesale closure of Cornish railways (the destruction of the North Cornwall network aggravated the peripheral characteristics of the locality), the failure of the campaign to achieve a Cornish university, and the fact that the Cornish Development Area was run from Bristol (despite the fact that Bristol was nearer to London than it was to Penzance), he warned that "Nor has the Economic Planning Council for the South-West (SWEPC) been more discerning than Whitehall in its dealings with this outlying county".[55] He questioned the socio-economic assumptions of "Overspill", drew attention to Cornwall's "blighted character" but ". . . its potential for development given the right leadership",[56] and concluded that — in a system where real economic planning might be devolved to regions — Cornwall should be defined as one such region in its own right. Here, of course, Banks had located the tangental point of contact between the critique of socio-economic policies and the demand for political "accommodation", an intimation that in practice the two would often proceed hand-in-hand in political debate within Cornwall.

Later, in 1983 at the first Conference on Cornwall at Perranporth, Banks developed the economic concept of "Cornwall as a Region", using demographic and economic statistics to compare Cornwall with regions within Europe (Zeeland, Saarland, Luxembourg, Iceland — each one in varying degrees responsible for its own economic planning policies).[57] Chosen for their similarities in terms of population size and density, these regions nevertheless showed sharp contrast with Cornwall in areas such as unemployment, industry, earnings, and gross domestic product per head. In unemployment, for example, Cornwall had in 1979 ". . . twelve times the unemployment rate of Iceland, three times that of Luxembourg, a third more than the average for the UK . . . In fact, unemployment in 1979 was higher in Cornwall than in no fewer than 29 out of the 52 statistical areas of the . . . EEC."[58] Similarly, "Cornwall emerges as the least industrialised of all the areas under review, even compared with distant Iceland".[59] Gross domestic product in 1979 ". . . in Saarland and Zeeland is nearly half as much again as it is in Cornwall, with Luxembourg and Iceland having a small edge on even these levels . . .",[60] with further comparisons showing that "Cornwall is seen as eighth from the bottom in this league of EEC regions and small States. The other seven were the two parts of Ireland and five provincial groupings in the Italian south".[61] To Banks, such data was prima facie evidence of the failure of central government Regional

218

Planning in relation to Cornwall, a cue for criticism and action from within Cornwall.

The essential issue here, of course, is not whether Banks' analysis was valid, but rather the fact that he was encouraging a debate based upon the presumed shortcomings of Regional Development policies. Such debate was evident in the activities of the Cornwall Conservation Forum, a pressure group which was launched amidst great excitement and publicity in 1972 ("World Environmental Year", as Wight noted[62]) with the broad aim of co-ordinating and providing a platform for individuals and organisations working for the best interests of Cornwall. Although the Forum had apparently run out of energy by the late 1970s, and vanished very quickly thereafter from the public scene, it made a considerable impact during its relatively short life. Most importantly, the Forum in 1974 published its *Cornwall's Choice*,[63] a terse reposte to SWEPC's *A Strategic Settlement Pattern for the South West*[64] which had also been produced in 1974 and outlined the conventional wisdoms of Regional Planning, in particular the regional aid/population increase nexus. The Forum countered that Regional Planning had been of no value to Cornwall, and that regional aid was neither necessary nor desirable for Cornwall: "Regional Aid cannot be said to improve earnings or to significantly reduce unemployment . . . if Cornwall's Development Area status were abolished the existing population would not be adversely affected."[65] Indeed, the Forum argued that regional aid, through its attendant encouragement of in-migration, would actually exacerbate problems of employment while the economic activity that it did manage to create would be of a fragile and unstable "branch factory" nature. In this, the Forum anticipated the later work of Perry,[66] and was surprisingly accurate in its projections for Cornish society and economy in the 1970s and 80s.

By the mid-1970s, therefore, the inherent difficulties and weaknesses of the Cornish socio-economic framework in the era of "Third Peripheralism" were already becoming apparent. The foundation of the Cornwall Industrial Development Association in 1974 was in part a reaction to this, its policy document *The Economy of Cornwall*[67] — published in 1977 — advocating that, instead of encouraging new firms to come to Cornwall from elsewhere, economic development strategy should focus upon industries and companies already located within Cornwall. This would involve import substitution, more local processing, and an increased level of self-sufficiency. Like the Cornwall Conservation Forum, CIDA warned against the dangers of creating a "branch factory" economy, and it was similarly dismissive of central government Regional Planning policy:

If the view of Cornwall, as seen from London, is that of a colony whose raw materials and labour are to be exploited for the relative well-being of a non-productive central bureaucracy, while at the same time maintaining the appearance of raising regional incomes, then the regional policies of successive governments begins to make some sense . . . .[68]

The highly-charged, overtly political nature of such an attack revealed a deep-seated anti-metropolitanism within CIDA, a view also articulated in its ". . . expressions of the feelings of alienation from remote decision-making".[69] But, as Wight noted, CIDA's members and supporters were by no means traditional Cornish nationalists[70] (there seemed, for example, to be little or no overlap in membership with Mebyon Kernow). Paradoxically, however, their behaviour and attitudes reflected — indeed, were a part of — the emergence of Cornish politics from its "fossilisation" and the enhancement of a distinct Cornish political culture through the growth of anti-metropolitanism.

Despite this movement of opinion, the planners adhered to their initial assumptions, and CIDA, for example, was disappointed when the County *Structure Plan*[71] emerged with little signs of CIDA influence (it had not, for instance, taken up the idea of a Cornwall Development Bureau[72]) and with a strategy still aimed at the encouragement of industry and population growth from across the Tamar. Thereafter, criticism of socio-economic policy and planning was increasingly directed at the County planners, who were seen (rather unfairly, given the constraints in which they operated) by critics as the "willing tools" of central government's "deleterious" Regional Aid policies. Perry's analysis[73] of "counter-urbanisation" contained explicit criticism of the *Structure Plan*, and (as shown in Chapter 8) the shortcomings of the County strategy were themselves demonstrated and admitted in the *First Alteration* of the Plan in 1987. But instead of a search for a fundamentally different approach, the *First Alteration* sought to build upon the salvageable parts of the original Plan with a strategy ". . . much more based on housing and population factors rather than employment factors".[74] This represented the full manifestation of "Third Peripheralism" and prompted wide-spread criticism and disquiet, not only from nationalist groups but also (and rather more forcefully) from new pressure groups that had arisen in response to the situation. Although it was the "tin crisis" of 1986 (when the government was persuaded finally to advance funds to keep some Cornish mines open for a few years in the aftermath of the collapse of world tin prices) which caught the popular imagination outside of Cornwall, it was in fact the activities of Cornish Alternatives to the Structure Plan (CASP) and the Cornish Social and Economic Research Group (COSERG) which offered the most powerful and sustained critiques of the socio-economic situation in Cornwall.

CASP was formed in 1987 as a direct response to the *First Alteration*. In publications such as *Cornwall: A Breathing Space* and *Local Needs Policy*,[75] CASP attacked the conventional planning wisdoms and advanced instead its own "Arguments for radical change".[76] In a perceptive assessment of Cornwall's recent history, CASP recognised that "The decline of mining and the post-war re-population aimed at revitalising the Cornish economy set Cornwall's economic scenario somewhat apart from the general National picture".[77] This, argued CASP, meant that Cornwall had acquired a highly distinctive set of socio-economic problems which required novel and local solutions. In particular, CASP argued for an end to in-migration and the process of "counterurbanisation", pleading for a "breathing space" to "Enable communities which have expanded over the last

25 years to consolidate and absorb their new residents into the social fabric and structures".[78] In an attack upon the *First Alteration*, CASP asserted that "The concept that population growth will inevitably bring about a stimulation of the local economy can be seen to be wrong"[79] and that "The argument that increased provision of housing will stabilise prices and enable local people to compete in the market is spurious. It ignores realities such as high unemployment and low wages".[80] Instead, argued CASP, there should be a genuine local needs housing policy, complemented by an industrial development policy which would draw upon internal resources and not be reliant upon outside investment of the "branch factory" type. This would require, too, an attack on ". . . the psychological barrier that tourism is the central plank of the Cornish economy".[81] Significantly, in a manner that bore witness to the degree to which Cornish political activity had by now moved from its "fossilisation" and paralysis, CASP emphasised that Cornwall should continue to ". . . attack its own sense of inferiority and, in aspiring to self-reliance, demand a radical change in the way it is regarded by Central Government".[82]

In one sense CASP was successful in its last aim, for it mobilised such widespread opposition to the *First Alteration* that indecision became apparent within the County Council (but an attempt by some councillors to reject the *First Alteration* was defeated) and, more importantly, the Department of the Environment held an Examination in Public to inquire into the numerous objections. As the *West Briton* explained, it would then be up to the Secretary of State to decide eventually ". . . if the proposed level of housing is appropriate for Cornwall in light of the County Council's assessment of population, household formation and housing demand",[83] bearing in mind such considerations as "local needs", environmental constraints, and employment opportunities.

Operating in tandem and often in close co-operation with CASP was the Cornish Social and Economic Research Group (COSERG). Although also concerned with the *First Alteration*, COSERG worked to an even wider brief, addressing social and economic issues at the broadest levels and with a parallel interest in their cultural and political consequences. COSERG insisted that "Various economic and social forces are combining to marginalise us — soon we will be strangers in our own land"[84] and, in the belief that ". . . the first step needed in order to resist these forces is to identify them",[85] it published a report in 1987 entitled *The Cornish Community: Reclaiming Our Destiny*.[86] This proved to be the precursor of a fully-fledged book, published at the end of 1988 by the COSERG team (Deacon, George, and Perry) entitled *Cornwall at the Crossroads*[87] in which the condition of Cornish peripherality in the post-war era was examined at length. Contrasting the apparent success of "development" — its ". . . marinas, luxury yachts and millionaires' playgrounds . . ."[88] — with the ". . . submerged Cornwall that refuses to go away . . ."[89] of homelessness, unemployment and low pay, COSERG identified a "hidden agenda" which (it was alleged) had motivated planners at both central government and County level. This agenda was based upon the key assumptions that Cornwall was remote, that Cornwall and its people suffered from backwardness, that Cornwall was too small to be "viable" in its own right, and that the principal economic role of Cornwall was to provide a "playground" for people from elsewhere. This had led, argued the COSERG team, to the planners' insistence that all must ". . . accept, without question, that Cornwall must be developed and, in the process, effectively ignore its distinctiveness, its communities and its identity".[90]

In particular, *Cornwall at the Crossroads* attacked the strategy based upon population growth and the attraction of new firms from outside, highlighting the alleged admission of failure of that strategy contained in the *First Alteration* but also criticising the *First Alteration* for itself failing to come up with anything new. It was, said COSERG, "A plan without a strategy".[91] Like CASP, COSERG argued instead for a new and radical strategy, claiming that the first step was to replace the planners' conventional assumptions of Cornwall's "weaknesses" with a new set that emphasised "strengths". In this, COSERG postulated that it was the South East that was remote from Cornwall (and not vice versa) and that in fact Cornwall was geographically well placed to construct maritime links with Europe and the wider world. Equally, COSERG argued that Cornwall should be freed from the constraints of Regional Planning, building up its indigenous intellectual infra-structure and stemming the loss of young, dynamic Cornish people. "Smallness", insisted COSERG, was in fact a distinct advantage, something that was increasingly sought in the modern world, something to cherish and not to throw away in the pursuit of "bigness". Again like CASP, COSERG called for a "breathing space" in population growth, arguing for a "two-tier" housing market in which there would be a "Cornish weighting" in favour of "local needs". A Cornish Develop-ment Agency was also necessary, it was claimed, to control development in such a way that optimised the use of internal resources and benefitted the existing community.

Cornwall at the Crossroads concluded with a demand for "More power to Cornwall", for "Only decentralisation of authority can enable us to realise our opportunities".[92] Here again was the meeting point of the critiques of Regional Planning and the demands for renewed political "accommodation", a synthesis which represented the quintessential nature of Cornish political reaction to the socio-economic condition of "Third Peripheralism". It was, indeed, the fundamental political component of "Third Peripheralism", marking the emergence of Cornish politics from its "fossilisation", shaking off the old paralysis to insist that the political process should ". . . maintain and then strengthen the confidence of the Cornish identity"[93] and "Ensure that factors of ethnicity and identity are positive and creative factors in the planning process in Cornwall".[94]

In articulating the critiques of Regional Planning, CASP and COSERG had to a considerable degree absorbed (even eclipsed) the earlier role of the nationalist groups, which had proved organisationally ill-equipped to tackle the necessary specialist research and conceptual model-construction. This was not so much a criticism of the nationalist groups, but rather evidence of the extent to which concern for the condition of modern Cornwall had spread far beyond the confines of the nationalists. Once again the success of the "politicisation" of the

"Revivalists" was emphasised, revealing once more its all-pervading influence upon Cornish political activity and its underlying political culture.

Inevitably, this influence was felt in other areas of political activity in Cornwall, especially within the existing political parties. As noted in Chapter 8, Cornish politics had failed to participate in the great "alignment" of the inter-war years, with the intervention of Labour severely retarded and with the principal contest continuing to be between Liberals and Conservatives. Cornish politics in that era was also, like the rest of Cornish society, in a state of paralysis, of "fossilisation". The Conservatives proved the main beneficiaries of this paralysis but with the Liberals retaining their identity as the "Cornish" party through their continued adherence to localist attitudes (especially Methodism), and with Labour failing to make much headway except in Falmouth-Penryn under the energetic influence of A.L. Rowse. In the immediate aftermath of the war, there was some little evidence of apparent change. In the 1945 General Election, North Cornwall was won by the Liberals, St Ives by the National Liberals, Truro and Bodmin by the Conservatives, and with Labour taking the newly-created seat of Falmouth-Camborne in its first-ever victory in Cornwall, the local man (Harold Hayman) building upon Rowse's important ground work and benefitting from the UK-wide surge to Labour. Hayman was able to retain his seat despite the general swing against Labour in the 1950 General Election, with the Liberals losing North Cornwall to the Conservatives, and with the other Cornish seats remaining in Tory hands (although St Ives was still held by the theoretically distinct National Liberal Party, it was by now to all intents and purposes within the Tory fold). This set a pattern that was reproduced exactly in General Elections for a decade, in 1951, 1955, and 1959. To the casual observer, the Cornish political scene exhibited slow but perceptable movement, the features of note being the apparent decline of the Liberals and the relative success of Labour (in Falmouth-Camborne at least), an indication perhaps that Cornish politics was being eased at last from its "fossilised" paralysis and moving towards greater conformity with the "alignment" elsewhere.[95]

However, such superficial observation belied the complexity and reality of the situation. Given the socio-economic condition of post-war Cornwall, that Labour did not make even greater impact (in 1945 especially) was a clue to continuing Cornish political distinctiveness. Although without a Cornish seat in Parliament for the entire 1950s and early 60s, the Liberals nonetheless remained the effective opposition in Cornwall (except Falmouth-Camborne). As Bogdanor noted, Cornwall was one of the few areas where the Liberals remained highly active and contested a majority of seats in a period which represented the nadir of their fortunes elsewhere. Indeed, at a time when Liberal support was still declining in most parts of Britain,[96] there was in the early 1960s something of a Liberal revival in Cornwall, manifested in the 1964 General Election when Peter Bessell won Bodmin and later in 1966 when Bessell held Bodmin and John Pardoe won North Cornwall. Thereafter, bolstered by Liberal revival in the rest of Britain, the Liberals were confirmed in their role as the main opposition party in Cornwall, with Labour failing to build upon its early post-war breakthrough. Indeed, Labour lost

Falmouth-Camborne to the Conservatives in 1970, and experienced a continuing decline in electoral support in Cornwall. But despite the inherent strength of the Liberal Party (Liberal activity ". . . was on a spectacularly energetic scale"[97] in 1970 with 7,000 members in North Cornwall and 3,000 in Bodmin[98]), Liberal electoral performance tended to be volatile. Bodmin was lost to the Conservatives in 1970, to be regained in February 1974 and then lost again in the October, while in North Cornwall the Conservative candidate — Gerry Neale — successfully mobilised the "second homes" vote and managed to oust Pardoe in 1979. Meanwhile, however, Penhaligon had won Truro for the Liberals in February 1974, consolidating his position in the October and in 1979.[99] Following his untimely death, he was replaced in Truro in a by-election in 1987 by the Liberal Matthew Taylor.

In the post-war era, then, the Cornish political scene continued to be dominated by the Conservative-Liberal contest. Early indications of a Labour breakthrough and a Liberal decline were deceptive, the longer-term experience demonstrating the re-assertion of Liberal performance and the dwindling of Labour's support. In matching this to the experience of the United Kingdom as a whole, Lee had demonstrated that Cornish politics remained highly distinctive in this period. To obtain a measurement of gross diffences in party competition between Cornwall and the rest of Britain, Lee employed the technique developed by Miller to calculate the difference between the multi-party outcome in one area and another. Miller's method (the "MD formula") produced a measure of voting deviation ("MD") between one area and another — a measure of zero, for example, would indicate that voting patterns were identical between the two.[100] Employing this method, comparisons had been made between the other parts of the United Kingdom and England. In this way for example, scores of % MD for the 1979 General Election were: Wales — 15, Scotland — 17, and Northern Ireland (where there is a greatly different mix of parties) — 74. Having made the proviso that an exaggerative effect may have been introduced by the small number of constituencies involved, Lee proceeded to calculate the % MD score for Cornwall against England for each General Election between 1922 and 1987. As Lee concluded:

> The remarkable features of this gross measure of deviation are firstly its size and secondly its relative consistency over time. Variations range from 15.54% (1970) to 29.03% (1966) if the elections of 1931 and 1935 are discounted as having fewer than five contests in Cornwall. In both size and consistency the deviations compare with those found by Miller for Wales for a selection of elections. In no year does the average for Cornwall fall below the Welsh: in all others it is above, and from 1959–1966 substantially so.[101]

Lee's findings confirmed an apparent continuity between the inter-war and post-war periods. Not surprisingly, Lee explained that the main deviation was produced by the variation in the respective strengths of the Labour and Liberal Parties. But he also noted that while the Conservative Party had always performed

YEAR	Cornwall– % MD England
1922	17.87*
1923	26.45
1924	23.86
1929	19.05
1931	31.79**
1935	27.54*
1945	23.32
1950	24.41
1951	22.02
1955	18.12
1959	20.76
1964	23.34
1966	29.03
1970	20.44
1974 (F)	18.83
1974 (O)	18.80
1979	19.04
1983	16.23
1987	16.37

* 4 contests
** 3 contests

Measure of voting deviation (MD)
Cornwall — England

Source: Adrian Lee, "The Persistence of Difference? Electoral Change in Cornwall", unpublished paper presented to Political Studies Association Annual Conference, Plymouth Polytechnic, 1988, p3.

marginally above its general English level, its performance was nonetheless at a substantially lower level than one would expect for a group of constituencies falling as they do with one exception into the Government-designated CAC1 Cluster 31 — "Agricultural areas". The exception was Falmouth-Camborne, which is in Cluster 24 — "Small manufacturing towns with rural hinterlands".[102] Commenting upon this Conservative "under-performance", Lee considered that ". . . although the party has dominated the county's parliamentary representation in the post-war period . . . it could be argued that the party's share of the vote has reached a ceiling level from which little deviation has been experienced . . .".[103] Interestingly, the decline in Liberal variation from 1970 onwards indicated not only a similar ceiling but more importantly the growth of third party (Liberal-SDP) support within England: "Put another way, since 1970 rural England in this respect

Electoral Support in Cornwall: Five constituency average

Year	Con%	Lab%	Lib%	Other
1922*	45.6	9.6	42.8	2.0
1923	41.8	2.6	55.6	0.0
1924	48.8	9.4	41.8	0.0
1929	36.5	17.0	42.4	3.2
1931**	43.1	13.8	38.6	4.5
1935***	46.8	15.8	37.0	0.4
1945	42.1	25.2	32.6	0.2
1950	44.5	28.9	26.6	0.0
1951	50.6	32.5	17.0	0.0
1955	48.7	29.7	21.6	0.0
1959	44.2	26.4	29.4	0.0
1964	41.3	25.0	33.5	0.2
1966	41.5	26.7	31.8	0.0
1970	48.0	23.7	27.8	0.5
1974 (F)	41.9	18.9	38.8	0.4
1974 (O)	43.8	19.6	36.4	0.2
1979	51.3	12.9	33.1	2.7
1983	49.4	9.0	40.3	1.3
1987	47.3	12.8	39.8	0.1

*Average for 4 constituencies (Cornwall North (NLIB) unopposed)
**Average for 3 constituencies (Bodmin (LIB) & St Ives (NLIB) unopposed)
***Average for 4 constituencies (St Ives (NLIB) unopposed)
N.B. In 1951 the Liberals contested only three constituencies.
Source: Adrian Lee, 1988, p5.

has come to more closely resemble Cornwall".[104] This new-found similarly was shortlived, however, the European Paliamentary elections of June 1989 displaying a renewed divergence between Cornwall and rural England. In the wake of the Alliance collapse, the Liberal Democrats faired disastrously in much of rural England, apparently losing much of their traditional support to the newly-emergent Green Party (in the Devon EPC the Greens — who came second — achieved 53,220 votes, the Liberal Democrats 23,306, and the SDP 7,806), whereas in Cornwall (and Plymouth) the Liberal Democrats achieved their best result in Britain, challenging the victorious Conservatives' 88,376 votes with a very credible 68,559 and with the Greens appearing in fourth place with 24,581 votes.[105]

Labour failure, Liberal tenacity and Conservative "under-performance" were therefore the major features of Cornish electoral experience in the post-war era, an experience which was highly distinctive — even when set against ostensibly comparable rural English areas. The *ITN Election Factbook* in 1987 admitted that

Cornwall — Variations in party support against English average 1945–1987

General Election Year	Con	Lab	Lib	Other
1945	+1.9	−23.3	+23.2	−1.7
1950	+0.7	−17.3	+17.2	−0.6
1951	+1.8	−16.3	+14.7	−0.1
1955	−1.7	−17.1	+19.0	−0.2
1959	−5.7	−17.2	+23.1	−0.2
1964	−2.8	−18.5	+24.4	−0.1
1966	−1.2	−21.3	+22.8	−0.3
1970	−0.4	−19.6	+21.2	−1.2
1974 Feb	+1.7	−18.7	+18.8	−1.8
1974 Oct	+4.9	−20.5	+16.2	−0.6
1979	+4.1	−23.8	+18.2	+1.5*
1983	+3.4	−18.0	+13.9	+0.5*
1987	+1.1	−16.7	+16.0	−0.4

*Represents effects of MK's intervention
Source: Adrian Lee, 1988, p6.

"The further one proceeds towards Cornwall, the less 'English' the ambience, and the less firm the Tory grip",[106] while Curtice and Steed — in their examination of regional changes in the 1987 General Election — found it difficult to categorise Cornwall in the North/West-South/East divide that they were attempting to identify, complaining of: ". . . the Devon and Cornwall subregion which does not fit easily into either of these broad divisions and which we have consequently set aside in the analysis . . .".[107] Clearly, Cornwall remained politically distinct in several respects; the experience of the late 1940s and 50s had *not* been one of movement towards greater conformity with the "alignment" elsewhere.

This, as Lee's statistics had already indicated, suggested a high degree of continuity from the pre-war era. And yet, there *were* changes in the post-war period in the nature of Cornish politics, manifested only subtly at electoral levels but in fact profoundly affecting the conduct of local politics and serving to enhance what was already a distinctive Cornish political culture. There was indeed a movement from "fossilisation", from paralysis — not towards conformity, but towards a style of politics in which anti-metropolitanism became a major determinant of activity. This, inevitably, was allied to the increasing demands for the renewed political "accommodation" of Cornwall and to the increasingly vociferous critiques of Regional Planning. It also indicated the impact of Cornish nationalism upon the wider political scene where, as Andy Smith wrote, "Though an essentially powerless and split force, it has retained a powerful influence on politicians of the main national parties".[108] In terms of public opinion, the effects were not difficult to gauge, the British Election Survey in 1970 getting 57.7 per cent agreement in Cornwall to the proposition ". . . that Government is too centralised in London"[109] (as opposed to 36.8 per cent in the South West and 35.1 per cent in Britain as a whole), and in 1974 receiving 66.7 per cent agreement to the notion that it is ". . . 'very' or 'fairly' important that Goverment should decentralise power"[110] (as opposed to 43.1 per cent in the South West and 49.9 in Britain).

As Bogdanor noted, the Liberals were receptive to the claims of Cornish anti-metropolitanism as they emerged in the post-war era.[111] Deacon wrote that the "Liberals were much more successful in purveying an image of local patriotism in Cornwall than in Scotland and Wales . . .",[112] and Andy Smith has asserted that ". . . it is the Democrats, or the old Liberals which have most effectively stolen the nationalists' clothes".[113] Certainly, it was not entirely co-incidental that the rise of anti-metropolitan sentiment in the 1960s occurred against the background of the revival of Liberal fortunes in Cornwall, most notably the victory of Bessel in Bodmin in 1964 and that of Pardoe in North Cornwall in 1966. Both men were careful to join Mebyon Kernow and to publicly proclaim their membership, in 1967 declaring that " . . . the Cornish people have the same right to control their country, its economy and its political future, as the other Celtic peoples of Scotland and Wales".[114] When, in 1968, the Liberal Party document *Power to the Provinces* failed to specify a separate regional status for Cornwall, there were howls of disapproval from Cornish Liberals, with the Liberal leader intervening hastily to give assurances that "Cornwall would have the right to become a province of its own".[115]

The Liberal Party was, of course, well placed to assume the mantle of Cornish anti-metropolitanism. In Britain as a whole, the Liberals had become progressively the party of the Celtic periphery, adopting an early commitment to "Home Rule All Round" and attuning itself to the particular needs and concerns of peripheral Britain. In Cornwall specifically, the Liberal Party had always embraced "Cornish" issues and was firmly entrenched as the party of the Cornish radicalism, in particular the radical tradition wedded to Cornish Methodism. Hayden[116] demonstrated that the Cornish Liberal-Methodist link had survived into the post-war era, and Hearl suggested that it was no co-incidence that the Liberal "heartland" of central and North Cornwall — where the Liberals had performed especially well in recent decades — was also the "heartland" of modern Cornish Methodism[117] (and, one might add, the former "heartland" of the specifically Cornish Bible Christian Connexion, one of Methodism's constituent sects). The Liberals, then, remained closely identified with Cornwall during the period of paralysis, so that when Cornish politics emerged from its "fossilisation" in the new era of "Third Peripheralism", the Liberal Party especially was able to respond to the new "politicisation" of the "Revival", the new anti-metropolitanism with its demands for political "accommodation" and its critiques of central government "Regional Planning" policies.

Nowhere was this more apparent than in Truro constituency during the time that David Penhaligon was its MP, from his election in February 1974 until his

228

death in December 1986.[118] Penhaligon employed his obviously Cornish ambience and accent to good effect, both in appealing to the Cornish "ethnic" vote and in projecting his views convincingly as being those of the average Cornishman or Cornish woman. He embraced all the distinctly Cornish issues of his period with enthusiasm — seeking a Devolutionary assembly for Cornwall when others were proposed for Scotland and Wales, opposing Plymouth "expansionism" and demanding a Cornwall-only European Parliamentary Constituency, championing the cause of the Cornish mines during the "tin crisis". The nationalists hailed him as a "Cornish Hero".[119] Michael Williams, a Liberal activist in North Cornwall, considered that Penhaligon displayed ". . . firm commitment to the Cornish cause",[120] and that he was "A reforming radical, with something of the Cornish nationalist in him . . ."[121] who ". . . spoke for Cornwall with the same Celtic spirit that the young Lloyd George spoke for Wales".[122] After Penhaligon's death, the *Western Morning News* lamented the loss of the ". . . man who was regarded everywhere as the voice of Cornwall".[123] Incredibly, his memorial service in Truro Cathedral was listened to on Radio Cornwall by an estimated 100,000 people.

Penhaligon's death left something of a vacuum in Cornish politics, with other Cornish politicians clamouring to assume his role and to demonstrate their commitment to Cornwall and to the spirit of anti-metropolitanism. As Smith noted wryly, "Never was the nationalist influence more transparent than at the Truro by-election when each main candidate strained to prove his Cornish credentials, even though it was quite clear none had a complete set".[124] Nick St Aubyn, the Conservative, stressed his descent from an ancient Cornish family, and Londoner John King — for Labour — had learnt the Cornish language in an effort to acquire a veneer of Cornishness. But the seat was won by Matthew Taylor, Penhaligon's protege, who proceeded to articulate Cornish concerns at Westminster, most notably during the European Constituency debate when he presented a detailed critique of the Assistant Commissioner's report and called on Parliament to ". . . reject what the Boundary Commission says and recognise the backing given . . . for the distinct identity and voice that Cornwall demands".[125] Likewise, Taylor was at pains to highlight Cornwall's special socio-economic condition, claiming that Cornwall was the poorest county in Britain and one of the poorest regions in Europe:

> . . . the general sketch that people like to draw of the north-south divide between the economically wealthy and the poor areas of the country is no more than a caricature. In Cornwall the figures for poverty and joblessness regularly compete with those in the midlands and north-east. Cornwall is the poorest county in the country and has one of the lowest GNPs in Europe. Its poverty, which is unexpected in the south . . . is combined with house prices that compete almost with the south-east.[126]

In similar vein, Paul Tyler — briefly Liberal MP for Bodmin during 1974 — had embraced Cornish issues, claiming descent from no less a personage than Bishop Jonathan Trelawny himself.[127] As the Liberal Democrat candidate for the

1989 European Parliamentary Elections, Tyler also lent his support to the calls for a Cornwall-only EPC and, in a further demonstration of his concern for the political "accommodation" of Cornwall, claimed that alleged Conservative plans to abolish County Councils posed a severe threat to the territorial integrity and identity of Cornwall.[128] Liberal commitment to Cornwall's integrity, however, had come under suspicion during the period of its Alliance with the Social Democratic Party. The identification of the SDP leader, Dr David Owen, with the City of Plymouth might have been enough to ring alarm bells in Cornwall, but more significant was the SDP's 1983 "green paper" on regional government which advocated the creation of a unified Devon and Cornwall authority. As Stanyer observed. "Cornwall and Devon might well have lost their identities in their new joint regional government".[129] In the prelude to the 1987 General election, therefore, the Liberals in South East Cornwall found it politic to announce that "The Alliance will resist moves by Plymouth to take over parts of East Cornwall. Not only are Cornish members of the Alliance against this, but Dr Owen has also spoken out against moves by Plymouth into Cornwall".[130] Although in West Cornwall in particular the SDP did attempt some identification with Cornish issues, the formation of the Social and Liberal Democratic Party and its estrangement from Dr Owen's minority SDP was an opportunity for the new Liberal Democrats to assert their Cornish credentials, reminding the electorate that "Cornwall enjoys an enviable tradition of radical and progressive politics . . ."[131] of which they were the inheritors.

Indeed, the *Guardian* noted in September 1988[132] that the North Cornwall branch of the Liberal Democrats was the largest in Britain, and in the 1989 European Parliamentary Elections Tyler's campaign adopted an almost nationalist tone, exhorting voters to "Put Cornwall First", a photograph in the eve-of-poll *Cornish Voice* leaflet depicting Tyler (along with Matthew Taylor and Annette Penhaligon) at Twickenham sporting a "Trelawny's Second Invasion" sweat-shirt and holding a Cornish flag![133] This helped Tyler to deflect a potentially strong performance by the Mebyon Kernow candidate, Colin Lawry (who had produced an impressive and comprehensive election manifesto, *The Cornish Answer*[134]), MK in fact achieving a poor 4,224 votes as its potential supporters switched their allegiance to either the Liberal Democrats or the Greens.[135]

The Conservative Party in Cornwall was never as obviously "Cornish" as its Liberal rivals, notwithstanding its partial inheritance of the local Liberal Unionist and National Liberal traditions, but it too was able to respond to the new anti-metropolitanism, albeit in a more ad hoc manner. John Nott, as Conservative MP for St Ives, was quick to realise the electoral appeal of anti-metropolitanism, lending support to the Cornish stamp campaign and attacking the Redcliffe-Maud proposals with the retort that "I can see no reason why Cornwall, with its own traditions and culture, should not form the nucleus of one such authority and retain its separate identity"![136] Later, in 1975 Nott responded to the Cowethas Flamank report *Towards Self-Government*, explaining that "My own view is not radically different from your own conclusion . . . I have always been in favour of a far greater degree of devolution to the Cornish people".[137] This was a sentiment echoed in neighbouring Falmouth-Camborne by David Mudd, who wrote that "... I recognise the validity of much of the Report's case and feel that, on balance, Crown Dependency status is the most realistic goal",[138] arguing that Cornwall should enjoy the same degree of autonomy as that afforded to the Isle of Man.

Mudd, indeed, proved the most successful Conservative proponent of anti-metropolitanism, joining Mebyon Kernow as part of his campaign to win Falmouth-Camborne from Labour, as a journalist writing a number of popular books on Cornish themes to demonstrate his intimate knowledge of and affection for Cornwall,[139] distancing himself formally from the Parliamentary Conservative Party during the "tin crisis", and warning of the dangers of what he saw as Thatcher centralism. He perceived, he said, an aloofness and arrogance of government which was resented by the Cornish electorate: "They are told of the magical 'national prosperity', but can see little of it in Cornwall and are only aware of an obscenely rosy glow emanating from the fat-cats of the South East".[140] Similarly, in the European Constituency debate he distanced himself from the government's support for the proposed Cornwall and Plymouth EPC, arguing instead that Cornwall should have its own constituency.[141] Mudd's independence of thought and action was facilitated by his confirmed "back-bench" status in the Commons, which allowed him the luxury of unswerving commitment to Cornish issues, affording in turn a high degree of "ad hominen" support from the electorate. The Cornish propensity to lend "ad hominen" support had been apparent in the case of David Penhaligon, but it was also noticeable in Bodmin (later South East Cornwall) where Robert Hicks had built up a strong personal following and was also prepared to criticise his party on Cornish issues. Hicks was one of only a few Conservative MPs widely tipped to follow Brocklebank-Fowler into the SDP during its heady days, but he remained within the Tory fold.[142] He lent support, however, to the Cornwall Industrial Development Association, and — like Mudd — was increasingly prepared in the late 1980s to criticise what he considered an over-authoritarian and doctrinaire government.[143] At the European level, the Tory MEP Christopher Beazley had in 1988 and 1989 to counter criticism of his support for the perpetuation of the Cornwall and Plymouth EPC by vigorously publicising his sponsorship of a *Petition to the European Parliament in Support of Cornwall's Heritage and Culture* prepared by the Cornish Bureau for European Relations (COBER).[144]

Not all Conservative MPs possessed the style of Mudd and Hicks, however, and Piers Dixon — the sitting Conservative who was defeated by Penhaligon in 1974 — was one who failed to develop the necessary rapport with the Cornish electorate (despite his production of a little book on Cornish surnames![145]). It was Labour candidates, however, who consistently found it difficult to present themselves in a "Cornish" light. The great exception was Harold Hayman in Falmouth-Camborne, a local man acknowledged for his independence of thought within the Labour Party, generally characterised as a right-winger.[146] But after his death he was replaced by John Dunwoody, who conceived politics in a rigidly UK-wide framework (refusing, indeed, to recognise Cornwall's Celtic identity[147]), and who was defeated by the enthusiastically localist Mudd in 1970. Latterly, Labour has become much more aware of the need for a Cornish image, a requirement not lost on John King in his efforts in Truro constituency and in his broader determination to bring a Cornish dimension to Labour politics, and with Paul Clarke in South East Cornwall in the 1987 General Election turning to Cornish issues as a means to try to make headway against that constituency's formidable Conservative and Liberal machines.[148] More generally, frustration at Labour's failure to advance in a region of obvious relative poverty was voiced in Dalton's *Turn Left At Land's End* in 1987 where he noted "The need for Cornwall County Council Labour Group to do more . . . And . . . to raise the public and media profile of trade unionism in Cornwall."[149]

Labour's failure to capitalise upon the new anti-metropolitanism was, of course, also a function of the party's position (or rather lack of position) within Cornish political culture over a much longer period of time. Similarly, the Conservatives' consistent electoral "under achievement" was not necessarily a measure of their less successful adoption of anti-metropolitanism (vis a vis the Liberals) but also reflected the underlying differences between Cornwall and the ostensibly similar English rural areas with which she was being compared. These differences were socio-economic in part, but they were also differences in political culture. As to the strength of that political culture, it is interesting to note — as Lee has done — that the massive in-migration (much of it from South East England) had not benefitted the Conservatives to the extent that one might have expected.[150] This demonstrates, perhaps, the power of the Cornish political culture to assimilate newcomers. The actual mechanism of assimilation is more problematical, but an explanation might lie in the strength of the Liberals (now Liberal Democrats) and hence their credibility and attraction to former Conservatives who find themselves isolated from their former Tory heartland. Having moved to Cornwall from the South East, newcomers appreciate their distance from the centres of economic and political power, at the same time perceiving that a Liberal vote is not "wasted" in the way that it might have been at home. They vote accordingly, perhaps.

Be that as it may, the enduring strength of Cornish political culture was evident in another facet of local politics, namely at the County and other levels of local government. Here Cornwall had developed an "Independent" tradition, in which local politics were seen as divorced from and irrelevant to national politics, there being therefore no place for party-political conflict at local government level. This, of course, reflected Bulpitt's thesis of the estrangement of local from central government (the former essentially "de-politicised") and it was significant that local government had been introduced and developed during the period of Cornwall's political paralysis. Cornwall's "Independent" tradition, therefore, was largely a reflection and product of that paralysis. Specifically, it represented Cornish isolation from mainstream British politics, and locally it meant an understanding between Liberals and Liberal Unionists at County level which was expressed in the eschewing of party labels. In the first County Council of 1889, for example, the Chairman had been a Liberal Unionists and his Vice a Liberal — an attempt to achieve an apolitical balance — and thereafter local elections were fought on a non-partisan basis, with candidates offering themselves as "Independents".[151]

Indeed, such was the level of "de-politicisation" achieved, that habitually a majority of local government seats were uncontested, with candidates having already gained some form of local consensus and being returned unopposed — very much the image of a political system in paralysis!

As Lee has shown in some detail, this state of affairs persisted well into the post-war era.[152] In 1973, in the first elections fought within the reformed Local Government structure, the only Counties to fall under the control of "Independents" were Cornwall, the Isle of Wight, Dyfed, Gwynedd, and Powys (each of which exhibited "peripheral" characteristics).[153] As recently as 1977 a full 55 per cent of seats on Cornwall County Council were filled through unopposed returns, and although this figure had fallen to 21 per cent by 1985 it was still the highest proportion of any County. The number of "Independents" both standing and being returned was thereafter eroded, so that in the retiring Council in 1989 there were 26 "Independents" amongst a total of 78 councillors (ie 33.3 per cent). Nonetheless, the "Independent" tradition has survived (24 were returned in 1989) and indeed during 1988 and 1989 "Independent" candidates began to campaign in concert, holding an "Independents' Day"[154] to discuss their role and advertising their determination to "Keep Cornwall Independent . . . in the long standing Cornish tradition . . .".[155]

Superficially, the erosion of the "unopposed" and "Independent" traditions might have suggested the demise of a distinctively Cornish political culture at local government level, but in fact the pattern of party-political contestation that developed was in itself highly distinctive. As Lee explained, "The contrast between Cornwall and other counties, even near neighbouring ones such as Devon, Dorset and Somerset, is marked".[156] Instead of the standard Conservative v. Labour v. Liberal/SDP contest encountered elsewhere, the pattern in Cornwall was often less coherent, the great majority of contestations taking place between only two candidates, and with the pattern of contestation changing markedly even in specific seats between one election and the next. Added to this was the paradox that contestation also marked emergence from political paralysis, with the new imperatives of anti-metropolitanism manifesting themselves at local government level. It was no co-incideence that one of the first significant (and successful) "party political" interventions was by Mebyon Kernow in St Day in 1967, nor was it surprising that the resurgent Liberals — with their efforts to embrace "Cornishness" — should have set the pace in forcing contestation.[157] Local government, then, had become "politicised" against the background of a more wideranging change in Cornish politics that had resulted from the "politicisation" of the Cornish "Revival", particularly during the 1980s when the Cornish Liberals/Liberal Democrats could portray themselves as the defenders of Cornwall against a supposedly centralist, Conservative government. This was especially noticeable in the 1989 County elections where, in contrast to Devon where the Conservatives won control, the Liberal Democrats increased their representation in Cornwall, with the County Council continuing to be run in effect by an alliance of Liberal Democrats and Independents.

This, then, was further evidence not only of continuing "difference" between the politics of Cornwall and England, but of the enhancement of Cornish political culture in the post-war era. This itself represented the emergence of Cornish politics from its "fossilised" paralysis in response to and as a part of the "Third Peripheralism" (the new socio-economic conditions and the "politicisation" of the "Revival") that had arisen, a phenomenon manifested not only in the birth of the nationalist groups but also in a new anti-metropolitanism (the demand for "accommodation", the critiques of Regional planning) that had affected party political activity in Cornwall. Taken together, these disparate strands of political behaviour combined to produce a highly distinctive Cornish political profile in the years after the Second World War, constituting in effect the new politics of "Third Peripheralism".

Notes and References

1. Eric Hobsbawm and Terence Ranger, *The Invention of Tradition*, Cambridge University Press, Cambridge, 1983.
2. Glanville Price, *The Languages of Britain*, Edward Arnold, London, 1984, pp141-145.
3. Richard Gendall, *Kernewek Bew*, Kesva an Tavas Kernewek/ Cornish Language Board, St Ives, 1972, p136.
4. Ken George, *The Pronounciation and Spelling of Revived Cornish*, Kesva an Tavas Kernewek/Cornish Language Board, Torpoint, 1986.
5. To propogate his work Richard Gendall has formed the Cornish Language Council and Teere ha Tavaz (Land and Language — not to be confused with the pre-war Tyr ha Tavas) and produced learning/teaching packages such as Richard Gendall, *Laugh & Learn Traditional Cornish: A New Course in Cornish For the Beginner*, Teere ha Tavaz, Liskeard, 1988. Definitive statements of his work are contained in Richard Gendall, *A Student's Dictionary of Modern Cornish, Part I — English/Cornish*, Cornish Language Council, Liskeard, 1991, and Richard Gendall, *A Student's Grammar of Modern Cornish*, Cornish Language Council, Liskeard, 1991. See also, Rod Lyon, *Traditional Cornish*, Lyon, Nancegollan, 1989, and *Cornish Banner*, November 1986, May 1987.
6. For example, see Institute of Cornish Studies' *Associates' Newsletter*, Winter 1989–90.
7. Meic Stephens, *Linguistic Minorities in Western Europe*, Gomer Press, Llandysul, 1976, pp200-220.
8. Charles Thomas, *The Importance of Being Cornish in Cornwall*, Institute of Cornish Studies, Redruth, 1973, p9.
9. *Western Morning News*, 30 March 1989.
10. *Cornish Banner*, February 1986.
11. For example, "Trelawny" appeared in full in the programmes for both Semi-Final (Redruth 21 January) and Final (Twickenham 1 April 1989).
12. *Independent*, 3 April 1989.
13. Ibid.
14. *Guardian*, 2 April 1989.
15. Ibid.
16. *Cornish Times*, 7 April 1989.
17. Cited in P. Berresford Ellis, *Wales — A Nation Again*, Library 33, London, 1968, p184.

18. Mebyon Kernow, *A Stamp for Cornwall/Stamp Lyther Rak Kernow: The Little-Known History of the Cornish Nation*, MK Publications, Redruth, 1974.
19. E.J. Pengelly, *The Detectable Duchy*, Cowethas Flamank, Redruth, 1986.
20. Cited in Ibid., pi; *The Report of the (Kilbrandon) Royal Commission on the Constitution*, Cmnd. 5460, HMSO, London, 1973.
21. *Commission on the Constitution — Written Evidence 8: England*, HMSO, London, 1972, p41.
22. Cowethas Flamank Research Group, *Towards Self-Government*, Cowethas Flamank, Bristol, 1974, p9.
23. Ibid.
24. *Kilbrandon*, op. cit., para. 329.
25. Cowethas Flamank, 1974, op. cit., pi.
26. A.L. Dennis (ed.), *Cornwall County Council 1889-1989: A History of 100 Years of County Goverment*, Cornwall County Council, Truro, 1989, p97.
27. *Cornish Nation*, June-July 1969.
28. John Fleet, "The Cornish Border", in F.G. Thompson (ed.), *The Celtic Experience: Past and Present*, Celtic League, Dublin, 1972, p118.
29. Dennis (ed.), op. cit., p98.
30. Ibid., p1.
31. Ivan Rabey (ed.), *Cornwall: An Official Guide to Cornwall*, Cornwall County Council/British Publishing Co., Gloucester, n.d. c1988, p31.
32. *Cornish Guardian*, 30 April 1987.
33. *Boundary Commission For England Report: European Assembly Constituencies*, Cmnd 7348, HMSO, London, 1978, pp4-43.
34. David Butler and David Marquand, *European Elections and British Politics*, Longman, London, 1981, p133.
35. *Report of S.J.L. Oliver, Q.C.: 1983 Review of European Assembly Constituencies, European Assembly Election Acts 1978/81, Cornwall and Plymouth/Devon*, Boundary Commission For England, London, 1983.
36. *Daily Telegraph*, 11 July 1988.
37. Ibid.
38. This legal requirement was re-iterated by the Boundary Commission For England in its *News Release* dated 2 June 1988 and in its *Statement to be made on behalf of the Commission* by the Assistant Commissioner at the Bodmin Public Inquiry, 12 July 1988.
39. Campaign For A Cornish Constituency, *Campaign Submission to the Public Inquiry, Public Rooms, Bodmin, on Tuesday 12th July 1988*, 1988.
40. Ibid.
41. Feock Parish Council, *Boundary Commission For England: European Parliament — Cornwall and Plymouth Constituency, Public Inquiry, Bodmin, 12 and 13 July 1988, Representations of the Parish Council*, 1988, p1.
42. North Cornwall District Council, *Boundary Commission For England: Public Inquiry into the European Parliamentary Constituencies of Cornwall and Plymouth and Devon*, 1988, p1.
43. Kerrier District Council, *Boundary Commission For England: 1988 Review of European Assembly Constituencies, European Assembly Act 1978 and 1981, Cornwall and Plymouth Constituency, Local Inquiry . . . Representations of the Kerrier District Council*, 1988, p3.
44. Cornwall County Council, *European Parliamentary Elections Act 1978 (as amended):*

Representations to the Boundary Commission For England on Their Provisional Recommendations Published 17th March 1988, 1988, p4.

45. *Boundary Commission For England: European Parliamentary Elections Act 1978 (as amended): The Report by Mr Assistant Commissioner G.D. Flather, Q.C. upon the Local Inquiry held by him on 12 and 13 July 1988 in Bodmin, Cornwall, into the proposed changes in the European Parliamentary Constituencies of Cornwall and Plymouth and Devon*, Boundary Commission For England, London, 1988.

48. Ibid., p27.

47. Ibid., p30.

48. Campaign For A Cornish Constituency, *A Critique of: The Report For the Boundary Commission by G.D. Flather Q.C. upon the Local Inquiry held on 12/13 July 1988 into the proposed Cornwall and Plymouth and Devon Parliamentary Constituencies*, 1989

49. *Hansard*, 7 March 1989.

50. *Guardian*, 15 May 1987. See also *Western Morning News*, 5 November 1988.

51. John Fleet, "Heritage and Identity in the new Europe: The Cornish Bureau for European Relations", *European Access*, 1990: 3, June.

52. *Cornish Nation*, December 1971.

53. *Cornish Nation*, June 1972.

54. J.C. Banks, *Federal Britain? The Case For Regionalism*, Harrap, London, 1971.

55. Ibid., p255.

56. Ibid., p253.

57. J.C. Banks, "Cornwall as a Region", unpublished paper presented at the Conference on Cornwall, Perranporth, May 1983.

58. Ibid., p2.

59. Ibid., p3.

60. Ibid., p5.

61. Ibid.

62. Ian Wight, "Territory Versus Function in Regional Development: The Case of Cornwall", unpublished paper, University of Aberdeen, 1981, p15.

63. Cornwall Conservation Forum, *Cornwall's Choice*, C.C.F., Truro?, 1974.

64. South West Economic Planning Council, *A Strategic Settlement Pattern For the South West*, SWEPC, Bristol, 1974.

65. Cornwall Conservation Forum, op. cit., para. 23.

66. Ronald Perry, with Ken Dean and Bryan Brown, and with the assistance of David Shaw, *Counterurbanisation: International Case Studies of Socio-Economic Change in Rural Areas*, Geo books, Norwich, 1986.

67. Cornwall Industrial Development Association, *The Economy of Cornwall*, C.I.D.A., Truro?, 1977.

68. Ibid., p62.

69. Ibid., p69.

70. Wight, op. cit., p23.

71. Cornwall County Council, *Cornwall Structure Plan*, Truro, 1980.

72. Wight, op. cit., p21.

73. Perry et al, op. cit.

74. Cornwall County Council, *Structure Plan: First Alteration*, Truro, 1988, 1.8; cited in Bernard Deacon, Andrew George, and Ronald Perry, *Cornwall at the Crossroads? Living Communities or Leisure Zone?*, Cornish Social and Economic Research Group, Redruth, 1988, p55.

75. Cornish Alternatives to the Structure Plan, *Cornwall: A Breathing Space*, CASP, Truro, 1988; CASP, *Local Needs Policy*, CASP, Truro, 1988; see also, CASP, *Euro-constituency: Shotgun Marriage? Amicable Split?*, CASP, Truro, 1988.
76. CASP . . . *Breathing Space*, Frontispiece.
77. CASP, . . . *Policy*, p1.
78. CASP . . . *Breathing Space*, p1.
79. Ibid., p2.
80. Ibid., p1.
81. Ibid., p5.
82. Ibid., p8.
83. *West Briton*, 10 November 1988.
84. Cornish Social and Economic Research Group, *The Cornish Community: Reclaiming Our Destiny*, COSERG, Redruth, 1987, frontispiece.
85. Ibid.
86. Ibid.
87. Bernard Deacon et al, op. cit.
88. Ibid., p11.
89. Ibid.
90. Ibid., p27.
91. Ibid., p58.
92. Ibid., p181.
93. Ibid., p179.
94. Ibid.
95. Michael Kinnear, *The British Voter: An Atlas and Survey Since 1885*, Batsford, London, 1981, pp56-69, details General Election performances in Cornwall during the post-war period.
96. Vernon Bogdanor, *Liberal Party Politics*, Clarendon Press, Oxford, 1983, p79.
97. David Butler and Dennis Kavanagh, *The British General Election of 1983*, Macmillan, London, 1984, p326.
98. Ibid., p263.
99. Robert Waller, *The Almanac of British Politics*, 2nd ed., Croom Helm, London, 1983, pp246-250, provides a concise insight into Cornish constituency activity in this era.
100. William Miller, "Variations in Electoral Behaviour in the United Kingdom", in Peter Madgwick and Richard Rose, *The Territorial Dimension in United Kingdom Politics*, Macmillan, London, 1982, pp225-230; pp240-250.
101. Adrian Lee, "The Persistence of Difference? Electoral Change in Cornwall", unpublished paper presented to Political Studies Association Annual Conference, Plymouth Polytechnic, 1988, p4.
102. I. Crewe and A. Fox, *British Parliamentary Constituencies: A Statistical Compendium*, Faber, London, 1984, pp14-15.
103. Lee, op. cit., p6.
104. Ibid.
105. *Western Morning News*, 19 June 1989.
106. Independent Television Network, *ITN Election Factbook*, ITN, London, 1987; cited in Derek Hearl, "Regional Political Behaviour: The Case of Devon and Cornwall", unpublished paper presented to Political Studies Association Annual Conference, Plymouth Polytechnic, 1988, frontispiece.
107. John Curtice and Michael Steed, "Appendix 2 Analysis", in David Butler and Dennis Kavanagh, *The General Election of 1987*, Macmillan, London, 1988, p320.

108. Andy Smith, Political Correspondent in *Western Morning News*, 8 March 1989.
109. *British Election Survey*, 1970 and October 1974, cited in Colin S. Rallings and Adrian Lee, "Politics of the Periphery — The Case of Cornwall", unpublished paper presented to the Conference of the PSA Work Group on The Politics of the United Kingdom, Aberystwyth, 1977, Table 3.
110. Ibid.
111. Bogdanor, op. cit., p245.
112. Bernard Deacon, "The Cornish Revival: An Analysis", unpublished paper, Redruth. 1985, p43.
113. Smith, op. cit.
114. *Western Morning News*, February 1967.
115. Cited in Rallings and Lee, op. cit., p10.
116. Peter Hayden, "Culture, Creed and Conflict: Methodism and Politics in Cornwall, c1832-1979", unpublished PhD thesis, University of Liverpool, 1982, p377.
117. Hearl, op. cit., pp7-11.
118. Annette Penhaligon, *Penhaligon*, Bloomsbury, London, 1989.
119. *Cornish Banner*, February 1987.
120. *Cornish Scene*, March/April 1987.
121. Ibid.
122. Ibid.
123. *Western Morning News*, 23 December 1986.
124. Smith, op. cit.
125. *Hansard*, 7 March 1989.
126. Ibid.; see also *Western Morning News*, 7 July 1988.
127. Election Communication, *Paul Tyler: Liberal Democrat — Campaign For Cornwall '89*, 1989.
128. *Cornish Times*, 9 December 1988.
129. Jeffrey Stanyer, "Cornwall, Devon and the British System of Government", unpublished paper presented to Political Studies Association Annual Conference, Plymouth Polytechnic, 1988, p6.
130. South East Cornwall Liberal Association, *Focus: Partners For Progress — News From the Alliance*, leaflet, 1987.
131. South East Cornwall Social and Liberal Democrats, *Focus: Democrats in South East Cornwall*, No 1 Spring 1988.
132. *Guardian*, 26 September 1988.
133. Annette Penhaligon (SLD Campaign Agent), *Cornish Voice*, June 1989 (not to be confused with the earlier and shortlived Mebyon Kernow journal of the same title).
134. Mebyon Kernow, *The Cornish Answer*, MK, Liskeard, 1989.
135. *Western Morning News*, 19 June 1989.
136. *Western Morning News*, 17 December 1967.
137. Letter to Cowethas Flamank, dated 23 April 1975.
138. Letter to Cowethas Flamank, dated 13 May 1975.
139. For example, David Mudd, *Cornishmen and True*, Frank Graham, Newcastle-upon-Tyne, 1971; David Mudd, *The Falmouth Packets*, Bossiney Books, Bodmin, 1978.
140. *West Briton*, 10 November 1988.
141. *Western Morning News*, 25 June 1988.
142. Waller, op. cit., p249.
143. *Western Morning News*, 26 November 1988.
144. Conservative Party, *European Parliament Election Communication*, 1989; Cornish

Bureau for European Relations, *Petition to the European Parliament in Support of Cornwall's Heritage and Culture*, COBER, Mylor Bridge, 1988.

145. Piers Dixon, *Cornish Names*, Dixon, Probus, 1973.

146. Mudd, 1971, op. cit., pp112-115.

147. Berresford Ellis, op. cit., pp183-184.

148. *Cornish Times*, 22 May 1987.

149. A.J.P. Dalton, *Turn Left At Land's End*, Red Boots, London, 1987, pp93-94.

150. Lee, op. cit., p17.

151. Dennis (ed.), op. cit., p3.

152. Lee, op. cit., pp7-10.

153. Wyn Grant, *Independent Local Politics in England and Wales*, Saxon House, Farnborough, 1977, p2.

154. Bert Biscoe, *Independent's Day: A Conference for Representatives, Candidates and Supporters of Independents in Local Government in Cornwall*, leaflet, Truro, 1988.

155. *West Briton*, 27 April 1989. The actual composition of Cornwall County Council after the 1989 Local Elections was: Liberal Democrats 32 seats, Independents 24, Conservative 14, Labour 8, Mebyon Kernow 1.

156. Lee, op. cit., p8.

157. John Pardoe heralded the Liberals' onslaught on the Independents in *Cornish Nation*, June 1973; see also *Sunday Independent*, 22 April 1973.

Conclusion

This book has sought to investigate the making of modern Cornwall, adopting a model and strategy of analysis postulated by Rokkan and Urwin, and employing an historical inquiry to support the view that Cornwall's experience can be explained in terms of phases of peripherality, derived from Tarrow's assertion that in the relation between centre and periphery there was an original or "Older Peripheralism" of territorial and cultural isolation to which was added, in the era of industrialisation, a "Second Peripheralism" of economic and social marginality. Noting that the events of the 1960s and 1970s in Scotland, Wales, Northern Ireland and — to a lesser extent — the North of England had led academic commentators to abandon the conventional wisdom of the "homogeneous state" and to search for new explanations of the newly-apparent diversity within the United Kingdom, this study has shown that Cornwall too exhibited behavioural differences over the same period and which also attracted attempts at academic explanation. It has been argued that such explanation must be sought within the analyses of state formation within the British Isles and within Western Europe generally, accepting Rokkan and Urwin's typology and placing Cornwall within their framework as one of the Celtic-Atlantic peripheries of the West. Within this, the United Kingdom is seen as a highly "monocephalic" state, with political and socio-economic power vested in its "lowland" centre in South East England and with Cornwall characterised as part of the "Inner Periphery" of the "highland" zone, in modern times attracting only the minimum of political "accommodation".

From this analysis, Cornwall's status as a periphery emerges strongly, with important "constants of peripherality" which served to perpetuate elements of that status from one historical phase to another. But of overriding importance in determining the characteristics of peripherality in any one phase was, it has been argued, the changing relationship between centre and periphery over time. Here Tarrow's assertion has been adapted, extended and refined. An "Older Peripheralism", in which Celtic-Catholic Cornwall was indeed territorially and culturally isolated, has indeed been identified, and the processes by which that condition was eroded and finally destroyed have been examined. In the same way, the era of "Second Peripheralism" has been analysed in considerable detail, demonstrating how it was that despite the apparent technological advance in Cornwall, the Cornish experience of industrialisation was in fact over-specialised, imperfect and incomplete. This led, as has been argued, to early industrial collapse and consequent economic, social and political paralysis, the condition that exemplified "Second Peripheralism" in its most matured manifestation.

In a development of Tarrow's concept it has been argued also, however, that the post-war era — with a changing centre-periphery relationship based upon central government Regional Development policies — witnessed an emergence from the paralysis of later "Second Peripheralism" and the establishment of rapid social, economic and political change in what was a new era of "Third Peripheralism". Although this phase exhibited many stark contrasts when compared to that which had gone before, it nonetheless continued to mark the Cornish experience apart from that of the English "centre", with features ranging from the process of "counterurbanisation" to the rise of political nationalism serving to highlight Cornwall's continuing distinctiveness.

The experience of modern Cornwall, then, has been at root one of industrial change, from the rise and fall of technological prowess to the emergence of the post-war "branch factory" economy, the determining factor in this the changing nature of peripherality. It was this experience which moulded the distinctive social, economic and political identity of modern Cornwall, shaping and emphasising the differences between the Cornish "periphery" and the English "centre" (and even neighbouring Devon), and placing Cornwall firmly within the "multi-national" diversity of the British State.

Peripherality is thus an important determinant of identity — in Cornwall, but also by implication within other elements of the United Kingdom's "multi-national" diversity. The detailed elucidation of the experience of modern Cornwall contained within this study, therefore, not only contributes towards the fuller elaboration of the British diversity but also furnishes a method of inquiry (with its emphasis upon phases of peripherality) which — if applied equally to other components of the State — might shed yet further light upon the nature of that diversity. Indeed, the model may have yet wider applicability for the analysis and understanding of Western European states as a whole, the examination of Cornwall forming a case study whose significance extends far beyond the Tamar border.

Finally, given that it is the condition of peripherality that has ensured the perpetuation of Cornwall's separate identity, one must reflect that the price of distinctiveness has been so often economic hardship and deprivation, and that the changing nature of peripherality has brought so often in its wake trauma and upheaval. But this is no less true for the Scots-Irish Ulster folk, for the crofters of Barra or Skye, the Welsh-speakers of Gwynedd, the coal-miners of Lanark and Fife or Glamorgan and Gwent . . . in the final analysis, the extraordinary diversity, territorial inequalities, and enduring fascination of these islands are a function of the dynamic relationship between centre and periphery. The making of modern Cornwall is thus part of the broader experience of the British periphery.

241

Postscript

The "persistence of difference" thesis was posed a dual challenge in April 1992, as this book was in press and being steered towards publication. First of all, the long-awaited General Election came to pass. Trumpeted as the most significant election since 1979, would the influence of a distinctly Cornish political culture be observable in its outcome, or would polerisation around key personalities and key issues eradicate regional distinctiveness? Secondly, the Cornwall rugby team found itself on the road to the County Championship at Twickenham for the third time in four years. Had the novelty of success begun to wear thin for the team's supporters, or would forty thousand Cornish once again treat a bemused Capital and the home of international rugby to an exuberant display of separate identity?

In a General Election where, it turned out, there were clear distinctions in voting behaviour between (and sometimes within) the regional and national components of the United Kingdom, Cornwall managed one or two surprises but still produced a blend of results which was "true to type". Although the loss of Glasgow Govan and a generally lacklustre Scottish National Party performance had perhaps taken the sting out of the "Scottish question", at least in the short term, in Wales Plaid Cymru advanced quietly, its modest but measurable success startling many commentators. In Cornwall, the importance of distinctly Cornish issues was observable in North Cornwall, where Paul Taylor (for the Liberal Democrats) addressed local concern from the problems of rural poverty to the future of local government reform, unseating Sir Gerry Neale, the sitting Tory who had insisted that Cornish issues would be of secondary importance in determining voting patterns. Notwithstanding the possible influence of the Camelford "poisoned water" factor in achieving the Liberal Democrat victory, it was as if the North Cornwall constituency were re-asserting its old Bible Christian credentials, the latent rural radicalism of this sprawling and thinly-populated district re-emerging to re-affirm the political significance of Cornish Nonconformity at a time when Cornish issues were high on the agenda.

In neighbouring South East Cornwall, an energetic Liberal Democrat challenge was beaten off with apparent ease by Robert Hicks, the fiercely independent "local man" who commanded widespread "ad hominen" support and whose election leaflet — delivered to every household in the constituency — neglected to mention his Conservative Party affiliation but exhorted voters to "Return Robert Hicks to Westminster, for Moderation, Consistency and Continuity", reminding the electorate that he ". . . has always spoken up for what he believes to be right whether on local or national issues". Further to the west, in Truro and St Austell, it was Matthew Taylor who was picking-up the "personality" vote and increasing his majority, the china clay country villages in particular displaying a mass or orange-and-black Liberal Democrat posters during the campaign, a measure of the success that Taylor had continued to enjoy in presenting himself to the Cornish electorate as a worthy and natural successor to the late David Penhaligon.

The biggest electoral surprise in Cornwall was the victory of sporting celebrity Sebastian Coe in Falmouth and Camborne. Against the background of massive unemployment in the constituency (particularly in Camborne-Redruth) and the controversy surrounding the closure of nearby Wheal Jane and subsequent pollution of the Carnon River, it was felt by many that the Conservatives' campaign would commence at a severe disadvantage. Added to this was that Coe, unlike the retiring Tory MP David Mudd, was not a Cornishman, a deficiency which led (as *The Times* noted in its report for 21 March 92) to his being described variously as "foreigner", "emmet" and "up-country carpet-bagger". Written-off by the press and under-estimated by his opponents Coe managed nonetheless a convincing victory in what had become a "three-way marginal" seat, defeating the "favourite" (Liberal Democrat Terrye Jones) and the popular Labour candidate (John Cosgrove, a Cornishman from Looe). Significantly, Coe had been forced in the campaign to address himself to Cornish issues, in particular taking-up the old "nationalist" cry and demanding the creation of a Cornish Development Agency.

Although observers had seen the St Ives constituency as perhaps the least "winable" for the Liberal Democrats in Cornwall, the Liberal Democrat candidate (Andrew George) fought an impressive campaign, coming within just 1600 votes of victory in what was now a "marginal" seat, achieving a swing that was greater than that that had secured the Liberal Democrat success in North Cornwall (or, for that matter, North Devon, Bath and Cheltenham). Born within the bounds of the constituency at Mullion, Andrew George was one of the co-authors of the *Cornwall at the Crossroads* book that had caused such a stir when first published (in 1988) and had subsequently informed social, economic and political debate within Cornwall. Not surprisingly, George made great play of his Cornish credentials, a colour photograph in his election campaign leaflet showing him in the distinctive black-and-gold of a Cornish rugby jersey!

In assessing the Cornish dimension of the 1992 General Election, mention should also be made of the "Liberal Party", the group whose members had not accepted the merger of Liberals and Social Democrats (in 1988) and who, in Cornwall, fought an almost nationalist campaign. Appealing explicitly to Mebyon Kernow and Cornish Nationalist Party supporters, the Liberals called for a Parliament for Cornwall, their leader Paul Holmes (candidate for Falmouth and Camborne) claiming in his election leaflet that "The River Tamer is a recognised national boundary" and that "Europe now recognises the cultural heritage of Cornwall even if England does not". Holmes achieved a little over 700 votes in his difficult marginal constituency. Interestingly, the two nationalist parties proper failed (as in 1987) to contest the election. Perhaps a measure of their inability to pierce the electoral process, their inactivity also served, paradoxically, to remind observers that at one level the nationalists were victims of their own success, their hitherto "beyond the pale" demands now a routine element of the Cornish political agenda, their rhetoric and vision increasingly usurped by "mainstream" politicians such as Paul Tyler, Andrew George, and — even — Seb Coe.

A little over a week after the excitement of the General Election, "Trelawny's Army" was mobilised yet again, with new recruits this time who swelled the Cornish contingent at Twickenham to well over 40,000. Set amidst the trappings of the Falmouth Marine Band, the giant pasty, the giant chough, the Cornish kilts and Cornish flags, not to mention the collective euphoria of the Cornish (formerly Mexican) Wave, the rugby match itself might to the casual observer have seemed almost incidental, which was perhaps as well because the Cornish team — despite its verve and commitment — was in fact beaten by Lancashire. Nonetheless, despite this failure to achieve a "back-to-back" in the County Championship, the stirring, almost unnerving demonstration of "Cornishness" by some ten per cent of the Duchy's population, with their insistence upon recognition and respect for Cornwall's identity, served to impress not only the rugby fraternity but also a far wider world. The *Western Morning News* editorial (18 April 92), musing on the motives of those rugby fans ". . . who carry the Cornish cause into the capital of foreign England", understood the political implications of it all and opined that ". . . in the reorganisation of power in Britain that must surely come, Cornwall must keep its own identity and should have enhanced power."

Bibliography

Books, Pamphlets and Articles

Adburgham, Alison, *A Radical Aristocrat: Sir William Molesworth of Pencarrow*, Tabb House, Padstow, 1990.

Almond, G. and Verba, A., *The Civic Culture*, Little, Brown, Boston, 1965.

Alvey, Ada, *In Search of St James: Cornwall to Compostella—A Medieval Pilgrimage*, Dyllansow Truran, Redruth, 1989.

Baines, Dudley, *Migration in a Mature Economy: Emigration and Internal Migration in England and Wales, 1861–1900*, Cambridge University Press, Cambridge, 1985.

Balchin, W.G.V., *The Cornish Landscape*, Hodder & Stoughton, London, 1983.

Banks, J.C., *Federal Britain? The Case for Regionalism*, Harrap, London, 1971.

Bannister, John, *A Glossary of Cornish Names*, Williams & Norgate, London, 1871.

Barta, Gyorgyi and Dingsdale, Alan, "Impacts of Changes in Industrial Company Organisation in Peripheral Regions: A Comparison of Hungary and the United Kingdom", in G.J.R. Linge (ed.), *Peripheralisation and Industrial Change: Impacts on Nations, Regions, Firms and People*, Croom Helm, London, 1988.

Barton, D.B., *A History of Copper Mining in Cornwall and Devon*, Bradford Barton, Truro, 1961, revised ed., 1968.

The Redruth and Chasewater Railway 1824–1915, Bradford Barton, Truro, 1961, 3rd ed., 1978.

The Cornish Beam Engine, Bradford Barton, Truro, 1965, republished Cornwall Books, Exeter, 1989.

A History of Tin Mining and Smelting in Cornwall, Bradford Barton, Truro, 1967, republished Cornwall Books, Exeter, 1989.

Essays in Cornish Mining History: Volume I, Bradford Barton, Truro, 1968.

Essays in Cornish Mining History Volume II, Bradford Barton, Truro, 1970.

Barton, R.M., *A History of the Cornish China Clay Industry*, Bradford Barton, Truro, 1966.

Berg, Maxine, *The Age of Manufacturers 1700-1820*, Fontana, London, 1985.

Berrington, Hugh, "Centre-Periphery Conflict and British Politics", in Yves Meny and Vincent Wright (eds.), *Centre-Periphery Relations in Western Europe*, George Allen and Unwin, London, 1985.

Best, R.S., *The Life and Good Works of John Passmore Edwards*, Dyllansow Truran, Redruth, 1981.

Betjeman, John, *Betjeman's Cornwall*, John Murray, London, 1984.

Bice, Christopher, *A Stamp For Cornwall: Stamp Lyther Rak Kernow*, MK Publications, Redruth, 1974.

Biggs-Davison, John and Chowdharay-Best, George, *The Cross of Saint Patrick: The Catholic Unionist Tradition in Ireland*, Kensal, Bourne End, 1984.

Birch, Anthony H., *Political Integration and Disintegration in the British Isles*, George Allen and Unwin, London, 1977.

Nationalism and National Integration, Unwin Hyman, London, 1989.

Blackwell, Henry Cecil, *From A Dark Stream: The Story of Cornwall's Amazing People and their Impact on the World*, Dyllansow Truran, Redruth, 1987.

Blake, Robert, *The Conservative Party From Peel to Churchill*, Eyre & Spottiswoode, London, 1970.

Blewett, Neal and Jaensh, Dean, *Playford to Dunstan: The Politics of Transition*, Cheshire, Melbourne, 1971.

Blondel, J., *Voters, Parties, and Leaders: The Social Fabric of British Politics*, Penguin, London, 1963, 6th edition, 1974.

Blundel, J.R., "The Redevelopment of the Cornish Tin Mining Industry: Its Problems and Prospects", in K.J. Gregory and W.L.D. Ravenhill, *Exeter Essays in Geography*, University of Exeter, Exeter, 1971.

Bochel, John; Denver, David; and Macartney, Allan (eds.), *The Referendum Experience: Scotland 1979*, Aberdeen University Press, Aberdeen, 1981.

Bogdanor, Vernon, *Liberal Party Politics*, Clarendon Press, Oxford, 1983.

Bottrell, William, *Traditions and Hearthside Stories of West Cornwall*, 1870, republished Frank Graham, Newcastle-upon-Tyne, 1970.

Bowen, E.G., *Saints, Seaways and Settlements in the Celtic Lands*, University of Wales Press, Cardiff, 1969.

Boyle, Kevin and Hadden, Tom, *Ireland: A Positive Proposal*, Penguin, London, 1985.

Bradley, T and Lowe, P. (eds.), *Locality and Rurality: Economy and Society in Rural Regions*, Geo Books, Norwich, 1984.

Brown, H. Miles, *A Century For Cornwall: The Diocese of Truro 1877-1977*, Oscar Blackford, Truro, 1976.

Bryant, Arthur, *Protestant Island*, Collings, London, 1967.

Buckley, J.A., *A History of South Crofty Mine*, Dyllansow Truran, Redruth, n.d. c1982.

Tudor Tin Bounds: West Penwith, Dyllansow Truran, Redruth, 1987.

A Miner's Tale: The Story of Howard Mankee, Penhellick Publications, Redruth, 1988.

Bulpitt, Jim, *Territory and Power in the United Kingdom*, Manchester University Press, Manchester, 1983.

Burke, Gillian, "The Cornish Diapora of the Nineteenth Century", in Shula Marks and Peter Richardson (eds.), *International Labour Migration: Historical Perspectives*, Temple Smith, London, 1984.

Burt, Roger (ed.), *Cornish Mining: Essays on The Organisation of Cornish Mines and the Cornish Mining Economy*, David & Charles, Newton Abbot, 1969.

Cornwall's Mines and Miners, Bradford Barton, Truro, 1972.

John Taylor: Mining Entrepreneur and Engineer, 1779–1863, Moorland, Buxton, 1977.

The British Lead Mining Industry, Dyllansow Truran, Redruth, 1984.

and Timbrell, Martin, *Diversification as a Response to Decline in the Mining Industry: Arsenic and South-Western Metal Production 1850–1914*, University of Exeter, Exeter, 1984.

and Waite, Peter, *Bibliography of the History of British Metal Mining*, University of Exeter, Exeter, 1988.

Waite, Peters and Burnley Ray, *Cornish Mines: Metalliferous and Associated Minerals, 1845–1913*, University of Exeter, Exeter, 1987.

Butler, David and Marquand, David, *European Elections and British Politics*, Longman, London, 1981.

and Kavanagh, Dennis, *The British General Election of 1983*, Macmillan, London, 1984.

The General Election of 1987, Macmillan, London, 1988.

246

Cable, J.R., "Industry", in A.R. Prest and D.J. Coppock, *The UK Economy: A Manual of Applied Economics*, Weidenfeld & Nicolson, London, 9th ed., 1982.

Calder, Angus, *Revolutionary Empire: The Rise of the English- speaking Empires from the Fifteenth Century to the 1780s*, Jonathan Cape, London, 1981.

Celtic League, *Celtic League Annual*, C.L., Dublin, 1971.

Central Statistical Office, *Regional Trends 23: 1988 Edition*, HMSO, London, 1988.

Regional Trends 24: 1989 Edition, HMSO, London, 1989.

Chadwick, N.K., "The Colonization of Brittany From Celtic Britain", Sir John Rhys Memorial Lecture, 1965, *Proceedings of the British Academy*, Vol L1.

Early Brittany, University of Wales Press, Cardiff, 1969.

Champion, Tony and Green, Anne, *Local Prosperity and the North-South Divide*, Institute for Employment Research, University of Warwick, Warwick, 1988.

Clemo, Jack, *Penguin Modern Poets*, Penguin, London, 1964.

Coate, Mary, *Cornwall in the Great Civil War and interregnum 1642-1660*, 1933, republished Bradford Barton, Truro, 1963.

Collins, Wilkie, *Rambles Beyond Railways, or Notes in Cornwall taken a-foot*, Richard Bentley, London, 1851.

Combellack, Myrna, *The Camborne Play*, Dyllansow Truran, Redruth, 1988.

The Playing Place, Dyllansow Truran, Redruth, 1989.

Cook, Christopher, *The Age of Alignment: Electoral Politics in Britain 1922-29*, Macmillan, London, 1975.

Corin, John, *Fishermen's Conflict*, David & Charles, Newton Abbot, 1988.

Cornish Alternatives to the Structure Plan, *Cornwall: A Breathing Space*, CASP, Truro, 1988.

Local Needs Policy, CASP, Truro, 1988.

Euro-constituency: Shotgun Marriage? Amicable Split?, CASP, Truro, 1988.

Cornish Chamber of Mines, *Mining in Cornwall Today*, C.C.M., Truro, 1977.

Cornish National Party, *Cornwall—Forward with Confidence*, CNP, Liskeard, c1969.

Cornish Social and Economic Research Group, *The Cornish Community: Reclaiming Our Destiny*, COSERG, Redruth, 1987.

Cornwall and Devon County Councils, *Towards 2001: The Future of the Plymouth Sub-Region*, Truro/Exeter, 1975.

Cornwall Conservation Forum, *Cornwall's Choice*, C.C.F., Truro?, 1974.

Cornwall County Council, *Development Plan 1952: Report of A Survey*, C.C.C., Truro, 1952.

West Cornwall Study, C.C.C., Truro, 1970.

Cornwall Structure Plan, C.C.C., Truro, 1980.

Structure Plan: First Alteration, C.C.C., Truro, 1988.

 and Institute of Cornish Studies, *Cornish Studies For Schools*, C.C.C., Truro, 1987.

Cornwall Industrial Development Association, *The Economy of Cornwall*, C.I.D.A., Truro?, 1977.

Cornwall, Julian, *Revolt of The Peasantry 1549*, Routledge & Kegan Paul, London, 1977.

Cowethas Flamank Research group, *Towards Self-Government*, Cowethas Flamank, Bristol, 1974.

Craig, F.W.S., *British Parliamentary Election Results 1885- 1918*, Macmillan, London, 1974.

Crewe, I. and Fox, A., *British Parliamentary Constituencies: A Statistical Compendium*, Faber, London, 1984.

Cunliffe, Barry, *The Celtic World*, Bodley Head, London, 1979.

247

Curtice, John and Steed, Michael, "Appendix 2 Analysis", in David Butler and Dennis Kavanagh, *The General Election of 1987*, Macmillan, London, 1988.

Dalton, A.J.P., *Turn Left at Land's End*, Red Boots, London, 1987.

Daniell, S., *Old Cornwall: Life in Cornwall About a Century Ago*, Tor Mark Press, Truro, n.d., c1969.

Davitt, Michael, *Life and Progress in Australia*, Methuen, London, 1898.

Deacon, Bernard, "Attempts at Unionism by Cornish Metal Miners in 1866", *Cornish Studies* 10, 1982.

"Is Cornwall an Internal Colony?" in Cathal o' Luain, *For A Celtic Future*, Celtic League, Dublin, 1983.

"The Electoral Impact of Cornish Nationalism", in Cathal o' Luain, *For A Celtic Future*, Celtic League, Dublin, 1983.

Migration and the Mining Industry in East Cornwall in the Mid-Nineteenth Century, University of Exeter, Exeter, 1985.

"Heroic Individualists? The Cornish Miners and the Five-Week Month 1872-74", *Cornish Studies* 14, 1986.

"Cornish Culture of the Culture of the Cornish?", *Cornish Banner*, November 1986.

George, Andrew; and Perry Ronald, *Cornwall at the Crossroads? Living Communities or Leisure Zone?*, Cornish Social and Economic Research Group, Redruth, 1988.

Dennis, A.L. (ed.), *Cornwall County Council, 1889–1989: A History of 100 Years of County Government*, Cornwall County Council, Truro, 1989.

Devon and Cornwall Development Bureau, *Engineering in Devon and Cornwall*, DCDB/ Cambridge Consultants, Plymouth, 1988.

Dickason, Graham B., *Cornish Immigrants to South Africa*, Balkema, Cape Town, 1973.

Dixon, Piers, *Cornish Names*, Dixon, Probus, 1973.

Doble, G.H., *The Saints of Cornwall*, Parts 1-5, Dean and Chapter of Truro, Truro, 1960-70.

Dodd, A.H., *A Short History of Wales*, Batsford, London, 1979.

Drucker, Henry (general ed.), *Developments in British Politics*, Macmillan, London, 1984.

du Maurier, Daphne, *Vanishing Cornwall: The Spirit and History of Cornwall*, Victor Gollancz, London, 1967.

Dunkerley, David and Faerden, Ingrid, "Aspects of Seasonal Employment in Devon and Cornwall", in Peter Gripaios, *The South West Economy*, Plymouth Business School, Plymouth, 1985.

Dunstan, Alan and Peart-Binns, John S., *Cornish Bishop*, Epworth Press, London, 1977.

Durkacz, Victor Edward, *The Decline of the Celtic Languages*, John Donald, Edinburgh, 1983.

Ellis, P. Berresford, *Wales—A Nation Again*, Library 33, London, 1968.

The Creed of the Celtic Revolution, Medusa, London, 1969.

The Story of the Cornish Language, Tor Mark Press, Truro, n.d. c1970.

The Cornish Language and its Literature, Routledge and Kegan Paul, London, 1974.

Celtic Inheritance, Muller, London, 1985.

The Celtic Revolution: A Study in Anti-Imperialism, Y Lolfa, Talybont, 1985.

Ellis, Steven, "Not Mere English: The British Perspective 1400- 1650", *History Today*, December 1988.

Faull, Jim, *The Cornish in Australia*, A.E. Press, Melbourne, 1983.

Feiling, Keith, *A History of the Tory Party 1640–1714*, 1925, republished, Oxford University Press, Oxford, 1950.

Fleet, John, "The Cornish Border", in F.G. Thompson (ed.), *The Celtic Experience: Past and Present*, Celtic League, Dublin, 1972.

"Heritage and identity in the new Europe: The Cornish Bureau for European Relations", *European Access*, 1990: 3, June.

Foot, Sarah, *Isaac Foot: My Grandfather*, Bossiney Books, Bodmin, 1980.

Fox, Harold S.A., "Outfield cultivation in Devon and Cornwall: a reinterpretation", in Michael Havinden (ed.), *Husbandry and Marketing in the South West 1500–1800*, Exeter Papers in Economic History No 8, University of Exeter, Exeter, 1973.

Freeman-Grenville, G.S.P., *Atlas of British History From Prehistoric Times Until 1978*, Collings, London, 1979.

Fudge, Crysten, *The Life of Cornish*, Dyllansow Truran, Redruth, 1982.

Gendall, Richard, *Kernewek Bew*, Kesva an Tavas Kernewek/Cornish Language Board, St Ives, 1972.

Laugh and Learn Traditional Cornish: A New Course in Cornish For the Beginner, Teer ha Tavaz, Liskeard, 1988.

A Student's Dictionary of Modern Cornish, Part I—English/Cornish, Cornish Language Council, Liskeard, 1991.

A Student's Grammar of Modern Cornish, Cornish Language Council, Liskeard, 1991.

George, Andrew (ed.), *Planning: A Guide For Cornish People/Steeva: Gwerez lever rag Kernowyon*, Cornish Rural Community Council and Cornwall Association of Parish and Town Councils, Truro, n.d. c1985.

Homes For Locals in Cornwall/Chyow Rag Genesygyon Yn Kernow, Cornwall Rural Community Council, Truro, 1987.

George, Ken, *The Pronounciation and Spelling of Revived Cornish*, Kesva an Tavas Kernewek/Cornish Language Board, Torpoint?, 1986.

Gibbs, R.M., *A History of South Australia*, Balara Books, Adelaide, 1969.

Gill, Grispin (ed.), *The Duchy of Cornwall*, David & Charles, Newton Abbot, 1987.

Gilligan, J. Herman, "The Rural Labour Process: A Case Study of a Cornish Town", in T. Bradley and P. Lowe (eds.), *Locality and Rurality: Economy and Society in Rural Regions*, Geo Books, Norfolk, 1984.

Grafton, D. and Bolton, N., "Planning Policy and Economic Development in Devon and Cornwall 1945-84", in Peter Gipaios (ed.), *The Economy of Devon and Cornwall*, South West Papers in Geography, Plymouth Polytechnic, Plymouth, 1984.

Grant, Wyn, *Independent Local Politics in England and Wales*, Saxon House, Farnborough, 1977.

Greenberg, William, *The Flags of the Forgotten: Nationalism on the Celtic Fringe*, Clifton, Brighton, 1960.

Gregory, P., "Low Pay in the South West", in Peter Gripaios (ed.), *The South West Economy*, Plymouth Business School, Plymouth, 1985.

Gregory, K.J. and Ravenhill, W.L.D, *Exeter Essays in Geography*, University of Exeter, Exeter, 1971.

Griffin, C., "Economic Change in Cornwall: An Overview", in Gareth Shaw and Allan M. Williams (eds.), *Economic Development and Policy in Cornwall: Proceedings of a Regional Studies Association—Institute of Cornish Studies Conference, Spring 1982*, South West Papers in Geography, Plymouth Polytechnic, Plymouth, 1982.

Griffiths, Andrew, *Changes in the Countryside: The Cornish Perspective*, Cornwall Rural Development Committee/University of Exeter Enterprises, Exeter, 1989.

Gripaios, Peter, *Manufacturing Industry in Devon and Cornwall: An Analysis of Decision*

Taking, Industrial Linkages and Locational Perceptions, Plymouth Business School, Plymouth, 1984.

The Economy of Devon and Cornwall, South West Papers in Geography, Plymouth Polytechnic, Plymouth, 1984.

The South West Economy, Plymouth Business School, Plymouth, 1985.

The South West Economy II, Plymouth Business School, Plymouth, 1988.

and Consultancy South West, *The South West Economy: Trends and Prospects*, Plymouth Business School, Plymouth, 1989.

Haig, Christopher (ed.), *The Cambridge Historical Encyclopedia of Great Britain and Ireland*, Cambridge University Press, Cambridge, 1985.

Halliday, R.E. (ed.), Richard Carew's *The Survey of Cornwall, 1602*, Melrose, London, 1953.

A History of Cornwall, Duckworth, London, 1959.

Hanham, H.J., *Scottish Nationalism*, Faber, London, 1969.

Harris, T.R., *Arthur Woolf, 1766–1837: Cornish Engineer*, Bradford Barton, Truro, 1966.

Harvie, Christopher, "Scottish Politics Since 1901", in Christopher Haigh (ed.), *The Cambridge Historical Encyclopedia of Britain and Ireland*, Cambridge University Press, Cambridge, 1985.

Hatcher, John, *Rural Economy and Society in the Duchy of Cornwall 1300–1500*, Cambridge University Press, cambridge, 1970.

Havinden, Michael (ed.), *Husbandry and Marketing in The South West 1500–1800*, Exeter Papers in Economic History No 8, University of Exeter, Exeter, 1973.

"The South West: A Case of De-Industralization?" in Marilyn Palmer (ed.), *The Onset of Industrialization*, University of Nottingham, Nottingham, 1977.

Hechter, Michael, *Internal Colonialism: The Celtic Fringe in British National Development*, Routledge, London, 1975.

"Internal Colonialism Revisited", in Edward A. Tiryakian and Ronald Rogowski, *New Nationalisms in the Developed West: Towards Explanations*, George Allen and Unwin, Boston, 1985.

Hobsbawm, Eric, *Labouring Men*, Weidenfeld & Nicolson, London, 1964.

and Rude, George, *Captain Swing*, Penguin, London, 1973.

and Ranger, Terrence, *The Invention of Tradition*, Cambridge University Press, Cambridge, 1983.

Hooper, E.G.R. (ed.,), *Gwryans an Bys or the Creation of the World*, Dyllansow Truran, Redruth, 1985.

Hopkins, Ruth, *Where Now Cousin Jack?*, Bendigo Bicentennial Committee, Bendigo, 1988.

Hoskins, W.G., *The Westward Expansion of Wessex*, Department of English Local History Occasional Paper No 13, Leicester University Press, Leicester, 1960, 2nd edition, 1970.

Hudson, W.H., *The Land's End: A Naturalist's Impressions of West Cornwall*, 1908, republished Wildwood, London, 1981.

Hunt, Robert, *Popular Romances of the West of England*, 1871, republished in part as *Cornish Customs and Superstitions*, Tor Mark Press, Truro, n.d. c1971.

Husband, Charles, *'Race' in Britain: Continuity and Change*, Hutchinson, London, 1982.

Hutchinson, John, *The Dynamics of Cultural Nationalism: The Gaelic Revival and the Creation of the Irish Nation State*, Allen & Unwin, 1987.

Independent Television Network, *ITN Election Factbook*, ITN, London, 1987.

Jackson, Kenneth H., *Language and History in Early Britain*, Edinburgh University Press, Edinburgh, 1953.

250

Jenkin, A.K. Hamilton, *The Cornish Miner*, 1927, republished David & Charles, Newton Abbot, 1972.

Cornwall and Its People, 1932–34, republished David & Charles, Newton Abbot, 1983.

Jenkin, Richard and Ann, *Cornwall: The Hidden Land*, West Country Publications, Bracknell, 1965.

Jenkins, T.A. (ed.), *The Parliamentary Diaries of Sir John Trelawny, 1858-1865*, Camden Fourth Series, Volume 40, Royal Historical Society, London, 1990.

Jenner, Henry, *A Handbook of the Cornish Language*, David Nutt, London, 1904.

"Cornwall: A Celtic Nation", *Celtic Review*, 16 January 1905.

Jewell, Andrew, "Some Cultivation Techniques in the South West of England", in Walter Minchinton (ed.), *Agricultural Improvement: Medieval and Modern*, Exeter Papers in Economic History, University of Exeter, Exeter, 1981.

John, Catherine Rachel, *The Saints of Cornwall*, Lodenek Press/Dyllansow Truran, Padstow/Redruth, 1981.

Johnston, R.W., "The Nationalisation of English Rural Politics: Norfolk South West 1945-1970", *Parliamentary Affairs*, 26, 1973.

Jones, Fred, *The Honourable Sir Langdon Bonython KCMG: An Eminent South Australian*, Royal Cornwall Polytechnic Society, Camborne, 1931.

Jones, R. Tudur, *The Desire of Nations*, Christopher Davies, Llandybie, 1974.

Jupp, James, *The Australian People*, Angus & Robertson, Sydney, 1988.

Keast, John, *The King of Mid-Cornwall: The Life of Joseph Thomas Treffry 1782-1850*, Dyllansow Truran, Redruth, 1982.

Kearney, Hugh, *The British Isles: A History of Four Nations*, Cambridge University Press, Cambridge, 1989.

Keating, Michael, *State and Regional Nationalism: Territorial Politics and the European States*, Harvester Wheatsheaf, London, 1988.

and Bleiman, David, *Labour and Scottish Nationalism*, Macmillan, London, 1979.

Kedourie, Elie, *Nationalism*, Hutchinson, London, 1960.

Kellas, J., *The Scottish Political System*, Cambridge University Press, Cambridge, 3rd edition 1986.

Kennedy, Brian, *A Tale of Two Mining Cities: Johannesburg and Broken Hill 1885–1925*, Melbourne University Press, Melbourne, 1984.

Kinnear, Michael, *The British Voter: An Atlas and Survey*, Batsford, London, 1981.

Kohr, Leopold, *Is Wales Viable?* Christopher Davies, Llandybie, 1971.

Koss, Stephen, *Nonconformity in Modern British Politics*, Batsford, London, 1975.

Krejci, Jaroslav and Velimsky, Vitezlav, *Ethnic and Political Nations in Europe*, Croom Helm, London, 1982.

Lane Davies, *Holy Wells of Cornwall*, Federation of Old Cornwall Societies, Truro?, 1970.

Langdon, Arthur G., *Old Cornish Crosses, 1896*, reprinted Cornwall Books, Exeter, 1988.

Langton, John and Morris, R.J. (eds.), *Atlas of Industrializing Britain, 1780–1914*, Methuen, London, 1986.

Lean, Thomas, *On the Steam Engines in Cornwall*, 1839, republished Bradford Barton, Truro, 1969.

Leifchild, J.R., *Cornwall—Its Mines and Miners*, 1857, republished Frank Graham, Newcastle-on-Tyne, 1968.

Lewis, G.R., *The Stannaries: A Study of the Medieval Tin Miners of Cornwall and Devon*, 1908, republished Bradford Barton, Truro, 1965.

Lewis, Robert, *De-Industrialisation in the South West: Background Paper*, University of Exeter, Exeter, 1984.

251

Linge, G.J.R. (ed.), *Peripheralisation and Industrial Change: Impacts on Nations, Regions, Firms and People*, Croom Helm, London, 1988.

Lingenfelter, Richard E., *The Hardrock Miners*, University of California, Berkeley, 1974.

Lyon, Rod, *Traditional Cornish*, Lyon, Nancegollan, 1989.

Madgwick, P.J., *The Politics of Rural Wales*, Hutchinson, London, 1973.

and Rose, Richard, *The Territorial Dimension in United Kingdom Politics*, Macmillan, London, 1982.

Mais, S.P.B., *The Cornish Riviera*, Great Western Railway, London, 1934.

Markale, J., *Celtic Civilization*, Gordon and Cremonesi, London, 1978.

Marks, Shula and Richardson, Peter, *International Labour Migration: Historical Perspectives*, Temple Smith, London, 1984.

Massey, Doreen, "In What Sense a Regional Problem?", *Regional Studies* 13, 2, 1979.

Mayo, Patricia Elton, *The Roots of Identity: Three National Movements in Contemporary Politics*, Allen Lane, London, 1974.

McNabb, R; Woodward N., and Barry, J., *Unemployment in West Cornwall*, Department of Employment, London, 1979.

Mebyon Kernow, *What Cornishmen Can Do*, MK Publications, Redruth, 1969.

The Cornish Answer, MK Publications, Liskeard, 1989.

Mellor, Roy E.H., *Nation, State, and Territory: A Political Geography*, Routledge, London, 1989.

Meny, Yves and Wright, Vincent (eds.), *Centre-Periphery Relations in Wester Europe*, George Allen and Unwin, London, 1985.

Miles, Robert, "Racism and Nationalism in Britain", in Charles Husband, *'Race' in Britain: Continuity and Change*, Hutchinson, London, 1982.

Miller, Amos C., *Sir Richard Grenville of the Civil War*, Phillimore, Chichester, 1979.

Miller, William L., *The End of British Politics? Scots and English Political Behaviour in the Seventies*, Clarendon, Oxford, 1981.

"Variations in Electoral Behaviour in the United Kingdom", in Peter Madgwick and Richard Rose, *The Territorial Dimension in United Kingdom Politics*, Macmillan, London, 1982.

Minchinton, Walter (ed.), *Capital Formation in South-West England*, Exeter Papers in Economic History No 9, University of Exeter, Exeter, 1978.

Agricultural Improvement: Medieval and Modern, Exeter Papers in Economic History, University of Exeter, 1981.

Miners, Hugh, *Gorseth Kernow: The First Fifty Years*, Gorseth Kernow, Penzance, 1978.

Moorhouse, Geoffrey, *Britain in the Sixties: The Other England*, Penguin, London, 1964.

Morgan, Kenneth O., *The Oxford Illustrated History of Britain*, Oxford, 1984.

Morgan, Prys, "From a Death to a View: The Hunt for the Welsh Past in the Romantic Period", in Eric Hobsbawm and Terrence Ranger, *The Invention of Tradition*, Cambridge University Press, Cambridge, 1983.

Morrison, T.A., *Cornwall's Central Mines: The Northern District, 1810–1895*, Alison Hodge, Penzance, 1980.

Mudd, David, *Cornishmen and True*, Frank Graham, Newcastle-upon-Tyne, 1971.

The Falmouth Packets, Bossiney Books, Bodmin, 1978.

Muir, Richard, *Reading the Celtic Landscapes*, Shell Guides/Guild Publishing, London, 1985.

Murray, John and The Survey Committee, *Devon and Cornwall: A Preliminary Survey*, Wheaton, Exeter, 1947.

252

Nairn, Tom, *The Break-Up of Britain: Crisis and Neo- Nationalism*, New Left, London, 1977.

Nelson, D. and Potter, D., *A Survey of Employees in the Manufacturing Sector in the South West*, Regional Research Series No 3, Department of Industry, London, 1982.

Noall, Cyril, *Smuggling in Cornwall*, Bradford Barton, Truro, 1971.

Tales of the Cornish Fishermen, Tor Mark Press, Truro, 1970.

Cornish Seines and Seiners: A History of the Pilchard Fishing Industry, Bradford Barton, Truro, 1972.

O'Callaghan, M.J.C., *Separatism in Brittany*, Dyllansow Truran, Redruth, 1983.

O'Luain, Cathal, *For A Celtic Future*, Celtic League, Dublin, 1983.

Osmond, John, *Creative Conflict: The Politics of Welsh Devolution*, Gomer, Llandysul, 1977.

The Divided Kingdom, Constable, London, 1988.

Overton, Mark, "The 1801 Crop Returns for Cornwall", in Michael Havinden (ed.), *Husbandry and Marketing in the South West 1500–1800*, Exeter Papers in Economic History No 8, University of Exeter, Exeter, 1973.

Pacey, Arnold, *The Culture of Technology*, Blackwell, Oxford, 1983.

Padel, O.J., *A Popular Dictionary of Cornish Place-Names*, Alison Hodge, Penzance, 1988.

Page, Edward, "Michael Hechter's internal colonial thesis: some theoretical and methodological problems", *European Journal of Political Research*, Vol 6, No 3.

Palmer, Marilyn (ed.), *The Onset of Industrialization*, University of Nottingham, Nottingham, 1977.

Parsons, Wayne, *The Political Economy of British Regional Policy*, Routledge, London, 1988.

Pascoe, W.H., *The History of the Cornish Copper Company*, Dyllansow Truran, Redruth, 1981.

Payton, Philip, "The Celtic Fringe: A Review of Hechter's 'Internal Colonialism'", *Cornish Banner*, June 1979.

The Cornish Miner in Australia: Cousin Jack Down Under, Dyllansow Truran, Redruth, 1984.

Cornish Carols From Australia., Dyllansow Truran, Redruth, 1984.

The Cornish Farmer in Australia, Dyllansow Truran, Redruth, 1987.

"Labour Failure and Liberal Tenacity: Radical Politics and Cornish Political Culture, 1880–1939", *Cornish Studies* 17, 1992.

"On Centre and Periphery", *Journal of Interdisciplinary Economics* Vol. 4 No 2, 1992.

"Socio-Economic Change in Post-War Cornwall", *Journal of Interdisciplinary Economics* Vol. 4 No 2, 1992.

(ed.) and Noall, Cyril, *Cornish Mine Disasters*, Dyllansow Truran, Redruth, 1989.

and Syme, Victoria, "Eastern Europe: Economic Transition and Ethnic Tension", in Michael Pugh, *European Security: Towards 2000*, Manchester University Press, Manchester, 1992.

Pearce, John, *The Wesleys in Cornwall*, Bradford Barton, Truro, 1964.

Pearce, Susan, *The Kingdom of Dumnonia: Studies in History and Tradition in South Western Britain, AD 350–1150*, Lodenek Press, Padstow, 1978.

Pearse, Richard, *The Land Beside The Celtic Sea: Aspects of Cornwall's Past*, Dyllansow Truran, Redruth, 1983.

Pelling, Henry, *Social Geography of British Elections, 1885–1910*, Macmillan, London, 1962.

Pelmear, Kenneth, *Carols of Cornwall*, Dyllansow Truran, Redruth, 1982.

Pengelly, E.J., *The Detectable Duchy*, Cowethas Flamank, Redruth, 1986.

Penhaligon, Annette, *Penhaligon*, Bloomsbury, London, 1989.

Pennington, Robert R., *Stannary Law: A History of the Mining Law of Cornwall and Devon*, David & Charles, Newton Abbot, 1973.

Perry, Ronald, "The Role of the Small Manufacturing Business in Cornwall's Economic Development", in Gareth Shaw and Allan M. Williams (eds.), *Economic Development and Policy in Cornwall: Proceedings of a Regional Studies Association—Institute of Cornish Studies Conference, Spring 1982*, South West Papers in Geography, Plymouth Polytechnic, Plymouth, 1982.

The Impact of Counterurbanisation on Cornwall: A Preliminary Examination of Conceptual and Empirical Issues, South West Papers in Geography, Plymouth Polytechnic, Plymouth, 1984.

with Dean, Ken and Brown Bryan and with the assistance of Shaw, David, *Counterurbanisation: Inter-National Case Studies of Socio-Economic Change in Rural Areas*, Geo Books, Norwich, 1986.

Population Turnaround in Cornwall and Finistere: Contrasting Models of Development in the Rural Periphery, South West Papers in Geography, Plymouth Polytechnic, Plymouth, 1987.

"Is there a Solution to the Cornish Problem?", in Peter Gripaios (ed.), *The South West Economy II*, Plymouth Business School, Plymouth, 1988.

Philip, Alan Butt, *The Welsh Question: Nationalism in Welsh Politics 1945–1970*, University of Wales Press, Cardiff, 1975.

Plumb, J.H., *The First Four Georges*, Batsford, London, 1956.

Pool, P.A.S., *The Death of Cornish*, Cornish Language Board, Penzance, 1975.

Porter, Jeffrey, *Education and Labour in The South West*, Exeter Papers in Economic History No 10, University of Exeter, Exeter, 1975.

Pratt, Andy C., "Industrial Estates and Local Economic Development in Cornwall", in Peter Gripaios (ed.), *The South West Economy*, Plymouth Business School, Plymouth, 1985.

Prest, A.R. and Coppock, D.J., *The UK Economy: A Manual of Applied Economics*, Wiedenfeld & Nicolson, London, 9th ed., 1982.

Price, Glanville, *The Languages of Britain*, Edward Arnold, London, 1984.

Price, L.L., "West Barbary", 1895, reprinted in Roger Burt (ed.), *Cornish Mining: Essays on The Organisation of Cornish Mines and the Cornish Mining Economy*, David & Charles, Newton Abbot, 1969.

Probert, John C.C., *The Sociology of Cornish Methodism*, Cornish Methodist Historical Association, Truro, 1971.

Pryor, Oswald, *Australia's Little Cornwall*, Rigby, Adelaide, 1962.

Pugh, M., *The Tories and the People 1880-1935*, Blackwell, Oxford, 1985.

Punnett, R.M., *British Government and Politics*, Heinemann, London, 2nd edition, 1971.

Rabey, A. Ivan, *Hurling at St Columb and in Cornwall*, Lodenek Press, Padstow, 1972.

(ed.), *Cornwall: An Official Guide to Cornwall*, Cornwall County Council/British Publishing Co., Gloucester, n.d. c1988.

Rawe, Donald R., *Padstow's 'Obby 'Oss and May Day Festivities: A Study in Folklore and Tradition*, Lodenek Press, Padstow, 1971.

A Prospect of Cornwall, Robert Hale, London, 1986.

Ravensdale, Jack, "The China Clay Labourers' Union", *Historical Studies* 1, 1968.

"The 1913 Clay Strike and the Worker's Union", in Exeter Papers in Economic History No 6, University of Exeter, Exeter, 1972.

Robbins, Keith, *Nineteenth-Century Britain: England, Scotland, Wales—The Making of a Nation*, Oxford University Press, Oxford, 1989.

Roche, T.W.E., *The Withered Arm: Reminiscences of the Southern Lines West of Exeter*, Forge Books, Bracknell, 1967.

Rogers, K.H., *The Newcomen Engine in the West of England*, Moonraker, Bradford-on-Avon, 1976.

Rokkan, Stein, *Citizens, Elections and Parties*, Universitets for leyet, Oslo, 1970.

and Urwin, Derek, W., *The Politics of Territorial Identity: Studies in European Regionalism*, Sage, London, 1982.

Roots, Ivan, *The Monmouth Rebellion: Aspects of the 1685 Rebellion in the West Country*, Devon Books, Exeter, 1986.

Rose, Richard, *The United Kingdom as a Multi-National State*, University of Strathclyde Survey Research Occasional paper No 6, Glasgow, 1970.

Understanding the United Kingdom: The Territorial Dimension in Government, Longman, London, 1982.

Rowe, John, *Cornwall in the Age of the Industrial Revolution*, Liverpool University Press, Liverpool, 1953.

Cornish Methodists and Emigrants, Cornish Methodist Historical Association, Truro?, 1967.

The Hard-Rock Men: Cornish Immigrants and the North American Mining Frontier, Liverpool University Press, Liverpool, 1974.

"The Declining Years of Cornish Tin Mining", in Jeffrey Porter, *Education and Labour in the South West*, Exeter Papers in Economic History No 10, University of Exeter, 1975.

"Cornish Mining Crisis in the 1920s", *Cornish Banner*, August 1986.

Rowse, A.L., *Sir Richard Grenville of The 'Revenge'*, Jonathan Cape, London, 1937.

Tudor Cornwall, Jonathan Cape, London, 1941, republished, Dyllansow Truran, Redruth, 1990.

A Cornish Childhood, Jonathan Cape, London, 1942.

The Cornish in America., Macmillan, London, 1969, republished, Dyllansow Truran, Redruth, 1991.

The Expansion of Elizabethan England, 1955, republished Cardinal, London, 1973.

Matthew Arnold: Poet and Prophet, Thames & Hudson, London, 1976.

A Man of the Thirties, Weidenfeld & Nicolson, London, 1979.

A Cornish Anthology, Alison Hodge, Penzance, 1982.

The Little Land of Cornwall, Alan Sutton, Gloucester, 1986.

"The Essence of Cornishness", *Cornish Banner*, November 1987.

Quiller Couch: A Portrait of Q, Methuen, London, 1988.

The Controversial Colensos, Dyllansow Truran, Redruth, 1989.

Rush, Michael, *Parliamentary Government in Britain*, Pitman, London, 1981.

Salmon, Tom, *The First 100 Years; The Story of Rugby Football in Cornwall*, CRFU, Illogan, 1983.

Schonfield, Andrew, "The Politics of the Mixed Economy in the International System of the 1970s", *International Affairs*, Vol 5, No 1, 1980.

Schmitz, Christopher, "Capital Formation and Technological Change in South-West England Metal Mining in the Nineteenth Century" in Walter Minchinton (ed.), *Capital Formation in South West England*, Exeter Papers in Economic History No 9, University of Exeter, Exeter, 1978.

Shaw, Gareth and Williams, Allan M. (eds.), *Industrial Change in Cornwall: Proceedings*

255

of a Seminar on the Collection and Analysis of Data, South West Papers in Geography, Plymouth Polytechnic, Plymouth, 1981.

Economic Development and Policy in Cornwall: Proceedings of a Regional Studies Association—Institute of Cornish Studies Conference, Spring 1982, South West Papers in Geography, Plymouth Polytechnic, Plymouth, 1982.

Shaw, Thomas, *The Bible Christians*, Epworth Press, London, 1965.

A History of Cornish Methodism, Bradford Barton, Truro, 1967.

Shorter, A.H.; Ravenhill, W.L.D.; and Gregory, K.J., *Southwest England*, Nelson, London, 1969.

Simmons, Jack, "The Railway in Cornwall, 1835–1914", in *Back Track: Recording Britain's Railway History*, Winter 1987 (first published in the *Journal of the Royal Institution of Cornwall*, 1962).

Skues, Keith, *Cornish Heritage*, Werner Shaw, London, 1983.

Smith, Anthony D., *Theories of Nationalism*, Duckworth, London, 1971.

Ethnic Revival in The Modern World, Cambridge University Press, Cambridge, 1981.

"Nationalism, Ethnic Separatism and The Intelligentsia", in Colin H. Williams, *National Separatism*, University of Wales Press, Cardiff, 1982.

Smith, Dai, *Wales! Wales?*, George Allen and Unwin, London, 1984.

Smith, M.G., *Fighting Joshua: A Study of the Career of Sir Jonathan Trelawny, bart, 1650–1721, Bishop of Bristol, Exeter, and Winchester*, Dyllansow Truran, Redruth, 1985.

Soulsby, Ian, *A History of Cornwall*, Phillimore, Chichester, 1986.

South West Economic Planning Council, *A Region With A Future: A Draft Strategy For the South West*, HMSO, London, 1967.

A Strategic Settlement Pattern For the South West, SWEPC, Bristol, 1974.

Spence, W.G., *Australia's Awakening: Thirty Years in the Life of an Australian Agitator*, Workers' Trustees, Sydney, 1909.

Spooner, D.J., "Industrial Movement and the Rural Periphery: The Case of Devon and Cornwall", *Regional Studies* 6, 1971.

"Some Qualitive Aspects of Industrial Movement in a Problem Region of the UK", *Town Planning Review*, 45, 1974.

Stephens, Meic, *Linguistic Minorities in Western Europe*, Gomer Press, Llandysul, 1976.

Stevenson, John, *Popular Disturbances in England, 1700–1800*, Longman, London, 1979.

Stucley, John, *Sir Bevill Grenvile and His Times*, Phillimore, Chichester, 1983.

Sturt, John, *Revolt in The West: The Western Rebellion of 1549*, Devon Books, Exeter, 1987.

Svensson, Organ, *Saxon Place Names in East Cornwall*, Lund University Press, Lund, 1987.

Tarrow, Sidney, *Between Centre and Periphery: Grassroots Politicians in Italy and France*, Yale University Press, New Haven, 1977.

Temperton, Paul (ed.), *Up North! How to Unshackle a Forgotten People*, Campaign For The North, Hebden Bridge, 1978.

Thayer, George, *The British Political Fringe: A Profile*, Anthony Blond, London, 1965.

Thomas, Charles, *The Importance of Being Cornish in Cornwall: An Inaugural Lecture*, Institute of Cornish Studies, Redruth, 1973.

Celtic Britain, Thames & Hudson, London, 1986.

Thomas, D.M., *The Granite Kingdom: Poems of Cornwall*, Bradford Barton, Truro, 1970.

Thomas, David St John, *A Regional History of the Railways of Great Britain—Volume I: The West Country*, David & Charles, Newton Abbot, 5th edition, 1981.

Thompson, F.G. (ed.), *The Celtic Experience: Past and Present*, Celtic League, Dublin, 1972.

Thorne, Caroline and Frank (eds.), *Domesday Book—Cornwall*, Phillimore, Chichester, 1979.

Thorpe, Lewis (ed.), Geoffrey of Monmouth's *The History of The Kings of Britain*, Guild Publishing, London, 1982.

Tiryakian, Edward A. and Rogowski, Ronald, *New Nationalisms and the Developed West: Towards Explanations*, George Allen and Unwin, Boston, 1985.

Todd, A.C., *The Cornish Miner in America*, Bradford Barton, Truro, 1967.

Beyond the Blaze: A Biography of Davies Gilbert, Bradford Barton, Truro, 1967.

The Search For Silver: Cornish Miners in Mexico, 1824- 1947, Lodenek Press, Padstow, 1977.

and Laws, Peter, *Industrial Archaeology of Cornwall*, David & Charles, Newton Abbot, 1972.

and James, David, *Ever Westward The Land*, University of Exeter, Exeter, 1986.

Todd, Malcolm, *The South West to AD 1000*, Longman, London, 1987.

Tomlin, E.W.F., *In Search of St Piran: An Account of his Monastic Foundation at Perranzabuloe, Cornwall, and its Place in the Western or Celtic Church and Society*, Lodenek Press, Padstow, 1982.

Tremenheere, Seymour, "Notice respecting the Lead and Copper ores of Glen Osmond Mine, three miles from Adelaide, South Australia", *Transactions of the Royal Geological Society of Cornwall*, Vol VI, 1841-46.

Trounson, John H., *Historic Cornish Mining Scenes at Surface*, Bradford Barton, Truro, 1968.

and Burt, Roger (ed.), *The Cornish Mineral Industry: Past Performance and Future Prospect 1937–1951*, University of Exeter, Exeter, 1989.

Truran, Leonard H., *For Cornwall — A Future!*, MK Publications, Redruth, 1976.

Thomas Merritt: Twelve Cornish Carols, Dyllansow Truran, Redruth, n.d. c1970.

Tyron, F.G. and Schoenfeld, Margaret H., "Mineral and Power Resources" in *Recent Social Trends in the United States*, McGraw-Hill, New York, 1933.

Urwin, Derek W., "Territorial Structures and Political Developments in the United Kingdom", in Stein Rokkan and Derek W. Urwin, *The Politics of Territorial Identity: Studies in European Regionalism*, Sage, London, 1982.

"The Price of a Kingdom: Territory, Identity and the Centre-Periphery Dimension in Western Europe", in Yves Meny and Vincent Wright (eds.), *Centre-Periphery Relations in Western Europe*, George Allen and Unwin, London, 1985.

Val Baker, Denys, *The Timeless Land: The Creative Spirit in Cornwall*, Adams & Dart, Bath, 1973.

Vivian, John, *Tales of the Cornish Wreckers*, Tor Mark Press, Truro, n.d. c1971.

Wakelin, Martyn, F., *Language and History in Cornwall*, Leicester University Press, Leicester, 1975.

Waller, Robert, *The Almanac of British Politics*, 2nd edition, Croom Helm, London, 1983.

The Atlas of British Politics, Croom Helm, London, 1985.

Walke, Bernard, *Twenty Years at St Hilary*, 1935, republished Anthony Mott, London, 1982.

Ward, Stephen V., *The Geography of Inter War Britain: The State and Uneven Development*, Routledge, London, 1988.

Weiner, Martin, J., *English Culture and the Decline of the Industrial Spirit, 1850–1980*, Cambridge University Press, Cambridge, 1981.

Whetmath, C.F.D., *Railways of Looe and Caradon*, Forge Books, Bracknell, 1974.

Whetter, James, *Cornwall in the Seventeenth Century: An Economic Survey of Kernow*, Lodenek Press, Padstow, 1974.

A Celtic Tomorrow, MK Publications, St Austell, 1973.

Cornish Essays 1971–76, CNP Publications, St Austell, 1977.

"The English in Kernow in the Thirteenth Century", *Cornish Banner*, February 1988.

The History of Glasney College, Tabb House, Padstow, 1988.

The History of Gorran Haven, Part I 0-1800 AD, Lyfrow Trelyspen, St Austell, 1990.

The Bodrugans: A Study of a Cornish Medieval Knightly Family, forthcoming.

White, G. Pawley, *A Handbook of Cornish Surnames*, White, Truro, 1972.

Whitehouse, P.B., *Britain's Mainline Railways*, New English Library, London, 1977.

Wilson, R.B., *Go Great Western: A History of GWR Publicity*, David & Charles, Newton Abbot, 1970, republished 1987.

Wickes, Michael J.L., *The Westcountry Preachers: A History of the Bible Christians 1815-1907*, Wickes, Bideford, 1987.

Wigfield, W. Macdonald, *The Monmouth Rebels*, Sutton, Gloucester, 1985.

Williams, Colin H., *National Separatism*, University of Wales Press, Cardiff, 1982.

Wilson, Tom, *Ulster: Conflict and Consent*, Blackwell, Oxford, 1989.

Wood, Michael, *In Search of The Dark Ages*, British Broadcasting Corporation, London, 1983.

Woodfin, R.J., *The Cornwall Railway to Its Centenary in 1959*, Bradford Barton, Truro, 1960, republished, 1972.

Worgan, G.B., *General view of the Agriculture of the County of Cornwall*, London, 1811.

Theses

Brayshay, Mark, "The Demography of three West Cornwall Mining Communities 1851–1871: A Society in Decline", PhD, University of Exeter, 1977.

Burke, Gillian, "The Cornish Miner and the Cornish Mining Industry 1870–1921", PhD, University of London, 1981.

Crook, Denise A., "The Early History of the Royal Geological Society of Cornwall", PhD. Open University, 1990.

Dawe, Richard, D., "The Role and Influence of the Cornish Miner in South Africa 1886–1925", MA, CNAA (Middlesex Polytechnic), 1986.

Eastlake, Rosalie, "Cornwall: The Development of a Celtic Periphery", MA, McGill University, 1981.

Faerden, Ingrid, "The Social Impact of Seasonal Employment in Devon and Cornwall", PhD, CNAA (Plymouth Polytechnic), 1986.

Fox, H.S.A., "A Geographical Study of the Field Systems of Devon and Cornwall", PhD, University of Cambridge, 1971.

Freeborn, Sally, "The Royal Institution of Cornwall and its Role in Adult Education during the Nineteenth-century", M Phil, CNAA (Cornwall College), 1986.

Heyden, Peter, "Culture, Creed and Conflict: Methodism and Politics in Cornwall c1832–1879", PhD, University of Liverpool, 1982.

Luker, D.H., "Cornish Mehodism, Revivalism and Popular Belief c1780–1870", D Phil, University of Oxford, 1987.

McArthur, Mary, "The Cornish: A Case Study in Ethnicity", MSc, University of Bristol, 1988.

Mungles, N.J., "A Study of Cornish Nationalism in the Twentieth Century", BA (Hons), Nene College, 1991.

Patrick, Amber, "The Evolution of Morwellham: A Tamar River Port", M Phil, CNAA (Plymouth Polytechnic), 1980.

Payton, Philip, "The Ideology of Celtic Nationalism", BSc (Hons), University of Bristol, 1975.

"The Cornish in South Australia: Their Influence and Experience from Imigration to Assimilation 1836–1936", PhD, University of Adelaide, 1978.

"Modern Cornwall: The Changing Nature of Peripherality", PhD, CNAA (Polytechnic South West), 1989.

Piper, Laurence, "The Development of Technical Education in Cornwall from the Early Nineteenth-Century until 1902", M Ed, University of Leicester, 1977.

Rule, J.G., "The Labouring Miner in Cornwall c1740–1870: A Study in Social History", PhD, University of Warwick, 1971.

Spooner, D.J., "Industrial Development in Devon and Cornwall 1939-67", PhD, University of Cambridge, 1972.

Unpublished Papers

Banks, J.C., "Cornwall as a Region", unpublished paper presented at the Conference on Cornwall, Perranporth, May 1983.

Dawe, Richard D., "The Effect Chinese Labour Had on the Cornish Miner in South Africa", unpublished paper, Middlesex Polytechnic, 1984.

Deacon, Bernard, "The Prospects for Cornish Politics— Constructing an Ethnic Politics", unpublished paper (in Redruth Cornish Studies Library), Redruth, 1984.

"The Cornish Revival: An Analysis", unpublished paper (in Redruth Cornish Studies Library), Redruth, 1985.

Gamble, A., 'Thatcherism and The Politics of Inequality", unpublished paper presented to the Institute of British Geographers' Conference, Portsmouth, 1987.

Hearl, Derek, "Regional Political Behaviour: The Case of Devon and Cornwall", unpublished paper presented to Political Studies Association Conference, Plymouth Polytechnic, 1988.

Hoskins, W.G., "Celt, Saxon and Norman in the Rame Peninsula", lecture at Millbrook, in unpublished MSS *Essays and Notes on Rame Peninsula*, Torpoint Public Library, Cornwall.

Lee, Adrian, "How Cornwall Votes", unpublished paper presented at the Institute of Cornish Studies, 1977.

"Cornwall: Aspects of Regionalism and Nationalism", unpublished paper presented to Workshop on Nationalist and Regionalist Movements in Western Europe, University of Strathclyde, 1978.

"The Persistence of Difference? Electoral Change in Cornwall", unpublished paper presented to PSA Annual Conference, Plymouth Polytechnic, 1988.

Page, Edward, "Michael Hechter's 'internal colonial' model of political development in the British Isles: some theoretical and methodological problems", unpublished paper presented to PSA Conference, Aberystwyth, 1977.

Payton, Philip, "The Cornish Radical Tradition: Its Background in Cornwall and Development in South Australia", unpublished paper, University of Adelaide, 1977.

"Territorial Politics in Cornwall: The Impact of the Eighties", unpublished paper presented to the Conference of the PSA work group on The Politics of the United Kingdom, Oxford, 1990.

"Territory, Identity and Development: Cornish Politics in the Eighties", unpublished paper presented to the Cornish Bureau for European Relations' Conference on Cultural Identity and Regional Development, St Austell, 1991.

"Understanding Cornwall: Centre and Periphery in the Multi- national State", Unpublished paper presented to the Conference of the PSA work group on the Politics of the United Kingdom, Newcastle Polytechnic, 1991.

"Cornish Emigration in Response to Changes in the International Copper Market in the 1860s", unpublished paper presented at the Centre for Maritime Historical Studies, University of Exeter, 1991.

Rallings, Colin and Lee, Adrian, "Cornwall: The 'Celtic Fringe' in English Politics", unpublished paper, ECPR workshop, Brussels, 1979.

"Politics of The Periphery—The Case of Cornwall", unpublished paper presented to the Conference of the PSA work group on The Politics of the United Kingdom, Aberystwyth, 1977.

Rokkan, Stein, "Peripheries and Centres: The Territorial Structure of Western Europe", unpublished paper (in Adrian Lee Collection), 1979.

Smart, N., "The Age of Consolidation: South West Electoral Change in the Age of Alignment", unpublished paper, Plymouth Polytechnic, 1988.

Stanyer, Jeffrey, "Cornwall, Devon and the British System of Government", unpublished paper presented to Political Studies Association Annual Conference, Plymouth Polytechnic, 1988.

Urwin, Derek, W., "Territorial Structure and Politics in the United Kingdom", unpublished paper presented to ECPR workshop, Brussels, 1979.

Wight, Ian, "Territory Versus Function in Regional Development: The Case of Cornwall", unpublished paper, University of Aberdeen, 1981.

Newspapers and Periodicals

An Gannas
An Kenethlor
An Weryn
Chambers Journal
Cornish Banner (19th century, Bible Christian)
Cornish Banner (1970s and 80s, CNP)
Cornish Guardian
Cornish Labour News
Cornish Magazine
Cornish Nation
Cornish Post
Cornish Scene
Cornish Stannary Gazette
Cornish Times
Cornish Voice
Cornubian
Daily Telegraph
Free Cornwall
Guardian
Gwyn ha Du
Independent
Kernow (pre-war, Tyr ha Tavas)

Kernow (early 1970s, MK youth magazine)
Kernow (late 1980s, independent nationalist)
Kevren
Mining Journal
New Cornwall
New Statesman
Old Cornwall
People's Weekly (Moonta, South Australia)
Private Eye
Royal Cornwall Gazette
Sunday Independent
Wallaroo Times (South Australia)
West Briton
Western Morning News
Yorke's Peninsula Advertiser (South Australia)

Miscellaneous Sources

Biscoe, Bert, *Independents' Day: A Conference For Representatives, Candidates and Supporters of Independents in Local Government in Cornwall*, leaflet, Truro, 1988.
Boundary Commission for England, *Boundary Commission for England Report: European Assembly Constituencies*, Cmnd 7348, London, 1978.
Press Release, 2 June 1988.
Statement to be made on behalf of Commission by the Assistant Commissioner (at the Bodmin Inquiry, 12-13 July 1988).
Boundary Commission For England: European Parliamentary Elections Act 1978 (as Amended): The Report by Mr Assistant Commissioner G.D. Flather, Q.C. upon the Local Inquiry held by him on 12 and 13 July 1988 in Bodmin, Cornwall, into the proposed changes in the European Parliamentary Constituencies of Cornwall and Plymouth and Devon, 1988.
Report of S.J.L. Oliver, Q.C.: 1983 Review of European Assembly Constituencies, European Assembly Election Acts 1978/81, Cornwall and Plymouth and Devon, Boundary Commission For England, London, 1983.
British Election Survey, *British Election Surveys*, 1970 and October 1974.
Campaign For A Cornish Constituency, *Campaign Submission to the Public Inquiry, Public Rooms, Bodmin, on Tuesday 12th July 1988*, 1988.
A Critique of: The Report For Boundary Commission by G.D. Flather Q.C. upon the Local Inquiry held on 12/13 July 1988 into the proposed Cornwall and Plymouth and Devon European Parliamentary Constituencies, 1989.
Conservative and Unionist Party, *European Parliamentary Election Communication*, 1989.
Cornish Assembly, Cornish Assembly policy leaflet and membership form, c1980.
Cornish Bureau for European Relations, *Petition to the European Parliament in support of Cornwall's Heritage and Culture*, COBER, Mylor Bridge, 1988.
Cornwall County Council, *European Parliamentary Elections Act 1978 (as amended): Representations to the Boundary Commission for England on Their Provisional Recommendations Published 17th March 1988*, 1988.
Cornwall Record Office, DDX 384/3, *Kilkhampton Bible Christian Circuit Minute Books 1891–1910*, 19 June 1902, Resolution 11.
Feock Parish Council, *Boundary Commission For England: European Parliament—*

Cornwall and Plymouth Constituency Public Inquiry, Bodmin, 12 and 13 July 1988, Representation of the Parish Council, 1988.

Fleet, John, "Cowethas Flamank and the Conference on Cornwall", unpublished memorandum, Camborne, 1986.

Hansard (British Parliamentary Debates)

Institute of Cornish Studies, *Associates' Newsletter*, Winter 1989-90.

Kerrier District Council, *Boundary Commission For England: 1988 Review of European Assembly Constituencies, European Assembly Act 1978 and 1981, Cornwall and Plymouth Constituency Local Inquiry, Representations of the Kerrier District Council*, 1988.

Mebyon Kernow, Mebyon Kernow policy leaflet and membership form, c1969.

North Cornwall District Council, *Boundary Commission For England: Public Inquiry into the European Parliamentary Constituencies of Cornwall and Plymouth and Devon*, 1988.

Penhaligon, Annette (SLD Campaign Agent), *Cornish Voice*, election leaflet, June 1989.

Royal Commission on the Constituion, *Royal Commission on the Constitution—Written Evidence 8: England*, HMSO, London, 1972.

Royal Commission on the Constitution, Report Volume I, Cmnd. 5460, HMSO, London, 1973.

Social and Liberal Democratic Party, Election Communication, *Paul Tyler: Liberal Democrat—Campaign For Cornwall '89*, 1989.

South East Cornwall Liberal Association, *Focus: Partners For Progress—News From the Alliance*, leaflet, 1987.

South East Cornwall Social and Liberal Democrats, *Focus: Democrates in South East Cornwall*, No 1 Spring 1988.

The Duchy of Cornwall, *Preliminary Statement Showing the Grounds on Which is Founded The Right of The Duchy of Cornwall to the Tidal Estuaries, Foreshore, And Under-Sea Minerals Within and Around The Coasts of The County of Cornwall*, Duchy of Cornwall, London, 1855.

The Tidal Estuaries, Foreshore, And Under-Sea Minerals Within and Around The Coast of The County of Cornwall, Duchy of Cornwall, London, 1857.

Index

264

Fife 241
Finistere 185
First World War 119, 123, 125, 126, 155, 169
Flamank, Thomas 59
Flanders 194
Fleet, John 201
Foot, Isaac 157, 159
Forbes, Stanhope 126
Forest of Dean 50
Foster, K.G. 25, 212
Fowey 55, 56, 61, 63, 76, 77, 126
Fowey, River 179
Foweymore 50
Fox family 77
Fraddon 89
France 12, 18, 50, 55, 61, 108, 126, 126
Frederick Louis, Prince 84
Free Cornwall 202
Frere, Bishop W.H. 133
Furness 112

Galicia 44
Gendall, Richard 208
George I, King 84
George II, King 84
George III, King 84
George IV, King 82
George, Andrew 243, 244
George, Ken 208
George Augustus, Prince 82-84
Geraint, King 46
Germany 8, 50
Germoe 107
Ghandi 149
Giddy, Pascoe 61
Gilbert, Davies 77, 85, 129, 134
Gilbert, Humphrey 61
Gilpin County 110
Glamorgan 146, 241
Glasgow Govan constituency 9, 217, 242
Glasney College 54, 60
Gloucestershire 77, 151, 173
Godolphin, Sidney 84
Gorran Haven, 55
Gorsedd of Brittany 134
Gorsedd of Cornwall 28, 134, 208-210
Gorsedd of Wales 134
Grampound 49, 53
Grand Union Canal 77

Granville, George 84
Grass Valley 108, 110, 146
Great County Adit 73
Greater London Council 9, 182, 187
Great War (see First World War)
Great Western Railway 125, 126
Green Party 226
Grenwich 59, 123
Grenfell, Pascoe 78
Grenville, Sir Beville 62
Grenville, Sir Richard (of 'Revenge') 61,
Grenville, Sir Richard (of Civil War) 62, 63
Grimond, Jo 28
Grose, Samuel 75, 76
Guernsey 108
Gulf, the x
Gulf Stream 105
Gulval 60
Gunnislake 74, 109, 142
Gwavas 61
Gwent 241
Gwennap 74, 75, 87, 100, 109, 142, 149
Gwinear 75
Gwithian 75
Gwynedd 233, 241

Hafod 78
Halton 61
Hampshire 152
Hanoverian era 84
Hardie, Keir 140
Harris & Co 76,
Hawker, Robert Stephen 129
Hawkins 61
Hayle 76, 78, 121, 168
Hayman, Harold 25, 195, 223, 231
Hebden Bridge 217
Helland 60
Helston 49, 52, 53, 61, 63, 74, 93, 144
Hendra 46
Henry V, King 48
Henry VII, King 51, 58, 59,
Henry VIII, King 43, 56, 60, 61,
Hensbarrow Downs 50
Hereford 46
Hicks, Robert 28, 231, 242
Highlands, Scottish 56, 58, 104, 131, 151, 179

266

269

271